on some of the warnings I might look out for, based on a scientific but more importantly a compassionate approach. These readings have improved the quality of my life."

—Dominic Miller, guitarist for Sting, The Pretenders; composer, solo CDs *First Touch* and *Second Nature.*

"One of the first appointments I made after the birth of my daughter was for an astrology reading with Steven and Jodie Forrest. Now, fifteen years later, I still refer to its contents and am grateful for their insight in helping me honor her uniqueness and support her strengths and weaknesses. I can't imagine a more valuable gift that parents could give to their child."

—Susan B. Reintjes, psychic, author of *Third Eye Open: Unmasking Your True Awareness.*

"From their insight and understanding, you'd think Jodie and Steven were your closest childhood friends. They have an uncanny ability to gently unravel the tightest knots of your inner self."

—Eric Silver, award-winning songwriter: Dixie Chicks, Donna Summer, Diamond Rio. Record producer: Michelle Wright, Neal McCoy, Reba McEntire.

Praise for *The Inner Sky*

"Steve's book manages to disarm the skeptic, as well as debunk the charlatanism that surrounds popular astrology, with language that is as intelligent and cogent as it is poetic."

—Sting

"No matter what you think of astrology, if you appreciate humor, insight, poetry and astute, articulate observations of human nature, you will appreciate Steven Forrest's fascinating book."

—Calli Khoury, screenwriter, *Thelma and Louise*

"Steven Forrest's down-to-earth approach is refreshing, funny, and void of pompous claims."

—*The L.A. Times*

"One of the best and sharpest books for beginners that I've ever come across."
—Mark Lerner, *Welcome to Planet Earth*

"One truly outstanding book . . . The best part is that it is intelligent, well-written and actually fun."
—*Esquire*

"Even if you feel that you are well past the beginner's stage, *The Inner Sky* can give you insights in the basics of astrology that you never dreamed possible."
—*American Astrology*

"Beautifully written in simple language, yet amplified with stunning verbal imagery throughout, the book is a reading experience worth savoring. Throw in the fact that it is undoubtedly one of the clearest, simplest astrology primers ever written and you begin to glimpse the miracle Steven Forrest has wrought."
—Richard Nolle, Dell *Horoscope*

Praise for *The Changing Sky*

"Steven Forrest . . . One of the most gifted writers on astrology to emerge in the last quarter of a century . . . You will be delighted with *The Changing Sky*."
—Richard Nolle, Dell *Horoscope*

Praise for *The Book of Pluto*

"This book is as scary as Chernobyl and as utterly beautiful as a summer night sky. It's Pluto, so don't expect bikini day at the beach. Still, you'll be so struck by Forrest's profundity and humanity that his work will inspire you."
—Michael Lutin

"We all have Pluto somewhere in our chart, and this is where something wolf-like in us knows no surrender, no compromise . . . Without sounding preachy or self-righteous, Forrest has brought a moral compass to

astrology. His spiritual messages permeate the detailed descriptions of Pluto, making him not only a premier astrologer, but also a wise man."
—Dell Horoscope

"Steven Forrest's writing in *The Book of Pluto* is so good and riveting it's scary . . . [an] illuminating, penetrating, humorous and revolutionary volume on the planet of universal mysteries. Steven is a master storyteller—the Ernest Hemingway of astrologers—and you will be transformed during and after this visit to Pluto's realm of enchantment, soul purpose and spiritual power. The instant classic on distant Pluto has finally arrived on earth."
—Mark Lerner, *Welcome to Planet Earth*

"Since its discovery in 1930, astrologers have noted a tendency for the planet Pluto to loom large in our birthcharts during life's darker moments. It does not cause painful events, but it does symbolize them and, handled consciously, a passage through this planet's domain can actually change our perspective on crisis for the better. [This book] shows ways to understand the meaning of the planet's passage through the chart. . . . Pluto may dump us in hell, but its purpose is also to guide us to heaven."
—*Bodhi Tree Book Review*

"This is by far a most definitive book about the work of the planet Pluto . . . The author describes Pluto as the harbinger of the dark pages of life, the master of death and regeneration, sexual energies, and all such drives. His placement in the chart looms large in the native's life. . . I found this book riveting and it spurred my intense drive to research and experiment."
—*The Rosegate Journal*

Praise for *The Night Speaks*

"A must for all astrologers and everyone . . . they know."
—Demetra George, author of *Asteroid Goddesses*

"This book contains one person's thinking. But what thinking. . . It is the kind of book which you will want to share and discuss with your friends."
—Michael Munkasey, author of *Midpoints: the Power of the Planets*

"Finally, a richly-textured reading that combines astrological insight with poetry."
—Michael Lutin, author of *Childhood Rising*

"Steven Forrest is an excellent astrologer as well as a superb writer, so he might be one of the few to successfully carry out the task he set himself, namely 'to produce a book an intelligent "believer" could offer his or her skeptical friends . . . to demonstrate that astrology is intellectually plausible.' As far as I am concerned, he has succeeded, in fact better than I expected. This book is not only instructive to the skeptic, but a jewel and a 'must read' for all astrologers."
—Marion March in *Aspects*

Praise for *Stalking Anubis*

"The stars are right for astrologer Steven Forrest's mystery debut, *Stalking Anubis*. Astrologer Plato Mims has to rely on psychological insight as well as the power of the planets to help his friend Sinker Crenshaw when Sinker's new romance takes a deadly turn. "
—*Publishers Weekly*

"I began caring about the main characters right away. They were human and endearing. Halfway through the book, I noticed that I had become *completely* engrossed. The next thing I knew, I had read two thirds of the book, the dishes were piling up in the sink, dust bunnies were collecting under the furniture . . . and I was dying to know (no pun intended) what the next plot twist would be and what would present itself as the characters' next challenge, requiring yet another cleverly devised solution."
—Mary Plumb, in *The Mountain Astrologer*

**Praise for *Measuring The Night, Volumes One and Two*
(co-authored with Jeffrey Wolf Green)**

"In creative echo of one another in this book, their lectures together capture the core of what each of these celebrated astrologers stands for as teachers of our art, our philosophy, our practical discipline."
—Noel Tyl

"Astrology can deepen and grow when astrologers dare to explore new ways of working with astrology . . . Two well-known and creative astrologers share their experience and insights in this book in a thought-provoking way."
—Karen Hamaker-Zondag

"Two of astrology's leading lights, Steven Forrest and Jeffrey Wolf Green, have each written excellent books on Pluto. Their personal styles and terminology differ, but they have far more in common than do most individuated astrologers. Recognizing this, they have pooled their talents to put on a series of lectures . . . the wonderful result is *Measuring The Night*."
—Chris Lorenz in Dell *Horoscope*

"Some of astrology's most lively and provocative work is being modeled by Steven Forrest and Jeffrey Wolf Green . . . . if you are not already one of their many fans, I invite you to treat yourself to this book and enjoy the camaraderie of two vibrant astrological minds."
—Mary Plumb, in *The Mountain Astrologer*

**Praise for *Skymates, Volumes One and Two*
(co-authored with Jodie Forrest)**

"A book made for anyone who dreams of having a match made in the heavens! I can't recommend it enough!"
—Trudie Styler, actress, producer, U.N. Ambassador for UNICEF

"The Forrests make their science and their art accessible to us all, and provide avenues of growth far deeper than reflection or even psychotherapy could provide . . . This book is a must-have for anyone doing the spiritual work of relationships."
—Tracy Gaudet, M.D., Director, Duke Integrative Medicine

"A fantastic guide for those looking to discover or recover that romantic spark!"
—Kelli Fox, founder of Astrology.com

"Steven and Jodie's intuitive approach makes this a wonderful guide to

personal relationships. Their sound astrological principles are undeniably helpful, informative, and make good practical sense."
—Danny Kee, Director of A&R, Warner Bros Records

"A simple step-by-step approach with lots of encouragement. An invaluable reference book, with exciting new interpretations and guidelines to keep your analysis on track and innovative. I highly recommend *Skymates*."
—Marilyn Harquail, *The Astrologers' Newsletter*

"Teachers will want to use *Skymates* as a basic text; anyone interested in astrology and relating will find this book an intriguing and marvelous guide."
—Chris Lorenz, Dell *Horoscope*

"*Skymates* can teach the complex art of synastry to beginners, although astrologers at all levels will appreciate this book. The authors speak imaginatively and compassionately to the very sensitive issues of love and intimacy."
—Mary Plumb, *The Mountain Astrologer*

"*Skymates* is a revolutionary signpost of wisdom for anyone who wants to uncover the secrets of successful relationships in the horoscope. It also responsibly demonstrates how astrology can be used with sensitivity and integrity. This book is invaluable to new students of astrology and to experienced astrologers."
—Jan Angel, AstrologyOnline.info

"Properly practiced, astrology attempts to address the apparent consonance or dissonance between our lives and the sky. Jodie and Steven Forrest bring us into that space, and into the spaces between us, with grace, humor and informed awareness. In this book, astrology is the portal through which you will examine relationships in a manner worthy of any of the world's wisdom traditions. We should also describe the book this way: 'Astrology—Not Just for Astrologers Anymore.'"
—Scott Ainslie, musician (CDs: *Jealous of the Moon, Terraplane, Feral Crow, Thunder's Mouth*) and author of *Robert Johnson: At The Crossroads.*

"Like all of the Forrests' work, *Skymates* is rich with wisdom and humor. Their well-documented research is deftly folded into lyrical parables that reveal the mysteries of relationships and offer equipment for living."
—Linda Belans, host of the medical ethics radio show *Do No Harm*, http://donoharm.duke.edu.

"Steven and Jodie take astrology to a whole new level by returning it to its original intent: to offer an outline for our evolutionary paths so we can discover our own meaning in life. Their work infuses you with wit, wisdom, and humor, and with a wealth of information found nowhere else."
—Keith Cleversley, record producer: Flaming Lips, Sound of Urchin, Moses Leroy, Hum.

"To write a powerful book on the astrology of relationships takes two things: a vast knowledge of astrology and a fantastical, loving relationship in life. When these two things merge, well, the results are nothing short of miraculous. The Forrests have both. Caution: insight and miraculous relationship knowledge inside."
—Philip Sedgwick, author of *Astrology of Deep Space,* and *The Sun at the Center.*

"A marvelous combination of good writing and good information. The deep insights authors Jodie Forrest and Steven Forrest provide are a beacon that illuminates a path to success and joy from a soulmate relationship!"
—Richard Fuller, *Metaphysical Reviews.*

"Please treat yourself to the deep insights that these two wonderful souls offer within this book."
—Jeffrey Wolf Green, author of *Pluto: The Evolutionary Journey of the Soul*, and *Pluto, Volume II: The Soul's Evolution Through Relationships.*

"I'm glad to see a book go beyond sun signs, stereotypes and platitudes. And this opus from Steve and Jodie Forrest is nothing but a pleasure to read, while being comprehensive and clear."
—Robert Griffin, keyboardist for The Squirrel Nut Zippers, and for Katharine Whalen and the Jazz Squad; solo pianist (CD *North Carolina, A State of Music*).

"*Skymates* is an unforgettable literary journey that will enrich your personal consciousness while ultimately leading to more fulfilling relationships."
—Laure Redmond, author of *Feel Good Naked.*

Yesterday's Sky:

Astrology and Reincarnation

by

Steven Forrest

Seven Paws Press

Published by Seven Paws Press

PO Box 82, Borrego Springs, CA 92004
Tel 760 767 4720; Fax 760 767 4730
www.sevenpawspress.com

ISBN 978-0-9790677-3-0
Library of Congress Catalog Card Number: 2008935357

First edition
First printing, September 2008

For information about other titles and to order, please contact
Seven Paws Press at the above address.

Acknowledgments

Special thanks to Paige Ruane, Patrick Kearney, and Dr. Hadi Ali of the Integrative Medicine Foundation for providing the grant which allowed this book to come to fruition.

Some of the material in Chapters Three and Four appeared originally in *The Mountain Astrologer* magazine. I thank the staff there for their enthusiastic support over the years and for permission to re-use that particular material here.

Most of the charts I have used as illustrations in this volume come from the extensive files of Astro*Data*Bank. The debt that the astrological community as a whole owes this institution is incalculable.

Special thanks to artist Michelle Valborg Kondos for the magnificent painting you see on the cover of this book. Treat yourself to a look at her website at www.mvkondos.com. Of this work, she writes, "I've incorporated quite a bit of sacred geometry, including the Golden Section, into it—that seemed appropriate considering the subject. Also nine visible stones (if you could see all the stones, there would be twelve) representing half the nodes' cycle, plus the numerological significance. And the four stones in front that the light hits strongly representing the four elements, the four Angles, etc."

Infinite gratitude to the four hundred or so members, past and present, of my apprenticeship program. They provided the laboratory in which most of the wrong ideas which might otherwise have made their way into these pages were weeded out. I am particularly grateful to the people who have risen to the cat-herding challenge of organizing the program over the years: Karen Briggs, Ingrid Coffin, David Friedman, Barbara King, Carrie Nash, Vinessa Nevala, Cristina Smith, Joyce Van Horn, and Paula Wansley.

My thanks to all the following people for support and friendship: Scott Ainslie, Bobbie and Willard Aldrich, Lynn Bell, The Blue Sky Ranch Fellowship, Ceci and Chella of La Casa del Astrólogo in Mexico City, Cheryl Cooper, Beth Darnall, Janette DeProsse, Robert Downey, Jr, Amy Dye, Rona Elliot, Michael Erlewine, Nancy Fantozzi, Robert Finnegan, Hadley Fitzgerald, Chris Ford, Bunny Forrest, Rishi Giovanni Gatti, Tracy and Ryan Gaudet, Nan Geary, Martha Goenaga, Jeffrey Wolf Green, Robert and Diana Griffin, Baris Ilhan, Kathy Jacobson, Bill Janis and Shannon Glass, Barbara Jensen, Cheryl Jones, Lisa Jones, Rhiannon Jones, Alphee and Carol Lavoie, Michael Lutin, Christy Mack, Kim Marie, "P" and Michie McConnell, Jean McKinney, Chris McRae, Ray Merriman, Rafael Nasser, Dorothy Oja, Melanie Reinhart, Paul Richard, Evelyn Roberts, Moses Siregar III, Herb and Barbara Stone, Sting and Trudie Styler, Tem Tarriktar, Kay Taylor, Mark and Ingrid Tighe, Patricia Walsh, Jan and Jeff Ward, Roger Woolger, Bob Wilderson, Scotty Young and Diane Swan, Christal Whitt, and Cindy Wyatt.

Finally, to my partner in life, love and work, Jodie Forrest, on the occasion of our twenty-fifth wedding anniversary—my inexpressible thankfulness for sharing this journey with me, again.

YESTERDAY'S SKY: ASTROLOGY AND REINCARNATION
TABLE OF CONTENTS

FOREWORD

This book is Steve's gift to us. He used his own gifts, his intellect, heart, wisdom, time, care, understanding, humility, humor and compassion to make this offering. Key to a treasure chest, Yesterday's Sky contains nothing short of one compelling version of the meaning of life. This version rests on, and harmonically converges with, many other versions. Included within, like 17 the offering of any art, we discover maps and sparks to future personal and professional insights. And also to future paradigmatic movements like the one he has been elemental in creating here: evolutionary astrology.

In these pages he leaves a trail of treasures like a mischievous Easter bunny. He leaves gorgeous, painted, intricate, fertile eggs everywhere. Steve can paint with the tiniest brush, laying out technical revelations and, in a blink, throw wide swaths of philosophical landscape on everything in his path. These strokes all work with rhythmic cadence, seamlessly, into the beauty he reveals.

To me, his work is, in essence, about relationship in the grand sense of the word. We are part of a perfect system and Steve triumphs in helping us remember that on many levels. Such recall is not only useful, it is sublime. He helps us remember where we are located in relation to ourselves, each other and all that is. He mastered conventional astrology and then tapped into something greater. What he found points to a more harmonious relationship between us and our heavenly surrounds than most before him, in recent memory, had imagined. Aided by the astrological tools available in his youth, he experimented. He kept watch on his inner divining rod, looking for subtleties and deeper truths in the eyes of his clients, until it was clear there was a deep river running beneath conventional astrology.

What, beyond the phenomenological and empirical observations he made with his clients, led him to blaze this path? A similar question would be, "Why did certain animals and indigenous people—the Motecs, for example—know to head for the hills just before the 2004 tsunami and thus survive?" Because of a remembering. This remembering has everything to do with our relationship to the natural world and there are consequences to forgetting. How much are we willing to work on this relationship? To honor it? To see it as symbiotic to survival and our ability to thrive? What

Steve reveals succinctly, is one way to remember.

To paraphrase Steve in service of describing him, he asks thoughtful questions about things hidden in plain view. If we fail to do this, we miss richness available to us in relationships that hold greater intricacy than we imagined and there is loss. Steve is a guide; he brings us back to ourselves and back to a meaningful view of life in a way that I find startling.

A childhood friend of mine married a high school biology teacher. About ten years ago I visited them in Idaho. We were lying on their lawn, in the magnificence of their environs, talking about how things worked. I will never forget his saying that he could explain to his students in endless detail how things worked, but not why. What a wonderfully humble perspective. It invites possibility. It made me think of how absent such a view was in our eighth grade biology classes. In fact, I had a distinct fear of my biology teacher, an unhappy woman, always blowing her nose, angry about her allergies, shaming us into memorizing every last detail of enzyme and neuron function with a reign of terror. It felt flat, devoid of meaning, giving me just enough to be frustrated. Our physics teacher on the other hand made things exciting, placing "how things worked" in a larger context, passionate about it all himself, demonstrating experientially.

The more we look with a microcosmic perspective, the more our individual philosophies develop: how the parts make a whole and what it means. What it might mean. Steve has that rare combination of lighting mind and depth of heart. With the strength of both, he holds micro and macro together for us so we can stand back and really turn 360 degrees to take in the whole. He is painting those Easter eggs; he doesn't allow things to go flat. And this book, his basket of eggs, will land powerfully in fertile imaginations, I suspect. It will serve to empower the minds and hearts of astrological practitioners and lay people alike.

I have a precious friendship with Steve and in the process of reading this wonderful book, I found commonalities that add new dimension to that preciousness. Rich intricacy in the relationship between what we each do has been hidden in plain view. Pursuing my own work on truly integrated systems of medicine, I cofounded the Integrative Medicine Foundation in 2005 whose mission, in part, supports the research and development of traditional systems of medicine. We support traditional medicine practitioners and their communities while collaborating with and learning from them. Basically where my partners and I are devoting our time and energies, like Steve, is to a search for succinct ways to honor our relationship to the natural world and provide that for people. Ways to prevent loss in that relationship's potential, and beautiful examples of that prevention, offer a reminder that the relationship is symbiotic to our survival and ability to thrive. We are trying to correct the loss of the relationship's healing potential—a loss which runs epidemic through scientific paradigms of Western culture.

One aspect of our relationship to the natural world that traditional medicines cultivate is an understanding of plant life. Plants have riches for us, like the planets, which infer profound responsibility to respect and care for them. Until I began working with traditional healers in Africa, until my partners and I started trusting our own inner divining rods, watching for subtleties in the way of science, I thought it was great that pharmaceutical companies were "finding cures" for ailments in plants and creating drugs from them. I thought it was great that I could go to a health food store and buy a "natural" shampoo or an "herbal" remedy. But one surprising truth made me reassess all of that. Whole plants are an entirely different thing than any convenient dissection of them for use that we might make, let alone the additives we throw in so that we might patent or preserve them. Whole plants operate in ways our instruments cannot yet measure, and our scientific paradigms cannot yet embrace. If their nature, and therefore use, is understood, as fine traditional medical practitioners do, the whole is far less toxic than the part. What a revelation to understand that there is knowledge pointing to great harmony. And it is waiting to be remembered by those of us who have forgotten; asked of (not stolen from) people who have not forgotten and, as Steve points out here with astrology, there is more to be discovered.

This turns the "manifest destiny" need to control nature attitude on its head and makes things infinitely more relational, and interesting. Much the same way, Steve's work alleviates a malaise of suspicion, apathy or disconnection with the planets and their relevance to our lives. Without this alleviation, why value the planets? Have we ever had a greater need to value our natural environment than now? To experience the natural world's gifts helps us to stop compartmentalizing our investments.

Conventional allopathic medicine gives us just enough to be frustrated in my opinion, much like my biology teacher did and perhaps conventional astrology did for Steve. There is a lack of philosophical framework within it, as Steve shows similar dearth in conventional astrology. This dearth ultimately causes fault lines which, if handled well, can be inspiration for higher thought and practice. If handled myopically, these limitations can get us lost.

The wisdom encouraged in the ethical application of traditional systems of medicine has parallels to the wisdom Steve encourages. There is a valuing of free will underlying his practice that should also be applied to medicine of any kind. People must be given the right to make informed treatment choices and be encouraged to do so. This, really, is what Steve helps and encourages us to do with the threads of our lives. I hope that like him, my foundation can bring a 360-degree view of choices for people. He emphasizes the need for the heart to be central to any astrologer wise enough to take heed. The mind is capable of fantastic mental gymnastics, valued in American culture, but it is the heart, he shows, that humanizes any healing work and in the end makes it possible. He makes reference to knowledge that he finds perhaps having been guarded as sacred, true also of traditional medical knowledge. As with evolutionary astrology, it is powerful! Just as someone can clumsily or egotistically hurt a client using evolutionary astrology, so too can plants be toxic in the wrong hands. In these wrong or untrained hands, technique, as with any unskilled representative of evolutionary astrology, can be misunderstood, thereby at the least dismissed as nonsense. This reinforces a forgetting.

If we can remain open, and listen closely to masters like Steve who clearly strive to "do no harm" while pioneering ways to soothe the challenges of being human, then not only will our lives be enriched by what our natural world has to offer but we will come to value our place in a perfect system. Just as we need clean water, nourishing food and non-toxic medicine, we need meaning. *Yesterday's Sky* opens the gate, not only to a fun, poignant, instructive garden of meaning, like a prepared gourmet meal, but invites you to engage in your own harvest, however that may look. Astrologers, philosophers, people of all cultures, enjoy this revolutionary masterpiece. May it remind you of our rich differences, our commonalities and the vital relationships we share.

—Paige Ruane, Cofounder and President, Integrative Medicine Foundation

INTRODUCTION: MY SECOND WIND

Lucky me—in my fiftieth year I caught a second wind. Like most writers, my youth was a paradise of inspiration. Visions seemed to coalesce out of thin air, cloaked in feelings of earth-shaking significance. Doubtless, I proudly re-invented the wheel many times. But fresh ideas, plus excitement and energy enough to execute them, were thick as pollen in the springtime air. I was on a roll.

And the universe cooperated spectacularly: in my early thirties, I signed a contract with Bantam Books. My popular *Sky* trilogy emerged out of those merry days—*The Inner Sky, The Changing Sky,* and, with my then-new wife Jodie Forrest, the original *Skymates* (since re-written in two volumes). By then I had essentially laid the foundation of the rest of my life's work—or so I thought.

My inward orientation had always been metaphysical, more than my early books reflected. Little did I know how far those tidal currents would carry me. As I recount in the coming pages, when I was about twelve years old I had encountered the work of the famous psychic Edgar Cayce. Based on his teaching, the evolution of consciousness through successive lifetimes was my belief even as a teenager, even though I attended a Protestant church. I wanted to write my first book, *The Inner Sky*, along those philosophical lines. Trouble was, in those days in the New York publishing scene, spirituality was still seen as a marginal topic. I was told to go lightly on the word "soul," if I had to use it at all. I snuck a few references to prior lifetimes into that volume, buried about two hundred pages deep. That was all I could do.

Thus it remained for many good years. I was essentially a psychological astrologer, placing a big emphasis on the power of choice and personal responsibility, and fighting the good war against the astrological fatalists. I presented my work against the metaphysical backdrop of the notion of an evolving soul, and spiced it with vague references to past lives. Gradually, in my private work with clients, my sense of the relevance of prior-life dynamics to present-life challenges and circumstances was becoming clearer. Still, my public persona in the astrological world was over-shadowed by the *Sky* trilogy and its essentially psychological perspective.

Then along came Jeffrey Wolf Green—and my second wind. Jeff's techniques were, and still are, quite dissimilar from mine. And a more different human being than me would have been tough to find. But we quickly realized that we were coming at the same questions and working from the same assumptions. In an interview in *The Mountain Astrologer* (issue #94, Dec. 2000/Jan 2001)), Hadley Fitzgerald asked Jeff point blank about any differences between us regarding our point of view on astrology. Jeff responded, "Nothing. We're saying the same thing in different ways. I can't even imagine where there'd be something of a conflicting nature."

Jeff and I had both been successful as astrological authors and we both tended to draw big audiences at the astrological conferences. Comparatively, he was much more of a maverick—his time in combat as a Marine in Viet Nam had left its mark on his style and his social reflexes. We each had the natal Moon in the fourth house—and few people could believe mine was in Aries and his, in Pisces. With Jeff's more combative exterior and my comparatively diplomatic one, it seemed the other way around. But we bonded, and certainly for me, Jeff's work was like yeast in my bread. To me, it felt like we had each been holding half the deck of cards.

Two books came out of our friendship, *Measuring the Night*, Volumes One and Two. They were based on transcripts of a series of talks we gave together in California and Arizona in the late 1990s. For many people, the publication of those works marks the emergence of Evolutionary Astrology as a distinct, widely-recognized branch of modern astrology, something bigger than the work of a single individual. In fairness, years earlier Raymond Merriman had already published a volume entitled *Evolutionary Astrology: The Journey of the Soul Through States of Consciousness*. Neither Jeff nor I knew of his work—it first came out in a limited edition of 1440 copies of a hand-written original in 1977. Like ours, Ray's approach was also centered on reincarnation, although his techniques were as distinct as mine were from Jeff's. Still, Ray Merriman, so far as I know, is the one who can rightly lay claim to originating the term, Evolutionary Astrology. Strangely, Jeff and I had also independently been using the same term at least since the early 1980s. And others, notably Stephen Arroyo, Alan Oken, Martin Shulman, David Railley and A.T. Mann, had been working in approximately similar philosophical territory.

Simply said, a synchronistic wave was passing through the collective and many of us surfed it. In private communications with both Ray and Jeff, it has become clear to me that, while we all want the record straight, none of us are feeling proprietary about the term, Evolutionary Astrology. It is bigger than any of us, and we all recognize that. In our *Measuring the Night* books, Jeff and I listed a set of specific principles which would define the field, at least for the two of us and our students. What they boil down to in my own mind is simply that anyone who speaks simultaneously of astrology and of the evolution of consciousness through many lifetimes, and frames it in a context of free will, is an evolutionary astrologer. It's a big tent.

I learned a lot from Jeff Green, and much of what I learned came more from a kind of soul-transfusion than from technical exchanges. He is a wise man, more prophet than scholar. One of his gifts to me was his knack for presenting this kind of astrology unabashedly, without apologies or the need to win friends in academia. Technically, most of what I got from Jeff was a deeper sense of the importance of planets in aspect to the nodes of the Moon, and of planetary rulerships in connection to them. Those of you reading these pages who have cut your teeth on Jeff's "Pluto School" style of astrology will see that the techniques I am about to introduce are quite dissimilar. For one thing, Pluto does not play so central a role in my work, although it is profoundly important in its own way. For another, I have not done much with the phase relationships of planets to each other, nor with polarity points. I have no disagreement with Jeff about any of these techniques. It is just that my own work has gone down different roads.

Different roads that lead into a glittering, seemingly endless gold field! Adding Evolutionary Astrology's philosophical perspective—and its attendant bag of tricks—to basic psychological astrology is like putting away the recipe book and instead sitting down at a five star restaurant in Provence. For me, the excitement is compelling. It is as if I am seeing astrology as it should be, no longer "approximately right," but as God intended it.

Some of my "second wind" comes from the sheer exhilaration I feel just thinking of what remains to be discovered. Evolutionary Astrology, quite emphatically, is a work in progress. Many of us are now working in the field, exploring in different directions. These different directions all seem productive—and more complimentary than contradictory. No one has truly put it all together yet. That is the work of the next generation—or two.

Already I feel that Evolutionary Astrology is by far the most accurate form of "psychological" astrology ever devised. I have come to believe that unresolved prior-life dynamics play a far more pivotal role in shaping the adult psyche than do misadventures in potty training in the so-called "formative" years of childhood. I value psychological astrology very highly—in fact, one could define Evolutionary Astrology quite succinctly as a form of psychological astrology which is integrated with metaphysics. Where a twentieth century psychological astrologer might focus on the dynamics of childhood, the evolutionary astrologer focuses on the *childhood of the soul*—prior lifetimes, and the issues left unresolved from them. It is a *sacred* psychology, in other words. But it is also a *demonstrable* one, grounded in observable, present-life realities. There is nothing flaky here—Evolutionary Astrology is as hard-hitting and clear as a laser beam. If your experience is anything like my own, once you have grasped its basic concepts you will never look at a chart the same way again.

I could never have played my role in the development of Evolutionary Astrology had I not been exposed to teachers outside the astrological world. Basically, the state of the astrology I encountered as a young man forty years ago, while technically advanced, reflected no overriding philosophical framework or purpose. It was basically descriptive. I had to turn elsewhere in order to put astrology into a larger *context of meaning*. Earlier I mentioned cutting my teeth on the work of Edgar Cayce, the "sleeping prophet." If you have not heard of him, you will soon learn more.

Above all, my understanding of reincarnation has been guided by the Buddha, his teachings, and the continuing fellowship of those who keep that flame burning. I have made an effort since my late teens to understand and practice that path, and I have been fortunate enough to sit with many living masters within that tradition. *Yesterday's Sky* is not formally or overtly "Buddhist literature," but if anyone smiles at me conspiratorially and suggests as much, I will gladly wink back at them.

Buddhist notions of prior lives are quite subtle and complex. I avoid speculating on much of that richness in these pages, instead taking refuge in the simpler, more western notion of a reincarnating "soul." As a westerner raised in the Christian tradition, I am comfortable speaking of God, where a Buddhist might prefer the less personalized notion of the *dharmakaya*. Often Buddhism is described as an "atheistic" religion. More precisely, the Buddhist view is that the ultimate reality is beyond all specific qualities and descriptions. To a sophisticated Buddhist practitioner, insisting that the *dharmakaya* has the quality of "impersonality" is no more accurate than imputing "personality" to it.

Make of all that what you will. If there is any core message in astrology, it would have to be a respect for human individuality. In other words, you can compose your own theological position papers, with my blessings. You certainly do not need to be a Buddhist to understand this book. You don't even really need to be convinced of reincarnation as a literal fact. As Carl Jung said in a lecture he gave in 1939, "The mere fact that people talk about rebirth . . . means that a store of psychic experiences designated by that term must actually exist."

A reality or a metaphor—you decide.

So, if I have accomplished what I set out to do, you will not find my words particularly preachy . . . well, with one exception! I unabashedly preach the primacy of free will in shaping our experience. In some more "deterministic" astrological circles, this is blasphemy. I am personally confident that we humans are capable of changing ourselves, capable of evolution. None of us is limited to a "nature" that is cast in stone by the positions of the planets. As we change ourselves, we make different choices and thus create different futures. The first words of the first chapter of my first book were, "People change." I suspect that when I take my last breath, that faith in our capacity for self-transformation will still be there. Going further, I believe that most of the realities we experience in our lives are the result of the collision between our free-will and vast archetypal fields of astrological possibility. We make choices within that wide but still definable context. It is our "fate" to face that astrological context. Our freedom is to make choices within it.

Those of you who are familiar with the rest of my work have already heard me rant about the subject of personal freedom. I will not belabor it here. I only bring it up because the notions of past lives and karma are so often represented as the ultimate in fatalistic determinism. ("You burned down someone's house in 1492, so now your own house must burn down.")

Karma *can* work that way, but the mechanisms are often much more subtle. For one thing, karma is more likely to *repeat* than anything else—if you burned someone's house down in 1492, you may *still* be burning down people's houses today, just putting it all on your karmic VISA card!

More deeply, let me defer to one of the finest living teachers of the Buddhist tradition, Dzoghen Ponlop Rinpoche. In *Turning Towards Liberation: The Four Reminders*, he quotes Patrul Rinpoche, who says that "the quantity of our negative or positive karma is very much connected to our thoughts, our motivations. If our motivation is pure and full of compassion, though the action may seem rather negative, the karma is still positive. If the motivation is not so pure, even when we seem gentle and kind, the karma is not so positive. This means the creation of positive or negative karma is very much within our mind."

Consciousness, in astrology and in karmic matters, is the prime variable, in other words. It is not, after all, the physical body that reincarnates. It is the consciousness. Thus, throughout this book, while we will explore ways of learning about prior life dynamics, the focus will remain on healing and releasing ourselves through conscious work in the present tense. Very simply, the purpose of Evolutionary Astrology is to promote choices that support evolution. Prior-life *post mortems* are part of it—but only insofar as they help us clarify the questions we face in the present life. Quoting the well-known Zen Buddhist monk, Thich Nhat Hanh, in *The Heart of Understanding*, "This is an invitation to go on a journey to recognize yourself. If you do well, you can see your former lives as well as your future lives." He adds, "Please remember that we are not talking about philosophy; we are talking about reality."

Loudly and clearly, let me emphasize that all astrology is about symbolism, not literalism. We evolutionary astrologers cannot look at a chart and tell anyone definitively that she was once a snaggle-toothed 250 pound prize-fighter named Joe who fought in Philadelphia in the 1930s. That is not what Evolutionary Astrology is all about. Like every astrologer operating in the psychological domain, we see *images* and *metaphors*. We believe they *parallel* the actual realities of prior lifetimes. Failure to grasp this utterly simple notion has lead to a lot of needless bloodshed in the astrological world. Our detractors have claimed that "anyone could say *anything* about past lives and who could ever prove them wrong?" Fair enough—agreed! But that kind of literalism is not where Evolutionary Astrology makes its stand. We make our stand in the present tense, where our perspectives can be compared directly with experienced reality. As William Faulkner put it, "The past is not dead. In fact, it's not even past." Our hypothesis is very simple and totally testable. In a nutshell, we believe that *unresolved issues from prior lives, as revealed by these techniques you are about to learn, make themselves felt in the present lifetime.*

Listen to what your chart says about your prior lifetimes. Look at your present lifetime. If the horseshoe doesn't hook the stake, forget about Evolutionary Astrology!

I have thanked Edgar Cayce, Jeffrey Wolf Green, and the Buddha. My indebtedness extends much further. In 1998, in response to my second wind, I instituted my Astrological Apprenticeship Program. Several hundred students have now passed through it, and I am grateful to all of them. Each group meets twice a year for four days. The atmosphere is informal, but the work is rigorous and often quite emotional. That is because its essence is not abstract astrological theory. It is about the heart's direct experience. We work with our own charts and with the reflected realities of our own lives. I cannot begin adequately to thank everyone who has been involved with the "AP." My own clarity and confidence regarding the material in this volume is their gift to me. The actual life-experiences of several hundred people provide an excellent reality-check, should my enthusiasm for an idea lead me too far afield from actual reality. I wish I could name everyone in the program here—they deserve it. Let me instead call your attention to the Directory of astrologers whom my wife Jodie or I have trained in this work: Jodie's astrological Mentoring Intensive program also meets two or three times a year. Go to www.sevenpawspress.com, then click on Training up at the top of the screen, and scroll down the menu and click *Forrest Trained.*

Similarly, I want to express my gratitude to my private astrological clients. Once again, there is no reality check so effective as the look on a client's face when you are veering off into fantasy land.

Finally, I want to thank the Integrative Medicine Foundation for providing the generous grant that allowed me the time to finish this book. Under the able guidance of Paige Ruane, Hadi Ali, and Patrick Kearney, the Foundation is doing brilliant, life-saving work exploring indigenous herbal wisdom in Africa and elsewhere. Underlying the paradigms of Integrative Medicine is the equilateral triangle of body, mind, and spirit. Paige, Hadi and Patrick recognized that Evolutionary Astrology can provide powerful support to the health of mind and spirit, and thus decided help me bring this book to fruition. I applaud them for their courage and their generous spirits.

So fasten your seatbelts. Behind your familiar birthchart lurks another chart entirely, one whose existence you may never have suspected. It carries your treasures and your wounds. Where the predictions of your chart and the realities of your life might not in all honesty have lined up quite precisely, this chart-behind-the-chart will help you see why.

I count myself very fortunate, here in my sixtieth year, to have found my second wind—a way of looking at our inner skies which restores to me the kind of astrological excitement I felt when I was nineteen years old. I hope that what you read in the following pages benefits you as much as it has benefitted me.

—Steven Forrest
Chapel Hill, North Carolina
Spring Equinox, 2008

Part One:

The Technique

CHAPTER ONE:
EVERYTHING IN THE CHART IS KARMIC

Maybe, as Buddhists and Druids teach, we have all lived many other lifetimes.

Or maybe not.

Since neither belief can be refuted or definitively proven, I doubt the question will ever fully be settled at the intellectual level. In the next chapter, we will see that the objective evidence for reincarnation is compelling. Still the issue is forever at least partly in the category of faith—or of direct intuitive experience. We can't *know* about past lives, at least not in the way we know that two plus two equals four.

Two points, however, are objectively certain. A third one flows naturally from the first two:

1. All who accept reincarnation agree that our present personalities and circumstances are rooted in our previous lives.

2. All astrologers agree that our personalities and circumstances are reflected in our birthcharts.

Logic draws us to a third point:

3. If we accept both astrology and reincarnation, we are compelled to recognize that our present chart must reflect prior-life dynamics—that hidden in our natal configurations are clues, however subtle, about who we were and what we were doing in previous lifetimes.

If we accept both astrology and reincarnation, no other position is logically defensible.

We can take this reasoning a step further. Ask yourself a truly primordial astrological question: *Why* do you have the birthchart that you have? Not what does it "mean," but why do you have those particular configurations in the first place? Count nine months after your conception, and pop goes the weasel? Random chance, in other words? Logically, it *could* be that way. Astrology could work in a random universe. It could simply reflect some geocosmic laws that science has not yet unraveled.

The alternative is to reckon with the notion that there is a deeper reason behind your having the particular chart that you do—that the cosmos is not random at all, and that the fact that you face the challenges reflected in your astrological symbolism is woven into some larger mystery underlying the surface appearances of life. This means that something *caused* you to take your first breath at that particular place and time. God? An intelligent universe? Karma?

Take your pick.

In this latter view—where something larger than chance was involved in your being born when you were—there is one more fact we must include in our reasoning: *You have had your birthchart since the day you were born.* Irrefutable, eh? Well, then it follows that anything that *caused* you to have it must have happened before you were born.

This is not a specific proof of reincarnation, of course. All it really proves is that once we have observed the visible power of astrology, we have got some hard thinking to do. Unless we want to accept the idea that life is inherently random, we have got to assume that *something* was going on before your birth that would make your present chart exactly right for you.

We could say "that's the way God made you." We could point to DNA—and say that your chart reflects your ancestral "past lives" living on inside you in the form of little molecules of deoxyribonucleic acid. Or we could start listening to the Buddhists, Druids, Gnostics, Hindus and the rest who tell us that we are all born again—and again and again.

From now on in these pages, we are going to assume that reincarnation is a reality. You can switch to other metaphors, if you like—and that is actually a good skill to cultivate for when you are faced with a client who might not be comfortable with the idea of past lives. But we will not go through the exercise of phrasing everything several ways any longer. We will speak the language of the evolution of consciousness through a succession of physical incarnations.

For Everything There Is A Reason

Behind each configuration in your chart lies buried treasure—an implied biographical tale from long ago, from before you were a bulge in your present mommy's tummy. We cannot know the whole karmic story, at least not through astrology alone. But what astrology can give us is a set of hints about your past lives, and more importantly, a set of instructions for how to get on with the evolutionary journey in the present day.

An inherent ambivalence exists in every configuration in your natal chart: it is simultaneously a statement about your soul's pre-existing evolutionary condition—and a formula for advancing beyond it.

That is a critical concept to absorb, and it lies close to the healing heart of Evolutionary Astrology. Every configuration represents a kind of challenge we face—and that challenge can be grasped most deeply in the context of its being "left over" from another lifetime. Yet as we rise up and embrace the *higher potentials* of that configuration, we resolve the karmic wound and expand into new possibilities. In a moment, we will see an example of this and the idea will seem less abstract.

Chaos Theory

Your present life, as you have probably noticed, is complicated, full of loose ends and contradictions. Choices you have made and values you sincerely hold are hard often to reconcile with each other. We believe in truthfulness, but we lie. We think of ourselves as environmentalists, but we don't drive the car that gets the best mileage.

When we start thinking about prior lifetimes, we need to multiply that complexity. We are talking about *many* lives, after all. Furthermore the very meaning of the word "evolution" implies that in your prior lifetimes you were less evolved—and presumably you made messes that you would not make today. All these disjointed, often atavistic, elements come together, in chaos, to be reflected in the planetary patterns of one's present birth. Thus karma is complex and disorderly—and the shadow it casts onto the current birthchart is chaotic.

Let's bring this idea to life. It is easy, for example, to imagine someone who had lived two lifetimes—one of monastic celibacy and another one in which he or she was quite spoiled and protected within a safe marriage. In each case, patterns were established—patterns which "reincarnate" in the present chart. Thus there might presently exist both a habit of withdrawing from intimacy or of being confused by it, left over from the monastic lifetime—and simultaneously a kind of compulsion to enter into very "dependent" kinds of relationships, based on the lazy married lifetime.

A train wreck of contradiction, in other words.

Translating into astrological language, we might for example see Venus conjunct Saturn in Capricorn in the twelfth house—but also a seventh house Moon in Cancer. Today that chart belongs to one particular person, but "one" person is very slippery concept. Karmically each one of us is more like a crowd of very different people trying to come to a consensus.

In Chapter Three, we will begin to explore the royal road into karmic analysis: how to decipher the Moon's South Node and its planetary correlates. That will bring us to the heart of the matter: the *core* karmic story in terms of direct impact upon the present life. Those techniques bring clarity and crispness to our understanding—and the single, unitary past life story we learn to uncover there will very likely startle you with its demonstrable relevance to your present life.

The power of that kind of analysis should never blind us to the fact that in each birthchart there are also many fragmentary pieces of information, some of which do not readily fit into the main storyline. They reflect the jigsaw puzzle of the past, its loose ends, its contradictions. That confusion should not surprise us.

The critical point is to remember that *everything* in the chart is karmic.

This Is Not A Book About the Lunar Nodes

For reasons we will soon be exploring in considerable detail, the north and south nodes of the Moon provide the entry point into the *emotional underpinning* of the primary past life story. We could not do Evolutionary Astrology without them. But, as we have just described, everything in your chart is there for a karmic reason. Many planets or sensitive points make no aspects to the nodes and do not have any direct astrological relationship to them. No matter; they are still part of your karmic inheritance. We use the lunar nodes as a doorway into the heart of the issue. They are a good starting point and a foundation. But, as you will see, this is not simply a book about the nodes of the Moon. This is a book about astrology and reincarnation, which is a far wider subject and one which requires a consideration of the entire chart in every detail. Ultimately nothing is left out.

Because much of what follows does revolve around the lunar nodes, just to underscore our broader agenda, let's proceed with an evolutionary analysis of a configuration which has nothing to do with the nodes at all.

Saturn in the Seventh House

Traditionally, Saturn is often viewed as a "malefic" planet, bringing misfortune and difficulty to whatever house it touches. The seventh house is the classical house of marriage. Thus having Saturn in this position would conventionally be viewed as a bad omen for love. In *Astrology: A Cosmic Science*, Isabel M. Hickey writes, "A separative tendency deep within makes it difficult for this person to relate to others." In the classic book *Astrology*, Ronald C. Davison warns of the possibility of "unfortunate partnerships" or of a "cold, over-ambitious partner." In *Saturn: A New Look at an Old Devil,*: Liz Greene explores the configuration in depth, but also writes, "The most basic interpretation of Saturn in the seventh house is sorrow, difficulty, or constriction in marriage or other close relationships. Generally these sorrows appear to be the hand of external fate and often do not seem to be connected with any fault in the individual himself."

The cornerstone of Evolutionary Astrology is the life-shaping power of conscious choice—a willingness to work on one's self. Thus, any kind of dead-end or fatalistic astrological interpretation is too narrow. We can always reach for the higher ground. This is not just a philosophical statement. We see many living, breathing examples of it. You probably are one yourself! Still, the conventional kind of astrology, however depressing, often delineates quite effectively what we might think of as the evolutionary "starting line." It reflects the raw *re-expression* of the old karmic pattern. Thus, Padmasambhava, the great saint of Tibetan Buddhism, says, "If you want to know your past life, look into your present condition." The challenges of the present, in other words, are rooted in the past. (Padmasambhava added one more point, by the way: "If you want to know your future life, look at your present actions.")

Thus most of the negative interpretations that run through conventional astrology are typically accurate at least at some early point in a person's life. The toxicity of such interpretations derives from the way they imply that the starting line and the finish line are the same. They ignore the fact that human beings can learn and grow.

Accordingly, examples of sorrow or difficulty in marriage for people born with Saturn in the seventh house abound. Eleanor Roosevelt, the wife of American president Franklin Delano Roosevelt, is a classic example. Born with Saturn in the seventh house, she certainly married an ambitious man. Thirteen years after they married, she discovered evidence of an affair he had been having: juicy love letters penned to him by her own personal secretary. (Note the double betrayal.) Their marriage continued another twenty-seven years until Franklin's death, but apparently it was a marriage in appearance only. Evidence suggests they were no longer physically or emotionally intimate. And of course FDR was confined to a wheelchair for a good part of that time—another "Saturn manifestation" in Eleanor's house of marriage.

Elizabeth I of England, the famous "Virgin Queen," also had Saturn in the seventh. She likely was not a virgin, but she never married. She had apparently been sexually abused by a stepfather in her youth, and went on to have a long affair with the married Earl of Leicester in her adult life—again, feel the frustrating, limiting hand of Saturn, the "old devil."

In the more modern context, musician Kurt Cobain of Nirvana also had Saturn in the seventh house—and was married to the famously erratic and difficult Courtney Love until his death by apparent suicide.

There is a higher side to Saturn too—commitment, faithfulness, maturity, self-discipline. Those are qualities that contribute rather obviously to lasting intimacy. Alongside the pessimistic astrologers who see Saturn in the seventh as an intimate High Jinx, there are also those who would roll out their more encouraging view—and bolster it with case files of long-lasting marriages with the configuration. They are right too! One of the most famous long-term love stories of my generation was the bond between Paul and Linda McCartney, which ended tragically when she died of breast cancer in 1998. Prior to her passing, Paul and Linda had not spent a single night apart in twenty-nine years, apart from a ten day period when Paul was in jail for marijuana possession. (Note that twenty-nine years is one Saturn cycle!) Linda had Saturn in the seventh house, retrograde in Taurus.

Actress Michelle Pfeiffer has Saturn in that house. After an unsuccessful first marriage, in 1993 she got together with her present husband, David Kelley, with whom there is every evidence of commitment and happiness despite the madness of Hollywood life.

Similarly, Danny DeVito, with Saturn in the seventh, has been with his partner, Rhea Perlman, since 1970.

Conventional astrologers love to squabble over issues such as this. Is it "good" or "bad" to have Saturn in the seventh house? They will often quibble over whether the Saturn is "well-aspected" or "afflicted," and try to sort it out that way. But even that astrological illusion breaks down when we are brave enough to look at reality—Danny DeVito's Saturn opposes his Venus and is squared by Neptune! Linda McCartney's Saturn was conjunct another allegedly-unfortunate marital indicator—Uranus in the seventh house!

These astrologers are ignoring the single most powerful force in human affairs: *consciousness.*

To me, arguing about the meaning of Saturn in the seventh house this way is similar to observing a public school and arguing about whether "students are six years old" or "students are sixteen years old." Like school, Saturn in the seventh house—or, for that matter, any other astrological configuration—represents a *spectrum of evolutionary possibilities.* With it, we see people who are lonely all their lives. We see people who are caught in unsatisfying relationships. We see people who are accepting of solitude and celibacy, and who do not seem to suffer from it. And we see long, stable, exemplary relationships.

Silly astrologers squabble, while ignoring the evidence of their own direct experience and the testimony of their colleagues. Critics of astrology shrug their shoulders and suggest that the configuration can "mean anything" and that therefore it means nothing at all.

What they all miss is the *underlying, unifying principle of Saturn's archetypal field.*

Where Saturn lies:

You are born with a blockage.

You are invited to admit that fact—and to work on it with the realism, discipline, and honesty of high Saturn.

If you don't, then your life will be defined by the blockage. If you do, you can make progress.

Let's bring this analysis of Saturn in the seventh house fully into the realm of Evolutionary Astrology.

Psychodynamically, the seventh house is about *trust.* Thus with Saturn in the seventh house, there is an inborn *blockage to the trust-function.* Its origins pre-date the birth. They are karmic, and we will look at that in the next section, below. Present-tense, there is an invitation to work on these intimate issues.

Relationship is a vast piece of human experience and too big a subject to explore in full detail here. If you are interested in the astrological details, I recommend the two volume *Skymates* set that I co-authored with my wife, Jodie Forrest. Suffice it here to say that there are a number of different ways that Saturn can make itself felt in the interpersonal sphere, and each one will overlap with the ideas we are currently exploring.

Cutting to the chase, *people cannot learn very much about trust all by themselves!* By its very nature, trust is an interactive phenomenon. We can benefit from quiet, solitary reflection, but ultimately our progress can only be measured and tested in the context of intimacy. Thus Saturn in the seventh house says as much about one's *natural partners* and friends as it does about one's self. The bottom line is that we cannot do our evolutionary work without their help, and we can recognize them by their classic Saturn signature: *they are trustworthy people!* It seems painfully obvious, but the idea is quite fundamental: if you are born with issues around trust, as Saturn in this position indicates, you simply cannot resolve them without the help of people who are worthy of your trust.

Saturn, by its nature, loves *vows* and *commitments.* With Saturn in the seventh, your natural partners are people who are not afraid of those kind of promises—and their courage helps you be less afraid too. Saturn likes *ritual* too, and appreciates rites of passage: an exchange of rings, promises spoken aloud. It likes to see a track record and to celebrate it. Anniversaries of various sorts become important, for example.

Trust builds over time. Saturn is patient—if you have it in your seventh house, an unseemly eagerness to "get in your pants" on the part of a prospective partner is a turn-off. What's the rush? Who can trust anyone so quickly? Worse, such urgency could pander to your own willingness to remain self-protective—that is, untrusting—within a relationship. Plenty of people have sex without trusting each other!

Indications of *respect* are quite central here too. Saturn is formal that way—and that does not mean "stiff." But it does imply courtesy, boundaries, and a higher-than-normal chance that the bathroom door will be closed when the plumbing is in use.

From an evolutionary perspective, *all of these conditions must be met in order to create the intimate environment in which the trust-function can heal*. And, if you have Saturn in the seventh house, that is a big part of what your life is about.

Saturn in the Seventh: The Karma

Why might someone be born with Saturn in the seventh? What happened before this lifetime that leads a person to take birth with this configuration? There are a multitude of possibilities. All have the common denominator of the intimate rug being pulled out from under someone in a prior life—and of *that wound having not been resolved prior to that death*. Most of the possibilities fall into two main categories: *abandonment* and *bereavement*.

Imagine that in a prior lifetime you were abandoned at the altar—your partner failed to appear on your wedding day and was never heard from again. Or he or she went on to live a happy life with someone else, richer and cuter than you, in the same small town. How long does it take to get over something like that?

Alternatively, imagine that in a prior lifetime you were happily married to your true love. You were young and lovely, and you had started a family. And your partner was hit by a lightning bolt, dead and gone.

Again, how long does it take to get over something like that?

The question of "how long it takes to get over" such a blow is of course unanswerable. Grief must run its course, and everyone's experience of it is different. One can repress grief for a while, but it does not go away. And one can cling to grief and become identified with it, to the point that mourning is unnaturally extended. We often observe people going to their graves with unresolved—or unowned—grief.

Metaphysically, the next time we observe those people may be as they emerge from the other end of the grave's pipeline, which we call the womb. Their grief may still be fresh as a daisy—and in their new birthchart we might see Saturn in the seventh house.

Many Possible Stories

Abandonment and bereavement are very different phenomena, yet we lump them together here. We do that because of the way they overlap in terms of their emotional impact. If someone we trust fails us, or if someone we trust dies, in either case *we internalize the reasonable idea that trusting someone else is risky business.* While there are very obvious distinctions between the two situations; either one could manifest as Saturn in the seventh house in a subsequent lifetime. That is because in either case we are born with a blockage to the trust-function—and an evolutionary intention of healing it.

With a little imagination, we can add other past-life possibilities to our list. Perhaps in a prior lifetime, you took a premature vow of celibacy in some religious order. Your natural urge to bond sexually became a danger and a threat to you, so you had to repress it, make it an enemy. You developed a fearful reaction toward anyone whom you found attractive. There's some karma!

Or maybe in a prior life, you were a prostitute: you learned to seal your soul away from the natural bonding effects of human sexuality.

Maybe you were terribly abused. Maybe you were tortured in another life. Maybe you were a courtier in some Italian palace full of poisoners.

The list of trust-destroying possibilities is vast. It should be—there are a lot of sad human stories out there! One out of every twelve people has Saturn in the seventh house, so it must represent a very large number of those possibilities.

As you delve deeper into this book, you will discover a set of techniques that will help you narrow down the possibilities and focus the karmic story much more crisply. But just knowing that Saturn lies in the seventh house teaches us quite a lot. Let's summarize what we have learned:

Trust betrayed you in a prior life. You died with that issue unresolved. You have now been reborn with that wound unhealed—and with the power to heal it through certain specific methods. First and foremost, you need "Saturnine" partners, as we described above. With their help, you need to take the plunge: to make serious commitments. Do that, and you have created an incubator for your own healing.

The alternative to the higher evolutionary path is to have your life defined by this unhealed Saturnian blockage. In that dark scenario, you will go down one of two roads. On one hand, you might *adapt to a life of solitude,* never betting very big on intimacy, if at all. On the other, you might marry *symbols of your fear—people whom it would not be too hard to lose,* thereby minimizing your investment and vulnerability.

Unified Field Theory

Note how this evolutionary interpretation of Saturn in the seventh house embraces *all* of the possibilities we read about in more conventional kinds of astrological literature: "unlucky in love," a chosen life of solitude—or "long, happy, committed friendships and relationships." Evolutionary Astrology provides a kind of unified field theory that links all the possible behavioral manifestation under one theoretical umbrella. We see kindergarten through the twelfth grade, all in the same little red schoolhouse. Neatly, this kind of astrology also links ancient metaphysics with the funky, work-on-yourself methodologies of modern psychotherapy at its best.

Compassion

More importantly, this evolutionary view of Saturn in the seventh house is *compassionate.* We can understand *why* a person might be experiencing a certain set of existential difficulties. And we achieve those insights in a "no fault" way. We do not need to make anyone "sick" or "defective."

Say you have a dear friend who lost her partner in a car accident just six months ago. A well-meaning idiot has offered to arrange a blind date for her. She recoils, saying that she is really not yet ready to consider the possibility of intimacy with anyone. She is still in grief.

Would you have the slightest difficulty understanding your friend's emotional position? Would you paste onto her some psychiatric label? Of course not! Instantly and without effort, your heart would fill with compassion, support, and understanding toward her. *Six months after her bereavement, she is naturally not ready to date yet.* You have no problem with that! You would also have at least an approximate sense of the nature of the long healing road ahead for her—and you would have faith that she could walk that road whenever she was ready.

Take it a step further. Say that you yourself lost your mate in a car accident *in a prior life.* You now have Saturn in the seventh house. Maybe you have had some difficulty in love. Maybe you have had a failed relationship or two. Maybe you have grace enough to recognize that all this misery is at least partly "your own fault," deriving from your attitudes, blockages, psychological dynamics—not to mention your choice of partners.

Now imagine that you go to a conventional astrologer who, in essence, tells you that in terms of intimacy there is something "wrong" with your chart. *That statement resonates with your actual experience.* But it is toxic. The translation is that there is something inherently wrong with *you.* That astrologer has shamed you and discouraged you—and failed to describe the way forward.

Contrast that interpretation with the healing impact of Evolutionary Astrology: You were *hurt* in another life. It takes a while to get over that. And here's how to do it. Such an analysis reveals deeper truth, and it does so in a spirit of sympathetic respect, true insight—and ultimately of encouragement.

With the crystalline understanding that Evolutionary Astrology engenders in us about any human condition, two angels arise simultaneously:

One is the angel of compassion—whether it is for another person or for one's self.

The other is the angel of hope.

CHAPTER TWO: WHY BELIEVE IN REINCARNATION?

Were a thousand celestial pigs to raise their joyous voices in the *Alleluia Chorus*, wouldn't that be a day to remember? Well, yes . . . but none of us are holding our breath. Were all the politicians honest, were the legal system always fair, were oil as cheap as it was in '57 . . .

The wish-list goes on and on. All wonderful and desirable, but all unlikely.

Reincarnation is, in some ways, that kind of idea. It sounds good, but that alone doesn't make it true. The good parts of "coming back again" are obvious. For starters, nobody really dies—there goes that worry! For seconds, you don't really need to get it totally right in this one lifetime. You've got time. For thirds, justice is always done—the kid who stole your bike will get his bike stolen someday, as he deserves. Immortality, a second chance, and ultimate fairness—it is an attractive package.

And it gets better. What about juxtaposing the starving kids in Africa with the flamboyant lifestyles of the conspicuously, frivolously wealthy? In the sweet by and by, each will be in the others' shoes. There is elegant beauty and balance in the idea.

Ditto for singing pigs.

Are There Actually Any Good *Reasons* to Believe in Reincarnation?

Obviously, you have some openness to the idea of "transmigration" or you would not have opened this book. You are not alone. In America, the reported percentage of people who believe in reincarnation varies between 20% and 35% (Yankelovich Partners, CNN, Gallup, Luitz Research, *et cetera*).

The numbers look even better in my own astrological practice, which has attracted a widely varied clientele. When I sit with someone for the first time, I always ask if it is all right if I use past life language. Only twice has anyone demurred. One time, it was a professor at Catholic University. He came back ten years later and said, "OK, tell me about my past lives."

I am always ready to go with alternative interpretations if I run into someone who really doesn't want to hear about prior lives. I can translate the karmic information easily into the language of "that's how God made you" or "that's how your ancestral DNA patterns may manifest in your present character." Those perspectives are all ready to roll, but so far, basically there are no takers. People generally like hearing about past lives.

Who comes to me for astrological consultations? Clearly, it is not a random sample of humanity. Getting a reading is a voluntary behavior, and it implies some self-selection. Many people imagine that I see mostly mystical vegetarian-sympathizers and tree-huggers, such as myself. That isn't actually true at all. Remember that the most egregious example of public astrological enthusiasm in the past two generations was Ronald Reagan.

Astrology is funny that way—it cuts across the obvious lines of the culture-wars. There are very few common denominators among my clients, other than an open mind. Collectively, we are taught not to believe in astrology, so people who appear at my door are independent thinkers. They are also people who are living examined lives—who would want an astrological reading if they weren't interested in self-knowledge?

Statistically, maybe a third of Americans are open to reincarnation. Close to 100% of the people who come to me to have their charts read are open to it. Why are my numbers higher than the Gallup poll? Obviously, there is a lot of self-selection reflected in my clientele. My conclusion is that the ones out there watching television and ignoring life's persistent questions are less likely to have reincarnation cross their minds—nobody ever urged them to consider it. The ones who come to me are people who are wrestling with the meaning of life, and for virtually all of them, reincarnation has emerged as at least a thought they are willing to entertain.

If you are an astrologer and you are afraid you will be "too out there" if you start talking about past lives with your clients, I don't think you need to worry. The kinds of people who want consultations tend to love it. If my own experience is any indicator, you will gain far more clientele than you will lose.

But of course, none of this makes reincarnation "true." Our initial question still remains: Why should we believe in it? Are there any rational reasons beyond the attractiveness and relative popularity of the philosophy?

The Evidence

Can we prove or disprove the reality of reincarnation? The question is slippery. "No" is a tempting response, but it is too glib. Maybe we don't need to be so dogmatic about it. "Proof" is an ambiguous word. For the fundamental laws of science, proof basically means that the principle works all the time, and can always be demonstrated—energy is always equal to mass times the speed of light, squared, period. That principle has never failed a test.

I doubt we can ever prove reincarnation that way.

Most science is fuzzier than that. We all know to take it with a grain of salt when we learn that there is a 35% chance of rain on Thursday. Meteorology is a science—but one for gamblers. Ditto for economics. And quantum mechanics. Similarly, "proof" in a court of law is often framed as knowing something "beyond a reasonable shadow of a doubt."

Reincarnation *can* pass those kinds of tests. I feel that it already has, as we will be briefly exploring here. My aim in this chapter is not to attempt an exhaustive overview of this fertile and vibrant field of research. That would be a different book than one I am writing. In fact, it would take a library. Follow-up on the upcoming references for those kinds of leads. In these pages, I just want to hit a few of the high points in terms of the emerging data in support of the objective reality of reincarnation.

Let's start off with a quote which Rafael Nasser, the fellow behind the *Under One Sky* project, sent me a few years ago:

At the time of writing there are three claims in the ESP field which, in my opinion, deserve serious study: (1) that by thought alone humans can (barely) affect random number generators in computers, (2) that people under mild sensory deprivation can receive thoughts or images "projected" at them, and (3) that young children sometimes report the details of a previous life, which upon checking turn out to be accurate and which they could not have known about in any other way than reincarnation.

Believe it or not, these are the words of the late arch-Druid of twentieth century science, Carl Sagan. They appear in his book *The Demon Haunted World*. He was almost certainly referencing research done by . . .

Dr. Ian Stevenson

Canadian by birth, Dr. Ian Stevenson was a psychiatrist working primarily at the University of Virginia. His primary interest was the study of young children who, typically between the ages of two and four, began talking about prior lifetimes. Tellingly, such children had usually forgotten about their prior lives by the time they reached the ages of seven or eight. Dr. Stevenson traveled all over the world in search of these mysterious stories. He documented them meticulously. By the time he passed away in 2007, he had amassed a couple thousand of these tales. He published extensively. His best known work is *Twenty Cases Suggestive of Reincarnation*, published in 1966, with an expanded second edition in 1974. His team, under Dr. Jim Tucker, has continued the work.

Here's an example of the kinds of tales he encountered and recorded:

While in Kornayel, Lebanon, in 1964 researching another case, Ian Stevenson heard a rumor of a local boy who seemed to be reporting a prior life. The boy, Imad Elawar, before he was even two years old, had begun talking about a lifetime in Khriby—a village twenty-five miles away in which he had been part of the "Bouhamzy" family. He made flattering references to a woman named Jamile, comparing her favorably to his present mother. All in all, the boy made fifty-seven statements which Stevenson recorded.

When the researcher got to the village— which Imad Elawar had never visited—he was able to verify that one Ibrahim Bouhamzy had died there of tuberculosis nine years earlier. He had had a lover named Jamile. Those two facts, plus forty-nine other statements made by the child, were verifiable. *Imad even knew Ibrahim Bouhamzy's last words.* He could identify family members. Once on a walk with his grandmother when he was four, young Imad had run up to a stranger on the street and hugged him, startling the man. Imad claimed that the fellow had been his neighbor.

Turns out that the stranger was from Khriby and had in fact been Ibrahim Bouhamzy's neighbor.

How can we explain this?

Here's another:

A child named William was born with a defect in his main pulmonary artery. At age three, it became apparent that he had an inexplicable emotional connection with his deceased grandfather, whom he had never met—a New York City police officer killed in the line of duty by a bullet passing though his main pulmonary artery. Young William, when threatened with a spanking by his mother, told her that *when he had been her father, he had never hit her!* He even knew the names of the pets his mother had owned as a child.

It seems that William had actually been his own grandfather.

These are just two stories. It would be easy to dismiss them with a shrug of the shoulders—*except that there are two thousand more to go*, all carefully documented. Ian Stevenson himself never framed them as "proof" of reincarnation. He was too much of a scientist for that. He called them "suggestive" of reincarnation. Fair enough.

Dr. Helen Wambach

A spontaneous recognition of a specific book that had belonged to her in a prior lifetime triggered a lifelong fascination with past lives for Dr. Helen Wambach. She was a psychologist and teacher working with hypnotic techniques, using them to bring people back into touch with their own prior-life memories. *Reliving Past Lives* and *Life Before Life* (both 1978), and the new edition *Reliving Past Lives: The Evidence Under Hypnosis* (1984), detail her work, which was meticulous and scholarly. Over a period of ten years, she hypnotically regressed 1,088 people and carefully recorded their "remembered" stories of previous incarnations. Generally, this work was conducted in the context of small day-long "workshops" with a dozen or so participants. Post-session, they were all encouraged to fill out forms with the same set of standard questions. What were you eating—and with what utensils? What was your gender? What were you wearing?

Less than 1% of these kinds of factual daily-life recollections proved inconsistent with the historical record—nobody drove to the Crusades in a '58 Chevy or lost their iPod overboard on the *Mayflower*.

Wonderfully, not a single one of Wambach's subjects recalled being anyone famous. There were no Cleopatras or representatives of the twelve apostles. Nobody had saved the world. Ten percent recalled lifetimes in which they were members of the upper class, while between 20 and 35 percent were middle class, and 60 to 77 percent were near poverty or actually in it. The definitions of these sociological terms are of course a bit fuzzy and variable over time, but impressionistically this distribution has the feeling of reality.

The magic is in the specificity of the details Wambach uncovered. For example, five subjects recalled living migratory lives in tents in Central Asia between three and four thousand years ago. Strangely they recalled themselves as blond and light-skinned, *leading each of them to dismiss their own "memories" as incorrect.* They "knew" no blondes had lived in Central Asia.

And yet, as a matter of historical fact, Caucasians had migrated to that region during that period.

Thus these prior-life memories existed independently of the beliefs and assumptions of those who were recalling them.

Details of the styles of clothing being worn often came up with Wambach's subjects. Constantly and consistently these were verified as accurate, which is quite impressive given the ever-evolving nature of clothing styles. Quick—what were the upper classes wearing in Egypt in 1000 B.C.? The answer is a half or full-length white cotton robe. Under hypnosis, one of Helen Wambach's subjects knew that.

How?

These kinds of results are profoundly affecting to me.

All together, 62 percent of Wambach's 1088 subjects died of illness and old age. Eighteen percent died in war or violence. Twenty percent died accidentally.

A reasonable distribution?

Perhaps the most compelling of Dr. Helen Wambach's findings is that after more than a thousand subjects and ten years of time, when she totaled up the results, *50.6 percent of the remembered lifetimes were male and 49.4 percent were female*—fifty-fifty in other words. Just about what one would expect in reality.

As with Ian Stevenson and his successors, one can dismiss Helen Wambach's individual stories as "anecdotal." Maybe a friend of yours swears he saw Sasquatch crossing the road a quarter mile ahead at dusk last night. He'd only had one beer, or two. What do you think? You trust your friend, but your opinion is colored by reason and experience—Sasquatch probably does not exist, according to the usual semi-reliable authorities. You shrug your shoulders. Who knows? Maybe it was a dog. Maybe it was a guy in a gorilla suit.

But what if a thousand of your friends saw Sasquatch independently? What do you think then?

Reading the complete work of Stevenson and Wambach has that kind of impact. I have only introduced them here. If your faith in reincarnation could use a little encouragement and support, spend some time with their books. The accumulated evidence will impress you.

Peter Ramster

Some truly fascinating hypnotic regression work has come out of Sydney, Australia, under the guidance of psychologist Peter Ramster. As with the other researchers whose work I am mentioning in this chapter, my aim here is only to give you a taste. If you are interested in learning more, read his book *In Search of Lives Past* or marvel at his video *In Another Life*.

One of Peter Ramster's subjects was a woman named Gwen MacDonald, who had never been outside of Australia. Like Ramster, she was initially skeptical about the whole idea of reincarnation, but she consented to the hypnotic regression. During it she recalled a lifetime in Somerset, England, in the eighteenth century. Taken there in the present day, she was able to navigate around the area, even knowing in which direction her former village lay. She described some stepping stones—and local people confirmed that the stones had been removed only forty years earlier. She knew the names of villages whose names had fallen out of use two centuries earlier. She led the team to a house she remembered which had long since been converted into a shed for chickens. When they cleaned the floor of the shed, they found a stone—*a stone that Gwen MacDonald had sketched back in Sydney before leaving Australia.*

Ramster's work is full of anecdotes such as this one. As with Ian Stevenson and Helen Wambach, their persuasiveness is leveraged by their sheer numbers. Explanations such as "Gwen MacDonald is psychic and doesn't know it" or even "it's a hoax" become harder to sustain in the face of the sheer onslaught of multitudinous, mysterious facts—facts which make perfect sense if we simply assume reincarnation to be a reality.

Arthur Guirdham

English psychiatrist Arthur Guirdham was presented with a "Mrs. Smith" who had been suffering from nightmares about being a peasant girl burned at the stake during the time of the Catholic persecution of the Cathars in southern France. Amazingly, as a schoolgirl, she had actually written verses in Languedoc, the nearly-forgotten language the Cathars spoke. In 1944 she wrote out from memory what she claimed to be songs of the period. *Copies of these songs were only discovered in library archives twenty-three years later!* She could describe buildings of the period in detail. She knew the jewelry of the time.

Fascinatingly, Arthur Guirdham had had similar Cathar nightmares himself since his youth. Mrs. Smith claimed that he had a been a priest named Roger de Grisolles, whom she had known in that lifetime. Impressed by the accuracy of the rest of her dreams and recollections, Dr. Guirdham began doing some academic research to see if he could recover any relevant historical records. Sure enough, there actually was a Roger de Grisolles, murdered in Toulouse in 1242. The karma of their shared prior-life connection had ripened. The priest had turned into a psychiatrist. They met again.

Once more, this is just a brief taste. If you are interested, read Arthur Guirdham's book, *The Cathars and Reincarnation.*

Brian L. Weiss

Psychiatrist Brian L. Weiss's 1988 book, *Many Lives, Many Masters* became a major bestseller. Up until then, his career had been impressive, if rather conventional—Phi Beta Kappa at Columbia, Yale Medical School, University of Miami where he became an Associate Professor of Psychiatry and head of the psychopharmacology division, as well as Chief of Psychiatry at a major Florida hospital. In writing about reincarnation, Weiss of course took a monumental professional risk. Describing it, he delightfully quotes his old grandfather, "Vat the hell, vat the hell."

The trigger for this perilous leap of faith was the arrival in Weiss's office of a twenty-seven year old woman, "Catherine," in 1980. She presented with anxiety and panic attacks, which only worsened during the course of eighteen months of conventional psychotherapy. She was not interested in being drugged. She persisted in verbal therapy.

In 1982, Catherine visited a museum in Chicago where there was a guided tour of some ancient Egyptian artifacts. To her surprise, she found herself correcting the tour guide on some details—and being proven right. This tale piqued Dr. Weiss's curiosity, so he decided to try hypnosis on Catherine. His view, still conditioned by conventional psychology, was that the origin of Catherine's anxieties presumably lay in her childhood. Weiss took her back, in trance, and sure enough, they encountered early childhood sexual abuse. No surprise.

But her symptoms remained as bad as ever. Still baffled, in a subsequent session Weiss unwittingly crossed the Rubicon. He told Catherine simply to "go back to the time from which your symptoms arise."

"I see white steps leading up to a building," said Catherine. *"A big white building with pillars, open in front . . . I am wearing a long dress, a sack made of rough material . . . My hair is braided, long blonde hair."*

Weiss asked her what her name was and what year it was. *"Aronda. I am eighteen . . . There are baskets . . . You carry the baskets on your shoulders . . . The year is 1863 B.C."*

I will leave the rest of the story to Brian Weiss. He tells it well in *Many Lives, Many Masters,* and he has gone on to write a lot more in the field over the years. The beauty of his work to me lies in watching the healing impact of Catherine's unraveling her own karmic story. (In the course of it, we learn that she had lived eighty-six prior lifetimes.)

Four years after the end of their therapeutic relationship, Catherine remained free of the symptoms of anxiety, panic and depression which had driven her into Dr. Weiss's office in the first place. Weiss writes, "Since Catherine, I have done detailed regressions to multiple past lives in a dozen more patients. None of these patients was psychotic, hallucinating, or experiencing multiple personalities. All improved dramatically."

Many Lives, Many Masters is just one story. From an evidentiary perspective, it is not as compelling as the work of the other researchers we have mentioned. One could dismiss it as Catherine's fantasy. But in spirit Weiss's work is closer to the actual work of Evolutionary Astrology, as we will explore it later in this volume. Our aim, like that of Brian Weiss, is healing.

Edgar Cayce

No one was more surprised than Edgar Cayce when he woke up from a trance in 1923 and was told that he had diagnosed the origins of someone's present physical ailments as the results of experiences in a prior lifetime. Cayce, who lived from 1877 until 1945, was a devout southern Christian. He had read the Bible cover to cover once for each year of his life. For twenty years he had been going into trance and offering diagnoses and cures for people's illnesses. He gave about 14,000 readings all together, only 2500 of which were explicitly about prior lifetimes.

I remember finding a copy of Edgar Cayce's biography, *There Is A River* by Thomas Sugrue, in my parents' bookcase when I was twelve years old. Even at that hormonally-addled age, I valued that book above the *National Geographics* with their photos of naked Africans. Reading about Edgar Cayce changed the course of my life. It is the foundation of half of my adult beliefs and understandings. I have been fortunate enough to experience many honors and dignities in my life, but among the greatest of them was being invited to speak twice at the Association for Research and Enlightenment in Virginia Beach, Virginia, which Edgar Cayce founded and where his work is enshrined.

Unlike the work of Wambach or Stevenson, Edgar Cayce made no attempt to be scientific. His aim was purely one of service. Still, meticulous records were kept of his readings and, like that of Wambach and Stevenson, it is most impressive when taken as a body of work. The complete archives are available for perusal at the A.R.E. library in Virginia, and much of it is available in a multitude of books that have appeared about him over the years.

Here is one example, taken from the book *Edgar Cayce on Reincarnation* by Noel Langley. A psychologist by the name of Calvin Mortimer came to Cayce for a reading during the time between the two World Wars. Quoting from the text of the session, *"Before this, the Entity was in the land of the present nativity, during the period just following the American revolution . . . among the soldiery of the British, acting in the American land in what would be termed the Intelligence Service. Not as a spy but rather one of those who mapped and laid out the plans for the campaigns by Howe and Clinton. However the Entity remained in the American soil after hostilities ended, not as one dead, but as one making for the cooperation between the peoples of the Entity's native land and those of the land of adoption. Then in the name Warren, the Entity gained by successfully establishing those relationships. Hence in the present we will find diplomatic relationships, the exchange of ideas and plans of the various nations, becoming of interest to the Entity."*

When World War Two broke out, Mortimer was too old for active combat duty, so he joined the Coast Guard—but was quickly transferred to the Domestic Intelligence Service. There, he came to work closely with the Office of Strategic Services—the predecessor of the C.I.A.. By the end of the war, he was in charge of a school for spies, "training men to drop behind enemy lines on the selfsame spot in Long Island where he had once mapped and laid out the plans for the campaigns of Howe and Clinton in the War of Independence."

Remember: Edgar Cayce did this reading before World War Two had begun.

Over and over again in Edgar Cayce's readings we see these kinds of precognitions of future developments in people's lives based upon the repetition of old past-life patterns. There are the geographical and professional associations, as we observe with Calvin Mortimer—but also relationships, physical illnesses, talents. Throughout Cayce's work, there is a sense of strong moral philosophy. A better way to phrase it might be a sense of the natural laws of cause, effect, and consequence—karma, in other words.

For example, Cayce did a reading for a woman struggling with alcoholism and sexual compulsivity in her present life. He related it to a prior life during a wildly libertine period in French history—counter-intuitively, one in which she was judgmental and Puritanical, condemning others for their "contamination" and finally withdrawing into a convent. In trance, Cayce said to her, *"Ye condemned those whose activities were in direct disobedience to the law. But he who is weak in the flesh, is his error the greater? For one should know that the condemning of others is already a condemning of the self. Which is the greater sin?"*

Edgar Cayce, in trance, was more than a psychic. He was a powerful spiritual teacher. I owe him a great debt.

Roger J. Woolger, Patricia Walsh, and "Deep Memory Process"

When it comes to healing and release, there are tremendous advantages to the active reality of actually recalling one's own prior lifetimes. Alternatively, we can sit with a psychic—or an evolutionary astrologer—and hear about a prior incarnation. But then maybe we aren't sure. Maybe we don't know what to make of it. But when the memory comes roaring straight up out of your own unconscious, there is a certain undeniable immediacy to the experience. That can occur through meditation or dreams, but *hypnotic regression and other forms of trance work* are the classic gateways into that kind of direct experience. We have seen examples of that process already, most notably with Helen Wambach. One of its pioneers is an Englishman, Roger J. Woolger.

Woolger trained at the C.G. Jung Institute in Zurich, after studying at Oxford. His book, *Other Lives, Other Selves*, is generally recognized as one of the seminal works in the field of past life regression. His work is distinct from what we normally think of as hypnosis. His associate, Patricia Walsh, about whom you will learn more below, put it this way in a private communication:

Yes, regression does happen with eyes closed and in an altered state, but there is a main difference technically between hypnotic regression and the Jungian principle of 'active imagination' which we employ. Hypnosis attempts to get the person to 'relax,' to induce a trance state, while in our form we work with whatever affect is arising, be it a physical, emotional or mental symptom and guide the person deeper into it, this puts one into an altered state naturally. The story or the past life character is already in the symptom, there is no need to look any further. This is actually a more 'shamanic' approach as shamans typically exaggerate symptoms to have someone go deeper into them. Bradford Keeney, Ph.D., a psychotherapist who has studied extensively with shamans around the world and has been recognized by them as an elder, says, "The Bushmen and indigenous healers do exactly the opposite of what we do to help people in our culture. We calm, medicate and tranquilize people. We teach them meditation and relaxation techniques in an attempt to de-escalate their conflicts. The shamans often advocate something completely different: They instruct people who are troubled and disturbed to rev up their energy even further." What Keeney is pointing out is that just like in homeopathic medicine, a little bit of like cures like, the healing is in the pain of the symptom and one must dive into the depths to find the pearl of healing. When one exaggerates the problem it opens up a deeper layer of the complex and subsequently a deeper level of healing and resolution can occur. In hypnosis, not always, but typically, a person 'observes' the past life, and especially when traumatic events happen they are often encouraged to 'watch from the sidelines.' In our work we want the person to become the character fully as we are fundamentally doing trauma therapy that aims to heal the spilt and dissociated consciousness. "

Back before he was famous, Roger Woolger came to North Carolina to offer a weekend workshop, which I eagerly attended. My own first book, *The Inner Sky*, had just come out. Through a mutual friend, Roger and I were introduced. We had lunch. He was as eager to pick my brain about the mysteries of how to get published as I was to pick his about the mysteries of reincarnation. Synchronistically, our fates seemed to be linked. Within a short while, he had a contract with the same publisher as I did—Bantam

Books. And even though I had been drawn to reincarnation ever since I had been a child reading Edgar Cayce, Roger's presentations that weekend really inspired me to see the therapeutic possibilities in past-life recall and encouraged me to pursue its astrological dimensions.

Like the work of Brian Weiss, Roger Woolger's work—which he calls *Deep Memory Process*—has, sad to say, relatively little value in terms of convincing skeptics. The work is for open-minded people who want to dive into their own psyches and experience their own prior lives directly. It is not about "proving" reincarnation at all, except perhaps subjectively—in fact, Woolger distances himself from any such concerns. In his own words from *Other Lives, Other Selves*, " . . . past life therapy, as a rule, does not set out to prove anything. Proof or disproof of reincarnation is strictly the province of parapsychology and research. . . Be this as it may, any concern with explanation must remain secondary to the immediate task of the therapist, which is to help his or her clients to obtain relief from and to understand troublesome symptoms and behavior patterns over which they have no control."

Roger Woolger's aims are so like my own that it is no surprise that our journeys wove together many years ago. The rest should be no surprise either: several years ago while teaching an astrology workshop in Hartford, Connecticut, I encountered a bright, enthusiastic woman who said she had been working with Roger. Her name was Patricia Walsh. She had studied the principles of Evolutionary Astrology with my own friend and writing partner, Jeffrey Wolf Green, and she was connecting Jeff's past-life work very effectively with people's own recovered memories from the hypnotic work that Roger Woolger had pioneered. In other words, *Patricia Walsh was proving that trance-work and Evolutionary Astrology were coming up with the same results.* Her work is meticulous and very concrete. Case studies are compared, with the parallels between the two systems leaping out dramatically.

Patricia will have a book out soon. If you are interested, I encourage you to Google her name from time to time. For now, I would draw your attention to her article "Astrological Observations from Past Life Therapy." It appeared in *International Astrologer, the Journal of the International*

Society for Astrological Research in the Leo issue, 2006, Volume XXXVI, #3.

I find the work that Roger Woolger and Patricia Walsh are doing particularly exciting for two reasons. First, and more importantly, there is tremendous potential for a healing synergy between hypnotic regressions and Evolutionary Astrology. A regression in which a person actually has direct experience of a prior life trauma can be tremendously cathartic, adding dimensionality and punch to the more abstract astrological analysis. Turning it around, the astrological analysis can direct a person's attention to the most charged—and most relevant—unresolved karmic issues. In other words, if you were the captain of a slave ship (or one of its passengers) in a prior life, you might vastly prefer to recall lifetimes as a French pastry chef! Astrology strategically directs the attention in the most therapeutic direction, while Deep Memory Process can better trigger highly specific memories, plus release, confidence in the reality of the experience, and healing.

The second reason I am so excited about this coming together of Deep Memory Process and Evolutionary Astrology is that the combination is just so incredibly convincing. If Joe tells you he saw a UFO around sunset last night over the reservoir, you are interested, but you are not sure. If an hour later Carol, *who has never even met Joe*, tells you the same thing, you are far more compelled to belief. Seeing the karmic story in astrological symbols, then hearing it come independently out of someone's mouth can give pause to even the most dire skeptic.

Roger Woolger himself in a private communication says, "What I have seen of the application of Evolutionary Astrology illuminates more of what I understand to be the inherited psychological dynamics of past lives than anything else I have come across."

Many Avenues

As you can see from the foregoing pages, there are many ways people might encounter information about their prior lifetimes. Like Calvin Mortimer, we might sit with a psychic such as Edgar Cayce and simply have the story given to us. Like Brian Weiss's clients, participants in Deep

Memory Process therapies, or Helen Wambach's subjects, we might employ hypnotic regression or trance work, and, with the help of a guide, discover the tale ourselves. Like Arthur Guirdham's Mrs. Smith, the images might come to us in dreams or by direct recollection. Many, especially the very young, just seem to "know," as evidenced in Ian Stevenson's studies.

Evolutionary Astrology is taking its place among these other methods. In common with the others, it has certain advantages and disadvantages. Positively, its techniques are quite objective and replicable. They are not so subject to the impacts of people's wishes and fears nor so vulnerable to confusions created by forgotten memories—memories, for example, of movies we saw when we were three years old, which can honestly be mistaken for prior-life images.

Negatively, Evolutionary Astrology provides only symbols and metaphors. It will not tell you that you worked for Generals Howe and Clinton on Long Island in the War of Independence. It won't send you cleaning up the floor of a chicken coop in Somerset, England, looking for a certain etched stone.

As we will see, if healing and release are our primary aims, as they are for Brian Weiss or Roger Woolger, then the literal past-life facts are less important than the emotions that are locked up in them—emotions which can be accessed just as effectively through metaphors as through literal facts.

And there is ultimately no metaphorical system so powerful and so primal as that of astrology.

The Tulku of Saraha

In Tibet before the Chinese annexation, the monastery of Tsé-Chöling had lost its abbot. In the customs of Buddhism, the solution was not simply to choose a successor, but rather to simply await the late abbot's reincarnation.

Meanwhile, a boy took birth not far away and soon began to speak of a "monastery on a hill where he had lived as a monk."

The choir-master of Tsé-Chöling chanced to hear rumors of this boy and arranged to pay him an informal visit. The boy was by then three or four years old—the typical age of Ian Stevenson's subjects as they began speaking of prior lifetimes. Following Tibetan custom, the choir-master carried a bag full of objects, some of which had belonged to the deceased abbot and some of which had not. The objects were spread out before the child, who was casually invited to chose some for his own. Immediately he picked out a damaged bell, favoring it over another unflawed bell.

"Why do you want that old thing when there is a much better one?" asked the choir-master. "Won't you have the nice new one?"

"No, I would rather have my old bell," responded the boy.

"How do you know this is *your* bell?"

"Because one day it fell down and got chipped at the rim," responded the boy, pointing out where a piece of metal was missing from the inner rim.

This account is taken from the wonderful book, *The Way of the White Clouds*, by Lama Anagarika Govinda. He goes on to write, "Every single object that had belonged to the former abbot was immediately recognized by the boy, who firmly rejected all other things, though many of them were identical in shape."

Thus did the monastery of Tsé-Chöling recover its rightful abbot.

Tibetan Buddhism

1997 was a good year for bringing the reality of Tibetan society and religion to the attention of westerners. Two films came out that year, *Seven Years in Tibet* and *Kundun*. Both explored, among other things, the life and times of His Holiness the Dalai Lama. As a child, he too, like the Tulku of Saraha, had proven himself the reincarnation of his predecessor through the device of recognizing certain objects which he had possessed in his previous incarnation. (The word "Tulku," by the way, simply refers to the rebirth of a recognized spiritual figure from the past.)

In a culture which assumes reincarnation, such as traditional Tibet, these kinds of events are relatively commonplace. And the recognition of previous possessions is not the only way this certainty of identification across the abyss of death and rebirth is demonstrated, as we will now see.

The Karmapa

Perhaps the highest being to reincarnate successively within the sphere of Tibetan spirituality is called the Karmapa. The 16th Karmapa died in the United States in November 1981 after a long bout with cancer. His faithful attendant Akong Rinpoche had asked him for only one thing—one of the Karmapa's teeth, to be given to Akong after the Karmapa had died and been cremated. Somehow in the general chaos around the 16th Karmapa's passing in faraway America, the tooth had never gotten to Akong Rinpoche. He had been too distraught by his master's passing to attend the cremation, where he might have asked for it.

A few years later, Akong Rinpoche was in the party of lamas who set out to search for the Karmapa's reincarnation. The tale is very complex, unfolding at the byzantine intersection of Tibetan and Chinese politics. If you are interested, I would recommend the book, *The Dance of 17 Lives* by Mick Brown. The short version of the story is that basically the 16th Karmapa, following a common Tibetan tradition, had a written a letter just before his death detailing where he intended to take his next birth, naming a village, the parents and so forth. It took a while for that letter to surface, which created considerable confusion.

In the end, Akong Rinpoche and a band of monks followed the instructions in the letter, and at the end of the trail they encountered a boy named Apo Gaga who had been born on June 26, 1985.

In the words of Akong Rinpoche, *"So when I first saw Karmapa, I said to him, before you died you promised me something. So where is it?"*

Akong Rinpoche goes on to say that the young boy "had a small carpet, and under the carpet there was one of his milk teeth. And he gave it to me. So that solved the problem."

The 17th Karmapa had been born.

As I mentioned previously, for compelling, rational evidence of reincarnation, the broad samples, rigorous methodology, and statistical analysis of researchers such as Ian Stevenson and Helen Wambach are so far unparalleled. For an understanding of the therapeutic and healing applications of the work, I would look to Roger Woolger, Patricia Walsh, Brian Weiss, and their colleagues and contemporaries. But for whatever real understanding that I, at least, have of the larger logic of the long-term evolution of our beings, I can only thank the lineage of Buddhist teachers who have so kindly and generously shared their understanding with all those who care to hear it.

Personal Experience

Ian Stevenson found more kids who remembered previous lifetimes in societies that were collectively open to the idea of reincarnation—such an India—than he did in societies where there was no widespread belief in reincarnation, such as the United States or Western Europe. Intuitively, it is easy to understand why that would be so. A child from West Virginia who starts "babbling nonsense" about having been a monk in a Himalayan monastery is not going to get much positive reinforcement for continuing to insist upon it. Still, as we saw earlier, between 20 and 35 percent of Americans actually "believe in" reincarnation despite the common impression that it is an exotic, foreign notion. I am not sure what the corresponding figures would be in Europe, Latin America, or elsewhere in the Western world. Perhaps not so different.

Where do all these people get their belief? Going out on a limb, where do *you* get your own (however tentative) belief in reincarnation—my evidence being that you are reading this book?

Nothing remotely objective or scientific here . . . but if you get a few open-minded folks relaxing around a table talking about their past life impressions, you quickly strike a motherlode of intriguing stories. Mostly these stories take the form of *intuitive impressions* of prior lifetimes, typically based on a felt affinity with certain lands or certain times in history. "I have always felt that I was a nun in a convent in France." "I have always known that Quincy and I were among the Knights Templar."

Often there are "little miracles" that reinforce the images—details known or sensed, amazing "coincidences." For one personal example, when

I was a young man I went backpacking in Europe for a few months with my partner. In the deserted ruins of Pompeii on a gray November day, we encountered a guard. With his eye on my pretty blond girlfriend, he told me with a wink that I, as a man, should not miss the *fine* murals in the ruins of the old brothel. Lamentably, said he, women were not allowed in there due to the stimulating nature of the art—but that I shouldn't worry a moment because he would protect my girlfriend for me while I was gone. Even at that tender age, I saw through his deception—but the weird thing was that as soon as he launched into giving me directions to the brothel, I finished his sentence for him.

I *knew* where the brothel was in ancient Pompeii!

Years later, looking through a book of color plates of mosaics from all over the world, I came upon one of a mildly erotic nature and I immediately knew it was from that same Pompeiian brothel. Referring its plate number to the Index, my identification was confirmed.

Given the evolutionary nature of life, I like this Pompeii story of mine a lot. Had I "remembered" that I had been Jesus Christ's meditation teacher, I pray I would have been suspicious of myself! But knowing that I had enjoyed the pleasures of the local brothel a couple of thousand years ago has the ring of truth to it. (I have done nothing of that nature in this lifetime, nor do I find the notion attractive—perhaps I got it out my system back then!) The point is, I was *less evolved* then.

Somehow too, I know in my bones that while I once lived in Pompeii, that it was basically a happy lifetime. I am quite sure I was gone from that body before the famous "unpleasantness" for which the city is best known.

My point with indulging myself in this personal story is not to prove anything in particular or to make any claims about myself. My point is that I confidently believe that there are several billion such stories floating around the world. All that stands between us and them is a collective paradigm of "official" disbelief in reincarnation—a paradigm which is collapsing.

History

Most of us in the western world have been conditioned to consider reincarnation an "eastern" belief. And certainly it would be impossible to contemplate Buddhism or Hinduism without prior and future lives. Earlier we saw the practical relevance of reincarnation to Tibetan Buddhist culture. In the roots of Hinduism, Krishna himself in the Bhagavad-Gita says, "As a man throweth away old garments and putteth on new, even so the dweller in the body, having quitted its old mortal frames, entereth into others which are new . . ."

Less commonly known is that the Celts held a belief in reincarnation as well. Looking around the faces I see attending my classes and the conferences where I am invited to speak, I think it is fair to say we are talking about the distant grandmothers and grandfathers of an awful lot of modern Western astrologers! A common historical error is the belief that the Celts were basically British and Irish. While they did make their last stand against the Romans there, Celts were once spread out over much of Europe—and thus are the ancestors to a great many of us who hold the lamp of modern astrology in the West. Of that nation, Julius Caesar wrote, *"They wish to inculcate this as one of their leading tenets, that souls do not become extinct, but pass after death from one body to another."*

History is of course written by the victors, and when the Celtic kingdoms fell before the Romans and their Druids were put to death, the loss of spiritual treasure to the human race as a whole was incalculable. The tragedy was multiplied by the fact that the Celtic people kept no written records of their beliefs. The culture was an oral one, based on memorization and mentoring. That loss is particularly acute to those of us with northern European blood who have had most of our root-spirituality ripped from our souls, and the rest buried beneath layers of "foreign" Middle Eastern and Mediterranean philosophy—the Judeo-Christian tradition, in other words, with its theological overlay of Greco-Roman philosophy and logic.

What Would Jesus Do?

Nominally reincarnation is not a Jewish or Christian belief. And yet, peppered throughout the scriptures are many clear references to it. Try these passages from Matthew 17: 10-13 in the Revised Standard Version of the Bible:

"And the disciples asked him, "Then why do the scribes say that first Elijah must come? He replied, "Elijah does come, and he is to restore all things; but I tell you that Elijah has already come, and they did not know him, but did to him whatever they pleased. So also the Son of man will suffer at their hands. Then the disciples understood that he was speaking to them of John the Baptist."

Elijah was a prophet in the ninth century BC. He lived eight hundred years before Jesus spoke these words.

In the Old Testament book of Malachi 4:5-6, we read *"Behold, I will send you Elijah the prophet before the great and terrible day of the Lord comes. And he will turn the hearts of fathers to their children and the hearts of children to their fathers, lest I come and smite the land with a curse."*

The Book of Malachi is hard to date accurately, but internal clues put it no earlier than 515 BC and no later than 445 BC—at least a couple of centuries *after* Elijah had lived and died. Clearly, the prophecy here is for the *reincarnation* of Elijah. And much later, Jesus himself recognized Elijah's "Tulku" in John the Baptist!

The unparalleled giant of a poet and scholar, Robert Graves, pulled no punches on this matter. In his words, "No honest theologian therefore can deny that his acceptance of Jesus as Christ logically binds every Christian to a belief in reincarnation—in Elias's case at least." (Elias and Elijah are equivalent.)

What is going on here? What happened to reincarnation in the west? It is clearly "in the Bible," and yet Bible-thumping Fundamentalists who hold the belief that everything in the Bible is the literal word of God tend to view reincarnation as a blasphemous idea. How did that happen? To condemn reincarnation, they have to ignore some rather straightforward Biblical passages, as we just saw.

In the words of Brian Weiss, "In A.D. 325 the Roman emperor Constantine the Great, along with his mother, Helena, had deleted references to reincarnation contained in the New Testament. The Second Council of Constantinople, meeting in A.D. 553, confirmed this action and declared the concept of reincarnation a heresy."

That is one view, although the balanced academic perspective is murkier. Quoting Roger Woolger, "Contemporary Christian theologians don't seem to be able to agree, despite mountains of scholarship, on whether early Christianity accepted the doctrine of reincarnation or not. Leslie Wetherhead maintains that 'reincarnation was accepted by the early church for the first five hundred years of its existence.' Head and Cranston provide texts to support him. John Hick, on the other hand, claims this view to be totally erroneous and misleading, saying 'reincarnation was taught within the Gnostic movement from within the Church, but that it early distinguished itself and was treated as a dangerous foe.'"

At the risk of diverging too far afield, I do know that some of the disagreement over reincarnation's role in early Christianity stems from the intertwining of two ideas: past lives and *the pre-existence of the soul*. The latter is simply the idea that all souls were created by God at the beginning of time—versus "print-on-demand" souls which God would create at the moment of conception or the moment of birth. This was a hot debate a millennium and a half ago. You can have pre-existent souls that simply wait their turn for their single shot at incarnation, or pre-existent souls that reincarnate over and over again—either way those souls have "pasts." What you can't have are fresh, made-to-order souls with a history of prior incarnations.

The "pre-existence" issue was a contentious one in early Christianity. It seems that by the time the language and the texts age for a couple of millennia, then go through translations, honorab*-le scholars can read reincarnation into "pre-existence" or out of it.

So it is a muddle.

But clearly it is impossible to make sense of certain passages in the Bible without thinking literally of reincarnation, as we have demonstrated by simply quoting from the Gospel of Matthew. The Gnostics, who were so intimately bound up in the early history of Christian thinking, most definitely believed in it. Though subject to debate, there is also good evidence that Plato and Pythagoras assumed reincarnation. And, as we have seen, up north in the "barbarous" forests of the Celts, reincarnation was simply a fact of life.

If not universal, it at least seems to pop up everywhere, in other words. The notion that prior lifetimes are an "Eastern" concept is simply too restrictive. The fact is that belief in reincarnation was once widespread—but only survived as a mainstream belief into modern times in the East.

Other Cultures

I had the pleasure of speaking in Australia recently. My sponsors there, Lisa Jones and Cheryl Cooper, very kindly arranged a surprise for me. Just before I was to begin my five-day presentation, an Aboriginal man stepped out of the wings. He arrived in a loincloth, his body caked ceremonially in mud-patterns, ready to tell us stories and play his digiridoo.

He wove a spell on us all, then he was kind of enough to remain and listen to the first couple hours of my presentation. During that time, I spoke quite a lot about the lost relationship between astrology and past lives. When I took a break, he came up to me and told me that his people share the same belief. I had entertained no idea of that! Perhaps the most distinguishing mark of the Aboriginal people of Australia from a historical perspective is their utter, hermetic isolation from the rest of the world for perhaps *fifty thousand* years prior to the European conquest. Isn't it interesting that they too would accept the cyclicality of life? Their own hearts told them the same truth the Buddha saw.

In their book of collected quotations about prior lifetimes, *Reincarnation: An East-West Anthology*, Joseph Head and S.L. Cranston (cited earlier by Roger Woolger) list the so-called "primitive" peoples who show evidence of accepting the idea of reincarnation. Here is a slightly shortened version:

North America: Algonquins, Dakotas, Hurons, Iroquois, Koloshes, Mohaves, Hopi, Natchez, Nutkas, Powhatans, Tacullis, Tlingit , Eskimos, Haidas.
Central and South America: Caribs, Chiriguanos, Maya and Quiches, Patagonians, Peruvians, Soutals, Popayans, Icannas and Abysones.
Europe: Finns, Lapps, Danes, Norse, Icelandic peoples, Early Saxons, Celts of Gaul, Wales, England, and Ireland, Old Prussians and Early Teutonics, Lithuanians.

Africa: Suks of Kenya, Wanikas, Akikiyus, Mandingo, Edo, Ibo, Ewes, Yorubas, Calabar, Siena, Twi, Zulus, Bantus, Barotse, Maravi.

If you believe that you have lived before, you may seem slightly eccentric in modern North America or Europe. Keep perspective though: even today in those societies, statistically your "minority group" is—well, for one fun metaphor—about the size of all the gay folks and all the Fundamentalists combined.

You are in a minority, but it is a *big* minority.

And, from an anthropological perspective, across the millennia and across the spectrum of human cultures, you are probably in a majority.

A Last Word

My intent in writing this chapter has, in essence, been to make it "safe" to consider reincarnation to be a fact. I will be operating on that assumption from here on out as we move into exploring and mastering the technical realm of Evolutionary Astrology.

I believe that astrologers in general are no wiser than the cultures in which they are operating—we drink the same water and breathe the same mythic air as everyone else. I believe that the strange rejection of reincarnation in the West for the past fifteen hundred years has ripped astrology from its roots in the universal mysticism of nearly every culture. I feel that it is time to restore those roots, to put the soul and the mystery back into the astrological wind.

CHAPTER THREE: THE ESSENCE OF THE TECHNIQUE

Under the Bodhi tree, Gautama the Buddha "remembered many, many former existences . . . one, two births, three, four, five . . . fifty, one hundred . . . a hundred thousand."

In the previous chapter, we saw that Brian Weiss's patient Catherine claimed to have lived eighty-six human lives before her current one.

Whatever the typical number of prior lifetimes may be, if we had symbolism for all of them in every birthchart, it would be enough to paint the chart black! That is not the case, so there must be some kind of filtering mechanism involved. Not everything makes the cut. I believe that, rather than the entire past life panorama, the chart simply tells us *what we need to know* in order to most effectively navigate this present life. It describes prior lifetimes that are *relevant* to the present one, typically in a potentially vexing or undermining sort of way.

In rigorous terms, I believe the past-life filter built into astrology has two stages. For anything to manifest in the chart it must pass both tests.

First, the issue must be one that was *left unresolved* in a prior lifetime.

Second, there must be either a *soul intention* or an *evolutionary necessity* to work on the issue in this lifetime. The "karma has ripened," in other words.

Thus, while you may indeed have actually been Henry VIII in a prior life, if you have already resolved that formidable karma and moved beyond it in the evolutionary sense, it will not appear in your chart. And again, if you are *just not ready yet* to face those issues and are working on a different evolutionary angle, they too will not appear in the present astrological symbolism.

For psychologically transparent reasons, my ego might be enthusiastically receptive to the notion that I was "among the first to recognize the true nature of Jesus Christ, who was a close personal friend of mine" in a prior lifetime. That makes me look noble and wise. I might be less eager to recall that I had stolen my beer money from poor old blind woman in Elizabethan England! Evolutionary Astrology by-passes those ego-traps. It simply tells us what we need to know with objectivity and precision, and with no regard for our wishes or our fears.

Order Out of the Chaos

As we saw in Chapter One, everything in your chart is karmic in origin, and can be understood that way. Were we to apply the philosophy that we learned there as we explored Saturn in the seventh house to the analysis of each configuration in your natal chart, we would have a lot of deep information—but it would be a mish-mash of unrelated ideas and images. It wouldn't really be a "story" at all, just a bunch of fragments.

With some mindfulness, we might sense the way themes interconnected. One planet might seem relevant to themes connected with another—Saturn in the seventh house, as we explored in the previous chapter, could connect thematically with an aspect such as Pluto squaring Venus. In the latter aspect, we might very well be looking at an issue of exposure to *intimate treachery* in a prior life. That might lead us to underscore *abandonment themes* rather than bereavement themes in our interpretation of Saturn. Each configuration would flavor the other one.

But mostly we would still have a mish-mash. In Chapter One, we called it "chaos theory." Your karma is an amalgam of often-unrelated themes, just as is your biography in this present lifetime.

Since karma itself is typically a mish-mash, this perception of chaos does not mean we are off target! Still it would be helpful if we could bring a sharper focus to our work. In this chapter, we concentrate on the royal road into that sharper focus: *the lunar nodes.* They are immensely powerful, as you will see—but always remember that the full evolutionary perspective ultimately involves all the planets, especially the ones that rule or are in aspect to the nodes.

In this chapter, we sketch a brief overview of the entire system. I hope that this approach will provide you with a kind of *Mappa Mundi* that will help you navigate through the details of this methodology which comprise the rest of the book.

After you've digested the overview, in the following chapters we will expand on that foundation by doing three things.

We will offer "cookbook" interpretations of all the basic elements.

We will explore deeply all of the major planetary aspects to the lunar nodes.

We will bring it all to life with a number of concrete examples.

The Lunar South Node

(Note: for those of you with a technical, astronomical bent, in Chapter Five we define precisely what we mean physically by lunar nodes, learn about their cycles, and clarify the distinction between the Mean Node and the True Node.)

All the astrological planets except the Sun have south nodes, and all south nodes make reference to the past. But it is the *Moon's* south node—historically called the *Dragon's Tail*—that we generally interpret.

Why?

There is actually a simple answer, and knowing it illuminates the foundation of the system you are about to learn. The Moon is above all *emotional*. What survives the trauma of death and rebirth is not our *factual* memory—not our "Mercury memory," so to speak. It is our *emotional* memory—the Moon memory—that endures. We typically do not remember names or addresses from prior lives. We don't clearly recall our nationality or our religion. But we do carry an underlying *mood* or *attitude* forward from the past. Beyond that, at best we recall only fragmentary impressions of names, details, history.

> **That remembered mood or attitude is what you can see and feel in the south node of an individual birthchart. It is what automatically survives death and rebirth.**

Arguably, those deep-seated emotional memories are the only things from the past that have any present-tense importance anyway. They are what live on. It is the heart's memories that endure.

Imagine a two-year old child grievously abused. She grows up, but the trauma of her early life is repressed. At a conscious level, she has no idea that it happened. But everywhere she goes she carries an attitude of shame, fear, suspicion, and insecurity. It taints her relationships, her attitude toward her body, and her self-image. You can feel the mood surrounding her like a dark cloud. And yet she remembers nothing—in the Mercury sense. But the Moon carries the emotional memory intact, as perfect as a butterfly encased in glass.

The heart's memory is stronger than death; the mind's memory is not.

That is precisely how the Moon's south node works, except that it operates over longer time-scales. Not just childhood-into-adulthood, but lifetime into lifetime. Always there is the basic lunar fingerprint of karma: disproportionately strong emotions. "The heart's memory." Jeff Green nailed it beautifully in an interview in *The Mountain Astrologer* (issue #94). He said, "The simplest way to know a past-life issue is being triggered is when you have a disproportionate response to an existing stimulus." Let me add that often the karmic material reflects "childhood issues" as recovered via conventional psychological work. This should be no surprise, as little in our lives is more karmic than our "choice" of parents!

Karma is Habit

These attitudinal heart-memories persist into the present. If you have resolved issues from a prior life, they will not appear in your present birthchart—nor will they have much biographical relevance to your present life, except perhaps in a positive sense. But if they were left unresolved, you will experience certain consequences in your daily reality. *Karma, above all, is just habit.* It is not a very romantic or exotic concept—only the tendency that we all have to repeat old patterns, or to be defined by our knee-jerk reaction against them. If, for example, I was raised in an unnaturally repressive sexual environment, will I be sexually repressed in my adulthood? Maybe, even probably—but I might also be seeing how many notches I can put on my bedpost! Either way, I am still in the grips of the past. Maybe I am re-enacting it—or maybe I am reacting against it. But I am still in its grip.

Beware too of the tendency to think that karma is always about "getting what you deserve." It can work that way, but more often it is simply about deadening repetition. If you stole from someone in a prior life, it does not mean that they will steal from you in this lifetime. More likely, you will simply continue to steal, habitually. In the words of the Venerable Khenchen Thrangu from his booklet *Buddhist Conduct: The Ten Virtuous Actions:*

> *For example, if one has killed someone, then in the next lifetime one will experience various unpleasant things with the ripening result of this action. A corresponding result could be that one experiences short life in the next lifetime from having killed somebody. The second corresponding result which continues is that if one has killed in this lifetime, the result is that in the next lifetime one still has the tendency and will want to spontaneously kill again. Or if one steals in this lifetime, one will continue stealing in the next lifetime and so on. Even as a child, one will like stealing or killing.*

Thus the south node of the Moon defines a habitual, underlying attitude—a set of emotional assumptions—which underpin and drive a whole set of repeating dramas. Until you become conscious of them, they rule your life, just as surely and invisibly as did nineteenth century gender assumptions. As the great Dane Rudhyar wrote in his monograph, *The Planetary and Lunar Nodes*, the south node "refers to a type of experience which one can easily take for granted; that is, one tends to allow the experiences to control the consciousness, instead of the conscious mind controlling the experiences. One is naturally good at meeting such experiences and therefore they represent the line of least resistance and thus of least exertion. Because of this, one tends to repeat and indulge in them."

Habit, in other words.

The Helpfulness of a Negative Attitude

In all counseling work, there is an obvious case to be made for an upbeat, positive approach. But with the south node, a negative bias should permeate our interpretations—and that is completely appropriate. This can be a stretch for astrologers with warm hearts, but here is the reasoning: what we carry forward from the past—or at least what manifests through the symbols of the chart—is *material on which we need to work.* With the lunar south node, we learn about things we *got wrong* in prior lifetimes—or things we got right, but in getting them right, we sustained damage which haunts us today. It is inherently "negative."

Happier material does get through the after-death pipeline, but it doesn't seem to be reflected nearly as clearly in the astrological symbolism. There is an efficiency here: as we saw earlier, the chart seems to tell us only "what we need to know." It does not paint a complete and full picture of the soul's history. It illuminates issues that must be faced and resolved.

The south node primarily represents unresolved wounds, tragedies, limitations and failures from the past, which potentially interfere with our ability to fulfill our soul-contract in this lifetime.

The south node is always rooted in the past—and by definition, since evolution carries us forward, we were *less* evolved then. We are haunted by this unresolved, atavistic part of our soul history and vulnerable to repeating it.

Even the "good stuff" in the south node feels tired and overly familiar. We already know it, so there is no compelling need to learn it again.

Finding the Karmic Story

Any novel worth reading is full of made-up facts that come together to cast light on some great truth. Our aim in prising the karmic story out of the nodal structure is very similar. We are not really expecting to unearth specific, verifiable past-life facts: for that, go to a good psychic or experience hypnotic regression, as we described in Chapter Two.

What surfaces through nodal analysis is a *parable* that parallels the actual past-life realities. The core point is simply that *the story doesn't have to be "factual" for it to be "true."* Even without any particular intuition, the technical procedures we explore here can produce powerful, evocative, and psychologically-relevant results—stories that resonate with the deep soul-unconscious.

Maybe a person, for example, was actually a pioneer in the American west in a prior lifetime and was killed by beleaguered, desperate Comanche warriors. But maybe in our analysis of the south node, we come up with a a story describing her as an immigrant crossing the Atlantic on a ship taken by hungry pirates.

Our "facts" are completely incorrect—but the story is still "true" psychologically. Emotionally, it boils down to the same dynamics. That is what we are doing here.

The South Node's Sign and House

The sign the south node occupies tells us about the *nature* of the person and what his or her *soul-contract* was in the past. Here is a great trick for bringing that notion to life: just remember to tilt your interpretation a bit negatively, then *think of the south node's sign as you would a conventional Sun sign.* Just put it in a past life. Present-tense, the astrological Sun sign says a lot about your *core identity* and *values.* It is really the same for the south node: it describes your *core identity and values in a prior lifetime.* And remember, unlike the wide-open possibilities inherent in the Magical Now, that old soul-contract was not fulfilled successfully, at least not 100 percent. If it were, it would not be your south node today. It wouldn't haunt you that way.

South node in Aries? She had a *warrior's* nature and energy—but you'll be looking at dark issues of stress and fear, along with the damaging impact of violence received or violence offered. South node in Libra? Probably we are looking at a loving person—but watch out for too much "politeness," indecision, or concern with appearances. That is the Libran shadow.

In Chapter Six, you will find a kind of "starter kit" for looking at all twelve south node sign placements.

The *house* the south node occupies tells us about the *physical scene* of his or her life in the karmic past—what the person was actually doing and what their life looked like from the outside. It also offers some insight into *the circumstances which compelled or constrained the person.*

South node in the ninth house? Think about institutions of learning or religion. Consider travel or immigration. Eleventh house? Movements. Tribes. Large groups of people. The nearly irresistible force of mob psychology. Second house? Issues around money or the material basis of survival. Tenth house? Status questions linked to a defining public role—or a suffocating one.

In Chapter Seven, you will find a similar "cookbook" for understanding all twelve south node placements in terms of the astrological houses.

Next, put the house and the sign together. South node in Libra and in the eleventh house? Probably we are looking at a married person, crippled by indecision and by too much concern with what others thought (Libra)—living in the context of a *compelling, but suffocatingly proper society* (eleventh house, modified in the Libran direction).

Notice how much more vivid and precise everything becomes when we let the sign and the house modify and specify each other—and limit each other. Each detail brings additional focus.

Try switching to the south node to Aries, while keeping it in the eleventh house. No longer Libran, the person now emerges in a more belligerent, angry or adventurous way. That is Aries. He is still operating in the context of a group (eleventh house), but now that group is not so polite. It takes on an Arian edge of explosiveness and destructiveness—that's the eleventh house, now tilted in the Arian direction. That Arian eleventh house node sounds like it could be an *army*. That would at least be an evocative metaphor. It could as easily be an angry mob, or a highly competitive sports team. All those metaphors and images are consistent with people coming together (eleventh house) for a competitive or belligerent (Aries) purpose.

And metaphors are what we are seeking.

Run It Through The Filter

Linking the south node's sign and house, as we just saw, begins to narrow the field within which the karmic story will unfold. But it is still dauntingly vague. There are 144 possible combinations of sign and house. That is a lot—but there are a lot more than 144 possible human stories! Still we have made progress worth celebrating. We have winnowed the list down to less than one percent of all archetypal possibilities—0.69 percent of them, to be precise! That is what correctly choosing one out of 144 options means.

We can go much further toward precision.

What follows is a series of technical procedures. They may seem a bit overwhelming—and to succeed with Evolutionary Astrology, you do have to juggle a lot of balls! But there is one principle that overshadows everything. If you understand it, you will stay on top of the details.

Every new ball we juggle actually makes the work of finding the story easier.

Every technical modifier of the south node—its sign, house, aspects, and planetary ruler—serves to *narrow the focus*. Each one *adds* information, of course—but more importantly, it eliminates possibilities. It filters the information.

You saw how broad a field of possibilities the eleventh house represented. You also saw how much narrower it became when we were looking at *only* the Libran possibilities within that wide eleventh house range.

That is how it works. The complexity is your friend, not your enemy—even though as friends go, it can be a demanding one!

Thus, we start with the infinite field of all possible human stories. With each step, each new symbol, we winnow it down. In the end, what we have left is the essence of the karmic tale that underlies the emotional dramas of the present lifetime.

What we seek through our twin processes of discovery and elimination is a single story which is consistent with all the nodal information and which assumes nothing else of importance.

Working with the sign and the house of the south lunar node, we are really just beginning. For years, that was all I understood. And I still felt I was doing helpful astrology, getting good feedback from people, making a living. But then the world opened up. As I wrote earlier, I owe a lot of that to my students and my clients, and my soul-brother, Jeffrey Wolf Green.

Let's explore more deeply. We have only scratched the surface.

Planets Conjunct the South Node

When a planet is conjunct the south node, it further defines the nature of the individual's prior-life energy and circumstances. Again remember our trick of thinking of the south node as we would interpret the natal Sun in more conventional astrology. That planet was *deeply integrated with the individual's identity* in a prior life. In this case, you can view a planet conjunct the south node as you normally would work with a planet conjunct a person's natal Sun—except that you continue to tilt the interpretation toward sub-optimal expressions.

Say that Saturn is conjunct the south node. That would suggest a *long-suffering, disciplined* person faced with *extremes of responsibility, limitation, or privation*. We are probably looking at *exhaustion* or *depression*, or both, in the prior lifetime.

Jupiter conjunct the south node? Add an element of *expansiveness* and *victory* to the mix—a dollop of what the world would call "luck." And be alert to Jupiter's eternal shadows: all that glitters is not gold; pride goeth before a fall; be careful what you pray for, you might get it. Those themes are likely to be part of the past life tale.

A little while ago, we considered an Arian south node in the eleventh house, and we brought up the metaphorical image of an army. Now, armies have privates and cooks and latrine-cleaners. They have sergeants and they have generals. They have heroes and cowards. Half of the armies win and half of them lose—at least among the ones that actually fight. Many armies just sit there and don't do much at all. In other words, based only upon a sign and a house, our "0.69 percent of human possibilities" still contains a vast array of options!

Add Jupiter to that particular south node though a conjunction, and the focus gets a lot crisper. This soul was likely in a position of *authority, glory* and *power* (Jupiter) within that "army." Very probably, he "won the war" (Jupiter is victory). Pin some medals on him! Quite certainly, life offered him the chance to become *inflated* and *over-extended,* to overplay his hand, or to "play God." He got lucky—but he probably got into some soul-trouble because of it.

We can eliminate latrine-duty.

The Planetary Ruler of the South Node

If the south node lies in Gemini, Mercury is its ruler. Then, wherever Mercury lies in the chart we find another set of clues about the karmic story. If the south node is in Taurus, we need to look for Venus. In Cancer, we pay closer attention to the Moon.

In essence, the planetary ruler of the south node is an extension of the node itself. It describes *another dimension* of the karmic story. It provides *another angle* on the tale. Often, it seems to correlate with a *pivotal chapter* in the emerging tale of the prior lifetime.

If, for example, we see the south node in the ninth house, but its planetary ruler is in the twelfth house, we might reason this way: in a previous life, this person took a voyage (ninth house), *but the ship sank!* (Twelfth house: loss, trouble).

There are many other possibilities, but that is certainly one of them! The ninth house also correlates with *religion*. With the node there, and its ruler in the twelfth house, we might be looking at monastic life—religion (ninth house) and withdrawal from the world (twelfth house) come together seamlessly in that image. We might be looking at a nun or a monk.

Note that in the above example we have two very different storylines: a sinking ship and a monastic lifetime. Both stories are consistent with the symbolism. *Keep them both on the table—and keep exploring.* As more symbols get added to the pile, the storyline becomes increasingly focused.

Remember: each new astrological detail *further limits* the emerging picture. But it is still quite broad at this point.

In the example we are developing with the Arian south node in the eleventh house conjunct Jupiter, let's now place Mars—the nodal ruler—in the eighth house, the traditional "house of death." Warriors kill and are killed; they see a lot of death; they are face-to-face with the taboo and the extreme. All this is eighth house symbolism. *What impact does it have on a person to have faced death?* Or to have killed? Answer those questions, and you have added another pivotal psychological dimension to your emerging nodal story.

Now, instead of the eighth house, try putting Mars in the fifth house (play; creativity; pleasure). That is harder, simply because the connections between warfare and those happy subjects are not so obvious. But warriors are under a lot of stress. Their level of tension demands release. What does a soldier do when he's on leave? How does he behave? One answer is that he raises hell! The pent-up fires and stresses demand release, and they do so with pressing urgency.

Remember Jupiter: how might a solider carrying that kind of inner pressure respond to *victory*? After arduous battle, how are the citizens of the liberated town treated? There is more than one possible answer to that question, but since we are dealing with the south node, let your mind range toward the darker possibilities. Are sailors on leave famous for sobriety? Soldiers famously enthusiastic about chastity? Does the phrase *rape and pillage* ring a bell?

Because of the nature of rulership, the *planet* that rules the south node must always have the same basic tone as the *sign* of the node. Mars rules Aries, and they mean similar things. That means that the planet itself does not actually tell us much that we did not already know. Where the nodal ruler's usefulness emerges is through its placement in the chart in terms of sign, house, and aspects.

The planetary ruler of the south node essentially functions as a marker for another sign and house and aspectual framework that have relevance to the karmic story.

One specific situation demands highlighting. With the south node in Leo, the Sun is the ruler. Thus the very essence of the person today (his or her present Sun sign) is deeply imprinted with the mark of the past. Everyone has karma, but it is particularly essential that we understand that karma thoroughly with such an individual. Like the rest of us, for the sake of his basic vitality he needs to be true to his Sun sign. Yet, in so doing, he runs the danger of slipping into a lower, less-conscious version of that sign because of the downward pull of the ingrained karmic patterning. He is like a dried-out alcoholic who needs to sit soberly in a bar night after night.

More generally, we can see other ways that the nodal drama can move to center stage—or fade somewhat into the background. Strong aspects, prominent placement, significant alliances via rulership—all the standard ways of astrological thinking apply here as well.

The south node is like a planet—it can be prominent or obscure in a chart. As with a planet, its overall weight and centrality corresponds to the relative gravity or modesty of impact of the underlying karmic issues upon the present life.

The principle above is illustrated reliably by the Sun-ruled Leo south node. We know that the Sun will be central to any astrological interpretation. Experience has taught us that planets can become prominent in a chart by a variety of routes. Ruling the Ascendant. Conjuncting the Sun or the Moon. Being conjunct an Angle. Making a great many aspects.

All the same principles apply equally to the nodes. They may be very emphasized in a chart, or less so. This corresponds with the intensity and relevance of the karma to the present life—and that factor in turn often links to what we might think of as "fateful" events in life: the sorts of seemingly random windfalls and disasters that strike some people while by-passing others.

Rulerships: Modern Versus Traditional

One more point about the ruler of the south node. What do we do with a Pisces south node? The majority of modern astrologers would call Neptune its ruler. But traditionally the answer was Jupiter. It is the same with Aquarius—Uranus and Saturn are both named its ruler, depending on whom you ask. And Scorpio is shared—or fought over—by Pluto and Mars.

My experience suggests that in each case *both* planets simply have an affinity for the sign in question.

The word "rulership" is probably the real culprit. Linguistically, it sets us up to think that one planet should be "king." But it doesn't have to be that way: to me, it is better to think of rulership as indicating *affinity* rather than *hierarchy.* More than one planet can *like* a given sign! I suggest that with a south node in Scorpio, Aquarius, or Pisces, you simply recognize both rulerships. That complicates the pictures a bit, but as we have seen, more detail means a narrower focus and more precision.

I may be biased here, but what has produced the best results for me is to start with Uranus, Neptune or Pluto as primary rulers, then to let the traditional ruler add secondary detail. In my experience, the modern ruler seems to point closer to the interior heart of the matter, while the classical one gives useful concrete detail. I do encourage you to use them both.

Planets in Aspect to the South Node

All aspects to the south node other than the conjunction refer at least partly to *forces that acted upon the person* in the prior lifetime. They point to *external realities*, although they often have inward and subjective correlates as well. Since so much of human experience is about relationships in the larger sense, more often than not these planets refer to *other people*—human interactions that played some kind of shaping role on the person's experience.

Squares and *oppositions* correspond with people or situations which were experienced as challenges, resistance or negativity. *Trines* and *sextiles* are linked to people and circumstances which were felt to be supportive—but given our suspicious bias in all nodal analysis, we need to be careful about too glowing an appraisal of sextiles and trines. They might simply represent unambivalently good things in the context of otherwise difficult scenarios—safe havens or "tea and sympathy." Just as easily they can indicate ways in which we were supported in folly.

In our unfolding military karma example, let's add another element: Venus in Leo in the second house, making a trine to that Arian south node. Maybe our hero had money (second house). Maybe he had the "resource" of good looks (Venus in Leo).

Good news? Historically, how many children of wealthy, ruling class families have been bamboozled by their tribe into accepting military rank? And has it always worked out well for them? Remember too that we have a fifth house Mars—how does "too much money" interact with a compulsive, tension-driven need for ecstatic release?

The answer is, "supportively!"

With trines and sextiles, always be alert to ways in which the person could have been supported in folly or self-sabotage.

As we will soon learn, the most evocative aspects to the south node, other than the all-important conjunction, are squares and oppositions. These are powerful—and sufficiently distinct for us to treat them separately. We will look them specifically in a moment. In Chapters Eight, Ten and Eleven, we will explore all of these major Ptolemaic aspects in cookbook fashion, planet-by-planet. Here we simply introduce the basic concepts.

The so-called "minor aspects" can play a role in this kind of analysis too, but I tend to shy away from them, favoring a deeper look at the foundation rather than spreading myself too thinly over details.

Very briefly:

Quincunxes suggest tensions, wild cards, situations or people that came in out of the blue and *changed everything* or required a lot of *adjustment.*

Sesquiquadrates suggest situations and relationships that *tied the person in knots*, were intellectually confusing, and which smacked of "damned if you do, damned if you don't."

Semi-squares suggest chronic but tolerable vexations that take their toll by attrition. Annoyance. Think of mosquitos.

Quintiles suggest breaks in the action, temporary reprieves, "divine visitations," and creative interludes.

Planets in Opposition to the South Node

Any planet opposite the south node would be described more conventionally as "conjunct the north node." We will get to that! For our purposes here, we are concentrating on the south node of the Moon, and so it is the opposition aspect that draws our attention and focuses our understanding.

A planet opposing the south node represents something or someone who blocked, repressed, defeated or tantalized the person in the past. It either represents something insurmountable and irresolvable, or something unattainable. It symbolizes the brick wall of reality.

The Unattainable: Jupiter opposing the south node could indicate all the good things of life, just out of reach. Picture a Dickensian orphan, his belly empty—and his nose pressed up against the steamy glass of the elegant restaurant two nights before Christmas.

The Insurmountable: Imagine that the king (Jupiter) has declared war, and a gentle poet is conscripted into the army. He hates it. He does not believe in it. He didn't choose it. But how can you argue with the overwhelming might and authority of the king? His call-to-arms is the "brick wall of reality." You deal with it. You have no choice.

Those are two very different stories. Both are consistent with Jupiter opposing the south node. How can we know which story to tell? You couldn't—if you blundered by starting your analysis with this aspect, or by interpreting it in a vacuum. Again, remember that the techniques of Evolutionary Astrology are cumulative. We are building a story from a mass of hints and clues. As we said earlier, our holy grail is a tale that is consistent with all the nodal information and which assumes nothing else. So the first thing you do is to lay out all the clues.

Stories are the intersection of *character* and *plot*. By the time we consider aspects to the south node, we should already understand the basic past-life character. We've learned it from the sign and house of the south node, the placement of its ruler, and any planet conjunct it.

Now we add the dynamic element of plot through considering the aspects to the south node.

Planets Opposing the South Node, House by House

Any *first house* planet opposite the south node correlates with some dominant "significant other" whose authority defined the person in question.

Any *second house* planet opposite the south node correlates with overwhelming issues of a material nature: vast wealth or crushing poverty, perhaps the lack of the basic materials of survival: food, shelter, and so on.

Any *third house* planet opposite the south node correlates with limitations created by rapidly changing circumstances, smooth talkers, siblings.

Any *fourth house* planet opposite the south node correlates with the inescapable, pressing demands of family or clan.

Any *fifth house* planet opposite the south node correlates with the morally-unavoidable demands of children—or the labyrinth created by addictive or compulsive pleasure-seeking.

Any *sixth house* planet opposite the south node correlates with overwhelming responsibilities or duties, some dominant mentor figure, or the challenges that can be created by servants, staff or underlings.

Any *seventh house* planet opposite the south node correlates with the "brick wall" realities of marriage and partnership: the demands or needs, legitimate and otherwise, of a dependent partner.

Any *eighth house* planet opposite the south node correlates with extreme or nightmarish circumstances, perhaps involving exposure to death or the dark face of sexuality.

Any *ninth house* planet opposite the south node correlates with conflict with religion or law, or perhaps enforced migration: refugee status.

Any *tenth house* planet opposite the south node correlates with figures or structures of social authority existing in tension with the needs or desires of the person.

Any *eleventh house* planet opposite the south node correlates with the overwhelming force of public opinion, the will of the community or tribe, mob psychology, or conventionality.

Any *twelfth house* planet opposite the south node correlates with extreme and unavoidable losses, escapist behavior, monastic authority, prison authority, confining illness, or behind-the-scenes treachery.

Always, with planets opposite the south node, one fact is central: whatever the problem was, *there was no way around it.* Life is full of insoluble problems. Sooner or later, all of us face no-win situations, overwhelming forces, or other forms of existential checkmate. They are part of life. The opposition to the south node is the astrological symbolism for these kinds of circumstances, at least insofar as we faced them in prior lifetimes.

Planets Square the South Node

Any planet square the south node is naturally square the north node as well. As with the opposition aspect we just discussed, the aspectual link to the north node is best treated as a separate issue. At this point, we are only concerned with the south node—which is to say, with uncovering the karmic story.

A planet square the south node represents a person, circumstance or issue that crossed, vexed, afflicted or undercut the intentions or

needs of the person in the prior lifetime. It is therefore an issue left unresolved from the past, which presses for resolution again in the present.

Neptune square the south node? Explore a feeling of life slowly being leached out of the person. Take it further: perhaps Neptune was in the fourth house, and correlated with an endlessly needy, insatiably demanding, ever-dependent extended family. "Mom moved in and began to die when she was sixty. Now, she's ninety, still going strong, and still dying—and if she doesn't die soon, it will kill me."

Perhaps Neptune was in the fifth house or the twelfth house, either one of which can correlate with *escapist behavior*. With Neptune square the node from either one of those houses, we could imagine a person drinking herself into oblivion, gradually turning herself into a ghost of what she might have been.

In these Neptune-square-the-node examples, always recognize that *other options existed.* That manipulative mother could have been be told to stand on her own two feet. Boundaries could have been set. In terms of drinking, people can heroically break addictions.

Neither of these answers are easy ones and it is possible that the higher ground was simply not recognized at the time. But the key point is that squares (as distinct from oppositions) to the south node correlate with vexatious situations in which *our own blindness or error plays a large role.*

Blindness and error are part of life and we all succumb to them. And always remember one of our cardinal insights into spiritual evolution: *you were even dumber in the past!* These past-life lapses should not be greeted with guilt or shame, only with the recognition that we are all wounded, that we all run the risk of repeating old patterns, and that there are better choices available.

Not all nodal squares represent our own errors—that's just a useful possibility to try on when you begin framing the story. Some squares simply represent our frailty in the face of the enormity of life. Squares tend to "blind-side" us—thus they often link to circumstances "which we never saw coming." That is especially reliable when the edgier planets square the node—Mars, Uranus, or Pluto. These all tend to leave the mark of *trauma* on the person. We got clobbered somehow and we did not expect it.

Perhaps the south node is squared by an eighth house Uranus: a person is in the middle of life when suddenly he or she is taken unexpectedly by death. Terrorists crash the jet into the building and last night's bitter fight is the last conversation we will ever have with our partner in this body. How can we imagine the impact of such a sudden Uranian trauma? From a metaphysical perspective, we can assume that we would surely have some "unfinished business," if we were ripped from life that way! That is what these particularly hard squares are about.

Pulling the Karmic Story Together

All this juggling can be overwhelming, but remember that every piece of the puzzle, while it adds details, also simplifies the picture. By the time you have considered all the pieces of the puzzle, you have quite a lot of information—especially if there happen to be a lot of planets making aspects to the south node. Just knowing the sign of the south node gets the story down to about eight percent (one in twelve) of all human possibilities. Adding the south node's house, as we saw, gets it under one percent.

Progress!

A planet conjunct that node? Hooray! You've cut out 90 percent of the remaining possibilities. Every south node has a planetary ruler—another 90 percent of your possible confusion evaporates!

This is really the right way to think about the process—and not just because it is more encouraging. It is also sound methodology. What we are aiming to find, as we said earlier, is a story that is consistent with all the nodal information and assumes nothing else. Half of that is a process of discovery, but the other half is a process of *strategic elimination*.

Frying Pans

Every astrological symbol represents a very broad field of archetypal possibilities. The sixth house, for example, represents health and responsibilities—and mentors, daily routines, and humility. And that is just the psychological material! The sixth house also refers to pets, aunts and uncles and nieces and nephews, the tools in your toolbox, your sister's home, your children's finances . . . the list is overwhelming. And it should be, since we are dividing the universe into twelve (obviously huge) boxes.

Visualize each one of these archetypal fields as a gigantic frying pan full of icons representing each of its elements. Mars in Virgo in the ninth? That is three pans. Mars, Virgo, and the ninth house.

Mars: put icons in there for warriors, pioneers, adventurers, athletes, people under stress, angry people, scared people . . .

Virgo: in that frying pan, you need icons for motivations and attitudes involving meticulousness, responsibility, self-doubt, criticism, primness, nagging, martyrdom, craftsmanship, duty, skill . . .

The ninth house: conjure up icons for voyages, universities, religion, belief systems, the law, exploration, walking one's talk, jumping to conclusions . . .

Do the same with all the other archetypal fields pertinent to the nodal analysis—that is, with the ruler of the south node and with any planets in aspect to the node.

Now look for where the pans overlap. See where they have common ground. See what icons they either hold in common, or which daisy-chain together into a natural storyline, the way a gun might suggest a murder, or a ship a voyage, or loneliness a foolish relationship.

You have found it.

That is the chart behind the chart.

That is your karmic story.

Now it is time to begin seeing how to move forward with it. We have defined the problem—that is the tendency of this karmic story to repeat itself, or to otherwise make itself felt in the present lifetime. Let's frame some solutions and remedies. They are there in the chart too.

Projection

That orphan we met a while ago, the one with the hungry nose pressed against the glass of the fancy restaurant—what does she think of the rich people eating those lavish meals, leaving half the food on their plates? The gentle poet who is forced by the king to fight a war—what is his attitude toward law and authority?

When we are hurt, taunted or blocked by other people, we tend to think ill of them. We put our noses in the air. We say, *"I would never in a million years be like that."* And God writes it down in a little black book.

We reject things that harm us. We dehumanize our oppressors. We put them out of our hearts. In the language of psychology, we *project negatively* onto such entities. These projections are in fact rejections of part of what we ourselves are. Sooner or later in the journey, such projections must be withdrawn. And we hate that!

Planets square or opposed to the south node represent kinds of people we must learn to stop hating, judging and rejecting, or we will reject the very parts of ourselves which we need to employ if we are to go forward on our journey.

Please note that this is not a generic reference to the sweet virtues of forgiveness and acceptance! It is far more concrete in its relevance than that. Let's bring it down to earth with an example: with Jupiter on his north node, perhaps a person (who was a starving orphan in a prior lifetime) needs to experience wealth and status in this lifetime. Perhaps she needs to lose her *adaptation to poverty*, to anonymity, or to just "getting by." Why? As we will discover in a few moments, the north node of the Moon clarifies the answer, but maybe she has something important to do for her community in this lifetime—*and she can't succeed at it without being in a position to hobnob with the ruling class.* Maybe she has a soul-contract to play Chopin in this lifetime. Have you priced a grand piano lately? *For this woman to go forward, she must stop judging those whom she judged so vehemently in the past.* It is not about virtue; it is about the fierce, practical logic of soul evolution.

Withdrawing the projection is part of healing the past, and we need to do it in order to go forward. That work is just the price of admission. Here comes the real magic.

The Dragon's Head

The north node of the Moon is opposite the south node. Much of its meaning follows directly from that simple geometrical observation. Regarding the north node, we observer certain axioms:

It puts maximum tension on the south node—it represents an unexplored, unknown possibility for the person.

It answers the south node's questions; it resolves the south node's dilemmas.

It represents the person's evolutionary intention and soul-contract.
But:

Due to inexperience with it, the person will likely be tentative, awkward and confused in that part of life, inclined either toward avoidance or toward interesting and illuminating errors.

It has no intrinsic energy at all; it is nothing but an excellent suggestion.

Earlier we looked at an invented example of a person with his south node in Aries and the eleventh house, conjunct Jupiter and ruled by a fifth house Mars. We posited a background in military experience, probably as an officer selected from among the "good families."

His north node must therefore be in Libra and in the fifth house since they lie opposite Aries and the eleventh. Thus his soul-intentions are Libran: he is here to *deepen his ability to function in partnership,* and to experience *peace, grace*, and *serenity.* Libra is opposite Aries, as peace is opposite war and accord is opposite discord. Serenity is opposite tension—and, after the stress of war, there is a profound need to find tranquility. Libra also represents our *aesthetic functions*—our ability to respond to beauty and to appreciate the arts: these emerge as useful "yogas" for this individual. In general, there is a feeling of moving out of the inherent roughness and rawness of war (Aries) and into a more civilized framework reflecting gentler aspects of the human tradition (Libra).

With this north node, we observe an individual who has made a soul-contract to calm down, to heal from war.

Going further, with the north node in the fifth house there is also a hunger for *creative self-expression.*

We just hit pay-dirt: overlapping icons! Libra carries the archetype of the *Artist*. The fifth house urge to *express one's self creatively* links very directly to that same archetype. Thus we recognize an elemental piece of this soul's evolutionary strategy: *To find peace, release, balance and healing through the device of creative self-expression.*

These archetypes are more complex, of course. The fifth house is also about *joy* and *pleasure*. After war, we need them. Something hardens in us under that constant, brutalizing stress. Something grows stony when faced with chronic violence, ugliness, and fear. With the north node in the fifth house, there is a need to *soften and to open.* How? Art is one method, as we have already seen—a person thrilling to a live performance of Beethoven's ninth symphony, tears in her eyes at the final choruses, reaching for a partner's hand. Feel the opening to the shared heart? That is the overlap of Libran and fifth house energy.

Speaking of pleasure, remember that we learned that the south node-ruler, Mars, also fell in the fifth house, where it suggested a karmic vulnerability to potentially destructive pleasure-seeking. As we guide this person toward the higher ground, we have a tightrope to walk: we must, on one hand, affirm his evolutionary need for pleasure, while on the other hand cautioning him about damaging dissipation. The key is to emphasize the healthiest fifth house expressions, rather than setting strictures on the less healthy ones.

Children are yet another natural correlate of the fifth house. With the north node there—especially in Libra, the traditional sign of marriage—it is easy to imagine that having children could be part of this person's soul-intention. That is of course a very personal choice and it is not the astrologer's business to tell anyone to make babies. Having kids is consistent with that north node, but it is not the only possibility. It would be fair to say that part of his work is to move a relationship toward a place that is sufficiently *calm, settled, safe* and *stable* that he *could* comfortably choose to have kids.

In a nutshell, this soul needs to learn that *the war is over.*

Planets Conjunct the North Node

If there is a planet aligned with the north node, we have met it once already while exploring the karmic pattern—that same planet is of course opposing the south node. There, it represented something troublesome, insurmountable or unattainable. Now, in this new north node context, we see that same planet linked positively to the person's present evolutionary intentions. He is trying to integrate *the higher elements* of that planetary energy into himself.

Working with a planet on the north node is a good exercise in learning to see both the high and the low sides of *all* the planets. Saturn opposing the south node? In the karmic past, there was some basic, insurmountable *lack*—a poverty, in some sense—that stood between the person and what he or she wanted. There is a good chance it was embodied in some person who represented laws and limitations—someone saying "thou shalt not" or "impossible!" Now, in the present life, with Saturn conjunct the north node, he or she needs to withdraw the projection—to embrace that same Saturn energy, but also to move it up into its higher manifestations. There is an evolutionary need to *internalize the kinds of present-tense self-denial that allow a person to build a future which engenders self-respect.* Saving money so we can buy a house. Putting oneself through medical school. Raising healthy, sane kids. Staying together as a couple. Thereby, he or she overcomes an internalized karmic attitude of "coping" in a spirit of gloomy fatalism and the depressing assumption of ultimate defeat. It is replaced with the *dignity of accomplishment,* of goals attained. Saturn is still Saturn, but now on the north node we focus our attention on its more encouraging potentials.

A planet opposing the south node hurt you or stalled you in the past. Read it negatively.

That same planet, on the north node, shows you the way forward. Read it positively.

The key here is the simple idea, central to Evolutionary Astrology, that no symbol is inherently good or bad, lucky or unfortunate. Each represents a spectrum of possibilities, from dreadful to glorious. Consciousness and intention determine which possibilities actually manifest in the biography.

The Planetary Ruler of the North Node

The planet that rules the sign of the Moon's north node helps us get to where we need to go. It supports the realization of the evolutionary intention. It suggests helpful strategies and tactics. It is your ally.

The planetary ruler of the north node represents a useful tactic for fulfilling the soul-contract; or an important piece of the puzzle; or a helpful clue about how to get it right; or just the icing on the cake—a way to "make an A" in the north node work.

The critical theoretical point here is that the north node's ruler derives its meaning from the north node itself. We have to understand the two of them *in that order* or we will lose focus.

Here are two contrasting examples. In both, let's assume that a sixth house Venus is the north node ruler. Therefore "to make an A" the person must form responsible (sixth house) relationships (Venus).

Hold that part constant.

Put the north node in the tenth house. This person's basic soul-intention is to make a *mark in his community.* But remember that sixth house Venus: to succeed in making that mark, he will probably need to *hire* (sixth house) *artistic, creative, socially-skilled* people whom he *loves* (Venus).

Now switch things around: put the Moon's north node in the fifth house instead of the tenth. The evolutionary intentions now have to do with *creative expression.* To fulfill them, this individual will have to find *artistic* (Venus) *mentors* (the sixth house).

The thinking behind this process can seem confusing until you remember the fundamental principle behind it. Start with a thorough understanding of the north node, then apply common sense in trying to imagine how its planetary ruler might help the cause. With either the north or the south node, the principle is the same: *the context of the basic sign and house of the nodal structure determines the specific meaning of the nodal rulers.* Start with the nodes and then go to the rulers. If you do it backwards you will probably get into the kind of trouble that comes from losing perspective in a complex situation..

Planets Square the North Node

A while back we saw that planets square the *south* node represent something the person *left unresolved* in the karmic past. If that individual is to go forward, this leftover issue must be resolved—that is half the meaning of a planet square the *north* node.

According to Jeffrey Wolf Green, such a planet represents a "skipped step." It haunts us, and the only way for us to advance is to return to the old, unresolved question and get it right this time. It is like driving in a strange city: miss a critical exit on the highway and the only thing you can do is turn around and go back.

Maybe someone "solves" the problems in one relationship by escaping into another relationship. We all know that is not likely to work in the long run. Very probably, whatever you are not facing in the first relationship will emerge as a problem in the new relationship too. That, in common sense terms, is the way planets square the nodes feel.

We use the term "skipped steps," but the irony is that no one can really skip any steps at all. We can only defer them.

The energy of a planet square the nodal axis is *hanging in the balance* between the past and the future. Easily, it can fall backwards and help recreate the old south node dilemma. Ideally, it needs to move to a higher level and serve the north node.

Earlier we looked at Neptune squaring the south node. One possibility we considered is that, in the karmic past, the person lost his evolutionary focus in an alcoholic haze. Another possibility was that she allowed the life to be sucked out of her by a parasitic mother. Different stories, two out of many possibilities—but in both cases we see the dark Neptune signature: the uncreative, unproductive, unintentional *loss of self.*

Now in this present life, being square the north node, that Neptunian energy is *hanging in the balance.* The person needs to move it forward. It won't go away! If she does not get it right, she will surely get it wrong—again. This time, Neptune wants to flower as an *avid spiritual life,* a relationship with the transpersonal realm, or a deep engagement with the *image-making processes we call art.*

Looking at it integratively, if her north node lies in the tenth house, this developing spiritual or artistic life needs to manifest in her public, outward circumstances, perhaps in her profession.

If, on the other hand, the north node lies in the fifth house, it suggests "art for art's sake." In this case, there is ultimately no evolutionary need for any public expression.

In the ninth or the twelfth houses, such a north node would tilt more toward the spiritual and the mystical dimensions of Neptune, and less toward the imaginative and creative.

As always, our aim is to find points of overlap, and to let each symbol converse with all the others and come to accord with them.

It is critical to remember that resolving the issues connected with a planet square the nodal axis is the *price of admission for going forward*. Until those unresolved issues are addressed, we are blocked and stymied—stuck, whether or not we know it, in the past, and doomed to repeat it.

The blockages and distortions implicit in a planet square the nodal axis must be released and clarified before the soul-contract can be fulfilled. Otherwise, the north node is inaccessible.

A Common Dilemma—and its Resolution

The key to everything we have seen so far lies in understanding the *natural tension of the opposition aspect between the north node and south node.* Since opposite signs and opposite houses always represent different sides of the same coin, the nodes partake of the same polarity.

Libran peace "cures" Arian stress—as Arian courage and forthrightness "cure" Libran indecision and "politeness." Third house curiosity and open-mindedness cure ninth house dogmatism—as ninth house faith cures third house doubt and uncertainty.

This "oppositional" thinking underlies all of nodal theory—not to mention much of the rest of astrology, Jungian psychology and Hermetic philosophy.

But sometimes the north node and south node resemble each other so much that their natural tension seems to be dissipated. There are several expressions of this phenomenon, and all of them are resolved in much the same way. We might, for example, see a Gemini south node in the ninth house. That puts the north node in Sagittarius (the ninth sign), "but" in the third house—which has a natural resonance with the third sign: Gemini. So which way are we going?

We might see a Gemini south node—but Mercury (which rules Gemini) is conjunct the north node. The future looks a lot like the past! How can we leave Gemini, but move toward Mercury? We might see a Sagittarian north node—with Jupiter ruling it from its conjunction with that Gemini south node. Again, the past looks too much like the future.

In all these cases, the answer is the same: you need to keep a very clear distinction between the higher and lower expressions of the symbols. *Always the soul-contract is to go from lower to higher.* Where the past and the future bear symbolic resemblance to each other, sort it out through the high-low distinction.

Here's how:

Gemini south node? *Too much thinking or too much running around in circles, frantically but pointlessly, in the prior life.* Mercury on that Sagittarian north node? You are on a philosophical quest for a *meaningful existential framework* (Sagittarius) in this life—but to succeed, you will have to think, study, maintain intellectual openness and rigor, and be willing to discover surprising, even shocking, truths—that is the *higher* expression of Mercury (or of Gemini, for that matter).

When the ruler of the north node is conjunct the south node, think as we have just outlined: in the past, you were caught up in that planet's lower expression. Now you are trying to get to the higher ground, so you can go back and re-do the past, getting it right this time. Your route to the evolutionary future (north node) passes through the karmic past (south node). Literally remembering past lives can be particularly useful here. You will be presented with the same evolutionary crossroads. Last time you took a left turn. Try a right turn this time!

That is it, the whole theory, in just a few pages. The heart of evolutionary astrology lies in the skillful application of this handful of techniques. As with all other forms of serious astrology, practice and experience make a big difference. But if you know this much and apply it with imagination, respect for human freedom, and some compassion, you can not only find "the chart behind the chart," but also the way forward.

Conclusion

Coaxing the prior life story out of a chart at this level of detail is a relatively new technique. It has its own emerging principles and procedures, but most of the basic brain-programs that allow us to do conventional astrological interpretation work well here too, once we have made a few translations. In other words, if you are a conventional modern astrologer, you are already most of the way there. These techniques are really just an extension of what you already understand. Applying them is no more difficult than doing a middle-of-the-road astrological interpretation. But it is like staring at the stars from a desert mountaintop rather than from an urban parking lot.

Past lives can seem to be a vague area, one in which an astrologer could really "say anything" and no one would ever be the wiser. People ignorant of the actual techniques and values underlying this approach have sometimes leveled that charge. *The key here is that karmic patterns tend to repeat.* We may not be able to see past lives directly, but we can always see the relevance of the prior-life story to the person's *present* issues, often down to details. We invite the client to evaluate what we are saying—and to doubt it, if he or she so chooses!

It is in the *present tense* that Evolutionary Astrology can defend its claims and perspectives. The present is where we live. The present is the realm of magic—and of the choices that will create our futures.

CHAPTER FOUR: A PRACTICAL EXAMPLE

In the last chapter, we explored the nuts and bolts of Evolutionary Astrology. Now let's see how it works in practice with the chart of an actual human being—and please indulge my own secretive Scorpio south node by letting me keep the identity of our subject under my hat for a few pages.

Consider Figure 1 below, the chart of our Mystery Man, born on October 18, 1939, at 9:55 PM in New Orleans. Let's start by quickly scanning the chart from the perspective of modern psychological astrology, flying over the basic symbolism at a hundred thousand feet, snapping a few pictures, getting an overview.

The man is a Libran, with its implications of *relationship-orientation, aesthetic responsiveness*, and balance. The Sun is in the fourth house,

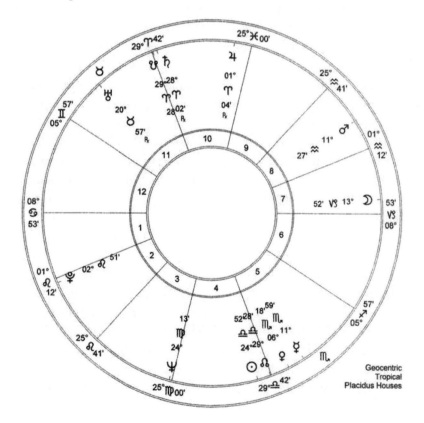

orienting the psyche toward *home and the inner life*. These two gentle themes—Sun in Libra; Sun in the fourth—are further underscored by his Cancer Ascendant, which echoes the inwardness of the fourth house Sun. That Cancer Ascendant also makes the Moon the ruler of the chart, further deepening, subjectifying and internalizing the consciousness. The predominance of the lunar theme also corroborates the *domestic* and *nurturing* motivations.

With the Moon ruling the chart from the seventh house, there is again a Libra-like accentuation of *empathy*, attention to others, and a general willingness and desire to get along with others. The chart-ruling Moon lies in Capricorn, adding *cautious* and *responsible* instincts, and introducing a paradoxical element of *solitude* into what is otherwise emerging as a very relationship-oriented birthchart. That theme of solitude is charged further when we notice Saturn opposing his Sun from Aries—a sign it shares with Jupiter. Along with Pluto in Leo, that puts three planets in Fire—which adds some "hot sauce" to the mix, but the thrust of the chart by most standards would remain dominated by its gentler, milder, more "internalizing" elements of Libra, Cancer, and Capricorn. That quiet interpretation is further bolstered by sensitive, surrendering Neptune right on the fourth house cusp, underlying everything in the man's psyche.

Always in astrology we must weigh contradictory testimony and come to balanced judgements. Certainly almost anyone practicing modern, psychological astrology would see this chart as representing a person who was sensitive, moody and perhaps a little depressive, but fundamentally gentle—someone probably focused on the simple pleasures of the quiet, intimate life.

The Chart Behind the Chart

Enter the karmic analysis, which clashes shockingly with all we have seen so far. The south node of the Moon lies in Aries on the cusp of the eleventh house. For purposes of efficiency, I used this configuration as an abstract example in the previous chapter—possibly you might find it helpful to review that material if you skipped it or it is not fresh in your mind. There we saw this nodal structure as indicative of a "warrior" (Aries) operating in a "group context" (eleventh house)—thus suggesting, for one obvious metaphor, *a solider in an army.*

Saturn is conjunct the south node, which points at *stoical, disciplined* adaptation to a difficult, long-lasting, hard situation—imagery which is again very consistent with embattled, relentless military circumstances. Remember: with Saturn conjunct the south node, he is identified psychologically with Saturn and appears that way socially.

A concrete picture of a hungry, exhausted solider slogging through the mud of a long winter enters my mind.

Mars rules the south node from Aquarius and the eighth house—the fabled House of Death. Facing one's own mortality every day, and confronting the reality of killing other human beings too—all that leaps out, echoing and strengthening the warrior metaphor. And it leaps out in a uniquely Aquarian way, suggesting an *emotional dissociation* (negative Aquarius) *from the act of killing,* as well as from the grind of endless (Saturn) mortal insecurity. Thus, our Mystery Man contemplated yet another bone-chilling day in which he might die, just like yesterday and the day before. He shrugged his shoulders. He shot another figure at a distance and watched him fall. He shrugged his shoulders again.

This quality of *emotional distance* is part of the Aquarian Shadow. To trigger it, all we need is trauma—which warrior-Mars in the house of death powerfully provides. Being the ruler of the south node, this coldly traumatized Mars represents a fundamental dimension of our Mystery Man's story and of his nature. As we saw in the previous chapter, it represents "another dimension" of his past-life psyche or "another chapter" in the parable.

There is more. Pluto squares the south node from Leo and the second house. The aspect is "out of quality," which means it is in the "wrong sign" to be squaring an Aries south node. But the aspect is close enough to an exact ninety degree angle, and thus quite real in its effect. From the square to the node, we know that Pluto represents an element that "vexed or blocked" him. In the context of a softer nodal story, such a Pluto might represent painful psychological or emotional issues. But we already have momentum in this story, and it is not looking soft at all. In this extreme framework such a Pluto likely indicates something very "real" and very much in the *nightmarish* category.

What, exactly?

Concretely, Leo is the archetype of the King, and here it can most readily be read as a Plutonian "authority" who vexed our Mystery Man—someone of a toxic, perhaps sadistic nature. Likely, in this developing military context, that would refer to the officers and the general hierarchy of inescapable coercion which towers above any solider.

Pluto is in the second house too. In a raw context such as the one emerging here, the second house goes far beyond "money." It suggests something closer to the basic necessities of survival—or, given Pluto's correlation with things that frighten us, the lack of them! There is no "noble" warrior's death here—it looks more like *malnutrition, exposure to the elements*, and *disease*. He probably died suffering from diarrhea in a puddle of freezing mud. That is, at least, an evocative metaphor.

There is still more. The Sun is conjunct the north node, and thus it opposes the south node. As always with the opposition aspect, here we see something our Mystery Man "could not get around." It was a "brick wall of reality." As the astronomical Sun's gravity is inescapable for the planets, similarly the astrological Sun represents *people with tremendous gravity*—people whose wills and demands we cannot escape, whether that power over us derives from their charisma or through their worldly position. Thus, this solar placement again echoes what we saw with Pluto: inescapable, undeniable *worldly authority* overwhelmed our Mystery Man with its requirements—requirements which opposed his own nature and desires.

The Sun is in the fourth house, which adds the further notion of inescapable demands created by *clan-loyalty*. What kind of person, for example, would not defend his own children or ageing parents? How could he face them again? How could he live with himself? Even if they made no "demands" in an aggressive or controlling way, their simple existence in that relationship to us constitutes a pressing moral necessity.

The nodal story has emerged. Time to reflect and integrate. Begin by adding a twist on conventional psychological thought. If someone you knew had a *childhood experience* of this nature—violence, starvation, and domination by abusive authority figures—what would be your guess about his or her present condition? Anyone who has read a few psychology paperbacks would have no trouble coming up with some dark guesses. Now just displace this obvious and familiar psychological perspective backwards, earlier than childhood, into the childhood of the soul:

View all this material as a set of underlying, unresolved issues from a prior life, warping the expression of the present birthchart like an invisible magnetic field, exactly as a hard childhood can warp an adult life.

Unless real healing had occurred, we would naturally imagine our Mystery Man to be vulnerable to alternating patterns of *rage* and *depression*. We would conjecture that he would have emotionally-charged *issues with figures of authority,* and a tendency toward projecting negatively onto them. We would fear a re-emergence of his karmic capacity for *detached or dissociated violence.* We would imagine a chilliness in the character that would potentially interfere grievously with the emotional surrender and gentleness inherent in human intimacy—an intimacy he desperately needs, as the more conventional reading of his chart demonstrates. We would thus see an *ambivalence* about family bonds and perhaps about national or cultural identity. And, because karmic themes tend to repeat, drawing us back into familiar old patterns, we would suspect that our Mystery Man would harbor a tendency to gravitate toward collective institutions carrying violent mandates, of which the military would be the most obvious example.

Here is the point of pivotal significance: *Note the striking tension between the karmic story on one hand, and, on the other hand, the gentle, domestic tone of our more conventional reading of the Mystery Man's basic astrological signatures.*

This haunted, pained soul came into this world to find peace and maybe a family, but it was not going to be easy. Pay particular attention to the fact that his Libran north node lies conjunct his Sun. Thus, rising to the most challenging point in all evolutionary astrology (the north node) was also the *key to his elemental solar sanity* and "centeredness." He desperately needed committed, stable intimacy. That was where the healing would happen. But living the natural life of a fourth house Libran in any healthy sense was an extreme soul-demand—all his karmic patterning ran counter to it.

And The Winner Is . . .

This is the birthchart of Lee Harvey Oswald, the man who allegedly assassinated John Fitzgerald Kennedy in 1963.

There is of course much controversy about Oswald's precise role in JFK's death. That issue is beyond the scope of this chapter. That he either shot Kennedy, alone or with an accomplice, or that he was somehow drafted or duped into taking the blame for it and then killed—either version of the story is consistent with the karmic perspective.

More pointedly, notice how *the factual, biographical reality of Lee Harvey Oswald's life is almost completely inconsistent with anything we might detect through more conventional astrological means.*

Yet it practically leaps out in the Evolutionary analysis.

Conclusion

Lee Harvey Oswald's chart provides us with a striking example of Evolutionary Astrology in action. I chose it here because it illustrates the true test of this new branch of astrology: a situation in which conventional astrological analysis would fail embarrassingly, but where integrating the evolutionary framework corrects our astrological vision to 20/20.

As you might imagine, not every nodal situation is so extreme. Sometimes the karmic story overlaps with the present birthchart, reinforcing it. There we obviously would not learn as much from these techniques. But we would be alerted to such a person's vulnerability toward simply repeating the old patterns in an empty, unproductive—or flat-out negative—way.

Other times, compared to Oswald's chart, the nodes are simply not so emphasized. They might, for example, make fewer planetary aspects. Then the karmic story is not quite as pressing.

Most of the time, as common sense might suggest, the karmic tale simply is not so dramatic. We can have a "lazy" nodal tale that pulls us toward lassitude and predictability in this life. That is karma too. It can take a myriad of forms, as it must if it is going to reflect life's full spectrum.

Still, I can honestly say that this nodal perspective has never once in my experience proven irrelevant to the realities of a client's present life.

Now you have a taste of how this system works. It has a few procedures with which you are probably unfamiliar, but nothing that strays too far away from the cognitive style of more routine kinds of astrology. If you are skilled with choice-centered, psychological styles of modern astrology, in learning Evolutionary Astrology you will be adding some tools, but not really deleting any.

In later chapters, we will look at many more concrete examples. Now, let's roll up our sleeves and actually master all the basic tools.

CHAPTER FIVE: THE ASTRONOMY OF THE LUNAR NODES

If you are a nerd, welcome to paradise. If you slept through science, but were wide-eyed when English class turned to the Romantic poets, you will probably make a very fine astrologer—but you might want to skip this chapter.

So, what exactly are the nodes of the Moon? Obviously, they are not planets. Since they are the foundation of Evolutionary Astrology and the gateway into karmic analysis, let's take a little while to understand them rigorously.

Earth orbits the Sun, but since we are sitting on the Earth, it doesn't look that way. For millennia, our ancestors assumed it was the other way around—that the Sun orbited the Earth. Since astrology is Earth-centered, we stick with that visual illusion in our language and perspective. What we actually *see* is that the Sun circuits the same band of constellations each year. Astrologers call that band the Zodiac. Astronomers call it the *Ecliptic*.

Imagine that as the Earth swings around the Sun, it sweeps out a flat circle of glass. That disk is the *Plane of the Ecliptic*. In our Earth-centered heads, we project this Plane of the Ecliptic out onto an imaginary Celestial Sphere—a kind of vast starry ball with us inside, right in the center. Where the Plane of the Ecliptic touches the Celestial Sphere, we have the "highway" in the sky that the Sun follows in its yearly path. Ditto, pretty much, for all the planets too. That is the Zodiac.

The Moon orbits the Earth. That cycle takes just under 27 days, 8 hours. Again, imagine that as the Moon does so, it too sweeps out another flat circle of glass. That is the *Plane of the Moon's orbit.* We project it out onto the Celestial Sphere as well, just as with the Ecliptic. (It is helpful to remember that even though in reality the Moon's orbit is a lot smaller than the Earth's orbit around the Sun, when they are both projected onto the inside of the imaginary Celestial Sphere, they are the same size.)

Here is the critical point: the Plane of the Moon's Orbit is inclined by about five degrees to the Ecliptic. (5° 8' 40"). They do not "lie flat," in other words. So half the time the Moon is above the Ecliptic, half the time it is below. (And here we shamelessly indulge in the European colonial fantasy that north is "above" and south is "below!")

If you have got all that, you are ready to understand the lunar nodes:

Where the Moon crosses the Ecliptic heading north is the Moon's north node. Where it crosses heading south is the Moon's south node. More precisely, *where the plane of the Moon's orbit rises above the plane of the Ecliptic*, we define the north node. Where it sinks below the Ecliptic, we define the south node.

The Moon itself could be anywhere in its journey around the circle. It only actually crosses the Ecliptic twice each month, once going up, once going down.

Those are the lunar nodes.

The Nodal Cycle

Spin a child's top. Say it is rotating really fast in a clockwise direction. As it gradually runs out of momentum, you see it begin a slow counter-clockwise wobble before it topples over. Similarly as the Moon speeds around the Earth every month, the plane of its orbit is gradually sliding backwards in the opposite direction. In other words, the places where the Moon's orbit crosses the Ecliptic—the nodes—do not remain in the same degree of the Zodiac for eternity. Instead they move slowly retrograde, taking 6793.39 days to get back to where they started. That works out to 18.5997 years—eighteen years, seven months, and a few days.

Another way to say it is that it takes either lunar node about a year and a half to move retrograde through each sign of the Zodiac.

Yet another way to say it is that the nodes take just under nineteen days to move through one degree.

Eclipses

Solar and Lunar Eclipses fit into all this nodal theory in a fairly obvious way, if you think about it. A solar eclipse, as everybody knows, is a big deal. People travel long distances to see one. What many do not realize is how close we come to a solar eclipse every month. Every 29 days or so, we have a New Moon. That means that the Sun and the Moon are aligned in the same degree of the Zodiac.

So why don't we have an eclipse?

The answer is because, even though Sun and Moon are lined up, the

Moon is a little above or below the Sun—*remember: the plane of the Moon's orbit and the Earth/Sun plane are out of whack by about five degrees.*

Where they are *not* out of whack is at the lunar nodes—as we have learned, the nodes are where the Moon's orbit actually crosses the Ecliptic, or aligns with it. So if we do experience a solar eclipse, that simply means that a New Moon has fallen close to a lunar node. Similarly, we will only have a lunar eclipse if a Full Moon falls near a lunar node.

Little hand-held calculators will figure all this out nowadays. Years ago, our ancestors built a big one to do the same thing. It is called Stonehenge.

Mean Versus True Nodes

There is a lot of fuss in the astrological community about whether to use the mean or the true nodes. People get very passionate about it, even though the difference between mean and true is never very great, not more than a degree and half or so. I have found that if such debates become annoying, a great way to silence them is to ask for a simple astronomical definition of the difference. That usually quiets people down.

The Moon orbits the Earth. That is a simple, practical statement, and basically true. But it is actually more precise to say the Earth and the Moon orbit a common center of gravity. That point is called the *barycenter.*

Think of the Earth as a big, heavy man dancing with his little tiny wife. Both pairs of hands are joined and they are spinning around merrily. Because he is so much bigger, at first glance he seems to be stable and she seems to be orbiting him. But if you look carefully, you see it is not quite that simple. The center of his body is making little circular gyrations as she pulls him first this way, then that.

It is exactly like that with the Earth and the Moon. Their common center of gravity—the barycenter—does not lie at the precise center of the Earth. In fact, it lies about three-quarters of the way from Earth's center to its surface. It is *within* the Earth, in other words, but just not at the center. So, like the heavy man, Earth wobbles as the Moon dances with it.

Let's make the language a little more technical. The small woman pulls the center of the big man's body toward her as she spins around him. She is much lighter, so the effect on him is slight. But it is real. Like the Moon, her "orbit" around him has a "plane," but the center of that plane—his hips—is not fixed and stable. It always pulls a bit toward her.

Earlier, we defined the south node of the Moon as the place where the plane of the Moon's orbit intersects the Ecliptic heading south—where the Moon would move "below" the Ecliptic. (And remember that we were visualizing the plane as circular piece of glass.) But, just as with our dancers, the "glass" plane of the Moon's orbit *wobbles*. So the exact position of those nodes wobbles too. The true nodes reflect that wobble. The mean nodes do not.

It gets a little more complicated.

The more closely we approach something, the more strongly we feel the pull of its gravity. That is the famous "Inverse Square Law" of physics—halve the distance and the force of gravity quadruples. The Moon's orbit around the earth is not perfectly circular. Like most astronomical orbits, it follows an *ellipse*, sometimes closer, sometimes farther from the Earth. This means that the strength of the Moon's tug on the barycenter varies over the Moon's monthly orbit. When the Moon is closer to the Earth, its pull is stronger. The effect is that the barycenter is basically made even more jittery.

Furthermore, the Sun's massive gravity is also part of the equation. As we learned earlier, the Moon's orbital plane around the Earth is not "flat" relative to the plane of the Earth's orbit around the Sun—it is tilted by about five degrees. So sometimes the tug of the Sun's gravity is "down." Other times it is "up." The effect is to add a further jiggle to the Moon's orbit.

One can take all of these factors into account, and see that the actual moment-to-moment position of the lunar nodes is quite twitchy. Essentially that is how the true node is calculated—although in reality most astrological computer programs do not take all of these effects fully into account. Even the "true" node is not really true. The bottom line is the calculated true node's motion is eccentric. It can even sometimes go briefly direct.

The mean node assumes the simpler view: that the Moon orbits the center of the Earth. The effect is to smooth everything out a bit.

As I mentioned earlier, the difference between the position of the mean and the true node is always slight, and thus generally inconsequential for our purposes.

I would never be dogmatic about it, but I work with the mean node myself. My reasons are practical more than theoretical. Here is what I have learned and experienced. Occasionally, someone sits with me who has the mean and true nodes separated, as is typical, by a distance of only a degree or so. But for this person that difference is enough to put the two nodes in different signs. Maybe the mean lunar south node is in 29°II 37' and the true one is in 0°   43', for example. I view such people as precious—or at least as excellent lab rats! When I was trying to sort all this out I have told such people both of the possible karmic stories and asked them which one felt right. I also compared the two versions with my subjective impressions of them as individuals and with the shapes of their outward lives. Far more valuable than any technical astronomical argument, these human truths are astrology's Supreme Court.

For me, more often than not, it is the mean lunar node that has carried the day. See what works best for you.

Two cautions:

First, do not apply this test to differences between true and mean nodal *house* positions. House cusps are inherently a little more blurry than sign cusps—they "flow" a bit more, like seasons changing, while sign cusps tend to operate with more distinct "clicks," like television channels. A great bugaboo in astrology is the accuracy of someone's birth time. Even a small error there can throw house cusps off enough to make them dubious for our purposes here. So, if the true node makes better personal sense to you than the mean one in terms of its house position—well, you are probably right about which house the node occupies, but my first guess would be that your birth time is off by a minute or two.

Second, in exploring the distinctions between mean and true nodes, avoid the temptation to look at only one or two charts. Half of the truly dumb ideas in astrology have arisen that way. "My best friend has Jupiter in her first house and she *loves* cats. Therefore Jupiter in the first house means you love cats."

We need to cast our nets more widely to see reliable patterns, and it is in those patterns that we mine the alchemical gold.

Part Two:

The Cookbook

CHAPTER SIX: THE LUNAR NODES THROUGH THE SIGNS

I am always a bit uncomfortable writing out rote interpretations of any astrological configuration. Nothing exists in a vacuum, and the heart of astrological skill lies in knitting everything together into a unique and specific kind of wholeness. In what follows, I purport to tell you "what the south node in Aries means." Please take it with a grain of salt! What if that independent, maybe angry, Aries south node is in the seventh house? Then, in a prior life, the person was *defined somehow by another person*, and likely that dependency was what the focus of the anger. The "war" happened in a very intimate environment. But what if that same Aries south node lies in the tenth house? Then the "war-story" was acted out on the stage of the world. What if it is opposed by Saturn and Pluto? The defeat was bitter. What if it were conjunct Jupiter? The victory was legendary. Context is everything.

Think of what follows merely as a starting point. Remember: each section that follows applies to one out of every twelve people. It must be vague—how could it be otherwise?

In the next chapter, we will do the same for the nodes in the houses, with similar caveats. But if you can put the two together—a node in both a sign and a house—you have taken a gargantuan leap. It is not one out of twelve people anymore—it is one out of one hundred forty four. Get there, and you are really . . . well, getting started!

SOUTH NODE IN ARIES
(NORTH NODE IN LIBRA)

Interpreting the south lunar node is like taking a defining moment out of a prior life drama, and putting a stethoscope on the condition of the human heart in that instant. We know what the person was *feeling*—but we have no idea what he or she was seeing, thinking, or doing. We take that emotional message, and using hints from other places in the chart, we attempt to discern the outlines of the actual story. With the south node in Aries, we know that this person was feeling the effects of a lot of adrenaline! In some sense of the word, he or she faced *war*. Often, given the human enthusiasm for war as evidenced in our collective history, we can take that Arian allusion to the violence of battle literally: this individual may very well have actually been in a do-or-die situation of combat. But "war" can also be a metaphor for any human situation involving danger, stress, intensity, and competition: climbing mountains, sailing a Spanish caravel through uncharted waters, traumatic childbirth, even being locked in business or political competition.

A young solider returns from Baghdad—or Vietnam or Monte Casino or Antietam—with a bad case of nerves. He is in bed asleep with someone he loves. A car backfires down the street. In one second, he is wide awake—and he has thrown a knife into the wall. His friend is whimpering, terrified. He feels insane in his overreaction. *Yet that same reflexive instinct kept him alive in the war zone!*

Much human craziness follows this pattern: we make a sane adaptation to an insane environment, then later, in another context, that adaptation looks like pure madness. With the south node in Aries, "throwing a knife into the wall" is a good metaphor for the karmic situation. There are, inborn in this soul, the reflexes of a warrior. Anger and fear may rise up out of the blue; discussions can go "over the top" with drama and intensity; there is an urgency and a sense of crisis. There may be internalized patterns of cruelty—cruelty expressed, or the marks of cruelty received.

Knowing that the north node lies in Libra helps give us perspective. The evolutionary intent of this individual lies in the general area of *calming down* and finding inner peace and equilibrium. To accomplish that aim, the person needs to understand the insidious ways he or she conspires to keep the existential situation more *dramatic, intense, and exhausting* than it needs to be or than is healthy. The person must weed out a kind of competitiveness that creeps in through the cracks in his or her self-awareness. He or she need to resist turning people into cartoonish "friends or foes," and instead take the time really to know them as nuanced, complex human beings. He or she benefits from exposure to civilizing influences: painting, music, graceful people. Above all, he or she need to absorb the notion that love is a bigger concept than passion.

Examples: Daniel Berrigan, William Bligh, Julie Christie, Jamie Lee Curtis, John Dillinger, Faye Dunaway, Fabio, Judy Garland, John Glenn, Sue Grafton, Jesse Helms, Don Imus, Ivan The Terrible, Jack Kerouac, Rudyard Kipling, Bruce Lee, Madonna, Charles Mingus, Isaac Newton, Lee

Harvey Oswald, Pele, Joseph Pulitzer, Gene Roddenberry, Grace Slick, Harry S. Truman, Jules Verne, William Butler Yeats, Frank Zappa.

SOUTH NODE IN TAURUS
(NORTH NODE IN SCORPIO)

Taurus is the most primal of the Earth signs. It echoes the nature of those "earthy" denizens of our planet we call the animals—and the natures of all of us "two-leggeds" who have not strayed too far from remembering our natural roots. Taurus is about *instinct*, and all the simple truths we "know in our bones." Like an animal, it is concerned with the basics: food, warmth, comfort, shelter, and love. It prefers the familiar. It avoids the unexpected. With the south node of the Moon in Taurus, a person's karmic past may very well have been agrarian, or otherwise close to nature. He or she might be carrying soul-memories of shared membership in a so-called "primitive" culture—Navajos or Gaels or Ashanti. That interpretation is far from certain, but it is consistent with the Taurean signature. So is any "simple" life: that of the farmer, the craftsperson, the fisherman. We will often see a natural way with animals in such an individual, or perhaps real ability as a gardener or naturalist. Commonly, there is some capacity to "work with the hands."

Generalizing a bit further, we can observe the Taurean south nodal signature in any lifetime that was motivated by the desire to keep everything *stable* and *predictable*—and therein lies the pitfall. An attachment to stability and predictability—a kind of conservatism—has suffused the logic of this soul. In the present life, he or she runs the risk of *stasis*. One manifestation of that issue often lies in becoming overly concerned with *financial stability*, to the point of "paying too much for one's money." Another lies in the avoidance of natural developmental conflicts within the context of relationship—being so preoccupied with "being happy together" that the work which actually maintains happiness in a relationship is avoided.

There is plenty of simple, instinctual goodness in Taurus. It represents a kind of "natural morality," without elaborate philosophical embellishment. By instinct, something inside us knows that killing for pleasure is wrong, or that it is wrong to take sexual advantage of children.

Thus a kind of *unselfconscious goodness* might very well exist in this person. One negative side to that positive quality is *naiveté*—a vulnerability to the predations of more Machiavellian types. We might be looking at the "simple Indian" tricked out of possessions, land or sexual favors by the "city slicker."

All of this helps us grasp the significance of the Scorpio north node. His or her evolutionary intention lies in making peace with life's *complexity, irony,* and *moral ambivalence.* This individual is ready for a psychological leap forward. In this lifetime, he or she intends to dance with the Shadow, and to integrate parts of it. This is a very delicate step for an evolving soul. Emphatically, the aim is not to become "bad!" Rather it is to make peace with one's own pre-existing "inner Scorpion." Like Adam and Eve, it is time for this person to "eat of the fruit of the tree of the knowledge of good and evil." Much of this work revolves around accepting one's own needs for power, one's sexual hunger, jealousies, control issues—all the "dirty games" people play. He or she must learn to accept these qualities, invite them to the table and make some accommodation with them. In this lifetime, he or she is going *beyond goodness,* into *wholeness,* which is really the highest form of love—a love that excludes nothing and shames nothing. In the jargon of psychology, he or she is learning to *withdraw projections,* which means to recognize in one's self the qualities he or she is most inclined to judge in others.

Examples: Tallulah Bankhead, Ludwig Von Beethoven, Ray Bradbury, Jerry Brown, Yul Brynner, Lon Chaney, Nicolaus Copernicus, Ellen Degeneres, Walt Disney, Betty Friedan, Alberto Giacometti, Kahlil Gibran, Franz Kafka, Abraham Lincoln, Guy Lombardo, Christopher Robin Milne (Winnie the Pooh), Michelle Pfeiffer, Pope John Paul II Mickey Rooney, Sharon Stone, Lily Tomlin, Ted Turner, Dwight Yoakam.

SOUTH NODE IN GEMINI
(NORTH NODE IN SAGITTARIUS)

Quick intelligence, verbal fluidity, and lightning reactions—those are Geminian qualities. Think of a fast-paced conversation, and how rapidly your mind free-associates. Now think of driving a car in heavy traffic on the freeway—again: stimulus, response. These improvisational skills, this sense of "making it up as you go along," is absolutely basic to our understanding of the Twins. With the south node in Gemini, the past-life experiences whose mood still overshadows this person reflect all those speedy mental energies and inner states. In the past, *he or she was shaped by situations that required light-speed reflexes, along with a capacity to recognize opportunity* and to seize it faster than a cat can snag a passing hummingbird. This focused the person's psychic energies in a *rational, cerebral* and rather stressed-out way—a necessary adaptation to the circumstances then, but perhaps too narrow a way of being human today. And yet, as soon as he or she is born, the gravitational field of the old rapid-fire assumptions make themselves felt. Life begins accelerating.

Gemini often refers to *siblings*. While we should not be rigid about this, it is easy to imagine such a person today encountering former-life brothers or sisters—that bond is very strong, and it may still have some unresolved components. Throw in a tale of siblings compelled to live by their wits, and you've got the right Gemini south node feeling.

The sheer speed and flexibility of Gemini also link it to *youth*. Again, no need to become fixated on the idea, but the south node in Gemini does often correlate persuasively with karmic experiences that are uniquely linked to the perils and opportunities of being young—it would strain credulity, for example, to imagine a traumatically premature marriage occurring at age forty! But such a marriage could be indicated by a Gemini south node linked to relationship symbolism. Ditto for sexual abuse, the student's experience, high school politics and follies—the whole range of youthful experience.

Perhaps most central is the orientation of the consciousness to *language*. The translation of human experience into vocabulary, grammar, and syntax is easy and natural here. Presumably, in a prior lifetime, there was much development of this communicative faculty—and look to the rest of the chart to sort that out, of course. A writer? A university professor? A con artist?

In the present life, an individual with the south node in Gemini must guard against a state of *chronic over-extension*. Also he or she must be wary of a pattern of having plenty of *effective tactics but no overarching purpose or strategy*. There are relentless pressures toward *chatter* and running around in circles. He or she will resolutely believe those pressures to be external, but that is really just the hangover of the karmic mood. The truth is, those pressures are mostly psychological and internal and do not have their origins in external reality.

The north node in Sagittarius, the sign of the philosopher, emphasizes the present-tense need for this person to *think deeply and intuitively about what is truly important in life*. Values, beliefs, and personal philosophies need to be the guide. Religion, in the broadest sense, might help the person keep perspective. A helpful "yoga" is to spend some time every year "on a mountaintop," thinking about where he or she is on life's big game board—and where he or she would like to be at the same time next year. Travel is an excellent Sagittarian vitamin in that it helps extricate a person from the clutches of the immediate dramas and distractions. He or she may also be guided intuitively to visit the literal scene of the prior-life Geminian trauma. The eerie experience of simply seeing the place, and half-recognizing it, can have a liberating impact.

Examples: Fred Astaire, Rona Barrett, Napoleon I Bonaparte, Jorge Luis Borges, George Carlin, David Copperfield, Bill Cosby, Cecil B De Mile, Henry Ford, Erich From, Bill Gates, Whoopi Goldberg, William Randolph Hearst, Ernest Hemingway, Jim Henson, Dustin Hoffman, Saddam Hussein, James Joyce, Nelson Mandela, Alanis Morissette, Friedrich Nietzsche, Richard Petty, Franklin D Roosevelt, William Shakespeare, Mickey Spillane, Swami Vivekananda, George Washington, Virginia Woolf, William Wordsworth.

SOUTH NODE IN CANCER
(NORTH NODE IN CAPRICORN)

Tell a decent mother or father that their child is in peril and one thing is certain: immediately nothing else matters. It is such a natural parental reaction that if we were to see anything less than that consuming focus in a mother or father, most of us would probably feel judgmental. Certain instincts—such as protecting kids—are so elemental to our humanity that they bypass the higher brain functions. Most of them have a lot to do with species-survival. They are so fundamental to us all that they form the basis of our moral and legal systems.

Cancer, ruled by the Moon, is the astrological epitome of *instinct* in general—and most especially of the instincts associated with *home, hearth,* and the *protection of the vulnerable.* With the south node in Cancer, this individual carries the mark of having been profoundly *identified with family*, and probably of having been touched deeply by parenthood. From birth, there is typically a deep and unquestioning feeling of *loyalty* and *bondedness* toward certain others—whether or not they deserve it! Emotion and instinct rule here.

Always with the south node it is helpful to be concerned with the potentially blinding or limiting effects of the karmic past, however laudable it might be in general. Family is typically a *cautious* institution. So much focus there naturally rests on the demands of nurturing that a deadening stability can arise. In families, we can see complex, passionate human beings reduced to roles and functions. There can be a kind of paradoxical invisibility—people who see each other every day in predictable circumstances are often less alert and savvy about each other than strangers conversing on a train.

Unconditional love, forgiveness, longsuffering acceptance of each other: these are precious qualities, often found abundantly in a person with the south node in Cancer. But these qualities can breed psychological pestilences! Such an individual must strive to see others as multi-dimensional adults, capable of standing on their own two feet—or at least of learning useful lesson if they land on their derrières. He or she needs to guard against the temptations of "working out" any relationship too effectively, letting it becoming numbingly comfortable. He or she needs consciously to come to decisions about where the *boundaries* should exist between self and kinship groups. Similarly, this person needs to navigate carefully around the risk that friends, especially needy ones, might become his or her "children." Even giving up too much life and autonomy for the sake of one's pets can be an issue here.

The point is that, with the south node in Cancer, this individual carries a tendency to *escape from psychic nakedness and also from facing others as naked souls by focussing attention on other people's needs rather than on their strengths.*

The north node lies in Capricorn, suggesting a kind of "toughening" occurring in this lifetime. This is the sign of the *Elder,* and by the time we become elders we have inevitably seen a lot of tragedy. Capricorn represents a developmental stage beyond parenting and nesting. There is more hard truth in it, and more willingness to be alone and separate. The evolutionary intentions for this person embrace a kind of *maturation*. He or she is learning to love solitude and to defend it. He or she is learning how not to be "cute," both in public and also privately in intimacy. The nurturer is giving way to the truth-sayer.

There is no incubator of psychological wisdom—and also dysfunction—more powerful than family. In prior lives, this person has been there, and learned a lot. With the north node in Capricorn, the time has come to move out of the narrow framework of the inward-looking family and to share this wisdom with the larger community.

Examples: Woody Allen, Julie Andrews, Jean Auel, Elizabeth Barrett Browning, Al Capone, Walter Cronkite, Benjamin Disraeli, Duke Ellington, Marsilio Ficino, Indira Gandhi, Buddy Holly, Ron Howard, William James, John F. Kennedy, Sandy Koufax, Leonardo da Vinci, Sri Ramana Maharshi, John McCain, Thelonius Monk, Luciano Pavarotti, Robert Redford, Oral Roberts, Jerry Seinfeld, Rabindranath Tagore, John Travolta, Denzel Washington Jr., Oprah Winfrey, Andrew Wyeth.

SOUTH NODE IN LEO
(NORTH NODE IN AQUARIUS)

Leo is the Lion—the King of Beasts—with dominion, at least in folklore, over all other creatures. The folklore is easy to appreciate—one look at a tabby cat and we see the "royal" qualities our ancestors noticed in the feline branch of the animal kingdom. With the south node of the Moon in this sign, thinking of this individual as "royalty" in a prior life gets our minds aimed in the right direction. With symbolism, it is of course essential to avoid the pitfalls of literalism: this does not mean the person literally wore a crown. But he or she was surely in a position of privilege and status, and probably therefore envied to some degree by others.

Sometimes people attain such positions of prominence through their own effort and accomplishment. But throughout history it has often simply been the circumstances of one's birth that determined one's place in the social pecking order. Thus the possibility of *privileged birth* in a prior life enters our equations. (Given the grim realities of poverty and powerlessness throughout history, there is a lot positive to be said for the comfortable implications of a Leo south node!) Always though our bias is toward the pitfalls rather than the joys of any prior-life situation. Being born into privilege entails severe social expectations in terms of role, marriage, work, values and behavior. It can be a straightjacket, stifling a soul's natural intentions.

In the present life, a person with the south node in Leo may not be born into wealth or hereditary privilege, but he or she will tend to *shine* somehow. Often such a person carries the burden of being seen as the embodiment of some kind of "perfection," or be framed as "lucky" in the minds of others, regardless of how hard she or she may have actually worked. Many times such a person is able to manifest create considerable *success*. Money may be part of it, but we should also be sensitive to the idea of success in creative areas or other vocations where the bank account is not always the final criterion. A simple observation is that such a person often dresses in a colorful or impressive style, not only looking good but also looking *natural* that way. That is another clue about the "royal" background.

Understanding the traps of the Leo south node is easy in the light of the north node, with its Aquarian evolutionary intentions. Aquarius always carries the energy of *true freedom*. It is the astrological reference to real individuality. Immediately, we understand the vulnerabilities inherent in the Leo karmic pattern: *the creation of a kind of success that is shaped more by a capacity to fulfill the expectations and values of others than by authentic soul-expression.* Easily, this individual can manifest a kind of *empty theatricality*. Typically, he or she has not set out to do that. It "just happens." But a deeper analysis reveals the core issue: the person was swept along by the *seductive currents of other people's projections*, both in a prior-life and perhaps in this present one as well. And even if those projections are positive, they still originate in others, rather than in one's own deep self. They are alien.

The Aquarian solution? *To do as he or she pleases!* To cultivate a blasé attitude regarding the opinions of others. To find the inner freedom to make what might appear "bad" decisions relative to conventional norms of behavior. To value freedom and honesty over applause and status.

Examples: Hank Aaron, Akbar The Great, Eddie Arcaro, Brigitte Bardot, Lionel Barrymore, Clara Barton, Benazir Bhutto, Tony Blair, Frank Capra, Catherine the Great, Anton Chekhov, Leonard Cohen, Oliver Cromwell, Legs Diamond, Sir Arthur Conan Doyle, Amelia Earhart, Albert Einstein, Jerry Falwell, William Faulkner, F. Scott Fitzgerald, Zsa Zsa Gabor, Jackie Gleason, Ulysses S Grant, Tonya Harding, Billie Holiday, Joan of Arc, Aga Khan, III, Sophia Loren, Charles Manson, Thomas Merton, Kate Millet, Bill Meyers, Edith Piaf, Elvis Presley, Frank Sinatra, Gloria Steinem, Marianne Williamson.

SOUTH NODE IN VIRGO
(NORTH NODE IN PISCES)

Poor Virgo gets teased a lot. But in common with the rest of the zodiac, there is something sacred and precious here. Jokes about Virgos alphabetizing their socks notwithstanding, this sign represents some of the best parts of human nature: the drive toward *competence, precision*, and *humility*. It is the archetype of the Servant, with all the attendant implications of *skillful helpfulness*. Virgo is the part of us that is willing to make the effort actually to get *good at something*. Still, since we are looking at the south node of the Moon, it behooves us to look at Virgo a bit more dubiously. For a person with the south node there, it is time to move beyond any blinding or limiting dimensions of the sign of the Virgin. What are they?

Perfection is a harsh and exacting standard. No one can ever live up to it. And yet this person, in a prior life, attempted it. And, of course, failed. To call this failure a "fault" is like lamenting the existence of gravity or taxes. But he or she *internalized a feeling of inadequacy*, and its dark cousins: *shame, guilt*, and a penitential, *self-punishing attitude*. Repressive, shame-based religion may be the culprit—but just as easily we might be observing the results of cultural puritanism, racial or ethnic shaming, the ego-shattering impact of discipleship under an overly-exacting master, or sexual abuse.

With the south node in Virgo, we may possibly be looking at "real" guilt—an unresolved response to some actual dark deed. That latter point must be handled with delicacy, since most of the time a Virgo south node is more reliably correlated with the "phony" guilt created by swallowing unnaturally demanding and unforgiving external standards. As usual, details of the karmic story only emerge through a more complex analysis involving the house position of the node and its planetary ruler, its aspects, and so forth. All we see here in terms of the Virgo south node itself is a *self-doubting, hassling, endlessly fussing* mood that can leach the joy and magic out of life, if it is allowed to stand.

The Moon's north node, and thus the evolutionary intention of this soul, lies in Pisces. To understand the meaning of this configuration, we must start with a line that almost inevitably doomed to go in one ear and out the other: *God's love is absolute.*

What those words signify is that there is nothing a human being can do to affect God's love—being absolute, it is beyond conditioning. Thus, in terms of love, God doesn't give a merry damn whether we feed the hungry children of the world or murder people at random. Stating the principle in shocking terms like that hopefully awakens us to the sheer, liberating Piscean power of the idea of *absolute* love. With the north node in Pisces, this person has reached a point in the journey where he or she needs to *let go of identification with the idea of struggling to evolve.* He or she needs to *play*—to "become as a little child." It is time to get out of his or her own way. Time to surrender.

That said, let's add a dangerous concept: an individual with the south node in Virgo needs to *meditate.* Why is that so dangerous? Because, by instinct and karmic reflex, he or she will interpret "meditation" as more struggle—and, quickly, as more evidence of failure. This true Piscean meditation is relaxing. It ends when we are tired of it, not when a timer goes off. It has no aim or goal. And in the end, this "meditation" merges with everyday consciousness. They become the same long dance under the benign eyes of a God who loves us already.

Examples: Andre Agassi, Pedro Almodovar, F. Lee Bailey, Andre Breton, Naomi Campbell, Pablo Casals, Johnny Cash, Edgar Cayce, Nicholas Culpeper, Joe DiMaggio, Fyodor Dostoevsky, Umberto Eco, Louis Farrakhan, Bob Geldof, Ruth Ginsburg, Hermann Hesse, Thor Heyerdahl, J. Edgar Hoover, Quincy Jones, Mata Hari, Emmaline Pankhurst, Steve Prefontaine, Dane Rudhyar, Babe Ruth, Jonas Salk, Starhawk, Gay Talese, Francois Truffaut, John Updike, Immanuel Velikovsky, Emile Zola.

SOUTH NODE IN LIBRA
(NORTH NODE IN ARIES)

We humans are dangerous primates, with aggressive qualities, strong emotions and sharp teeth. Because of that, can anyone imagine a relationship—or a civilization, for that matter—thriving without a generous dose of *respectful compromise, tact*, and *courtesy*? Let's throw in grace, empathy and love's blessed ally: *a sense of humor*. These are all Libran qualities. With the south node in Libra, no matter how heated this person's internal negotiations may become, an inner compass needle points back toward this pleasant, civilized mood. In the karmic past, he or she was very clearly *partnered* with someone in some way, and became skilled in the arts of "getting along." The impact of prior-life marriage is the most likely avenue to pursue, although of course there are many other kinds of human partnerships: partners in business, comrades in arms, life-long friendships. Because of this karmic pattern, such an individual will doubtless encounter many "familiar" relationships in this present lifetime. There will be many occasions to say, "I feel like I've known you before."

Furthermore, given Libra's natural associations with the more sophisticated aspects of civilization, such an individual probably carries into this world a soul-momentum of interest in the *arts,* in *justice,* and in the dissemination of all that is lofty and uplifting. There may be a high level of *creativity*, and an artistic talent may appear "miraculously" at an early age. It is of course simply being remembered, not learned.

So what's wrong with all that? Nothing! But we do need to recall that the core meaning of the Moon's south node is that it represents patterns that have already served their purposes, and which lead to evolutionary stasis unless challenged. We must also be alert to the Shadow.

The "fair" middle ground can be deadening for everyone. Compromise can mean answers that please no one. Courtesy and respect can hide truth, and provide cover for the parts of us that fear it. Aesthetic experience—music, film, television, beautiful clothing and beautiful people—can be used in shallow, escapist ways, helping us to avoid those nose-to-nose, eye-to-eye moments that are the heart of shared soul-process. These traps face anyone with the south node in Libra. For all the long soul-history this person shares with these ancient partners, there are ways in which they barely know each other. So much reality has been hidden behind walls of "appropriateness." *Justice, reason and dignity have robbed them of love.* The mask associated with their place in society has hidden their true faces—even from each other.

Now, with the north node in Aries, the evolutionary intention of this individual lies in embracing *fire, stormy passion*, and when necessary, *anger*. It is time to reveal the true nature of his or her inner experience, warts and all. He or she benefits enormously from risk and adventure—any situation that feels scary. Such stress and strain are far less threatening to this soul's well-being than the prospect of life foundering for a lack of drive and heat. Think of the depth of thought, reflection, and conversation that might arise in the wee hours between people in bomb shelters or riding out storms at sea! No need to take foolish risks, but this person does need to see how he or she feels in situations where everyone's conventional roles are stripped away: nakedness is exciting.

Examples: Michaelangelo Antonioni, Neil Armstrong, John Jacob Astor, Eva Braun, Edgar Rice Burroughs, Karen Carpenter, Ray Charles, Julia Child, Sir Winston Churchill, Sean Connery, Rene Descartes, Celine Dion, Sir Edward Elgar, Peter Frampton, Sigmund Freud, Peter Gabriel, Maurice and Robin Gibb, Jean Luc Godard, D.W Griffith,. Martha Graham, Aldous Huxley, Jay Leno, Meher Baba, Herman Melville, Florence Nightingale, Ram Dass, Bhagwan Shree Rajneesh, Dan Rather, Rainer Maria Rilke, Andres Segovia, George Bernard Shaw, Bruce Springsteen, Meryl Streep, Nikola Tesla, Twiggy, Walt Whitman, Stevie Wonder, Sir Christopher Wren.

SOUTH NODE IN SCORPIO
(NORTH NODE IN TAURUS)

There are things in life that can freeze the blood in our veins: human depravity and incomprehensible human suffering. A child in fearful agony. Dreadful bodily dysfunction. Sadistic violence. A person's state of mind one minute before jumping in front of a train.

None of us want to get very close to those places, but sometimes, unbidden, they get close to us. Terrible, dark events do happen, and when they do they leave marks on the souls that experience them. A person with the south node in the sign of the Scorpion has known such extremity in a prior life. One possible response to this kind of experience is to become numb—but Scorpio does not do that. It does not turn away. (Dissociation lies more in the dark side of Aquarius.) Here, we see the imagery of the heart as an open wound, shocked and dumbfounded, but still taking in the nightmarish perceptions, unable to break the gaze of the dragon.

There is an atmosphere of deep *seriousness* here—and a corresponding vulnerability to *loss of perspective*, to *gloom* and *suspicion,* especially regarding the lighter, more playful dimensions of human experience. There is also possibly some hard-won wisdom, and potentially compassion too. The key here, from the evolutionary point of view, lies in recognizing that souls often evolve rapidly when faced with extreme hardship, as this individual probably was in a prior lifetime. A man or woman captured and chained on slave ship, even one that sinks en route, may learn more about life and themselves in a year than a "more fortunate" person learns in a safe lifetime. Still, such a path of soul-growth obviously entails serious wear and tear on the attitude, not to mention the persistent scars that tragedy always leaves in its wake.

Taking it one step farther, we must recognize the *fascination* that the dark side of life exercises upon the psyche. A quick perusal of what is playing at your local movie houses will quickly confirm the existence of humanity's weird, ambivalent attraction to the dark. Strange as it may seem, the very realities we most fear seem most to pull us.

Back to the movies: can you imagine a sexy movie star who isn't also at least a little bit dangerous? Sexiness is a quality that cannot ultimately be separated from the Shadow—sexy people seem to beckon us to face our own hunger and need, and to *pay the price of passion.* With the south node in Scorpio, there is a good chance that in a prior lifetimes this individual carried a strong quality of *sexiness.* You can count on that if the south node is linked to relationship symbolism—if it is conjunct Venus, for example.

Along with the *depressive* psychic wear and tear, it is this *attachment to heaviness* that constitutes the deepest obstacle for a person with the south node in Scorpio. The gravitational field of his or her unresolved karmic wounds pulls the person ever into deeper waters—even when the higher path is a simple, pleasant stroll along the beach.

And that brings us to the north node, which lies in Taurus. Here the evolutionary emphasis lies in the area of *calming down*—literally of getting over the processes that brought this soul to its present state of agitated, psychologically complex wisdom. As always with the north node, the work is challenging and it goes against the natural grain. *This person has come into the world to find comfort.* In earthy Taurus fashion, that comfort must be concrete—a timely hug rather than a pithy insight. A bath and a nap instead of a serious talk. Such individuals benefit a lot from living away from urban areas, if possible—or at least in getting out of town as often as possible. Animals have a lot to teach them; it is helpful to have a cat or dog, with the homey comforts these creatures imply. In relationship, such a person benefits from trying to move toward a simple, instinctual acceptance of the partner. We hear so much how complex the process of relating is, but for a person with the south node in Scorpio, that is the last notion he or she need to emphasize. What he or she needs is more like the idea that life is *easier* with a partner, and that of course we humans are typically happier with a mate than without one! That last line may not apply to everyone on the planet, but for this person it conveys the right attitude. Calm, naturalness, and a return to the simple senses are the path forward.

Examples: Gregg Allman, Ian Anderson ("Jethro Tull"), Pamela Anderson, Yasser Arafat, John Belushi, John Wayne Bobbitt, Emily Bronte, Andrew Carnegie, Giovanni Casanova, Hillary Rodham Clinton, Gerard Depardieu, Francisco Franco, Anne Frank, Al Gore, L. Ron Hubbard, Martin Luther King, Linda Lovelace, Imelda Marcos, Josef Mengele, Edna St. Vincent Millay, Henry Miller, Mohammed, Stevie Nicks, Jacqueline Kennedy Onassis, Basil Rathbone, Arthur Rimbaud, Sir Ernest Shackelton, Cat Stevens, Mother Teresa, J.R.R. Tolkien, Mark Twain, Mike Tyson, Oscar Wilde, Tennessee Williams, Tom Wolfe, Paramhansa Yogananda.

SOUTH NODE IN SAGITTARIUS
(NORTH NODE IN GEMINI)

Sagittarius is the sign of the *Quest*—and with the lunar south node there, this individual had already logged many a searching mile before being born into this present lifetime. An exuberant spirit of *possibility* and *openness to life's being an adventure* suffuses this psyche. It is as if the backpack or the suitcase were loaded, the secret treasure-map carefully folded in the pocket, and the wandering road lay wide open. And what was the sought-after grail? Nothing less than the meaning of our existence. In the karmic past, this individual has felt a commitment to seek an *understanding* of life—and he or she has known instinctively that such understanding can only be gleaned through the total immersion of one's senses in all creation. Thus, this person experienced a past-life pattern of *breaking out of predictable molds,* of *doing the unexpected* and the extreme. In prior lifetimes, he or she has shipped out to far shores, leaving home behind, and gone crusading. He or she waited under the date palm when the moon rose in the wee hours and joined the caravan.

Sometimes, the underlying Sagittarian hunger for an understanding of life has been eclipsed behind a *sheer appetite for adventure.* Even then, at least unconsciously, the furnaces of philosophy were being stoked and fed—and that point is even more true when adventures have led this person into *spectacular miscalculations* and *errors*, as was often the case!

Other times, this philosophical hunger has been more obvious: this soul may have been deeply marked by *religion* and by adherence to compelling *belief-systems*. He or she may have lived monastic lifetimes or been involved with religious movements, especially if there are twelfth house influences. If there are hard influences from Pluto or Mars, we may recognize the mark of an experience of martyrdom—such is the power of sheer belief in the Sagittarian south node.

Often the religious impulses in Sagittarius combine with its geographical restlessness to produce a heady mixture of utopian beliefs and mass migration. With the south node in Sagittarius, such a person may, for example, have been a Mormon heading for Utah, a Jew returning to Israel, or a dissident Protestant heading for colonial America.

With the south node in general, we must always be especially alert to the darker side of these old patterns—and even where those patterns are intrinsically healthy, there is still something tired and worn-out about them. Believing in values and philosophies can be blinding. Even "believing in a relationship" can dull one's sensitivity to the need for processes of negotiation and adjustment. It is a short step from faith to a kind of unconscious editing of life's true complexity. In common with many religious people, in prior lives this individual has fallen into patterns of collusion that led to the *denial of truths that ran counter to expectations*—and it is a short step from fundamentalist Islam or Christianity in a past life to fundamentalist New Age thinking today. Karmically, with the south node in Sagittarius, the issue he or she has come here to resolve is a *compulsive addiction to certainty.*

That brings us directly to the evolutionary intention as symbolized by the north node of the Moon in Gemini. Here we find a focus on *listening* and *receiving*, and a willingness to be surprised, pleasantly or otherwise. *He or she needs amazement and wonder.* Gemini is the sign of the Twins, so it symbolizes *dialog* and thus, *relationship.* Two people, shoulder to shoulder, agreeing on everything—how dull! The soul-growth of this individual depends on vigorous, respectful *disagreement* with friends, followed by *long conversation.* Without differences, no one has anything to teach anyone. Let the Buddhist sleep with the Christian! Let the Existentialist try to love the astrologer! The formula this time around is endless dialog, fueled by floods of unexpected, mind-stretching experience, and seasoned with an appreciation of differences—and a wise affirmation that, regarding life, whatever we see, it is way more than that!

Examples: Kareem Abdul-Jabbar, Roald Amundsen, Maya Angelou, Sri Aurobindo, Aubrey Beardsley, Bjork, David Bowie, Charlotte Bronte, Jimmy Buffet, George W Bush, Che Guevarra, Bill Clinton, Charles de Gaulle, Bob Fosse, Enest and Julio Gallo, Michel Gauquelin, Jeffrey Wolf Green, Georges Gurdjieff, Ho Chi Minh, Jack Kevorkian, Francis Scott Key, David Letterman, H.P. Lovecraft, Robert Mapplethorpe, Groucho Marx, Terence McKenna, Emily Post, Gilda Radner, Django Reinhardt, Eddie Rickenbacker, Salman Rushdie, Bertrand Russell, Karen Silkwood, Steven Spielberg, Oliver Stone, Vincent Van Gogh, Orville Wright.

SOUTH NODE IN CAPRICORN
(NORTH NODE IN CANCER)

Necessity is a stern teacher. We rise to it or we are destroyed by it. As a result of prior-life experiences of that nature, there is a *grown-up, no-nonsense attitude* in this person. With his or her south node of the Moon in Capricorn, the *survival skills* are superb. He or she can add two plus two and come up with four every time—even when the numbers would put tears in anyone else's eyes. In prior lifetimes, he or she has squarely faced hard reality and steeled the heart to do the right thing. Furthermore, such realities were likely faced alone. Capricorn is the Hermit, and there is a deep mark of *adaptation to solitude* in this soul.

Nowadays our pop psychological culture places a great premium on "being in touch with our feelings." And of course only an ignoramus would argue against that idea. Still circumstances often arise in which *morality, ethics,* or *sheer practicality* demand that we set our feelings aside and take a course that reason supports—or that our conscience can accept in the long run. Anyone who has ever *resisted a temptation* understands this territory—and a person with this south node configuration understands it very well. In prior lifetimes, he or she has faced grim moral and practical requirements. Perhaps the person was a pioneer, eking out an existence in an unforgiving land. Perhaps he or she gave birth to a crippled child—or to a large, hungry brood of healthy ones. He or she has known grinding poverty—or the relentless demands of power and position. In prior lives, for this soul it has never been easy.

As always, we can get a better handle on the actual circumstances through a consideration of the house that contains the south node, along with the various associated planetary configurations. What we see here with the south node alone is simply the basic Capricorn signature: *strength, self-denial and character, bred in a harsh environment or in the face of relentless pressures.*

With the south node of the Moon in Capricorn, friends can rely on this person. If he or she has children, the kids will have their material needs met. Moving into a new neighborhood, he or she might chair the Neighborhood Watch committee. At work, the business runs efficiently—and survives downturns that catch competitors unaware. This individual is a magnet for duty and responsibility, and he or she handles them with maturity, realism and aplomb. As those duties and responsibilities proliferate, the person rises to the challenges without outward signs of falling apart.

Slogging along, putting one foot ahead of the other, becomes a habit. So does self-denial. So does stoical hopelessness. After a while, we stop noticing pain or need. And that brings us to the damage this soul has sustained. Such a person may be reliable, decent, and efficient—but is he or she having any fun? What about soothing the ancient wound that binds him or her to this wintry landscape of necessity? Giving himself or herself permission to feel, to cry, to need? Reaching out a comforting hand to his or her streetwise, *inner* orphans?

Those are the questions that bring us face to face with the north node of the Moon in Cancer. *This person has come into the world for healing.* And while that healing may eventually extend beyond one's self and reach out into the community, it is critically important that it begin with the Self.

In the karmic past, he or she did not have the luxury of tears. We certainly do not need to shame them for that; only to recognize that there was simply a realistic adaptation to inhumanly harsh realities. The intent now is to *soften.* There is a soul-contract to integrate, accept and comfort the weaker, more emotional, gentler parts of the psyche.

He or she must cry those old, unfallen tears.

With the south node of the Moon in Capricorn, underlying the karmic mood of this individual is an abiding hunger to be safe—at last. That hunger is inseparable from a need to establish an emotionally-secure place in the world. Physical and financial safety are part of it, but equally central is the feeling of heart-safety that comes from committed intimacy. That could mean marriage or a similar bond, but it can also as easily mean deep, long-lasting friendships. The guardian angels smile when they see this person feeling safe and stable enough to plant trees instead of seasonal marigolds. They jump for joy when he or she feels safe enough to express sorrow or fear or need or other "weaknesses." Cancer is the Great Mother, and with the north node there, it is time to rest a while in her arms.

Examples: Patch Adams, Louisa May Alcott, Johann Sebastian Bach, Bernard Baruch, Simone de Beauvoir, Hilaire Belloc, Robert Bly, William F Buckley, Robert Burns, Rachel Carson, Carlos Castaneda, Fidel Castro, Cesar Chavez, Eric Clapton, John Coltrane, Bette Davis, Danny DeVito, Johnny Depp, Daphne DuMaurier, T.S Eliot,. Queen Elizabeth II, Allen Ginsberg, Andy Griffith, George Friedrich Handel, Hugh Hefner, Adolf Hitler, Rock Hudson, Gary Kasparov, Elisabeth Kubler-Ross, Courtney Love, George Lucas, Bob Marley, Steve Martin, Marilyn Monroe, Maria Montessori, Baba, Gurudev Muktananda, Edward R Murrow, Maxfield Parrish, Maximilian Robespierre, Marquis de Sade, Pete Townshend.

SOUTH NODE IN AQUARIUS
(NORTH NODE IN LEO)

Could an ancient Egyptian have imagined a world without a pharaoh? A medieval European a world without kings, popes and dukes? The wheels of history turn. We look back over the pages of the history books and so much seems inevitable, as if there really were wheels of history turning like gears in some impersonal mechanism. But the truth is that the world changes because of individual people shaking things up. Those people are almost always a tiny minority of the population. Very typically they pay a price for the gift they give us—the figures of authority in the pre-existing culture are fiercely opposed to anyone who challenges the status quo.

When these revolutionaries reincarnate, they often display the south node of the Moon in Aquarius—the sign of the Rebel or the Exile. When we see that south node signature in a chart, we know that in a prior lifetime the person was an *outsider*, existing in tension somehow with consensual reality. There was a feeling of it being "me (or "us") against the world." And if it were "us," we are probably talking about some kind of *radical movement* of which he or she was a part. (In that case, the Aquarian south node would probably show some connection to the eleventh house, by the way.) In other words, we might be looking at a person who was among the slaughtered Cathars in thirteenth century France—or slaughtered civil rights activists in twentieth century Alabama.

If we are going along with the herd, believing what we are told to believe, our brains don't get a lot of exercise. But if everyone we meet imagines us to be wrong, that muscle between our ears gets a lot stronger! That is the case with this south node—it suggests a strong prior-life development of the urge to think for one's self. For an individual with the south node of the Moon in Aquarius, there is an instinct to do things his or her own way, to question the "received wisdoms," and to follow less-trodden pathways. He or she thinks independently, and therefore tends to be drawn toward the familiar ground of sub-cultures that are at odds with the social mainstream. Far more than most of us, such a person truly writes his or her own script.

Still, because of the unconscious karmic soul-conditioning, he or she may reflexively ignore the comfort and wisdom of "normalcy." He or she may become so identified with a set of colorful, rebellious *ideas* that there is a loss of contact with natural feelings and instincts. Such a person may needlessly alienate or isolate himself or herself from the human family.

Furthermore, because he or she may share soul-memories of persecution or even torture, there can be a *dissociative* tendency—basically a reflex to "go away" emotionally. That too can drive these people into a cerebral orientation which, while intellectually impressive, can also entail a gulf opening between mind and the soulful "belly" of our common humanity.

With the north node of the Moon in Leo, a person with this configuration holds the Lion's soul-intention: To roar! To be heard! Something was left undone in the karmic past. *Part of the reason he or she has reincarnated in this present life is to finish the business from long ago.* The message was not completely delivered. The exiled heretic must make his or her presence felt in the world.

To be "right" is one thing; to be *heard* is another. The first requires mental freedom and a willingness to question authority—and with an Aquarian south node, this individual has those bases covered. The second goal, actually being heard, requires a different set of skills—ones he or she did not master in the prior lifetime. Most of these skills are more *theatrical and political* than mental—Leo territory. He or she must find ways to appear *plausible and convincing*, especially to the unconverted. He or she must *build effective bridges* this time around. He or she needs to be appealing, non-threatening except where threat is absolutely necessary, and to *radiate confidence.* Even the message the *clothing* sends must be calculated. Ditto for language and word choices.

Do not be misled by the emphasis upon outward appearances here. There is an inward breakthrough trying to happen as well. With the Leo north node, it is time to "come in from the cold." As such a person has been judged by others, so he or she has become judgmental. As he or she has been isolated, there may be a separation from the larger community. The soul-contract is to find a way actually to make a positive difference in the lives of the very people who, formerly, would have burned him or her at the stake. This represents motion in the only direction higher than truth, and that is the direction of forgiving, unconditional love.

Such a person is moving beyond *rightness* into *effectiveness.*

Examples: Horatio Alger, Robert Altman, "Fatty" Arbuckle, Arthur Ashe, Chet Atkins, W.H. Auden, Lauren Bacall, Bart J. Bok, Pierre Boulez, Boy George, Garth Brooks, Truman Capote, Johnny Carson, Neville Chamberlain, John Constable, Tom Cruise, Alexandra David-Neel, John Z. DeLorean, Diana, Princess of Wales, Queen Elizabeth I, Bobby Fischer, Steve Fossett, Mohandas Gandhi, Newt Gingrich, George Harrison, Jimi Hendrix, Xaviera Hollander, Howard Hughes, Lee Iacocca, Eric Idle, Arthur Janov, Janis Joplin, Johannes Kepler, Soeren Kierkegaard, , k.d. lang T.E. Lawrence, David Livingstone, Joni Mitchell, Jim Morrison, Audie Murphy, Barack Obama, Georgia O'Keeffe, Jimmy Page, Elaine Pagels, Pol Pot, Diana Ross, Artur Rubinstein, Rod Serling, Sam Shepard, Bugsy Siegel, SwamiSivananda, Robert Louis Stevenson, Saint Teresa Of Avila, Gore Vidal, Venus Williams, Malcolm X.

SOUTH NODE IN PISCES
(NORTH NODE IN VIRGO)

Mystical traditions universally encourage us to look beyond the appearance of the world. They teach us the ancient Piscean truths: our true natures are not these transitory physical bodies; our true home is not this endless, three-dimensional passion play. For a person with the south node of the Moon in Pisces, such understandings are the glue that holds the psyche together.

But if he or she truly observes the world as if it were dream, does anything he or she does matter? Feeding imaginary starving children—or slaughtering imaginary rivals: does either action carry any significance? Is compassion any more relevant than hatred?

In prior lifetimes, this person has experienced a hallucinatory *loss of self.* He or she has learned to see the world as a dream—and felt a sense of moving through it like a ghost. There is a fair chance that in a prior lifetime this individual entered into spiritual practices: long meditations, devotional ritual, fasting. That he or she has been in monastic orders is a good guess, especially if we see other indications of religion in connection with the south node—ninth house elements, for example.

Those perspectives make the person sound "officially" holy. Perhaps the title is deserved. But Piscean energy can express itself in other, less holy ways. Just as likely, we may see the person drinking prodigiously in a bar in a prior-life, or floating through socially-defined roles in frivolous elegance, or experiencing the dull dream of a life defined purely by the expectations of others.

It is very possible that *all* the scenarios above apply to this person—and that the monastic existence came *first*. That might seem counter-intuitive, but spiritual practice is serious medicine. A soul that is not ready for the changes it engenders becomes disoriented and vulnerable.

Before we look at the actual evolutionary intentions for the person with this south node, we should spend a moment counting their treasures. The secret world holds a deep, authentic *sense of magic*. The *psychic sensitivity* is probably extraordinary—such a person often feels like he or she is reading other people's minds. There is an incredible faculty of *imagination* and *creativity*. He or she "gets the joke" about human egos, one's own included, and that helps with keeping perspective on conflicts, pride, and worldly razzle-dazzle.

What he or she has come here to do this time is symbolized by the north node of the Moon, which lies in Virgo. One big part of this intention leaps out when we recall that Virgo is an Earth sign: this person has a soul-contract to get "down to earth." To become grounded. He or she is learning to function in more *effective, orderly, efficient* ways.

Virgo is the *Servant*—but we need to be careful of that language. The aim here is not to become a "servant" in any literal sense, nor is it necessarily so lofty as becoming "servants of humanity." It is really about simply becoming *skilled enough at something in particular to be of use to other people.* Accepting specific responsibilities and discharging them competently is central to Virgo. *Making little things matter* is a huge part of the work of the Virgo north node.

Underlying this practical impulse to be helpful is an evolutionary strategy. With the south node of the Moon in Pisces, this individual has unwittingly become *self-absorbed* and *subjective.* He or she has fallen into the dreamlike trap of the "spiritual path," with its subtle, back-door reinforcement of the ego. He or she has reached a stage in the evolutionary trajectory where there is a need to take that ancient ego-antidote: *service. The person needs to make other people's dilemmas more central and compelling than his or her own dilemmas.* There is a deeply spiritual *self-*

forgetting in such a path. Thus, in becoming useful to others, this individual is profoundly useful to himself or herself.

Examples: Evangeline Adams, Muhammad Ali, Tammy Faye Bakker, Antonio Banderas, Karl Barth, David Ben-Gurion, Philip Berrigan, Clara Bow, Robert Browning, Luther Burbank, Leo Buscaglia, Joseph Campbell, David Crosby, Marie Curie, Jeffrey Dahmer, Salvador Dali, Charles Dickens, Emily Dickinson, Christian Dior, Bob Dylan, Henry Fonda, Jerry Garcia, Cary Grant, Dag Hammarskjold, Steven Hawking, Garrison Keillor, Henry Kissinger, Franz Liszt, Norman Mailer, Marcel Marceau, Marie Antoinette, Paul McCartney, Bridey Murphy, George Patton, Ezra Pound, Anne Rice, Jean Paul Sartre, Martin Scorsese, Percy Bysshe Shelley, Paul Simon, Barbra Streisand, Twyla Tharp, Paul Tillich, Arturo Toscanini, Kurt Vonnegut, Andrew Weil, Frank Lloyd Wright.

CHAPTER SEVEN:
THE LUNAR NODES THROUGH THE HOUSES

Beware, beware! What follows may endanger your astrological imagination! As I said at the beginning of the previous chapter, these kinds of "cookbook" interpretations can become addictive—and like most addictions, they do not contribute much to your soul or your creativity in the long run.

Please remember that the real meaning of the nodes emerges from their larger astrological context.

(Read the rest of the book, in other words!)

SOUTH NODE IN THE FIRST HOUSE
(NORTH NODE IN THE SEVENTH HOUSE)

Freedom: we all value it—and paradoxically we dread its constant companion, which is uncertainty. In every truly free situation, we must make choices. Sometimes we are free to choose between pleasant, positive courses. Other times, we are caught between a rock and hard place. Much of the time, we have no idea what kind of outcome a given choice will bring. There are no guarantees. Will marriage bring joy or sorrow? What about having a baby? Or moving to the coast? With the south node in the first house, this individual has felt *the weight of that kind of freedom* over and over again. In prior lifetimes, he or she has faced circumstances that demanded decisive action, typically without enough information to be absolutely confident. There was a certain hardening of the attitude, and bridges had to be burned.

These dramatic past life choices have affected not only the self, but also the lives of others. That is because first house energy correlates with *leadership*—and leaders have followers. Further, while leaders often appear to be clear and certain, their inner reality is often far shakier—such a person must make life-shaping decisions without any way of knowing if they are right or wrong. For this individual, these pressures created a *self-contained* quality, as if no one on the outside can see his or her inner processes with any clarity. He or she can be *impressive, radiant, and seemingly transparent—yet ultimately elusive.*

Even though the first house tends toward independence, we immediately know that there are relationship issues here—if only because the cutting-edge north node must be in the seventh house ("marriage"). Choosing—or not choosing—a mate is one of our ultimate, inalienable human freedoms. But once the hormonal veil of falling in love begins to lift, we recognize that, in loving, we give up a lot of precious freedom. With the south node in the first house, this individual has often come to that crossroads—and chosen to go down his or her own road alone. Often, there simply wasn't a partner with sufficient ego-strength available to hold up the other end of the relationship. Here we must also lay on the table the possibility of relationships forming in the past life scenarios—but relationships in which this person was isolated by his or her own dominance over a weaker or needier partner. Another scenario involves the *dependent* partner, a condition which may in origin be psychological or practical—the partner becomes debilitated.

This prior life conditioning had pumped so much energy into his or her natural authority and compulsion to take personal responsibility that the delicate interpersonal balancing act of partnership was no longer available.

With this nodal configuration, it is quite possible that this individual has had significant *rivals, enemies, or competitors* in previous lifetimes—look to planets in square or opposition to the south node for details. If so, we will see plenty of evidence for that tension in the present lifetime as well.

The north node lies in the seventh house, the traditional house of marriage. While it would be dogmatic to say that such a person *must* marry (or similarly bond) in this lifetime, it is essential to recognize that the evolutionary intention lies in the *direction of partnership and cooperation*. Countering that intention is the weight of the karmic pattern, pulling this person toward self-sufficiency, care-taking, insulated positions of authority, and clueless isolation. This individual needs to *learn to listen*, to *depend* on other people, and to *surrender* to certain (carefully-chosen) partners. The core evolutionary issues are *trust* and *commitment*. Many of the natural goals of the life can only be fulfilled in partnership—the kind of situation in which each person has talents and skills the other one lacks. Each holds half of the treasure map. Only by entering into a relationship characterized by seeing through each other's eyes and listening through each other's ears can this person—and his or her natural partners—actually do the great work.

Examples: Ralph Abernathy, Louis Armstrong, Antonio Banderas, Alexander Graham Bell, Annie Besant, Shirley Temple Black, Robert Bly, Art Buchwald, Barbara Cartland, Brian De Palma, David Duke, Queen Elizabeth I, Dale Ernhardt, Steve Fossett, Jean Luc Godard, Sue Grafton, Jeffrey Wolf Green, Herbie Hancock, William Randolph Hearst, Woody Herman, Billie Jean King, Thelonius Monk, Paul Newman, Richard M. Nixon, Barack Obama, Richard Pryor, Christopher Reeve, Rainer Maria Rilke, Norman H Schwarzkopf, Uma Thurman, Gianni Versace, Lawrence Welk, Marion Woodman, Tammy Wynette, Malcolm X.

SOUTH NODE IN THE SECOND HOUSE
(NORTH NODE IN THE EIGHTH HOUSE)

Calling the second house the "house of money" is like saying orchestras make loud noises—it is true, but it leaves out all the music! *Resources*, not just dollars, are the real issue here. Food and shelter are on the list. So are *skills* that empower us to survive—and that includes everything from the ability to start a fire without matches right up through professional talents that pay the bills in a complex, high-tech culture.

With the south node in the second house, prior life issues around such resources have left a mark on this person. Depending on the condition of the south node's sign and planetary connections, it is possible that this individual has known literal starvation—and this configuration is not uncommon in the charts of people with present-life eating disorders, simply because they starved in a previous one. It is possible that he or she has been exposed, perhaps fatally, to *extreme climatic conditions*: freezing to death for lack of shelter or wood to burn, for example. Reliably, in prior lives, he or she has known the distorting impact of financial extremes. *Poverty* may have taken its grinding toll—but *great wealth* can twist lives almost as easily, creating a spider web of expectations, manipulations, and mistrust. All these prior-life experiences have threatened this individual's actual survival—physically, spiritually or both. And that has left a mark of *fear, self-doubt*, and *insecurity* upon the soul.

Note that seeing the south node in the second house can equally indicate vast wealth or poverty, abundance or lack. Any time prior-life extremes or fluctuations relative to resources had a fundamental impact upon the quality of a life-experience, we may see a second house signature. The context of the south node fills in the details. Conjunct Jupiter? That looks like wealth. Conjunct Saturn? More like poverty. Conjunct Uranus? Sudden, unexpected changes in the resource base.

Underlying the outward circumstances which this nodal placement suggests, we encounter the interior psychological drama: a feeling of crippling self-doubt. Poverty and its focus on simple day-to-day survival does not offer much to support self-actualization. Maybe, in a prior life, we were capable of writing a brilliant novel—but if we never could afford an education and all we could think about was whether the kids had enough food to keep them alive, what were the chances of that novel getting written? Near zero, of course.

What are we left with? The feeling in the soul that we *could* have written a great novel, and *did not*. What does that feeling of failure do for our confidence and our dignity as we are reborn? There is a residual feeling of having missed the boat—and of being the kind of person who will *always* miss it.

I had a poignant talk once with a wealthy young man who had done many magnificent, generous things with his money. He complained of his heartbreak at overhearing comments along the lines of, "Well, if I had his kind of money, of course I could have done it too. Anyone could." All his successes were attributed to his money, never to himself. That was not accurate or fair, but the devaluation had sunk into his bones. Most of us are conditioned to believe that being rich is one of the best things that could happen to a person. For a reality check on that belief, ask the rich! This kind of past-life karma can manifest as a second house south node in the present birthchart. Be wary of always reading a second house south node in terms of lack or shortage.

How does this individual get on with fulfilling his or her soul intentions? With the north node in the eighth house, one point we recognize right away is that he or she cannot succeed alone. The eighth house is always about the *deepest kinds of intimacy*. Generally that implies sexuality, but only of the kind where two people become bonded or "mated," with all the attendant vulnerabilities and shared processes of psychic nakedness. This person is attempting to surrender sexually to someone in full, self-aware maturity. There is a pent-up need to consummate that kind of love. Why? *Simply to be seen clearly and nakedly by another soul.* This innocent human gift is one remedy for the prior-life distortions.

The eighth house is also about deep inner work. There, we dig down past resistance and denial, and find truth. As we saw, the second house south node suggests wounds to the fundamental *dignity* and sense of self-worth. Those layers of *self-sabotage* must be rooted out. For such people, there is often a dramatically cathartic result simply from remembering a prior life—understanding and self-forgiveness can arise, often very quickly.

Furthermore, the eighth house has a feeling of underlying *power* about it. People with strong eighth houses in their natal charts may not have worldly power or position, but when they walk into a room, you can feel a kind of intensity about them. Such a person is "someone to be reckoned with." With the south node in the second, this individual was disempowered somehow in a prior life. We can see the importance and helpfulness in the current life of *reclaiming natural power and authority.* This is supported by a feeling of having done brave inner work—and profoundly helped along by the fully adult sexual confidence that arises from having established a stable, satisfying bond with a substantial partner. *Examples: Kareem Abdul-Jabbar, Patch Adams, Pearl Bailey, Jim & Tammy Faye Bakker, Simone de Beauvoir, Craig Breedlove, Lenny Bruce, Mary Chapin Carpenter, Kurt Cobain, Billy Corgan, Bill Cosby, Mario Cuomo, Charles de Gaulle, Diana Princess of Wales, Albert Einstein, Friedrich Engels, Francisco Franco, Jimi Hendrix, Jesse Jackson, Robert Mapplethorpe, Groucho Marx, Camille Paglia, Marquis de Sade, Sri Sathya Sai Baba, Jean Paul Sartre, B.F Skinner, Oliver Stone, John Updike, Gore Vidal.*

SOUTH NODE IN THE THIRD HOUSE
(NORTH NODE IN THE NINTH HOUSE)

Maybe you are driving in the middle of six lanes of heavy, fast traffic. Maybe you suddenly realize that you've got only a quarter mile to get over into the right lane to make the exit. And maybe at that moment whoever is riding shotgun next to you asks you a question about your philosophy of life.

Probably you ignore him! If you think about anything other than navigating through the traffic, you might have an accident. If you make any response at all to his question, it is certainly short, and probably humorous or cynical.

Life gets like heavy traffic sometimes. Things are moving so rapidly and unpredictably that we simply do not have time to reflect. We are thinking, but the thoughts are focused on immediate concerns. In that mode, we are practical, concrete and reflexively logical. With the south node in the third house, an individual carries the karmic mark of that kind of nervous, speedy, mentally-driven reactivity. In prior lifetimes, his or her pattern has been one of *acceleration, improvisation*, and *rapid adaptation.* Perhaps he or she was orphaned, picking pockets in the marketplace to survive—with a belly full of hunger pressing harder than any moral analysis of thievery. He or she remained alive by recognizing opportunity and seizing it before it shifted away.

"Being orphaned" is of course only one of thousands of scenarios we could invent. In every one of them, reality hits hard and fast and we deal with it or things fall apart. If it is a heavy story such as being orphaned, look for heavy squares or oppositions to the south node, or for its ruler to be under some kind of pressure—in the twelfth house, for example.

Equally, we might be looking at a situation of worldly glory—a pop star feeling the need to improvise his next "hit," for example. A socialite with a smaller bank account than her appearances might suggest. Here too we see the basic third house signature: endless, malleable adaptation, driven by the wits and the reflexes. In this kind of situation, the ruler of the south node could be in the tenth house, and there might be some Jupiter involvements.

Trouble is, this person could be running on sheer momentum in this lifetime—still not able to take the eyes off the road and think about his or her philosophy of life. As always, the south node represents a pattern that has served its purpose, past tense. We need to recognize its dead-end qualities and move forward. If an individual fails in that challenge, then his or her life will be swept along by external currents. He or she will be fast, efficient and maybe astonishingly productive, but there will be no real strategy, only reaction and improvisation. He or she will communicate glibly, but never get down to the soul of things

Language and communication skills are central to the third house south node. There was much prior-life development in those areas. A simple fact is that the person, in the earlier incarnation, talked a lot. There could have been a compulsive element in that regard, or it may be connected with simply being a *raconteur.* Or a teacher, or a storyteller.

The good news is that this person does not need to remain locked in the cerebral or improvisational gravitational field of that south node. With the north node in the philosophical ninth house, the evolutionary intention is to go "sit on the mountaintop" and reflect a bit. He or she needs to think basic, grounding thoughts—such as, *why are we alive here on this earth in the first place?* What are the *core values* that underlie my life? What kinds of life does he or she want to look back on from the perspective of old age?

Religion, in some sense of the word, may help give perspective on these questions. So will anything conducive to broader views. For example, almost certainly as he or she moves toward this broader, more reflective style of thinking, the person will realize that one particular goal that simply feels very meaningful is *travel.* And with that simple idea, something amazing happens—instinct will then guide this individual *to the literal scene of a prior lifetime in which events happened too fast for reflection and integration*: back to that "marketplace," where he or she contrived to survive, for example. Seeing the "scene of the crime" can have a liberating effect on a person, which is why we must view travel here in positive evolutionary terms. It is one of the basic spiritual disciplines in this lifetime.

Examples: Douglas Adams, Robert Altman, Mary Astor, Cristobal Balenciago, Bjorn Borg, Ray Bradbury, Tycho Brahe, Helen Gurley Brown, Johnny Carson, Bill Clinton, Bob Dylan, Umberto Eco, T.S Eliot,. Peter Gabriel, Billy Graham, Adolf Hitler, Hazrat Inayat Khan, Courtney Love, Edgar Mitchell, Oral Roberts, Karen Silkwood, James Taylor, Mike Wallace, Oscar Wilde, Paramhansa Yogananda.

SOUTH NODE IN THE FOURTH HOUSE
(NORTH NODE IN THE TENTH HOUSE)

Cities only came into existence a few thousand years ago. Nations are practically a brand new concept. Throughout most of human history, our fundamental sense of our place in the world was defined by kinship groups: *families, clans and tribes.* And typically, that also meant a sense of *our sacred land.* Those are fourth house realities. When we think about a person with the south node in that house, we must be careful not to be bound by modern notions of "family." They are way too narrow. The idea that he or she came out of "family systems" in the karmic past is surely true, but so is the idea that he or she probably walked around on two legs—it is basically true of everyone, in other words. What we need to recognize is that such an individual was *defined* by family, and that the impact of familial expectations and familial mythology upon him or her was severe and limiting. That is the karma.

One immediate hypothesis is that, in the present lifetime, this individual is surrounded by people with whom he or she *had family bonds in a prior lifetime.* These people may not be "family," literally, now—although they will feel that way. For obvious psychological reasons, it is often hard for people in a present-day sexual relationship, for example, to think of themselves as brother and sister in a prior lifetime—but it can easily be the case. We can say the same for other possible kinship connections: one was the other's grandparent or niece or nephew.

In any case, there is typically a quality of *unquestioning, total loyalty* toward "family," however they define the term, among people with this south node—loyalty that may or may not be deserved. Often they feel an uncanny sense of familiarity between themselves and these "family members" right from the start of their present relationship. Living together feels very natural, and tends to happen quickly.

Note that I keep putting the word "family" in quotation marks. That is because these relationships are only sometimes recognizable literally as "family" in the present life. Other times, they take the form of friendships, romantic bonds, or professional relationships which are imbued with this "familial" sense of radical commitment and total identification. A person with this nodal configuration is likely to have deep and tangled relations with his or her literal family in this life. Those relations may be warm or they may be cold—and ditto for the prior life family scenario. It too could be warm or cold—and the answer to that question emerges from the rest of the planetary considerations. But warm or cold, it was *engulfing* and *defining*. That is the point, karmically.

We can honor the beauty of such human bonds. But always with the south node of the Moon, we must bias our attention in the direction of caution—families can be crazy and dysfunctional; people can be eaten alive by them, their individual destinies stripped away; loyalty can be offered where it is not earned or merited.

The karmic trap lies in the ease with which this person's individual identity can be subsumed by the requirements of the "family system." That pitfall can take two forms. The first lies in being crushed beneath the expectations of the literal family: enmeshment in the family dramas, and enslavement to the life-limiting realities of the family myth—"we Smith women always marry drunks," or "we Jones men always wind up working for the electric company." In cases such as those, we might find the ruler of the south node made vulnerable by Neptunian or Piscean contacts, or "defined by the group" via eleventh house contacts.

The second trap lies in a person with this south node creating crushing familial expectations all by themselves—having children too quickly, having too many of them, or becoming so preoccupied with being a couple that he or she forgets to be an individual with a separate life. In that case, we might see the ruler of the south node in the first house—for independent (if ill-conceived) choice and self-created realities. Or the ruler in the seventh house—for someone compelled by inner urges to be defined by another person.

With the north node in the tenth house, there is a great soul-desire to come out into the world. This individual *knows something* which can be of use to total strangers—to the community, in other words. It is time to offer his or her gifts to the world, not to hide them in the private, unexpressed imagination or to limit their expression to within the family. The essence of his or her evolutionary strategy lies in simply launching forth into the wild and frothy "white water" of life lived in the public context rather than in the withdrawn context of family.

Simply *prioritizing the professional life* is often a very big part of fulfilling this intention, in practice. "Will I move across the country to take this great job—or stay where I can be close to mom and dad?" In this case, moving would reflect the evolutionary intention, while staying home would reflect the now-deadening karmic pattern.

Extending this thinking, we recognize that with the north node in the tenth house, the soul has now reached a stage where thinking in terms of a *mission in life* becomes more rewarding than the quiet comforts of home. *Examples: Gianni Agnelli, Pedro Almodovar, Ian Anderson, Honore de Balzac, Tony Blair, Jon Bon Jovi, Tom Brokaw, Italo Calvino, Karen & Richard Carpenter, Jimmy & Rosalyn Carter, Coco Chanel, Cesar Chavez, Agatha Christie, Francis Ford Coppola, Celine Dion, Christian Dior, Carrie Fisher, Julio Gallo, Whoopi Goldberg, Germaine Greer, Maurizio Gucci, George Harrison, Jesse Helms, John Irving, Billy Joel, Charles Kuralt, Harpo Marx, Margaret Mead, Dolly Parton, Jean Piaget, Robert Redford, Julia Roberts, Carl Sagan, Willy Shoemaker, Meryl Streep, Pete Townshend, Sarah Vaughan, Johnny Weismuller.*

SOUTH NODE IN THE FIFTH HOUSE
(NORTH NODE IN THE ELEVENTH HOUSE)

Creativity, children, love affairs and issues around *hedonism* are the quaternity of factors that define the spectrum of possibility for this individual's karma. Which of those possibilities is emphasized is generally discernible through a consideration of the rest of the nodal factors, although all four are worth considering in every case.

Where we see significant nodal involvement with the Moon or Saturn or the signs Cancer and Capricorn, look especially to karmic entanglements involving children—those are the most "parental" symbols in astrology. This is a very common pattern, since the majority of people have children and kids are of course a potentially enormous source of complexity. For all the joys and rewards of raising the little ones, it is useful to remember that over and over again in human history, people have sacrificed much that was potentially important to them on the altar of parenthood. Furthermore, *unintended pregnancies* have always abounded—and bound people into premature, ill-fated marriages. Once children exist, their needs tend to eclipse the needs of their parents. This is natural, but it can also be tragic. With our suspicious bias toward the south node, these darker readings of the impact of children in prior life experiences are generally productive.

In the present life, this person may simply replicate the old patterns. Or there may be a lot of tension and questions around *whether or not to have children*, with obscure fears and resentments complicating the decision.

With the south node in the fifth house, the person may very well have been involved with the *creative arts* in some form in a prior life. One of the easiest ways to confirm that possibility is to see if the pattern is reproduced in the present life—if he or she is drawn to creative work in this lifetime, or shows some particular artistic talent, it practically clinches the karmic roots of the behavior. Think of the famous example of Mozart composing symphonies when he was barely out of his diapers. As with the issue of children, it is the *context* of the south node that focuses our attention on the creative possibilities: Libran or Venusian connections?

Generally, artists serve an experimental role in a society, going out to the ragged edges of emotion, passion and experience that more cautious citizens may find fascinating, but too risky to assay themselves. Thus we have the commonly observed linkage between the creative life and the "issues of hedonism." Drug-addled rock stars, and so on. With the south node in the fifth house, there may be a theme of *dissipation* linked to the creative life—or of course, simple dissipation with no creativity whatsoever is a possibility too! Freud famously observed that the libido never forgets a pleasure. Most *addictions* and *compulsions* are far easier to create than to shake. This person may very well have fallen into prior-life patterns involving debauchery or dissipation. And of course he or she need not have been an artist to go down that road!

Love affairs are yet another classic fifth house correlate, and often play an important role in this nodal interpretation. Love affairs can lead to pregnancy, neatly tying in this theme into issues around children. Even without thinking of children, it is worth considering that this person "broke the social rules" that governed the expression of sexuality in a prior life. That would be especially likely were there Uranian or Aquarian considerations in the mix as well. Also, look for a planet in the eleventh house opposing that south node—that can indicate the "judgment of the community," pinning the Scarlet Letter on this individual.

In the present life, with the Moon's north node in the eleventh house, the core of the healing process for this individual revolves around learning to *think strategically*. It is about taking a *longer view*, realizing that he or she *has time* to make decisions and develop dreams. He or she benefits enormously from pressing toward long-term goals: saving to build a home, or to complete an education, or to have a major adventure that requires preparation and planning. If children are on the radar screen, it is helpful for this individual to delay pregnancy for a while, putting that decision more under his or her own intentional control. In matters of creativity, there is a need to nurture *development* as an artist over time—perhaps taking instruction from masters and honing the craft over decades. Friendships are important here, and must be handled judiciously. Positively, he or she needs to develop *discernment* in terms of which kinds of people support what he or she most wants to become—and, negatively, to recognize people who, while fun, lead them nowhere, or worse.

It would be profoundly misleading to think that an individual with the north node in the eleventh house is trying to get past the need to enjoy life! It is really more that he or she is learning to be a little smarter about wringing the maximum amount of joy out of living, given two primordial truths: first, the joyless reality of pleasure's dark, compulsive side. And secondly, the reality of our need, given life's brevity, to live strategically. It is in such strategy that we truly honor the preciousness of each moment, each diamond in eternity.

Examples: Louisa May Alcott, Arthur Ashe, Jane Austen, Melvin Belli, Milton Berle, Otto Von Bismarck, John Wayne Bobbitt, Charles Boyer, George W. Bush, Frank Capra, Julia Child, Paquito D'Rivera, Marsilio Ficino, Harrison Ford, Jerry Garcia, Edward Gorey, Don Imus, Frida Kahlo, Stephen King, Queen Latifah, D.H. Lawrence, Liberace, Steve Martin, Guy de Maupassant, Jack Nicklaus, Shaquille O'Neal, Les Paul, Ross Perot, Dan Rather, Adolphe Sax, Arnold Schwarzenegger, George Bernard Shaw, Grace Slick, Bruce Springsteen, Twyla Tharp, Paul Theroux, Cheryl Tiegs, Donald Trump, Sir Christopher Wren.

SOUTH NODE IN THE SIXTH HOUSE
(NORTH NODE IN THE TWELFTH HOUSE)

Responsibilities have defined this individual for many lifetimes. Always, his or her own personal needs have been eclipsed by the dark lords of *duty, self-sacrifice* and *humility*. This is the traditional house of servants—and he or she may have literally been a servant, although we shouldn't always be too literal about that. There are plenty of "servants" in high social positions too. Given enough planetary harshness around a south node in the sixth house, we might even imagine this individual as a former slave—and by "planetary harshness," I mean hard aspects involving Pluto or Saturn, for example.

Bondage is not always coerced. This individual may have chosen his or her chains, and done so without masochism. In the days before birth control, a couple might simply find themselves swamped with children, with all the attendant duties and necessities. He or she—and probably the eldest siblings—would then live lives defined by the compelling needs of the young ones. (Look for some fifth house elements in the picture.) A beloved mate can become ill or incapacitated—again, duty calls. In that case, the flow of service is tilted from one partner toward the other, creating karmic impressions of imbalance, and perhaps resentment. (Look for the ruler of the south node in the seventh house).

Disciples or apprentices are profoundly bound by duty and obedience toward their masters. Again, this is a voluntary situation, but no less restrictive for that. Autonomy is sacrificed; devotion and surrender are the themes. And once the disciple "graduates," he or she is then compelled by another set of duties—those of passing on the torch to the next generation in the lineage. A south node in the sixth house can easily suggest all that—but look for some Piscean, Neptunian, or twelfth house correlates to confirm the "spiritual" context..

Traditionally, loving self-sacrifice is considered to be "good karma." Even the suffering of a slave might be viewed as "burning away bad karma." The conclusion, in a slightly blasphemous nutshell: *God owes this person something!* All that service has created an imbalance in the universe. There must be a flow *back* to him or her in this lifetime. He or she must *receive* something.

This brings us directly to the core soul intention, which is symbolized by the north node in the mystical twelfth house. Now, in the present life, it is pivotal that he or she let go of the karmic compulsion to disappear into a labyrinth of duties and responsibilities. He or she has served others—now the shoe should be on the other foot. How? By withdrawing from some of that reflexive engagement with other people's needs and ensuring that he or she has plenty of solitary, soul-nourishing time. Spirit wants to give this person a gift of magic and insight—or more precisely, he or she has already purchased such a gift with their karmic pattern of service. All that is necessary is to claim it. Where? In the great silence. On the mountaintop. In the wilderness. In the cathedral. In a peaceful bed.

There is nothing he or she has to do *first*. This person only needs to get out of his or her own way—and to think carefully before complicating life any further.

What about existing responsibilities? Given the nature of this karmic pattern, we can assume that such duties do already exist, unless the person is very young. Certainly we all have obligations we cannot in good conscience ignore. But very often for a person with the south node in the sixth house, those people towards whom he or she are feeling responsible have actually reached a developmental stage where "helping" them actually does more harm than good. Some little birds never learn to fly unless they are tossed from the nest. The universe is symphonic that way—one person's need to be less defined by responsibility harmonizes with the other's emerging need to fly solo—if we can only recognize that! The higher ground is not always defined by duty and self-sacrifice.

Examples: Charles Addams, Alan Arkin, F. Lee Bailey, Daniel Berrigan, Bjork, Edgar Rice Burroughs, Carol Burnett, Joseph Campbell, Charles Dickens, Johnny Depp, Alan Harvey Guth, Howard Hughes, k.d. lang, Jerry Lee Lewis, Bruce H Lipton, Lucky Luciano, Paul McCartney, Herman Melville, Thomas Merton, Maria Montessori, Toni Morrison, Bill Moyers, Benito Mussolini, Elaine Pagels, Prince, Bonnie Raitt, Steven Spielberg, Henri Toulouse-Lautrec, Vincent Van Gogh, Lina Wertmuller.

SOUTH NODE IN THE SEVENTH HOUSE
(NORTH NODE IN THE FIRST HOUSE)

When we see the Moon's south node in the seventh house, we immediately recognize that we are looking at a person who, in a prior life, *drew his or her identity from the context of a relationship*. This person was defined by another, and his or her reality was delimited by the power of that other individual. Three little words, nearly extinct today, nicely capture the situation: *Mrs. John Smith!*

Modern women—and modern men, for that matter—tend to be uncomfortable with that kind of title. It seems archaic. But there are still many of us who grew up hearing it. Women, under the patriarchy, drew their public identity from their husbands. That illustrates one possibility for the south node in the seventh house: a wife whose identity existed only as an appendage of her husband's identity.

Let's immediately recognize that such a condition does not imply personal tyranny or abuse—for those dark pieces to come up, look to that south node squared or opposed by Saturn, Mars, or Pluto, for example. Often, a woman in that very traditional situation was comfortable in it and not giving a thought to any alternatives. And of course her husband may have loved her and not been a monster at all. Still, since our bias with the south node is always negative, we must recognize that this person was somehow rendered powerless or voiceless.

Women have been particularly subject to this kind of definition, but they are not the only ones! Many men have often been defined by their dominant wives—so-called "henpecked husbands."

And we are not necessarily limited to the domain of marriage here, either. Life abounds with examples of other kinds of relationships with uneven balances of power—a client may be defined by a psychotherapist, for example. Or a charismatic friend might set the agenda for his or her "side-kick."

Here is a twist—sometimes the south node in the seventh house will correspond to a past life story in which the person emerges as the *more* powerful one in the relationship. The key to triggering this kind of interpretation lies in seeing the ruler of the south node in some position of great force—in a Fire sign and the first house, for example. How can we make sense of this? It seems counter-intuitive that a more powerful person could be defined by a less powerful one. Here is how it might happen: Say you marry well and for love—and your partner becomes crippled or chronically ill. Your love may bind you to forget about your own life and orbit that person's endless needs forever.

Always, with the south node of the Moon, we know that there is something left unfinished, wounded, or incomplete from the past. We understand that the soul-contract underlying this person's current relationships can only be fulfilled once the old patterns are recognized and released. What are they? Start by imagining a man and woman, both single, both living sanely and independently. They become involved. Within a few years, he has "forgotten" how to cook. She has "forgotten" how to get the oil changed in their car. Both lose pieces of their wholeness, *projecting* them onto the other person. Some of this division of labor is natural and healthy, and is one of the practical comforts of partnership. But there is a fine line between such division and pathological fragmentation. *In the karmic past, this individual lost himself or herself in someone else.* That simply must not be allowed to happen again.

Where to go from here? The aim is not to break up one's relationships or to stop loving. Instead it involves making more room for the true self within those bonds. With the north node in the first house, he or she is aiming for a kind of *enlightened selfishness.* Even in relationship, the aim is to be separate souls, on separate journeys. Sometimes two people need different experiences. Often, it boils down to each person being in a different place on a Thursday evening—or on different continents on their vacations this year. *The fear must be taken out of separation.* A respect for each other's autonomy needs to be seen as a precious gift of love. Naturally, as he or she evolves in this first house direction, there will be some butting of heads. And all the guardian angels will be cheering! Love revels in human differences; it can thrive on creative tension between people. Light and dark give meaning to each other. Female and male become conscious of themselves in each other's presence. Oneness is a deep wisdom, but Spirit knows itself through duality. For this individual, the time has come to let there be some breathing space in that loving duality. And in that separation, love evolves toward a deeper spiritual maturity.

Examples: Alan Alda, Hans Christian Andersen, Fred Astaire, William Blake, Nigel Bruce, Naomi Campbell, Johnny Cash, Billy Crystal, Isak Dinesen, Placido Domingo, Pancho Gonzales, Monty Hall, Werner Heisenberg, Jimmy Hoffa, Billie Holiday, Shirley Jackson, Garrison Keillor, Dr. Martin Luther King, David Koresh, Ursula K. Le Guin, Leonardo da Vinci, Henry Miller, Stevie Nicks, Pele, Sylvia Plath, Martin Scorsese, Nerine Shatner, Paul Simon, Mickey Spillane, Jimmy Swaggart, Theodorus Van Gogh, Sid Vicious.

SOUTH NODE IN THE EIGHTH HOUSE
(NORTH NODE IN THE SECOND HOUSE)

Storminess, strong emotion, and enormous intensity, all left over from prior lifetimes, define the mood of this person. With the south node in the eighth house, his or her character has been forged in fire—and very possibly in nightmare. How this individual handled such a nightmare is an open question. We certainly do not need to assume anything positively or negatively in that regard based simply on the node's house placement—drama can bring out the best in people or drive them into darkness depending on how they respond to it. We can safely assume that this person has had experiences which were extreme, as intimately revealing as a psychic X-ray, and quite possibly with tragic elements.

The eighth is the traditional house of death. Mortality is not the only issue here, but it probably figures prominently in the prior-life picture. Of course, we have all died in previous incarnations! But here death has drama. It is not "natural," as we would normally define that word. Perhaps nothing creates such strong emotions in us as such deaths—just think of the movie scenes that have put tears in your eyes. A friend has just given his life for a friend. The good guy whispers his last words.

Imagine a young man drafted into war and seeing mangled, decaying corpses for the first time. Imagine a medieval woman loading the dead onto the plague-wagons. Imagine a man holding his dying wife in his arms, hearing the cries of their newborn infant.

What do such experiences *do* to a person? How does he or she respond? The answers, of course, are as varied as individuals are. Perhaps we see profound, emotionally naked *honesty*. Maybe we see *shell-shocked denial*. Maybe evolution is accelerated; possibly it is stalled, overwhelmed by the horror of its experiences. And in every case, the mark of deep wounding is left: *fear, grief, anxiety*.

And, just possibly, fantastic sex. This is not a spurious remark. The greatest enemy of deep sexuality is emotional distance. Everything in the eighth house pulls in the opposite direction: toward *soul nakedness*. There have likely been such experiences of deep emotional bonding in this soul's history. Probably, he or she will meet these lovers again in this life—such is the power of the magnetism. Their level of familiarity with the normally hidden layers of each other's psyches will startle them from the outset of their present relationship. Whether that familiarity was forged in a bed or in a battle-trench is immaterial.

Let's also recognize that human sexuality can ally itself with the most depraved aspects of our natures. This individual may have been touched by those kinds of experiences too: *sexual humiliation, rape, molestation.* At the giving end or at the receiving end? We cannot tell from the node alone. Context will often reveal clues about anger, control-issues, and experiences of power if this person was at the giving end of such violence. Similarly, symbolism of loss or attack will abound if he or she were at the receiving end—the nodal ruler in the twelfth house, Pluto or Mars squaring or opposing the south node, for example. A very approximate rule-of-thumb is that conjunctions of hard planets with the south node incline more toward active experiences of perpetration, while hard planets squaring or opposing it tend more toward being the "victim." (And you can retain or delete the quotation marks around that word, depending on your own philosophy.)

Strangely the eighth house south node also correlates with *a sense of humor.* In the light of all we have seen so far, that statement, like the remark about "fantastic sex," might seem to come out of left field. But think of the last ten thousand jokes you have heard and analyze them for content: most of them, at root, are about very frightening things. How many jokes about death and disease have you heard? Infidelity? Sexual dysfunction? The horrors of aging? Dead babies? *Humans have always used humor as a way of dealing with the extreme and the unthinkable.* That mark of "gallows humor" is very often present in people with this nodal placement. Note, below, how many members of the famous Monty Python comedy troupe share this nodal placement, for example.

Long ago, some people with eighth house south nodes learned that "you laugh," while others learned that "you cry." Some learned both.

The soul-contract this time around? The north node lies in the second house, which is typically seen simplistically as the house of money. Actually it is pertinent to a far broader range of concerns, all of them related to *the resource base upon which survival depends*: food, shelter, appropriate skills, and social alliances. One piece of the puzzle for this person is that to heal the wounds of the past, he or she absolutely must create an environment which feels *safe*. To be precise, it must not only seem safe according to the logic of the human intellect, but it must also *feel* safe to the "inner animal."

The human intellect understands that most of us feel safer in this world if we have established financial security, live in a reasonably secure home, and have a supply of existential "parachutes," such as life insurance, health insurance, a retirement plan, and so on. It would be positively diabolical to suggest to this person that such concerns were somehow "unspiritual." Establishing such supports can be actively understood as a foundation spiritual practice. For this person, the "inner animal" needs the assurance and comfort of quiet and stability; it benefits from living in a natural environment, if possible. It likes to see food available. It wants escape routes. It might need weapons of some sort—and a prayer never to have to use them!

If this individual can create that reassuring second house environment, then in that ambience of security he or she begins to gain the deeper victory: the return of confidence in themselves and in life. *Faith*, in a nutshell.

And that is the whole point.

Examples: Muhammad Ali, Brigitte Bardot, Philip Berrigan, Napoleon Bonaparte, William F. Buckley, Charles Bukowski, Mark David Chapman, John Cleese, Miles Davis, Robert De Niro, Walt Disney, Benjamin Disraeli, Stephen Foster, Bob Geldof, George Gershwin, Terry Gilliam, Gene Hackman, Hermann Hesse, J. Edgar Hoover, Eric Idle, Carl Gustav Jung, Rush Limbaugh, Madonna, Karl Marx, Harvey Milk, Joni Mitchell, Randy Newman, Oliver North, Michael Palin, Sam Peckinpah, Elvis Presley, Vincent Price, Alexander Ruperti, Al Sharpton, Jim Thorpe, Tiger Woods.

SOUTH NODE IN THE NINTH HOUSE
(NORTH NODE IN THE THIRD HOUSE)

Kids in school learn that Christopher Columbus "believed the earth was round" and that he sagaciously contradicted the flat-earthers' fear that if we sailed far enough out into the ocean, we would sail right off the edge of the world. Even though the historical truths are more complex, this childhood imagery conveys a visceral sense of the power of belief and of *how it creates the reality we experience*—and therefore of the ninth house.

If we "believe" in something, we can accomplish great feats. Belief empowers people, just as surely as "believing in nothing" weakens them. With the south node of the Moon in the ninth house, this person's soul-memories are characterized by the *life-shaping impact of compelling belief.*

Given the realities of human history, we can make one more conjecture: most of the belief-systems that have shaped cultures in the past have been at least partly *religious* in nature. Thus, with considerable certainly, we can affirm that this person has been powerfully and indelibly marked in a prior lifetime by religion. Was he or she in "holy orders?" That is a possibility. We would look to other dimensions of nodal analysis to confirm it—the planetary ruler of the south node lying in the twelfth house (monasteries) would encourage such an interpretation, for example. But we need not assume an ecclesiastical past for this individual. Religion can impact life in many other ways, through community, family—even through its historical enthusiasm for war.

Let's weave another dimension of the classical ninth house into the picture: *journeys.* Maybe this individual's karma has nothing to do with religion—but before we dump the idea of religion and go traveling, take a moment to consider how often in history religion has caused people to travel and experience other cultures. Think of the Crusades—or a pilgrimage to Mecca, Rome, Macchu Pichu, or Benares. We might imagine the Puritans fleeing repression and coming to the New World, or Mormons heading west. Or Jews banished in the diaspora.

Education is another classic correlate of the ninth house. There may have been significant prior life experiences related to universities, for example. If so, such institutions might feel comfortable and attractive to the individual in this present life. It is helpful to recall here how endlessly cocksure the "academic view" of things has been throughout recent centuries—and how the "educated" truths of yesterday tend to be dismissed and replaced on a regular basis. Academia is, more or less, a religion too.

With the south node, our inquiries are always sharpened if we look a bit darkly upon the prior life orientation, seeking any limiting or distorting effects it might have upon the present experiences. The *need to believe* fogs our ability to see what is actually before our eyes. Arguing with "true believers" is impossible, as most of us have learned—they usually cannot imagine themselves wrong, regardless of the evidence. Such a person will kill, and fail to see the humanity of the victims. He or she will deny the evidence of their own senses. Such a person can "sail off the edges of the world" without stopping to consider their folly. How many nineteenth century physicists laughed at Albert Einstein? How many conquistadors simply disappeared into the wilderness, looking for the Seven Cities of Gold? How many pilgrims and crusaders never made it home again? This person has been *blinded by zeal* in the past.

Furthermore, he or she have may have been jammed into the tight shoes of *unnaturally repressive moralities.* Nothing can so estrange us from our bodies and natural instincts more certainly than religion and philosophy.

One bottom line about a core prior-life issue brought forward into this incarnation: *This person's world has been consistently mistaken for an idea—and the idea was at least partly wrong!* Out of "faith," in prior lifetimes this person has lost groundedness in instinct and common sense.

With the north node of the Moon in the third house, the soul-intention is to believe only the evidence of his or her own experience—and to gather a lot of such evidence! Thus, an *open mind* becomes a powerful evolutionary force. He or she is returning to *direct knowledge, sensory wisdom, and discovery.* The guiding star is *curiosity.* The person benefits from learning experiences—especially confusing ones! That may sound strange, but it comes down to this: if he or she meets an impressive New Age teacher, this individual needs immediately to seek out a Christian or a Muslim or a Scientist. Endless stretching is the key; all beliefs must remain tentative, subject to extension and questioning. A helpful strategy in accomplishing that aim lies in *conversation* with people who see things differently.

Giving life permission to be complex—and then comparing notes with trusted friends, sharing perceptions, endlessly conversing, with no perspective considered taboo or forbidden: that is the way forward for this soul. The aim is to learn to live with uncertainty and the unknown, with no solid ground and no retreat from the mystery.

Examples: Margot Adler, Jack Anderson, Richard Bach, Garth Brooks, Anita Bryant, Deepak Chopra, Jean Cocteau, Sean Connery, Nicolaus Copernicus, David Copperfield, Salvador Dali, Mia Farrow, Federico

Fellini, Erich Fromm, Stephen Gaskin, Joan Grant, Tom Hanks, Jean Houston, Joseph McCarthy, Loreena McKennitt, Muktananda, Edith Piaf, Dane Rudhyar, Stephen Sondheim, Tina Turner, Tennessee Williams, Emile Zola.

SOUTH NODE IN THE TENTH HOUSE
(NORTH NODE IN THE FOURTH HOUSE)

A reasonable criticism of reincarnation is that far too many people "remember" lifetimes in which they were somehow famous or in which they participated in pivotal historic turning points. Logic dictates that nearly all of us have lived mostly hum-drum lives and that once we were gone, we were forgotten relatively quickly! There is of course no shame in that anonymity—souls can do deep evolutionary work in absolute obscurity.

The same logic that compels us to accept that most of us aren't featured in history books also declares that *some* of us *must* be listed there! The most obvious astrological indication of that condition of prior-life *fame* is having the south node in the tenth house—the traditional house of honor. Seeing that configuration, we know that this person was well-known and somehow *symbolic* to the wider community. Saying that he or she was "Cleopatra"—or "Jimi Hendrix," for that matter—gets us roughly on the right track. But it is of course probably an exaggeration. One out of twelve people has the south node in the tenth house. There aren't enough truly "famous people" to go around. We need to penetrate the mystery of the tenth house more deeply. The issue here is not whether or not someone is remembered historically. It is the question of having become part of the collective symbolism of a community—and it does not matter if the entire community is subsequently washed away to sea and forgotten. The experience of *position* lives on inside the reincarnating soul.

With the south node in the tenth house, this person is marked by a prior-life experience of *prominence and leadership* within his or her society. Furthermore, given historical social realities, the chances are good that he or she was *born into* this prominence—famous dukes outnumbering famous serfs by a wide margin.

Fame and power have obvious attractions, but always with the south node of the Moon our approach begins with recognizing that, from an evolutionary point of view, something is hung up here. There are unresolved issues from the past that haunt this individual in the present tense. Is there a negative side to power? Are there soul-cages built into prominence and high birth? For this person, we must consider the damage done by *constant role-playing*, feigning affection for people whom he or she neither liked nor trusted, and constantly jockeying for position.

We must be cautious regarding this person's legacy of skills when it comes to "improving" his or her present-life status: he or she, by karmic reflex, might pay too much for career and status, for example. Climbing—or passively maintaining status—is an instinct here, not a conscious decision. Be careful too about assuming that we are speaking of conventional status. Every sub-culture is at least somewhat hierarchical; one can be prominent in the world of professional wrestling or stamp collecting.

Sometimes Venus or the seventh house will be involved in the nodal dynamic. In that case, one of the most uncomfortable perceptions we need to consider is that, perhaps, in a prior life, this individual married for social reasons, without any particular feeling of love. Such "political" marriages are naturally common historically—not to mention presently. In this life, such a person must make sure that what he or she is feeling for a partner is real, and that he or she is not carrying the "fortunate marriage" projections of their community. Every time he or she hears someone say, "you two *belong* together" (or "you can do better than *that* one"), there is a need to re-affirm that any such decision is purely a private matter.

There is a reason we emphasize this autonomy in matters of the heart. With the north node in the fourth house, the soul-contract for this individual, first and foremost, is to go down into his or her deep psyche and trust whatever is found there. The fourth house is where "psychology" unfolds within us: our innermost feelings and needs reside there. This individual aims to put a high premium on *honesty* and *reflectiveness*, and thus to attain true self-knowledge, free from the interference of the world and its ego-temptations.

Domestic needs are symbolized by the fourth house as well. If, after due inward searching, this person chooses to love a partner, then the goal here is to *create a home* together. Literally having a place to live that reflects their natures and their long-term commitment is a large part of this work. Single or in partnership, perhaps he or she might buy a house—a healthy fourth house move. But a house is just a building. A home is a place of nurturance, safety, and the sentiments created by shared history. Lacking a partner, even a dog or a cat can "warm" the house into a home. Human connections are critically important too though! With the north node in the fourth, this individual needs "family" in some broad sense of the word. They need not share strands of DNA. They need not live under one roof. But there must be a feeling of mutual commitment that transcends outward circumstance. Here is the question that should always have an answer—*if I lost everything I have in this world, if I were naked, condemned, and empty, who would still hold me in their heart?*

That is family.

Examples: Chet Atkins, Lucille Ball, Rona Barrett, Stephen Bechtel, John Belushi, William Bligh, Sonny Bono, David Bowie, Johannes Brahms, Jerry Brown, Patrick Buchanan, Jimmy Connors, Howard Cosell, the Dalai Lama XIV, Gerard Depardieu, Jerry Falwell, Gustave Flaubert, Judy Garland, Allen Ginsberg, Ernest Hemingway, Mick Jagger, Steve Jobs, Erica Jong, Linda Lovelace, Marie Antoinette, Peter Max, Bobby McFerrin, Lee Harvey Oswald, Louis Pasteur, George Patton, Richard Petty, River Phoenix, Gene Roddenberry, Erwin Rommel, Antoine de Saint-Exupery, Jonas Salk, Claudia Schiffer, Frank Sinatra, Upton Sinclair, Situ Rimpoche Tem Tarriktar, Tom Waits, Serena Williams, Brian Wilson, Walter Winchell, Tom Wolfe.

SOUTH NODE IN THE ELEVENTH HOUSE (NORTH NODE IN THE FIFTH HOUSE)

Ready for a little math? Stand back: here comes Forrest's First Law of Group Dynamics. *To determine the IQ of any group of human beings, take the average IQ of each member and divide by the number of people in the group.*

Fifty people, average IQ = 100. Group IQ = 2.

Okay, maybe it's not rocket science, but the formula does explain a lot of human history. The power of the lowest common denominator is always palpable in crowds. The darkest expressions of this principle are visible in lynch mobs, marauding armies, and in newsreels of fanatical preachers, mullahs, and rabbis. One can even feel it in a more benign form at major athletic events—thirty thousand people howling for blood is a formidable display of monkey-power.

With the south node of the Moon in the eleventh house, we are looking at the life-shaping impact of that collective social force upon the soul-memories of an individual. Somehow, in a prior life, such a person was *swept along by broad historical, social or cultural currents.* These currents carried the person away from authenticity, away from the actual soul-intentions, and away from natural values. *He or she lost individuality in the context of the will of the group.* Our fanatical images from a few lines ago may be quite relevant—but we don't necessarily need to assume such violent drama unless there are also serious Plutonian or Martial signatures connected with the Moon's south node. Given Venusian signatures, for example, we might be looking at the far more insidious impact of "polite society" on a person—the civilized pressure to "marry well," to "live normally," and to believe what others believe. Given Jupiter signatures, we might be looking at the way the collective definition of "success" can rob people of their direction in life, and even of their souls. As always, in other words, details emerge only in the larger nodal context. Our monkey-mind tendency to lose our identity in groups has soft faces and hard faces. We can be seduced; we can be threatened; or we can simply succumb to the lemming-pressure of collective delusion. Lynch mobs are murderous—but how many people in such a mob could actually kill another person, in private, face to face?

What we can count on, regardless of context, is that in this present lifetime, this individual has a soul-intent to claim more freedom from outside influences, whether those influences emanate from the tribe or from the corporation. That much is clear—but the fifth house north node takes us down some roads we might not anticipate quite so readily. The fifth is the house of *joy.* We learn a lot about it simply by thinking of the human need for *fun*—the pleasure principle. *For this person, it has become imperative from an evolutionary point of view to do as he or she pleases.* That is harder than it might seem. Why? Because, with that eleventh house south node pattern, the person is vulnerable to *internalizing collective beliefs* about what will give joy—the new car, meditating in Sedona, losing weight . . . whatever their cultural susceptibilities and socialized values dictate. And, for him or her, they may not work. There is an art to knowing in advance what might actually give us pleasure, at least beyond the obvious realm of food and orgasm.

The necessary foundation of the healing process lies in recovering his or her capacity to *know and recognize his or her own natural desires*, and to act upon them. This process often starts out with very simple things: listening to music that is not particularly popular, vacationing in places no one has ever heard of.

As he or she evolves, such a person will increasingly experience a desire to *express himself or herself creatively*. Perhaps he takes up painting or acting. Maybe she writes poetry. There is enormous joy in such self-expression.

In so doing, the individual finds himself or herself in the *company of artists*. And at that evolutionary juncture, he or she has reached a crossroads—and a serious rite of passage in terms of eleventh house discrimination. On one hand, there is the tribe of his or her natural soulmates—artists of life who are truly experimentalists, affirmative of exploration and risk, celebratory of life, and slow to judge others. Such artists are the real deal; they represent the polar opposite of "group think." They therefore apply a lot of useful tension to our protagonist's south node pattern by encouraging him or her simply to be natural, spontaneous and unselfconscious.

On the other hand, he or she will surely encounter many people who epitomize that outworn, conforming tribal consciousness—and probably he or she will have some compelling karma with them as well. That can happen even among "artists." There is nothing so conservative as the *avant garde*. There is no one less cool than someone concerned with looking cool. If he or she connects socially with these people and begins to be influenced by their opinions, the person has fallen back into the old south node pattern—except now it is congratulating itself on being "cool," something other than what it really is. But the sheep of the world have never thought otherwise.

So the cutting edge here—as ever, hard to attain—is individuality, joy, playful spontaneity, creativity, and a perfect freedom from the slightest need to appear successful, elevated, or elite.

Examples: Hank Aaron, "Cannonball" Adderley, Woody Allen, Karl Barth, David Brinkley, George Carlin, Enrico Caruso, Leonard Cohen, John Coltrane, Dino De Laurentis, Claude Debussy, Jeanne Dixon, Ralph Waldo Emerson, Rainer Werner Fassbinder, Galileo, Bill Gates, L. Ron Hubbard, Victor Hugo, Lee Iacocca, Quincy Jones, Henry Kissinger, Elisabeth Kubler-Ross, Marcel Marceau, Alanis Morissette, Jack Nicholson, Tip O'Neill, Luciano Pavarotti, Roman Polanski, Trent Reznor, Knut Rockne, Carl Sandburg, George Stephanopoulos, Ivana Trump.

SOUTH NODE IN THE TWELFTH HOUSE
(NORTH NODE IN THE SIXTH HOUSE)

Terrible loss and soul-growth: so often, the two are a matched set. A marriage ends, a career collapses, our doctor proffers ominous news—and we turn to Spirit. We turn to God or religion or some spiritual path. These changes can be completely authentic. Hospices are sometimes full of luminous eyes. With the south node in the twelfth house, this person has known *loss* and *grief* in a prior lifetime—that much is sure. There is an even chance that he or she has also forged a deep instinct for spirituality.

As always, a close consideration of the sign of the south node, along with the planets ruling it or in aspect to it, can fill in the details of the story. Just knowing that the Moon's south node lies in the twelfth is enough to invoke imagery of *bereavement, imprisonment, wasting illness,* and the loss of whatever gave this individual joy in a prior lifetime. It is also consistent with the notion that he or she spent time in a *monastery* or *convent*, or in the context of some mystical institution—a mystery school or a secret society, for example. Clearly, as this world became emotionally unacceptable to this person in a prior life, he or she put faith in the next world.

Thus, much that is rich and inspiring flows from this fountain of tragedy. The conscious connection between this individual and the raw realities of this transitory life is profound. Still, with the south node, our focus must always be on the issues left unresolved from the prior lifetime and on the ways those issues might interfere with the actual soul-contract in the present life. In that regard, we recognize that "loss of self" haunts this person. So might despair. Easily, people with this signature can fail to claim the outward, existential supports of simple happiness, instead losing themselves in their swampy inner lives. They can forget they have bodies—in fact, there may a powerful karmic memory of pain or privation in the physical body, which led to a dissociation from it. Such an individual could disappear into imagination, feeding it with endless film or reading or television. He or she could dissolve into escapist spiritual practice. The underlying soul-memories of pain can trigger a dependency on alcohol or drugs. Thus, without evolutionary effort, such a person can move through life like a grieving ghost.

With the north node in the sixth house, the soul-contract of this individual involves *coming back into the body.* The sixth has much to do with health and the physical realities of life. Exercise is helpful. So is making a happy ritual out of meals. Even more helpful is *touch;* this individual needs simply to hold someone, to cuddle, to relax into sleep with a friend.

Going further, the sixth house is concerned with the routines that allow us to thrive. Some of these are "boring" routines—paying the bills, grocery shopping. But many are the basic routines of physical and mental self-care: visits to a health-care provider, a reasonably conscious diet, exercise, enough sleep, avoidance of the various poisons the world offers us. For a person with the north node of the Moon in the sixth house, creating a life-style that reflects these priorities is a spiritual accomplishment. In fact, *self-care can be considered a spiritual accomplishment.* Finding balance in this area is a challenge. There can be *hypochondria*, as consciousness wakes up to its own natural self-monitoring functions—but more common is *hyperchondria.* (I am not sure if that is an official word, but its meaning should be obvious in this context—too *little* sensitivity to the signals of one's body.)

The sixth house is also about *service* and our need to feel *competent and useful to others.* With the north node there, this person's soul-contract involves giving a gift to the world. Despite the memory of pain and loss, he or she also carries real wisdom. Certainly, in a prior lifetime, this person at least began to integrate the lessons of unthinkable loss. Probably in response to that pain, he or she found true spiritual teachers. He or she was given some guidance, both from human sources and spiritual ones. Thus, this person carries something precious: an understanding of life's impermanence—and quite possibly the karmic memory of specific spiritual practices and perspectives. Going further, along with the hurt, there is therefore *gratitude* in a person with the south node in the twelfth—and that gratitude naturally wants to express itself as generosity toward other people. *The pain wants to abandon this world, while the gratitude wants to serve it.* This person's present evolution depends completely upon tilting the balance of those two conflicting emotions—revulsion from the world and gratitude—toward service.

This service, in the highest vision of it, naturally wants to express itself in that classic sixth house fashion: *lineage.* Once we have been taught something of value, we want naturally to pass it on. Our gratitude toward our teachers can never be repaid directly; so we defer it—and keep the flame burning by sending it on towards those who come after us. In a kind of feedback loop, the evolution created by this service toward others also opens such a soul up to further input from *spiritual preceptors.* With the north node in the sixth house, there may be meetings with gurus and guides in which great leaps are triggered very quickly. Lineage, of course, points in both directions—we are waking up to being part of a chain in which we both receive and give.

This participation in the passing on of the candle flame is the highest potential of a sixth house north lunar node.

Examples: Alois Alzheimer, Georgio Armani, Ingrid Bergman, Chay Blyth, Marc Bolan, Jorge Luis Borges, Luis Bunuel, Lord Byron, Albert Camus, Eldridge Cleaver, David Crosby, Clint Eastwood, Queen Elizabeth II, M.C. Escher, Sigmund Freud, Jim Henson, Elton John, Janis Joplin, John Lennon, Willy Messerschmitt, Jim Morrison, Jacqueline Kennedy Onassis, Sonny Rawlings, LeAnn Rimes, Maximilian Robespierre, Pete Rose, Percy Bysshe Shelley, Patti Smith, Gary Snyder, Sylvester Stallone, Starhawk, Robert Louis Stevenson, Barbra Streisand, Alfred Lord Tennyson, Michael Tilson Thomas, John Travolta, Rudolph Valentino, Jules Verne, Stevie Wonder.

CHAPTER EIGHT: PLANETS CONJUNCT THE SOUTH NODE

(Please note that much of what follows applies equally to the planetary ruler of the south node—see Chapter Nine for a fuller explanation)

Sir Arthur Conan Doyle gave the world one of its most enduring fictional characters, the famous *uber-detective,* Sherlock Holmes. In so doing he pretty much became the originator of the modern detective story. Literally thousands of authors have followed in his footsteps—Agatha Christie, P.D. James, Robert Parker, Sue Grafton. But Conan Doyle was there first. He broke the ground.

Unsurprisingly we find a classic indicator of originality and genius in his birth chart: his Sun is conjunct the planet Uranus. It even lies in Gemini (writing) and in the twelfth house, which is indicative of "things unseen" or "hidden matters."

Uranus always breaks the rules; it questions authority. If it weren't for Uranus, we would still believe the world was flat and had four corners. There would be no social change, no evolution. Conan Doyle illustrates this part of the planet very eloquently.

Keeping perspective, we must remember that not all traditions and "received wisdoms" are inherently wrong. They embody much of humanity's relationship with natural law—not to mention grounded common sense. In rebelling against cultural norms, Uranians can sometimes simply become quirkish or weird. Conan Doyle, for example, famously advocated the objective factuality of certain photographs of garden fairies, most of which would not have fooled a modern ten-year-old.

None of this is surprising. Most astrologers are quite familiar with the impact of planets conjunct someone's natal Sun, and how they become part of the person's core identity. In fact, since one interpretation of the Sun is *identity itself,* it follows that if you have a planet aligned with your Sun you are simply *identified* with it—you experience yourself that way, and it is no surprise to anyone else who knows you. They see it too. Sir Arthur Conan Doyle illustrates all this quite vividly. It is familiar territory—and in recalling it, we are most of the way toward understanding one of the most valuable tricks of the trade in evolutionary astrology.

Planets Conjunct the South Node

A planet conjunct your south node works very much the same way as a planet conjunct your Sun—except that now we are looking at your identity in a prior life. Back then, you were seen by anyone who knew you as the embodiment of that planet. And you would have agreed.

Of course, because of the way karmic patterns carry forward, we very likely see a significant fingerprint of this planet in your present life as well. Some dimensions of that classic Uranian potpourri are bound to be evident in your nature and your biography: genius, rebelliousness, tension with existing authorities, strange and unpredictable developments in life, quirks.

Film maker Michael Moore, famous for asking hard, outsider's questions in films such as *Bowling for Columbine, Fahrenheit 911,* and *Sicko* has Uranus conjunct his south node (in Cancer and the twelfth house). Oprah Winfrey does too. Again, in both of these figures we see the basic Uranian signature of *applying leverage* to the current cultural mythologies—except that the implication is that Moore and Winfrey have been doing it for lifetimes.

Knowing that we can think of the south node as part of your identity in a past life, our basic trick here is to . . .

Think of any planet conjunct the south node exactly as you would a planet conjunct the Sun, only recall that we are not talking about this present life. We are talking about a previous one.

Such a planet become inextricably bound to your nature and your fate in the prior life experience. You were the embodiment of it. Further, the laws of karma dictate that this planet's mark is still strong in you. You continue to see the world through its lens. And to evolve, you need to step outside yourself enough to recognize that other perspectives might be more helpful to you this time around. Furthermore, we know that it is usually most helpful and revealing to consider the south node with a particular openness to negative or critical points of view. It is most fundamentally a *problem of attachment or fixation.* You brought it into this lifetime in order to wrestle with it, to break free of the limits it has imposed on you. *The same attitude applies to our understanding of a planet conjunct the south node.* There is good in it too and those strengths will very likely be visible in the present life: again, just think of Michael Moore and Oprah Winfrey. Still, the rule of thumb is to look a bit askance upon the planet. Your interpretation will be closer to the mark.

Your Nature is Your Fate

I stole that line from my wife, Jodie Forrest. She puts it in the mouth of a wise old woman on the Viking island of Birka a millennium ago in her novel, *The Rhymer and the Ravens.* Those five words give us a good formula by which to live—especially when we underscore the notion that we can change our natures and thus alter what lies ahead for us.

The past is of course not so malleable! That karmic water is already under the bridge; our task is to unravel its signatures in the present chart and ultimately to untangle our lives from its grip. Even back then in a prior life, the principle held true: your nature determined your fate. That fate is now sealed—and indicated by a planet conjunct your south node.

In the end, we cannot separate nature and fate. Character and plot may be useful categories for analyzing fiction, but in practice they are as bound and intertwined as the cream and the coffee in your cup. Uranus conjunct the south node? Your past-life *nature* was Uranian—and that Uranian quality undoubtedly expressed itself somehow in your existential choices and thus in your "fated" circumstances.

Taking it further, we can add the Jungian concept of *synchronicity:* your inner life is bound to your outer life in *acausal* ways. In other words, if your soul has signed up to do Uranian work, you "by chance" seem to encounter a lot of *petty tyrants*—they are the ones who give you the opportunity to flex your developing Uranian muscles. You "stumble upon" official lies and errors. You "fall in" with the side of the rebels and the heretics.

In practice, the principle of synchronicity declares that when we see a planet conjunct the Moon's south node, we get insight not only into your prior-life nature, but also into your prior-life circumstances.

Planets, in other words, build a bridge between the *psychological* tone of the signs and the *circumstantial* tone of the houses. That is an elemental principle of astrology in general.

In Michael Moore's chart, as we have seen, Uranus is conjunct the south node in *the twelfth house.* The Uranian signature implies that he was a rebel by *nature* then as well as now. The twelfth house element implies that one strong possibility is that in a prior life his *fate* was that he came to grief and lost everything, perhaps for the simple reason that rebels often wind up on the gallows. That such an unfortunate development might have occurred *unexpectedly and suddenly* would be a synchronistic outward expression of the Uranian piece.

In Oprah Winfrey's chart, Uranus is conjunct the south node in *the seventh house.* That is an entirely different situation. Here, it is easier to imagine her escaping—perhaps triumphantly—from a repressive or stultifying marriage.

Those are two very different stories! Let them illustrate for you the perils of taking everything I write in the next few chapters too narrowly or literally. What follows is a set of general guidelines about the vast archetypal fields represented by each planet when it aligns with the south node. To make these techniques work, you must cherry-pick the suggestions according to which ones are most consistent with the main thrust of all the relevant symbols. A holistic, unified appraisal of the entire astrological context is our Holy Grail.

That may sound hard, but with practice you will get the hang of it. And it is literally the only path to success—these cookbook chapters can only carry you a certain distance. We'll go into detail about how to put it all together in Chapter Fourteen.

The Sun Conjunct the Moon's South Node

One fundamental property of the Sun is *brightness.* Another is *warmth.* A third is massive *gravity.* With the Sun conjunct the south node, any or all of these properties were central to your identity in a prior life. Somehow, people orbited you. Whether you wanted it or not, you were in a position of power. You may have displayed considerable personal charisma—that is a solar quality. At the very least you had the quality we call *gravitas*. People had reason to take you seriously, whether they liked you or not.

Maybe you are heading down the highway in a big rush, late for a critical appointment. But when the blue light of the police car flickers in your rear-view mirror, what are you going to do? You of course pull over, bowing to the authority of the police officer. To flee would be folly because, no matter how unimpressive the cop might be personally, he represents the power of the state. There's solar power! You will orbit him for while.

Maybe, in a prior life, you held *temporal, worldly authority* that way. You had a title. If so, look for other *signatures of position*—perhaps the south node is in the tenth house or in Capricorn, for example. One does not necessarily have to be colorful or impressive to hold power in this world. Leo? You had a regal glow! Capricorn or Virgo? You let your title do the impressing.

Many people report that in meeting someone famous they are struck by that person's intrinsic luminosity. Thinking of such luminosity might give us a sense of who you were in a prior lifetime. Is this "luminosity" a cultural projection (think of the way we react to our movie stars, rock stars, politicians)—or is it something elemental to them as people? Or both? In many cases, I suspect the third choice is the right one: charisma attracts power and position, and the two sometimes become inseparable. Again, "your nature is your fate." To see the signature of this kind of solar "luminosity," look for the south node to be connected, for example, with Jupiter or Leo or to be in the first house.

What are the negatives here? For one, we might simply be looking at too much attachment to ego. From the deepest wisdom in your heart, consider for a moment whether it is really "good luck" to be one of those folks whose faces you are always seeing on the covers of the magazines at the local grocery store. If you are one of them, what happens in your next lifetime when nobody cares about your favorite color or your political opinions?

Just because it is the Sun, do not assume that ego must be the issue. The *grievous weight of responsibility* can leave a terrible mark on the soul as well. Leadership is a burden. Power is isolating too—there may be a theme of *loneliness* within a public role here.

In any case, in the present lifetime there is a need for more human transparency and less public attention. It is good medicine for such a person to go somewhere and be a stranger—to step outside of any roles or expectations, to be "nobody special."

Examples: Julia Roberts (Scorpio; fourth house). Gianni Versace (Sagittarius; first house). Amelia Earhart (Leo; fourth house). Robert Bly (Capricorn; first house). Jeffrey Wolf Green (Sagittarius; first house). Jose Ortega y Gasset (Taurus; fifth house). Joseph Pulitzer (Aries; birth time uncertain). Cotton Mather (Pisces; birth time uncertain). River Phoenix (Virgo; tenth house).

The Moon Conjunct Its Own South Node

Let me jar the Moon in you, just so we know what we are talking about. Say you have just had a baby. You are holding the child in your arms, bonding. I appear and say, "Cute kid! I'll give you twenty bucks for her."

Naturally my offer does not tempt you even a little. You are probably offended. More to the point, it shocks something deep and fundamental within your psyche. *You simply do not abandon your children.* That principle goes beyond anything moral or ethical. It is hardwired into the human brain and soul. Mothers typically have the thermonuclear version of this instinct—but let's show the fathers a little respect here too. What man, out camping with his family, wouldn't charge a grizzly bear if that bear were dragging off one of his kids?

There is something beautiful in the Moon's instinct to nurture and protect. It is primal; it does not think, it only acts. When it comes to protecting the young, there is no price too great to pay.

Most of us, given obvious realities, have been parents in prior lives. With the Moon on the south node, that experience is somehow underscored. To love children, to raise them and see them launched, is almost as common an experience as being born, ageing, and dying. *When the chart asks you to look at a person's prior-life parenting experience, then something extreme happened.* Something went wrong. Were the children lost somehow? We all understand, at least vaguely, that there is probably no experience so extreme as the loss of a child. If that is the case, then this south node will surely be "afflicted" somehow—perhaps Pluto, Saturn, or

Mars squares it. What if the problem is the opposite one—we couldn't let go of the children? Look to Neptunian connections, for example. How about a child who could not move on for physical or mental reasons? A Down's Syndrome kid? One with cerebral palsy? Probably you will see heavy signatures from Saturn *(duty),* Virgo or sixth house connections—symbolizing endless, exhausting service.

The Moon is more than parenting: it also symbolizes *home, clan,* and *family.* Virtually all of us come from "families" in some sense of the word. That is often a wonderful thing. But what if, in a prior life, you were born into what we would nowadays call a "dysfunctional" family? To recognize that karmic imprint, look to anything flavoring that Moon/south node conjunction in an uncomfortable way. Alcohol issues? Consider pressures from Neptune, Pisces or the twelfth house. Incest? Typically, Plutonian afflictions, especially with Venus or Mars involved. Violence—hard aspects from Mars (and if the Mars is conjunct your south node, along with the Moon, it could mean that you internalized the violence. Simply square or opposed, then you were "victimized" by it).

Here is an alternative: What about families that are not crazy in obvious ways, just simply engulfing? If you were completely defined by family in a prior life, look to major underscorings of the basic lunar theme—the Moon/south node conjunction lies in Cancer or in the fourth house, for example.

As with all karmic patterns, the spooky thing is the way these old stories can repeat themselves in the present lifetime. Always with this configuration, there is a need to get beyond *defining ourselves through the nurturing we offer others.* Family does not become "bad" for us—but we must be careful to have a life outside it as well. Such a person is often great with kids. Again some judiciousness and some boundaries here are very helpful. One of the best single bits of advice for such an individual is simply to avoid having children too early in life—get your own identity established first. And while you are at it perhaps you need to put a state line between yourself and your family.

One of the primal expressions of the Moon is the act of giving food to another. What could be a more elemental expression of nurture? Often people with this configuration are good cooks! One also feels the lunar signature in them in their openness to hugging—and, generally, to a kind of "tea-and-sympathy" feeling they radiate. Those are precious qualities, but as always with the south node, the evolutionary aim lies elsewhere.

Finally, the Moon is elementally about *emotion* and *sentiment*. It is utterly subjective. Perhaps you have been striving to resolve a disagreement with someone. You find yourself frustrated because the person will not make obvious, logical connections. We cannot expect feelings to make sense—but for such a person the feelings have such compelling primacy that reason is eclipsed. Lunar people do not see it—and they may pay the price of adding two and two and getting three. That phenomenon may very well be reflected in the Moon's conjunction with the south node. *The identification with emotion* is so total as to eclipse rational function.
Examples: Julia Child (Libra; fifth house). Bruce Springsteen (Libra; fifth house). Martha Stewart (Sagittarius; second house). Princess Diana (Aquarius; second house). Emmaline Pankhurst (Virgo; seventh house). Ralph Nader (Leo; seventh house). Randy Travis (Aries; eleventh house).

Any of the Four Angles Conjunct the Moon's South Node

The Ascendant, Descendant, Midheaven and Astrological Nadir work the same way as planets when they are aligned with the south node. To understand these conjunctions, go back and read Chapter Seven about the south node in houses one, seven, ten or four, respectively. The four angles are, of course, only the cusps of these houses. The interpretation is the same—just add a few more exclamation points!

Mercury Conjunct the Moon's South Node

Hot little Mercury speeds around the Sun in eighty-eight days. No planet is faster. "As above, so below" works well and obviously here—Mercury corresponds to the fastest, most frenetic dimensions of the human psyche: the endless, zooming buzz of our *thoughts.* At an even deeper level, consider the soil from which all your thoughts must bloom: *sensory perception* itself. That is Mercury territory as well: the eyes and ears, and the spell they weave. We see. Then we think about what we see. Then we look again—and do we see what is "out there" or are we now only seeing an expectation we have created? It is an old question—and one that Mercury can think about for another eternity or two!

With Mercury aligned with the south node of the Moon, in a prior lifetime you were deeply marked by this *speedy, cognitive, reactive, cerebral* mode of perception. Likely you needed to be—Mercury on the south node often correlates with a lifetime in which a person was faced with rapidly changing circumstances requiring improvisation and constant adaptation. Much of the energy of the psyche was directed into that one part of the mind we call *intelligence.* This probably came at the expense of attention paid to other parts of the psyche, such as emotion, the inner world or body-awareness. Perhaps you were a pickpocket making your picaresque living in the streets of ancient Damascus—Mercury and the south node would then be linked to Mars or Pluto or Uranus, and maybe there would be some twelfth house components. Or perhaps you were a distinguished professor at Salamanca in medieval Spain—the configuration is in the ninth house, and lined up with Saturn. As always, context is everything.

Very likely, language played a huge role in such a prior lifetime as well. Mercury *talks.* And it *listens* too. The exchange of ideas is central here. Unless there are many afflictions to the configuration, we probably still observe this same verbal fluidity in the present life.

But what if you were deaf in a prior life, or mute? Those are Mercury themes too—and that is where we would be looking for harder aspects to be involved. Perhaps Saturn squares the Mercury/south node conjunction, for example.

Another common Mercury signature is *youth.* This is an old astrological idea, one that is often quite useful in this evolutionary context. Young people in general are far more "Mercurial" than older ones. They move around faster. They tend toward nervousness. They require more stimulus. These are all Mercury marks. Certain experiences and vulnerabilities are uniquely emphasized in younger people. Receiving education or mentoring is typically a young person's domain—and these processes capitalize on a classic Mercury skill: the ability to learn through *mimicry.* When we are getting educated in any sense of the word, we often pick up a teacher's style as well as the actual "material" of the educational process. A person with Mercury on the south node, even in this life, may have carried forward an ability to copy other people's accents and verbal quirks. Quite simply, Mercury is usually witty.

Younger people are more vulnerable than older ones to sexual abuse—and to sexual folly in general. To support taking your reading of Mercury conjunct the south node in this particular "youthful" direction, look, as always, for supportive indications. Perhaps the node is in the fourth house, suggesting a person "defined by family," but there are darker Plutonian, eighth house, or Scorpionic elements in the mix. That could indicate incest. Maybe the configuration lies in the fifth house, with its implications of "love affairs" or literally of "children." That could lean more toward sexual folly.

In any case, always stick with the bedrock: mental, cognitive energy, improvisation, and sensory reactivity.

Examples: The clown Marcel Marceau (Pisces, eleventh house). Evangeline Adams (Pisces; twelfth house). Pedro Almodovar (Virgo; fourth house). Jimmy Buffet (Sagittarius; second house). Amelia Earhart (Leo; fifth house). Chess champion Bobby Fischer (Aquarius; eighth house). Prince Charles (Scorpio; fourth house). Joseph Campbell (Aries; sixth house, with node in Pisces). Sue Grafton (Aries; twelfth house). Stephen Spielberg (Leo; sixth house). Arthur Rimbaud (Scorpio; second house).

Venus Conjunct the Moon's South Node

Venus, of all the planets, has the most nearly circular orbit. Follow its place in the sky for almost exactly eight years, marking its retrograde conjunctions with the Sun, and those five conjunctions sketch out a perfect pentacle. It is the brightest of the planets, and because it is never visually far from the Sun, we almost always see it against the violet sky of evening or wee-hours morning, where it glows like a pearl lit with inner fire. No planet is a purer white. No planet is lovelier. Can we even begin to wonder why our ancestors connected Venus with beauty and aesthetic perfection? With the things we love because they so attract us? With our very ability to love? With our ability to be thrilled by beauty—and to aspire to create it?

In practical terms, we associate two fundamental areas of life with Venus: *relationship* and *aesthetics*.

Virtually everyone establishes human connections, be they friendships, romances, or simply practical alliances, so we will begin there. If your south lunar node is lined up with Venus, we know that somehow you were *defined by relationship* in a prior lifetime. To maintain relationships requires a degree of *courtesy*—another Venusian quality which you presumably had in abundance. Courtesy does not have to indicate stiffness or formality. Mostly it is about sensitivity to the feelings of other people, which are conveyed through a set of culturally-specific signals—thus, the realization of how notoriously easy it is to blunder socially when relating in an unfamiliar culture. Courtesy is instinctive to you in this present life. It's in your blood, so to speak—but that courtesy may have odd elements to it from our present cultural point of view, rooted in your karmic memories of another culture's mores.

Were you actively an artist of some sort? We probably should not assume that to be the case unless the Venus-node conjunction is supported by another creative factor or two—perhaps the conjunction, or the ruler of its sign, lies in the fifth house, for example. That could support the idea of actual *artistic expression* in a prior lifetime.

Certainly, in any case, there was a marked affinity for beauty, elegance, or maybe simple luxury in that prior life.

Sexism has run like a dose of the flu through much of human history. Inevitably it has infected astrology. A prime example of this disorder lies in the association of Venus with women (and Mars with men). Modest reflection instantly proves to us that there are of course as many men as women with Venus in any position. You cannot determine someone's gender from a birthchart! Still, the power of collective mythology is strong, and when I see Venus on the south node, I am often inclined to imagine that I am looking at a female prior incarnation, simply because the set of experiences—and perils—to which females have been susceptible are often in the Venusian categories. Being defined by a relationship. Being valued solely for one's beauty—or one's docility and pliability. Men are not immune, and we may be looking at a male incarnation! But calling it a female one often snaps the story into plausible life—even if your client is presently manifesting as a profoundly heterosexual 280 pound football linebacker!

If you see prior-life indications of *social judgment* directed at this Venusian individual—the node/Venus in Aquarius or in hard aspect to Uranus, for example—it is quite possible that you are looking at someone who was a *gay male* in a prior life . . . someone who faced that whole train wreck of ignorant human prejudice and fear.

What if we do have reason to think this configuration might represent someone who was an artist in a prior life? Remember to aim your imagination in a somewhat negative direction. What particular perils do artists face? Maybe that fifth house Venus-node conjunction is squared by Saturn in the second house—the familiar face of the "starving artist" emerges instantly from the symbolism. What if there is a concentration of Piscean or Neptunian energy connected with the node? Artists, more than most groups, have always seemed susceptible to dissipation—alcohol or drug issues, sexual escapism, and so forth. What if the Venus-node conjunction is in the tenth house? Then we may very well be considering someone who was well-known in the arts in a prior life—someone "famous," at least within the context of their times and their community. There is nothing inherently wrong with that—but ask yourself, are there any soul-cages potentially connected with that kind of fame? How many "stars" wind up leading tragic lives, unable to cope with or to understand the projected energies they are receiving from their fans?

Examples: The Artist Formerly Known As Prince (Taurus, sixth house). Pedro Almodovar (Virgo, fourth house) Ingmar Bergman (Gemini; birth time uncertain). Robert Bly (Capricorn, first house). '50's sex goddess Sandra Dee (Pisces, twelfth house). Nelson Mandela (Gemini, birth time uncertain). Emily Post (Sagittarius, birth time uncertain). Barbara Streisand (Pisces, twelfth house). Grandma Moses (Leo; birth time uncertain).

Mars Conjunct the Moon's South Node

A few paragraphs back, we recognized that for historical social and cultural reasons, seeing Venus on the south node can often be helpfully interpreted as suggesting a *female* prior life, regardless of the nature of your "plumbing" today. For similar reasons, with Mars lined up with the south node, we might cautiously lean toward the idea of a male prior incarnation.

The reason is fairly obvious: males have typically been trained to carry the Martial burdens of *war* and *competition.* Please use this suggestion carefully—history, then and now, obviously has no shortage of male artists, or competitive females!

Why do we humans fight? It is always ugly, but most of us agree that it is sometimes justifiable. If you are attacked without provocation and you happen to hurt someone while defending yourself, who would criticize you? Every civilization recognizes, in principle, that we have a natural right to self-defense. But what if you kosh a bad guy over the head with a frying pan in order to stop him from hurting a child? Regardless of how you feel about the experience, you will get the Key to the City for it. *When the Warrior picks up the sword in defense of the innocent, it is almost universally recognized as an honorable act.* And the corollary is that we typically think less of someone who chooses not to defend the innocent when they are in a position to do so.

Sometimes the south node represents things we got wrong in a prior life. Other times it represents things we got right, but in so doing, we sustained damage. Mars on the south node could easily symbolize that second condition. You koshed the bad guy and saved the child. But you watched that bad guy die of a brain hemorrhage before your eyes. You may get the Key to the City—but you may also have nightmares for a long time after that. Such unresolved karma—honorable but complex—can be indicated by Mars conjunct the south node.

A lot of the action movies coming out of Hollywood begin with a scene in which the good guy—or someone innocent and defenseless whom he or she loves—experiences some grievous injustice. And from that moment on you merrily eat popcorn while watching 127 minutes of blood-letting and mayhem. It's OK now—*they deserved it!* See how they set you up? Again, *when the Warrior picks up the sword in defense of the innocent, it is almost universally recognized as honorable.* With that kind of premise, we can suspend our natural revulsion at violence and sadism. Not to be too judgmental here—this ancient formula has made some great movies, not to mention a lot of great literature. But has there ever been a war in which each government did not use the same trick? Claiming offended innocence, while pointing the finger at dehumanized evildoers? Claiming that the innocent are under attack and must be protected? Only now, unlike the movies, the bullets are real. How easily young men in particular are seduced by this ploy! Adding momentum to that seduction is the way young females have been conditioned to read the "warrior" as sexy, providing another stimulus for the young male's enthusiasm.

Given the realities of human history, how often have people—again mostly males—been thus bamboozled into murdering each other? And once the cycle of violence starts, the offences become real and self-sustaining. My personal guess is that this single phenomenon accounts for 90% of humanity's darkest karma.

If you have Mars on your south node, you might very well have been pulled into such a violent drama—war, literally, or "war" in some more personal framework. You might very well have blood on your hands. Were you a murderer? The word is probably unfair in this context. To convincingly read Mars conjunct the south node as indicative of prior-life commission of "murder most foul," it would help to see some influence from Pluto on the conjunction, for example. Probably also there would be some indication of social judgement or isolation—say, some pronounced Uranian or Aquarian themes.

And of course in speaking of literal killing, we are aiming our attention at the extreme end of the spectrum of possibilities. Mars more commonly manifests its dark side as *rage, pique, resentment*, and *annoyance*.

In any case, when we see Mars on the south node, we know that this soul has come into the present life carrying a burden of edgy anger, underlying fear, and big pain. There can be a fascination with extreme behaviors, and the passions they release in us all. Adventure still calls. "Normal life" can feel boring and enervating. Often there is a quality of *sexiness*. There may be a passion for justice, wise or misguided. The "heroic" looms large in the consciousness. Not to overdo this, but there is some potential for violence being repeated in this life, perhaps violence coming back at the person this time around.

Examples: J.R.R. Tolkien (Scorpio, third house). Willie Nelson (Virgo, first house). Gianni Versace (Sagittarius, first house). Lauren Bacall (Aquarius, eighth house). Agatha Christie (Sagittarius, fourth house). Bob Marley (Capricorn; second house). Leonard Cohen (Leo; eleventh house). Martin Luther (node Libra, Mars Scorpio; third house). Willy Shoemaker (Libra; seventh house). Sophia Loren (Leo; seventh house). Christa McAuliffe

(Mars Libra; node Scorpio; sixth house). Quincy Jones (Virgo; eleventh house). Ursula K. LeGuin (Scorpio; seventh house).

Jupiter Conjunct the Moon's South Node

Most of the stars in the galaxy are in binary systems—double stars. Single ones like our Sun are the exception. Our solar system barely escaped the more common fate. Had Jupiter been just a little more massive back when the planets were forming, its gravity would have sucked up enough dust and gas to trigger nuclear reactions in its core. It would have lit up as a little red dwarf star, married forever to the Sun, shining a little less brightly. And on Earth, getting a suntan would have been a whole lot easier—catastrophically so. This astrophysical fact tells us so much about Jupiter. *It is a planet that nearly became a star.* In fact, four planet-sized moons orbit it, almost like a miniature solar system. No wonder our ancestors called it the King of the Gods, even though they had no idea of the astronomy I've just mentioned..

With Jupiter on your south node, there is strong evidence of your having been a "star" in a prior life. Likely, you radiated a kind of charismatic magnetism. You were expansive and confident, and inspired people to look up to you. Probably you had a good sense of humor too.

Given that our interpretations of the south node always tend toward suspicion, we need to recognize the dangers Jupiter presents too—and to assume that to some extent you fell prey to them. Simple *over-extension* is the mildest element; perhaps in a prior life you bit off more than you could chew. Perhaps you illustrated the "Peter Principle," of having been promoted to a level at which you were incompetent. *Over-reaching, pride, self-importance*—those are soul-cages Jupiter offers, and which the world often thrusts on people who bear the mark of this planet.

Are we talking about prior-life worldly power? Yes—if the Jupiter-node conjunction falls in the tenth house. What about the ego-inflation that money can create? Look to the second house. Snooty "power family" stuff? The fourth house.

The Roman god Jupiter often annoyed his long-suffering wife Juno by getting nymphs pregnant. In the language of modern psychotherapy, he had "boundary issues." Paraphrasing Oscar Wilde, Jupiter "could resist anything except temptation." Look to this sexually voracious dimension of Jupiter operating in the karmic past if the south node is involved with Venus or the fifth house. Look to more alcoholic forms of escapism if the node is connected with Neptune or the twelfth house. What about another Jupiter shadow: *pomposity*? Look to associations of the node-Jupiter alignment with Saturn or Capricorn. Food-issues? Lunar and Cancerian associations. Religious dogmatism? Sagittarian or ninth house flavors.

Very likely, some of this tone of being "bigger than life" persists into the present incarnation. Confidence and healthy pride are wonderful qualities. They must be tempered now with a loss of self-importance. *Examples: Adolph Hitler (Capricorn, third house). F. Scott Fitzgerald (Leo; seventh house). Stephen King (Scorpio; fifth house). Arnold Schwarzeneggar (Scorpio, fifth house). Evangeline Adams (Pisces, twelfth house). Sue Grafton (Aries; first house). Tennessee Williams (Scorpio; ninth house). Willie Nelson (Virgo; second house). Martin Luther (Libra; third house).*

Saturn Conjunct the Moon's South Node

Cynics say that life's a bitch, then you die. This sentiment may not be a complete cosmology, but we all have days that fit the picture. The critical point with Saturn conjunct the Moon's south node is to realize that some people have *lifetimes* that fit that picture too. If we turn away from this sad truth in the name of positive thinking or any other philosophy, we have turned away from a demonstrable truth. People do suffer, and life is perceptibly unfair. Turn away from that and we have turned away from compassion too. Throughout history, there have been people who were born into slavery—and died there too. Often, in the spectacle of life, we see horrible conjunctions of disease, poverty, and mental illness. We see overwhelming circumstances colliding with human frailty.

Seeing Saturn conjunct the Moon's south node invokes such images. But Saturn can also indicate *responsibility*, and when it is in this position it can point to an enormous weight placed upon a person in a prior life. Picture a peasant woman suddenly widowed and with six young children to feed. Picture the decent, well-intended mayor of a medieval town faced with the onset of Black Plague in his community. Imagine having your beloved husband or wife struck down with lingering muscular dystrophy—and you are living in Massachusetts, 1673.

In any of the miserable situations I have just described, how might a person react internally? This is truly the critical question, since with any nodal configuration the heart of the matter is the *feeling or mood* that has been carried forward into the present life. The "facts" were only material vehicles for the soul's lessons. The facts have a much shorter life span than does their inward impact.

Faced with life's enormity, there are basically two kinds of people, although shades of gray naturally abound. There are the ones who rise to Saturn's challenges. And there are those who are broken by them. Either story is consistent with Saturn's conjunction with the south node. Let's look at each one.

Among those who rose to Saturn's challenges in a prior life, we find paragons of human *strength, endurance,* and *integrity.* Let's honor them, and know that we can recognize them in the present life because so often those same qualities are carried forward. These are people who seemingly can do anything and endure anything. They define the word "discipline." Inwardly, though, there is a terrible tightness in them. Relaxing and simply *feeling* are hard. That is because in a traumatic prior life, they became masters of self-denial, masters of maturity and focus. That was how they survived. They did not have the luxury of emotions, of self-care, or frivolity. They steeled themselves—and they were still "steeled" when they came out of their mothers this time around. They never learned to *count on anyone* simply because in the prior life there was no one there for them to count on except themselves. Astrologically, we distinguish these stalwart people because their Saturn-node conjunction is very strongly placed in the chart. It is Angular, for example, and perhaps in a Fire sign. Maybe Jupiter or Mars or the Sun are involved with it. When you look at it, you get the feeling that here was someone who would be determined to "die with his boots on."

What about those who were broken by Saturn in a prior life? Among those ground down under Saturn's relentless wheels, we see people who have carried forward into this life a sense of *defeat, pessimism and hopelessness.* Many will be *depressed.* They feel tired, and it is not the kind of tiredness that sleep helps. Loneliness is a common mood among them—and the loneliness often operates in vexing alliance with a tendency toward *self-isolation*. Working one's way out of such a soul-cage is difficult. Astrology can be a particularly helpful here by prescribing exactly the right medicine. That medicine is a willingness to engage long-term in the kind of life that is described in highest expression of the chart, with a special focus on the prescriptions of the Moon's north node.

Technically, we distinguish this sadder, more defeated population of Saturn-node people by a set of "overwhelming" factors connected with the configuration. Perhaps it falls in the twelfth house or is lined up with Neptune or in Pisces. Likely, the south node is under a lot of pressure through hard aspects too. We will learn more about them in Chapter Ten, but basically such hard aspects refer to painful, difficult circumstantial factors which may have simply overwhelmed the person.

For the sake of compassion and clarity, it is essential that we understand that *anyone can be broken*. Even a strong-looking nodal placement could represent a strong person shattered by catastrophe were it square a Mars-Pluto conjunction and opposed by the Sun.

Obviously, these are daunting nodal configurations. Never lose sight of the fact the that this person is ready to move on and to heal, and that the chart shows exactly how to do that.

Examples. Maya Angelou (Sagittarius; fourth house). Jack Kevorkian (Sagittarius, unclear birth time). Monica Lewinsky (Gemini; ninth house). Ted Turner (Aries; ninth house). President Felipe Calderon of Mexico (Aquarius; third house). The 17th Karmapa (Scorpio; 6th house—if we accept that he was born, as reported, "at sunrise.")

Uranus Conjunct the Moon's South Node

We have a lot of clichés to describe Uranian types. They are "square pegs in round holes." They "hear a different drummer" as they travel down "the road less traveled" being "their own person" while "thinking outside the box."

We generally use clichés to describe things about which we have not really done much original thinking. Humanity in general seems not to have done much thinking at all about its own oddballs. That is why we have so many clichés about them. Instead we often unwittingly apply pressure on these people to conform, to "return to normal." The pressure may be subtle mockery and the withholding of respect—or, failing that, it can burst into ostracism, even repressive violence. Pity, because without these Uranian types we would all still be hunting and gathering, while picking fleas off each other. Uranian energy is the mark of *genius* and of *revolution.* It breaks the rules, upsets the apple cart, and *allows change to happen.*

With Uranus conjunct your lunar south node, in a prior life you were an outsider. The archetype of the Exile played a big role in you. You simply had to develop independence and mental agility. Unlike "normal" people, you had very little choice.

Some people simply seem to be intrinsically divergent from the mainstream. They were just "born that way." We all know people for whom it would be psychologically impossible to work for a big corporation, for example. If you were that kind of Uranian in a past life, we might look for the node-Uranus conjunction to be in the first house or conjunct the Sun.

Say the conjunction lies in the ninth house or possibly in Sagittarius. Then we could be looking at a person who was socially isolated in a prior life because of his or her religion, or maybe simply because of some geographic situation: a refugee or an ex-patriot, for example.

Family ethnicity is something over which we have no control. The mildest, most pliant person in the world might have born into a Jewish bloodline in fifteenth century Spain. Late in that century, there was an attempt to drive Jews out of the "Christian" kingdom. Many fled—but many remained behind, with their mouths tightly closed, making the sign of the cross. Imagine that you had to live your life that way, constantly hiding what you genuinely were, forever exiled within your own land—and with your own nature actually conventional and not even slightly confrontational! How might we symbolize that kind of prior life astrologically? Put Uranus on the south node in the fourth house (family) and then make it milder by placing it in a Water sign and linking it to Venus, Saturn, the Moon, or Neptune.

Always, whether it is loud and flagrant or quiet, even timid, the Uranian signature on the south node carries the spirit of *isolation,* some immunity to consensual reality, and very likely at least a hint of innovative brilliance.

Uranus correlates with anything that happens suddenly. While what I am about to write is more typically associated with hard aspects between

Uranus and the south node, even with the conjunction we must be alert to the possibility of some sudden, shocking *change of condition* in the prior life. An unexpected collapse in one's status *(tenth house)*, one's finances *(second house)*, one's primary relationships *(seventh house)*—any of those catastrophes would illustrate the point. Such an experience often leaves a mark of some emotional distance or *dissociation* in the present character. *Examples: Michael Moore (Cancer; twelfth house). Henry Kissinger (Pisces; tenth house). Paramahansa Yogananda (Scorpio; third house). Marcel Marceau (Pisces; eleventh house). Oprah Winfrey (Cancer; seventh house). Hank Williams (Pisces; ninth house). Wolfgang Amadeus Mozart (Pisces; birth time uncertain).*

Neptune Conjunct the Moon's South Node`

Who gazes soulfully into space? Anyone who fits that description qualifies as Neptunian! The question is only five words long, but answering it fully would take quite a while—lots of different kinds of people fit the description.

The first and most obvious answer, though, is simply "everybody." Any one of us, pondering something vast, uncertain, and important, will gaze into space. We do that when we are looking for inspiration—for a visitation from the gods, or at least for a little input from the unconscious mind. Or the soul. Or the imagination. There are a lot of words we could use here, but all them point to that far country beyond the boundaries of the conscious, ego-centered, logical mind. All of them point to the mystery we carry inside ourselves. All of them point to Neptune.

Who, specifically, gazes into space? First and foremost, we might say that *mystics* do. And, with Neptune conjunct your south node, perhaps you were a mystic in a prior life. Link it to the ninth house *(religion)* or the twelfth house *(monasteries)* and you might very well have been a monk or nun in a prior life. Systematically, and with the support of a religion and some peers, you sought to *dissociate consciousness from personality.* Maybe you went too far too fast with that intention too. I remember a spiritual teacher of mine referring to a fellow who epitomized this issue. She said, "He is too heavenly to be of any earthly use at all."

While we speak of mystics, let's recognize that such people are forever giving things up—food, money, sexuality, and so forth. Such *non-attachment* plays a central role in many advanced forms of spiritual practice, but it leads us to recognize another potentially negative Neptune signature: someone with Neptune on the south node may have *unnecessarily given up something they actually really needed* in a past life. The giving up of committed love in a prior life might, for example, be indicated by Neptune-node in the seventh or eighth houses. A damagingly abstemious prior-life relationship with food could be revealed by the configuration being connected with the Moon or Cancer. Premature celibacy by links to Venus, Mars, or the eighth house.

Psychics and *visionaries* gaze into space too. So do *artists* and creative people—and to validate that signature, add some Venus or some fifth house to the stew.

When it comes to gazing into space, one of the most populous classes of practitioners are the *drunks, the addicts,* and the rest of the world's stoned-out souls. With Neptune conjunct the south node of the Moon, there may be karma in those departments as well. One of the best indicators of that particular prior-life issue would the person's present behavior. Either they are re-enacting the old problem in this lifetime, or, more to their credit, they are phobic about getting near anything of that nature—and for that we should respect them! Technically, if we are looking at addictive behavior in a prior incarnation, we are probably faced with a mix of twelfth house and Piscean energies, complicated by fifth house influences, and perhaps Jupiter or Venus signatures as well.

People escape into sex as often as they escape into alcohol. With the "sex addict," the karmic signature would be more Venusian or Martial—the former with a "romantic" addiction, the latter with a more frankly physical and "conquest-oriented" tone.

The next generation of evolutionary astrologers will be faced with Neptune-Mercury mixes manifesting in this "addictive" mode. Those disorders will beset the folks, now living, who will die in front of their televisions or computer screens, having forgotten actually to live. Next time around, many of them will have Neptune conjunct the south node.

Examples: Ernest Hemingway (Gemini; tenth house). Zelda Fitzgerald (Gemini; eleventh house). Billy Strayhorn—Duke Ellington's often-

forgotten musical collaborator (Leo; ninth house). Humphrey Bogart (Gemini; birth time uncertain). Jorge Luis Borges (Gemini; twelfth house). Richard Gere (Libra; time uncertain). Alfred Hitchcock (Gemini; time uncertain). Sigourney Weaver (Libra; sixth house). Edith Piaf (Leo; ninth house).

Pluto Conjunct the Moon's South Node

Much that is "unthinkable" actually happens. That is one of life's bitter paradoxes—many people *experience events they could not bear to contemplate or imagine.* Maybe you sat down to a festive meal with your family in your villa on the Amalfi coast of Italy on August 24, 79 A.D. And Mount Vesuvius blew. You fled in horror, only to choke to death on a mixture of hot ash and toxic gases. Maybe you were in Dachau or Hiroshima or My Lai or Wounded Knee. Or Gallipoli or Monte Casino or Appomattox or Waterloo or Trafalgar. Maybe you were cleaning third story windows in San Francisco when the earthquake hit in 1906 or in Indonesia when Krakatoa blew. Maybe the Pope decided to make a better Catholic out of you at Montségur in March 1244.

Any of those kinds of prior life experiences could be signaled by the presence of Pluto conjunct the Moon's south node in the present chart. History has no shortage of them. Most of the catastrophes I listed are public and collective, so we would probably see some relationship between the south node and the tenth or eleventh houses.

The underlying Plutonian key is here the possibility that you became *identified as a victim,* in your own mind and in the minds of others. People could not bear to contemplate or imagine what had happened to you.

Much that is extreme is more private and personal. What if you experience rape? *How long does it take to get over that?* That question is not meant to be insensitive. Obviously, one reflexive answer might be that you *never* get over it. What that actually means is that you might die with the experience unresolved—in which case, we might see Pluto on the south node in the present lifetime. In such a case, there would be eighth house and Scorpionic associations *(sexuality)* as well, along with some Mars-energy to represent the violence of the act.

There are even more uncomfortable notions to consider with Pluto on the south node. Fasten your seatbelts. I sat with a friend who had fought in Viet Nam. He was making reference to some awful things that he did there and how hard it was to live with the memories of them. I spoke to him of self-forgiveness. He said to me, "Steve, some things are just unforgivable." It was a very Plutonian moment. I couldn't argue with him. It is not that I really agreed with his statement; it was that I loved and respected him too much to trivialize what he had just said with a nit-picking philosophical argument.

If, with Pluto conjunct your south node, you did something truly dreadful in a prior life—you yourself committed rape or murder, for example—again I would ask that same, utterly Plutonian question: *How long does it take to get over that?* Ultimately, are not victimizers as damaged as their victims? With Pluto conjunct the south node of the Moon, you may be carrying some guilt from the past—something you did for which you might spend a lot of time unconsciously punishing yourself in this lifetime.

In that kind of "perpetrator" situation, look for the Pluto-south node conjunction to show strong first or tenth house energy, or associations with Mars or with Fire in general.

Winston Churchill chose to let the *Luftwaffe* bomb the city of Exeter rather than tip off the Nazis that their secret codes had been broken. In so doing, he may have secured the Allied victory on D-Day. Still a lot of people who were looking to him as their shepherd had to die because of his choice. For what it is worth, history seems to have decided he made the right call. His decision saved more lives than were lost. But how does one live with such a memory? We make a judgment call to the best of our ability and thousands die. *How long does it take to get over that?* We of course don't know if Winston Churchill has reincarnated, but if he has, I would not be surprised to see Pluto on his south node.

So, with this configuration, all you can assume is that this soul has contacted something extreme and died unhealed. Perhaps they were victims. Perhaps they were victimizers. Perhaps they had to make a morally-gray, high-stakes choice—and died still not knowing if it had been the right one.

Examples: Vladimir Putin (Leo; tenth house). Thelonius Monk (Cancer; first house). The Dalai Lama (Cancer; first house). Werner Erhard (Cancer; third house). Zelda Fitzgerald (Gemini; eleventh house). Christopher Reeve (Leo; sixth house). Rev. Jimmy Swaggart (Cancer; seventh house).

Other Points Conjunct the Moon's South Node

What about Chiron? What about the one-third of a million registered asteroids, or even the 13,000 or so named ones? Or even just the big asteroids, the so-called "big four" of Ceres, Pallas, Vesta, and Juno (although Hygeia should be included there—it is bigger than Juno). What about the new planet, Eris?

In principle I would take all of those seriously were they conjunct the south node. Experience has taught me to pay close attention to Chiron, to Ceres and to Eris, in particular.

In all honesty, I tend not to use any of these points very much in practice with my clients. This is probably a weakness of mine, which I hope to improve. But in writing my various books I am aware of the great responsibility that goes with the possibility that people will make choices based on what I write. I therefore follow the discipline of only writing in certain, definitive terms about configurations with which I have a lot of real, client-oriented experience. Let me tell you, there is no negative reinforcement that rivals falling flat with a client! Everything you read here has passed that hurdle, and emerged illuminated with a feeling of certainty.

With that caution stated, let me offer tentatively some brief guidelines about my current thinking with the three bodies I mentioned above.

Chiron. Look to one who was physically debilitated somehow in a prior life, or to one who spent much of a prior life as some kind of care-giver to someone in the former condition. To make the distinction between those two conditions, use the techniques I have described in the preceding pages. Where Chiron-node looks powerful and "in charge," think: *care giver*. Where it looks weakened and vulnerable or dependent, think: someone *ill or debilitated*.

Ceres: Now considered a "dwarf planet" by some astronomers, it is at least by far the largest asteroid, containing about one-third of the entire mass of the asteroid belt. "Mothering" and care-giving behaviors. Rites of passage. The insane, unthinking, all-consuming grief of the bereft parent.

Eris: This new planet needs a book. I am beginning to take it very seriously, but let me quote my better angels: "Steve, shut up about Eris until you've lived with it a while longer. This is a book, not email! You can't delete it."

Very cautiously, let me suggest that with Eris on the south node, there are prior life memories of situations of extreme competitiveness or of fierce rivalry—Darwinian themes of "the survival of the fittest." Vanity might be a factor. "Coyote" might have made an appearance—and for a definition, ask a Navajo!

CHAPTER NINE:
THE PLANETARY RULER OF THE SOUTH NODE

If your south lunar node lies in Gemini, then Mercury is its ruler. In Taurus, then Venus rules it. The planet that rules your south node makes a pivotal contribution to our understanding of your karmic story. It represents some *other dimension* of your situation and your character. Perhaps it gives us *another chapter* of the story, often a very specific one—maybe the lynch-pin of the whole drama.

For me, realizing the power of the south node's ruler was like going from black-and-white to color. It was like going from sitting before a bas-relief of Cleopatra to sitting down with her personally over a bottle of wine in the garden.

How do we use the south node's ruler? Let's map it into the larger theoretical context and let it takes its natural place alongside the other pieces of the puzzle.

To understand who someone *was* in a prior life, look at:
1. The sign and house of the south node
2. Any planet conjunct the south node
3. The ruler of the south node in terms of its sign and house

To understand what that person *faced* in the prior life, look at:
1. Any aspects other than conjunctions to the south node
2. The house of the south node (note redundancy—it is intentional)
3. Secondarily, any aspects to the ruler of the south node

This description of the system is overly pat—a moment's reflection and we realize that experience impacts our natures, and vice versa. We cannot ultimately separate them. Still these divisions are an effective way of organizing your thoughts as you dive into the morass of symbolism pertinent to sorting our prior life information and parables.

What if the south node lies in Pisces? What is the ruler? This question is the subject of much ferocity when astrologers gather, as we explored in Chapter Three. Traditional astrologers say Jupiter rules Pisces. Modern ones say Neptune does. I say they both rule it—and that we should dump the word "ruler." Planets are not giving orders to the signs! That is a transparently human projection onto the celestial realm. "Rulership" really means affinity or connection or harmony—and both Jupiter and Neptune have that kind of resonance with Pisces. And Pisces absolutely does not have to decide "who it likes best." This is the vast and mysterious universe we're talking about, not high school!

If you see a Pisces south node (or Aquarius or Scorpio), count yourself lucky in a way. You have a more complex situation to unravel, but you also have twice as much information to go on. An Aquarian south node? Look for both Uranus and Saturn. Scorpio? Pluto and Mars.

My experience suggests that the modern ruler often gives the deeper, more psychological information—or at least the most hard-hitting from an emotional perspective. The classical ruler typically leans toward more concrete, objective description.

Use them both, is my advice. Astrology is, as always, a work in progress. The one eternal principle is "as above, so below." If it is up there in the sky, it can be relied upon to have significance down here below.

The Meaning of the Ruler of the South Node

If your south node lies in Aries, we would naturally have already been thinking about the archetype of the Warrior, with all its implications of stress and courage and extremes of violence, rivalry, or competition. Knowing that Mars rules Aries does not really add very much—we know Mars is the Warrior too . . . but we already understood that part.

The main contribution of the ruler of the south node is to tie a new sign and a new house into the story.

The planet itself serves mainly as a marker—although it is central to our process to remember to bring that planet's energy into our reading of the ruler's sign and house. Mars still indicates "war." But now the original Arian war has spread to another province. The planet is essentially an *ambassador* of the south node's sign, carrying the message into a new territory.

Maybe the south node is in the second house conjunct Jupiter—we are thinking about prior-life issues around having lots of money. Say the ruler of the south node is in the tenth house. You might very well have then made that money yourself as a result of some public position or job you held. Maybe it is in the fourth house—the idea of "family money" leaps out.

To have earned a great fortune through one's own efforts, or to have been born into it: see how enormously different those two situations feel? This kind of clarification is the gift of the south node's ruler. We could not see it otherwise.

Sometimes, of course, the ruler of the south node will be in the same house or sign (or both) as the node itself. That intensifies the message of the node, but it really does not add very much that we did not know already. With experience, you will quickly discover how in some charts the nodal story is quite detailed. Other times, we only get a few hints.

Why this Is a Short Chapter

Once you have determined the ruler of your south node, here is a way to get started interpreting it:

Look at Chapter Eight, "Planets Conjunct The South Node." The ruler of the south node works essentially the same way as a planet conjunct the south node. You can use those same guidelines to get going with your interpretation. Both the planet that rules the south node and the one conjunct it represent *you* in a prior life.

It is critically important to place that planetary ruler in its own house and sign—and there you can use Chapters Six and Seven where we gave some hints about the node itself in each of the twelve signs and houses. Again, the planetary ruler of the node (just like the node itself) represents *you* in the past incarnation. The sign the ruler occupies shades it with a set of motivations and interests, and the house it is in puts it in a context.

In the next two chapters, we wrestle with how to understand the meaning of a planet in a hard or soft aspect to the south node. All the techniques we will learn there apply in a lesser way to learning more about the ruler of the south node through considering any aspects it receives.

That's why this is a short chapter. The ruler of the south node is hugely significant, but most of what you need to know about it is scattered around other parts of the book.

CHAPTER TEN:
PLANETS IN HARD ASPECT TO THE SOUTH NODE

Thinking about prior lifetimes boils down to two basic questions: Who were you and what were you doing? Character and plot, as we have mentioned earlier. The two are related, but only tangentially. Extroverts are more likely than introverts to meet strangers. That is an example of character driving plot. Bad things happen to good people: that is the other side of the coin, plot impacting character—unaccustomed bitterness might enter the character as a result of such a "plot twist."

As we penetrate more deeply, the distinctions between plot and character begin to break down a bit. Peering through the lens of synchronicity, we see all manner of "non-causal" connections between the inner life and outer experience: you start to feel lucky in a kind of peaceful, non-attached way. You roll the dice. Lucky sevens. You felt it coming. Ultimately "inner" and "outer" are lot more closely linked than simple reason might indicate.

Still, splitting character and plot is a useful mental device. We use the division all the time in every day life, and we use it in astrology too.

In parsing out the karmic story, there are two working hypotheses. Both over-simplify. Both are incredibly productive. I encourage you to use them as a starting point. They will build you a solid foundation.

To understand *character* in a prior life, concentrate on the sign and house positions of the south node, any planet conjunct the south node, and the position of the ruler of the south node, including any planets conjunct it.

To understand the *plot* of the prior life story, concentrate on any planets in aspect to the south node (except for the conjunction). Secondarily attend to aspects to the ruler of the south node—and take another glance at the house position of the south node itself.

Note that the house position of the south node plays a dual role here, covering both bases. Since houses are active and behavioral—so plot-like—they say as much about what you were up to in a prior life as they do about who you were. Say your south node is in the tenth house. Your *circumstances* were framed by a visible public role, and your *nature* was significantly defined by that experience of power or position.

Really, this plot/character "blur" we note in terms of the south node's house actually extends across the entire gamut of the past-life symbolism. Experience influences our inner reality, while our inner reality is reflected in the outward choices we make. Our distinctions here are a helpful fiction. They give you a reliable plot-and-character skeleton on which to hang the past-life "novel."

Over the past few chapters we have been focusing on trying to figure out who you were in a prior incarnation. We have covered the house and sign positions of the south node, the planets conjunct it, and its ruler. Now it is time to concentrate more on the storyline itself.

No Planetary Aspects?

Quite possibly, a given south node will make no aspects to anything except of course the north node, which it must always oppose. What can we make of that? Well, pretty obviously there is not much of a storyline available! This can be frustrating if we want something more detailed to emerge, but it is important not to "push the data." Better instead to think about what this lack of information actually signals. In this situation, we lack much plot-oriented, development-oriented data. There are lives in which, relatively speaking, not much happens—that is probably what you are looking at. Sometimes a set of circumstances arise which both utterly permeates a life, and is also going absolutely nowhere. For example, maybe the south node lies in Virgo in the sixth house conjunct Saturn. It makes no aspects. You were born a slave. You died that way too. Nothing "happened." And that is the story. Translation: there is an underlying karmic vulnerability to getting into similarly "stuck" situations, and adapting to them for the long haul, *even when that slavery is presently unnecessary.*

Never push the symbols beyond what they can support. Instead think deeply about what they *are* telling you.

One helpful trick: if the south node makes no aspects, do pay more attention to any aspects involving the ruler of the south node. They often add that missing dynamic element of plot.

Hard Aspects

Any aspect to the south node illuminates something of the past-life tale. "Easy" aspects—trines and sextiles, for example—are often not as easy as they sound! They are the subject of the next chapter. Here let's look to the hard aspects. By that, I mean primarily the square and the opposition. You can apply some of what I say here to minor aspects of a harder nature as well—quincunxes, sesquiquadrates, and so on. My practice, as I have described earlier, is to focus on the "major" Ptolemaic aspects because they are so compellingly evocative. Generally, they give me more than enough to contemplate. In a "no aspects" situation, stretching out to include the minor series would begin to make more sense to me.

In any case, *any planet in hard aspect to the south node represents something that created a problem for you in a prior life.* To use the grief-stricken language of traditional astrology, this thing *afflicted* you. Maybe that means it annoyed you. Maybe it killed you. In any case, it left a painful mark on your soul. In this present lifetime, the ghost of that planet still haunts you. Its damage was left unresolved. You put it on the cosmic VISA card and now the bill is due.

Make it Personal!

When we reflect on the troubles, pains and challenges we have faced in this lifetime, we realize that quite a lot of the stories that come spontaneously to mind revolve around other people. Love and friendship are grand gifts, and life without them would be hard to stomach. Still the lion's share of our frustrations and dramas involve other people: partners, rivals, enemies, teachers, lovers, children, parents.

When you see a planet square or opposed to the south node, start out by trying to think of it as *another person who created an issue for you* in the prior lifetime. The tack will not always work, but it often immediately opens a storyline.

Sometimes this kind of "personalized" interpretation is compellingly obvious. Maybe Venus *(love)* in the seventh house *(partnerships)* squares your tenth house south node. One reading of that would be that a marriage or an affair *interfered with* (square) your professional aspirations *(tenth house)*.

Other times, personalizing the planet may not be so compelling. Consider a fourth house Sun opposing your tenth house south node/Venus alignment. One reading of that configuration could be that your professional ambitions (tenth house) as an artist *(Venus)* were opposed by a powerful and demanding father-figure *(Sun in the fourth house)*.

If personalizing the "afflicting" planet feels forced or unnatural, or if it just does not seem to be getting you anywhere, drop it. Other things besides people can create trouble for us! An affliction from the second house? Try money-issues. South node in the ninth house squared by something in the twelfth house? You were flying to Brazil, but the plane crashed!

Always our goal is to listen to everything that the chart reveals about the prior life, and then come to a balanced integration—one that includes everything, does not invent anything pivotal, and just "sits" in the easiest and most unforced way possible. Very strange things happen in the world., of course. But the fact that we deem them strange means that they do not happen very often. Best to stick with past-life stories that do not ask too much of the imagination or the credulity. They are more likely to be correct that way. They are obeying the "law of averages."

As noted above, we will be concentrating on squares and oppositions in this chapter. All that we have seen so far applies to both of them—and they do overlap a lot. Trying to make too sharp a distinction between squares and oppositions is a triumph of theory over actual experience. But they are somewhat different. What they hold in common is a sense of resistance, vexation, and trouble. From now on, let's explore their unique signatures.

Planets Square the Nodes

Any planet square the south node is naturally square the north node as well. But those are two different aspects, and we read them differently.

Regarding the south node, we are getting information about things that limited us in the prior lifetime. Regarding the north node, we are seeing something about how to get on with one's evolution.

A planet square the south node is:
1. Something or someone that vexed or blocked you in the prior life; something that "hit you out of the blue;" something that felt unfair or random; something that attacked you; something that angered you and toward which you felt aggression.
2. The issue the planet represents was left unresolved in the past.
3. Therefore, resolving it is left over as a "skipped step." You must get it right or clear it somehow in order to go forward in this present life.
4. The planet is left "hanging in the balance." Will it echo the past—or help you toward your future?
(By the way, I owe my "Pluto Brother," Jeffrey Wolf Green, for the term, "skipped step.")

Say you have a Venus-Uranus conjunction squaring your south node. One reading of that configuration is that you were suddenly abandoned *(Uranus)* by someone you loved *(Venus)* in a prior life. This experience "hit you out of the blue;" and it felt unfair or random. Understandably, you have some "unresolved issues" around similar possible abandonments in this present life. Deeply, those issues are connected with the always-dicey balancing of love *(Venus)* and freedom *(Uranus)*. In the karmic past, maybe you drove your partner away through too much clinginess or dependency. Maybe you yourself were ambivalent around commitment, and chose someone who mirrored that issue. There are a lot of possibilities. But in any case resolving this issue is a "skipped step." You really have to make a serious and productive start on facing it and healing it before you are free to explore your north node intentions. It haunts you too much for you to get there otherwise; it is draining too much of your energy and your faith. And the issue is "hanging in the balance." Will you repeat the old karmic story? Or will you find dynamic partnerships characterized by a lot of respect for individual differences and the need for "space," relationships that will actually assist you critically in whatever your north node work might be?

These are a few guidelines about planets square the nodal axis. The specifics of the south and north nodes and the larger context will make the interpretation of the square much more crisp and specific. But always, these basic principles underlie the details.

Planets Opposing the South Node

. . . are of course conjunct the north node!

Seeing them as being in opposition to the south node shines a light on their role in the past life story. Their alignment with the north node underscores their role as positive "medicine" or "remedy" for the karmic predicament. We will get to that in a moment.

A planet opposing the south node can be considered in two fundamental ways, depending on the specifics of the configuration. Straightforwardly, it may be something that created an *overwhelming obstacle* for you in a past life: the "brick wall of reality." The second perspective is that it may also be something for which you *longed unrequitedly* but could never attain. This alternative reading of the opposition derives from the fact that anything opposite your south node is as *far away from you as it could possibly be.* And remember also that opposition aspect is the classic romantic one. "Opposites attract," famously. That idea is graven into astrological stone in the form of the first house-seventh house relationship.

How do we sort out these two possible interpretive frameworks for the opposition to the south node?

Generally, when the planet opposing the south node looks "hard" or "bad," incline toward reading it as an *overwhelming reality that hurt you.* When it looks softer and sweeter, see it as something *for which you longed.*

Pluto opposing the south node? Maybe you were enjoying a mountain picnic in Indonesia on the day Krakatoa blew. Maybe you were in Hiroshima or Dachau. There was nothing you could do: that is the brick wall of reality.

Maybe Jupiter opposes your south node? You pined away for wealth or success that always remained illusive. Venus? You loved someone unavailable. This kind of longing can become morbid. It can create a mark of hunger in the soul strong enough to survive death and rebirth.

A planet conjunct the north node is of course the same planet, but we read it differently. Such a planet becomes part and parcel of the north node. Attaining the highest reaches of its potential is the evolutionary goal. Pluto on the north node? There is an evolutionary need to do some very deep inner work, maybe grief work, for example. If you were in Dachau, that is not difficult to understand.

Jupiter on the north node? Your soul needs a victory! The attainment of some kind of success and abundance becomes a spiritual imperative. You longed for it for a lifetime. The most efficient evolutionary highway open to you is simply to feed the hunger—and see how you feel when you are satiated.

Venus? Experiencing one's self as worthy of love is the critical foundation. On it, we build lasting intimacy. Prior life romantic longing sapped your dignity and self-worth.

Again, these thumbnail interpretations are skeletal, aimed only at giving us a feeling for the action of the opposition aspect. As ever, the details emerge as we apply the entire evolutionary paradigm, integrating all the clues.

Distinguishing The Action of Squares and Oppositions

A helpful hypothesis to try on is that a planet *opposing* the south node is something you simply *could not get around,* while a planet *squaring* it represents a reality that *might have been circumvented,* had you been more aware. People stay in destructive marriages or in jobs which they, in principle, could actually leave. If you were in such a pickle and you did not leave, that will show up as a square to the nodes in one of your next lifetimes. Ships sink, bombs go off, disease wins, hurricanes slam into shore—if you were impacted in such a way and there was no possibility of getting out of it by thinking differently, that manifests as an opposition in a future lifetime.

Thus, the squares tend more toward *rage* and *frustration*, while the oppositions tend more toward *despair.*

Projection

As we discussed in Chapter Three, since a planet in square or opposition to our south node hurt us somehow in a prior life, it follows that we are annoyed at that planet! That is a problem because we actually need to make an ally of it in order to go forward—it is a skipped step if it is a square and it is our evolutionary goal if it lies on the north node. We must thus "withdraw the projection."

Maybe we have a conjunction of the Sun, Jupiter and Venus in the second house opposing our south node. Abundance looked pretty far away in a prior life, probably. If we were chronically impoverished back then, we may actually need to experience some prosperity this time. But, back then, the very existence of the rich, the beautiful, and the powerful seemed to taunt us. Today we might find ourselves haunted by an old promise. "I'd *never* want to be rich! I am just not materialistic. Jesus said it is harder for the rich man to get into heaven than for the camel to get through the eye of the needle. I thank God every day that I am living a simple life!"

If true transcendence lies behind those words, there is no limiting karma involved. But we can see how easily such language could be animated by a resentment against people who are more materially fortunate. And if you had experienced true transcendence in the prior life . . . well, this issue would not be appearing in your nodal structure now.

Let's look briefly at each of the planets as they square or oppose the south node. In what follows, we will be considering the common ground between squares and oppositions, and only making distinctions where it seems pressingly appropriate.

The Sun in Hard Aspect to the South Node

The Affliction: Often personalizing the Sun provides an effective start here. In a prior life, you lost your own identity and momentum because you were pulled into the "orbit" of another individual. That person either had some compelling worldly power or authority, or was simply so charismatic as to be irresistible to you. From a less personal perspective, the Sun in this configuration could represent some overwhelmingly life-shaping circumstance that defined you—political or social revolutions, for example. Look to it house and sign to narrow it down.

What Was Left Unresolved: In the wake of such a lifetime, a soul is left rudderless, unable to generate vision or momentum on its own. There is a great vacuum where one's own ego should go. This can lead either to a "lost sheep syndrome," or to a compensatory compulsion to aggrandize the ego.

The Possible Projection: Hatred, rage or jealousy directed toward those who are in power or who get attention.

The Resolution: The positive development of ego. The single most poisonous statement we could make to a person with this configuration is that spirituality is equivalent to ego-loss. Instead, this soul requires the active development of the capacity to be self-directed, an individual, and at times even selfish—ego, in other words.

Examples:

Squares: Agatha Christie (Virgo; twelfth). Eric Clapton (Aries; sixth). Zelda Fitzgerald (Leo; twelfth). John Glenn (Cancer; eighth). Jimi Hendrix (Sagittarius; eleventh). Billie Holiday (Aries; second). Bill Wilson, cofounder of AA (Sagittarius; second). Isaac Newton (Capricorn; time uncertain). Luciano Pavarotti (Libra; third house).

Oppositions: Ram Dass (Aries; tenth). John Lennon (Libra; sixth). Annie Bessant (Libra; seventh). Jack Kevorkian (Gemini; birth time uncertain). Elizabeth Kubler-Ross (Cancer; fifth). Karl Marx (Taurus; second) Eleanor Roosevelt (Libra; tenth).

The Moon in Hard Aspect to the South Node

The Affliction: Personalizing the Moon, we might imagine family or, specifically, a mother having a challenging impact on you in a prior life. Perhaps you were utterly defined by your expected role within the clan. Perhaps you were smothered or over-protected. Perhaps you were overwhelmed by the requirements of parenthood. At a less personal level, think in terms of emotional storminess afflicting you, a storminess exacerbated by external situations symbolized by the house and sign the Moon occupies.

What Was Left Unresolved: There is a residual moodiness when the Moon is in this position. Typically, there is a vulnerability to being defined again by the needs of others with whom there are "clan ties"—and that might not mean literal family anymore.

The Possible Projection: An ambivalent, moody mixture of dependency and resentment against care givers.

The Resolution: An embracing of positive, committed familial experience, with respect for one's individuality and for people's natural differences. A willingness to nurture one's self.

Examples:

Squares: Mick Jagger (Taurus; twelfth). John Glenn (Capricorn; second). Barack Obama (Gemini; fourth house). Jim Morrison (Taurus; third). Gianni Versace (Pisces; fourth). Tennessee Williams (Aquarius; first). Clint Eastwood (Leo; ninth). Maximilian Robespierre (Aries; second house).

Oppositions: Tony Blair (Aquarius; tenth). Jean Auell, author of Clan of the Cave Bear *(Capricorn; fifth). "Son of Sam," mass murderer (Aquarius; third). Prince Charles (Taurus; tenth). Rush Limbaugh (Pisces; second). Charles Manson (Aquarius; tenth). Pablo Picasso (Sagittarius; fifth). Jim Jones (Aries; third house.) JonBenet Ramsey (Aquarius; time uncertain).*

Ascendant/Descendant in Hard Aspect to the South Node

The Affliction: The horizon axis in the birthchart can be best understood as one single symbol which embodies the polarity of self vs. other—trying to find the balance between the need to be true to one's self on the one hand, and on the other, to be caring and loving. With the nodes square this axis, a prior life inability to find this balance is the affliction. Which direction the see-saw was tilted can generally be ascertained easily by looking at the nature of the south node: does it appear selfish or does it appear self-sacrificial?

What Was Left Unresolved: Finding a proper balance between relationship and independence.

The Possible Projection: Exaggerated anger at people for being "too dependent" or "too selfish and unable to commit."

The Resolution: The establishment of relationships which allow breathing room within the context of commitment; the finding of partners who are truly one's equals.

Examples:
Squares: Felipe Calderon, president of Mexico (Scorpio rising). Ram Dass (Cancer rising). George Patton (Gemini rising). Julia Roberts (Cancer rising). Prince Charles (Leo rising).
Oppositions: Johnny Cash (Pisces rising). Bill Moyers (Aquarius rising) Marion Woodman (Sagittarius rising). Kitty Kelley (Virgo). Auguste Renoir (Aquarius). Nerine Shatner (William's wife) (Libra). Theodorus Van Gogh (Aries)

Meridian Axis in Hard Aspect to the South Node

The Affliction: The MC/IC axis can be best understood, like the Ascendant/Descendant, as one single integrated symbol. It represents the polarity of the outer world vs. the inner world. This manifests as the tension between the needs of one's public life and the needs of one's family. It includes the idea of the argument between public responsibility and the inward drive toward reflection, simplicity, privacy and self-care. With the nodes square this axis, in a prior life one was afflicted by this dilemma. To learn which side carried the most weight, consider the nature of the south node—in which direction does it point? Toward domesticity? Toward career or public responsibility?

What Was Left Unresolved: The need to establish a sustainable, mutually supportive balance between public and private life, between the inner world and public responsibility.

The Possible Projection: Anger and judgment aimed at those who are perceived to be "too ambitious" (power-hungry; status-conscious) or those who are perceived to be "too domestic" (tame; uncool; irrelevant)

The Resolution: The establishment of both meaningful career and a solid sense of "home."

Examples:
Squares: Johnny Cash (nodes square Sagittarius MC). Georgio Armani (nodes square Taurus MC)). Albert Camus (nodes square Gemini MC). Werner Heisenberg (nodes square Leo MC)). Diego Rivera ((nodes square Gemini MC).
Oppositions: Chelsea Clinton (MC in Leo). Carl Sagan (MC in Aquarius). Meryl Streep (MC in Aries). Italo Calvino (MC in Virgo). Coco Chanel

(MC in Libra). Francis Ford Coppola (MC in Scorpio). Eleanor Roosevelt (MC in Libra)

Mercury in Hard Aspect to the South Node

The Affliction: Being convincing and being correct are two entirely different things. Ask any trial lawyer. In a prior life, you were tied in knots by someone whom you perceived as being smarter than you, or more informed. Perhaps you were intimidated by that person's education. Maybe you were flat-out tricked: Mercury can be a con artist or a brilliant liar. This individual may have been a brother or a sister, with you getting the short end of the stick in a classic sibling rivalry. Less personally, your intentions in that life may be have been hampered by a lack of education. You felt voiceless.

What Was Left Unresolved: Doubts about your own intelligence and voice. This may manifest as intellectual inhibition or under-achievement. As easily, it can manifest as a compensatory obsession with erudition, "rightness," and intellectual authority.

The Possible Projection: Passionate criticism aimed either at "intellectuals" or at "stupid people."

The Resolution: Finding your true voice through dialog with teachers and intellectual peers.

Examples:

Squares: Zelda Fitzgerald (Leo; first). Jimi Hendrix (Sagittarius; eleventh). Thelonius Monk (Libra; fourth). Michael Moore (Aries, ninth). Richard Nixon (Capricorn; fourth). Malcolm X (Taurus; fourth). Carl Sagan (Scorpio; sixth). Maya Angelou (Pisces; eighth). Bob Dylan (Gemini; seventh). Carl Jung (Cancer; fifth house).

Oppositions: Edgar Cayce (Pisces; seventh). Mick Jagger (Leo; fourth). Thomas Merton (Aquarius; twelfth). Annie Bessant (Libra; seventh house). J. Pierpont Morgan (Aries; second house). Jacques Cousteau (Taurus; eighth house). Burt Bacharach (Gemini; third house).

Venus in Hard Aspect to the South Node

The Affliction: The course of love, needless to say, does not run reliably smooth. Love can cause us terrible pain—the pain of heartbreak, or unrequited longing, or separation, or impossibility. Just listen to a country and western radio station for a couple of hours, and you will get a good survey of the territory in the unlikely event that you need a refresher course. Something of that nature afflicted you in the prior life. Additionally, we should be sensitive to the idea of Venus representing creativity, grace, and art—which were somehow blocked or forbidden in the prior lifetime, or used to taunt you.

What Was Left Unresolved: A consuming, tragic-romantic sense of being incomplete without another person. A need for an experience of being beautiful, and known for one's creativity and elegance.

The Possible Projection: Towards those who are perceived as "lucky in love" or towards those who are perceived as desirable, either a judgmental "sour grapes" bitterness or a blindly one-dimensional kind of worshipfulness and longing. Anger at *"artistes"* or generally at sensitive, civilized people. Jealous anger at people who seem to be loved and integrated into a community of affection.

The Resolution: Actually making grown-up love work. Often this literally entails partnering successfully in the present life with the one for whom one pined in the prior life. Claiming one's creative voice.

Examples:

Squares: Miles Davis (Aries; eleventh). Meryl Streep (Cancer; twelfth). Maya Angelou (Pisces; eighth). Matt Dillon (Aries; second). J.K. Rowling (Virgo; no birth time as yet). Christine Jorgensen (Aries; tenth house). Jimmy Swaggart (Aries; fourth house). Carl Jung (Cancer; sixth house). Oppositions: Edgar Cayce (Pisces; eighth). The 17th Karmapa (Taurus; eleventh, if the birth time is accurate). Duke Ellington (Aries; second). Timothy McVeigh (Aries; eleventh). John Wayne Bobbitt (Taurus; eleventh house). Connie Francis (Sagittarius; twelfth house). Whoopi Goldberg (Sagittarius; tenth house). Marcello Mastroianni (Leo; eighth house). Trent Reznor (Gemini; fifth house).

Mars in Hard Aspect to the South Node

The Affliction: Violence, in a nutshell. To be killed or hurt or maimed, or even to be manipulated by the threat of those things, leaves a deep gash in the soul. Violence is not necessarily physical, although often that is the simplest notion with which to start under these conditions. Verbal abuse, derision, and shaming leave their marks too. And remember, in real life, the good guys don't always win.

What Was Left Unresolved: Rage. Terrible fear. Feelings of powerlessness. Resentment.

The Possible Projection: A paradoxical feeling "that all violent people should be taken out and shot." Fear of strength. Fear of anger. Fear of being noticed.

The Resolution: To resolve this square, the individual must experience his or her own power and courage. Physical adventure is very helpful. So are relationships in which it is all right to be angry. Martial arts or weapons training can be helpful. Confidence in the inner warrior must be restored. There is not an evolutionary need to experience violence, but there is a need to experience a sense of being capable of self-defense—a sense of being "dangerous if crossed."

Examples:

Squares: John Glenn (Cancer; eighth). Ernest Hemingway (Virgo; first). Mick Jagger (Taurus; twelfth). Kenny Kirkland (Virgo; twelfth). The Dalai Lama (Libra; fourth). Jackie Robinson (Pisces; seventh). Tennessee Williams (Aquarius; first). Al Gore (Leo; first). JonBenet Ramsey (Taurus; birth time uncertain). Jimmy Swaggart (Aries; fourth house). Baghwan Shri Rajneesh (Capricorn; seventh house). Trent Reznor (Virgo; eighth house).

Oppositions: Albert Einstein (Capricorn; seventh). Jerry Garcia (Virgo; eleventh). William Bligh (Libra; third). Clint Eastwood (Aries; sixth). Hank Williams (Virgo; second house). Garrison Keillor (Virgo; first house).

Jupiter in Hard Aspect to the South Node

The Affliction: Jupiter is the King of the Gods, and it may simply represent some figure of superior authority who gave you trouble in a prior life. "You can't fight city hall." At a less personal level, abundance, charisma, "star power," prosperity, fame, position—the human ego naturally hungers for them all. Seeing others get them while we do not is a Jupiter affliction.

And, if the south node story suggests privilege and position, then attachment to soul-cages such as addictive conditions may be the issue.

What Was Left Unresolved: Craving for fame, money, or power. Craving to be noticed, to be taken seriously.

The Possible Projection: Jealousy, sometimes thinly disguised as judgmental resentment, toward people in enviable positions. "Get Rich Quick" fantasies. Obsession with the glamourous or with the "rich and famous."

The Resolution: There is a need actually to attain some kind of meaningful success, and to be noticed and applauded for it. Typically, this must be achieved through some risk-it-all act of faith.

Examples:

Squares: Ram Dass (Cancer; first). The 17ᵗʰ Karmapa (Aquarius; ninth, if birth time is accurate). Richard Nixon (Capricorn; fourth). Vladimir Putin (Taurus; seventh). Carl Sagan (Scorpio; sixth). Christopher Reeve (Taurus; fourth house). Jim Jones (Cancer; seventh house). Anne Rice (Gemini; time uncertain).

Oppositions: Zelda Fitzgerald (Sagittarius; fifth). Frida Kahlo (Cancer; eleventh). Madonna (Libra; second). Thomas Merton (Aquarius; twelfth). George Patton (Virgo; fourth). Trent Reznor (Gemini; fifth house).

Saturn in Hard Aspect to the South Node

The Affliction: Hard, practical limits are Saturn's territory. There is no money in the bank. The ship is sinking and we are two hundred miles from shore. We are freezing in bitter cold. There is no food. The General is insane, but we will be shot if we disobey. Any of these might be indicated by a hard aspect of Saturn to the south node. So could the endless grind of inescapable duty. Throughout history, human beings have risen to incredible challenges of endless endurance. That is all in the domain of Saturn.

What Was Left Unresolved: A stoical feeling of futility or impossibility. A kind of unconscious depression. Time-serving self-sacrifice.

The Possible Projection: Onto the canvas of the universe, such a person might project a sense of indifference or even active hostility. Authority may be assumed to be uncaring or unresponsive.

The Resolution: Great works. Earned success. The successful negotiation of vast and daunting challenges. Carrying through to the top of the mountain, to the end of the novel you are writing, to the altar.

Examples:

Squares: Ernest Shackleton (Aquarius; no birth time). Malcolm X (Scorpio; tenth house). Machiavelli (Taurus; third). Ram Dass (Capricorn; seventh house). Stephen King (Leo; second). Paul McCartney (Gemini; ninth). Pol Pot (Scorpio, no birth time). J.K. Rowling (Pisces; no birth time). Al Gore (Leo; first house). Louis Pasteur (Taurus; eighth house). Garrison Keillor (Gemini; tenth house).

Oppositions: Timothy McVeigh (Aries; eleventh). William Butler Yeats (Libra; eighth). Humphrey Bogart (Sagittarius; eighth - birth time suspect). Edgar Cayce (Pisces; seventh).

Uranus in Hard Aspect to the South Node

The Affliction: "Earthquakes and lightning bolts" are good Uranian metaphors. They represent anything that hits hard and suddenly, and which utterly changes the landscape. In a prior life, you were struck by shock. Out of the blue, the economy collapsed, you were crippled, your mate fled, the revolution occurred, the killers struck. You may have been vexed or overcome by someone operating outside the law or outside the bounds of the social contract. Perhaps you were abandoned.

What Was Left Unresolved: You were left in a gaping state of wide-eyed shock; a state of dissociation. You "went away;" you did not cry. You did not do the healing process. Quite possibly, you did not have time—sudden death is a distinct possibility.

The Possible Projection: A state of hyper-vigilance that often entails projecting onto situations an anxious sense of instability or the fear that everything will spin out of control. A discomfort with people who are perceived as chaos-bringers: criminals, trouble-makes, outsiders, abandoners.

The Resolution: Further individuation, which implies the attainment of a self-sufficient feeling that one's identity is not dependent on any outward social or practical circumstances.

Examples:

Squares: Catherine the Great (Scorpio; eighth). Jerry Garcia (Gemini; eighth). Jimi Hendrix (Gemini; fifth). Adolph Hitler (Libra; twelfth). Paul McCartney (Gemini; ninth). Chelsea Clinton (Scorpio; first). Pablo Picasso (Virgo; second). J.K. Rowling (Virgo; no birth time). Joseph Campbell (Sagittarius; third house). Rev. Jimmy Swaggart (Aries; fourth house). Garrison Keillor (Gemini; tenth house). Leonard Cohen (Taurus; eighth house).
Oppositions: Princess Diana (Leo; eighth). Gianni Versace (Gemini; seventh). George W. Bush (Gemini; eleventh). Bill Clinton (Gemini; ninth). Ram Dass (Aries; tenth). Zelda Fitzgerald (Sagittarius; fourth). Billie Holiday (Aquarius; first). Billy Strayhorn (Aquarius; third). Deepak Chopra (Gemini; fourth house). Jim Jones (Aries; third house). Stephen Spielberg (Gemini; twelfth house). Charles Darwin (Scorpio; birth time uncertain). Edith Piaf (Aquarius; third house). Barack Obama (Leo; seventh house).

Neptune in Hard Aspect to the South Node

The Affliction: Utopian idealism can sweep us into situations where the bottom falls out as soon as reality hits. This may manifest as a prior-life identification with some collective social or spiritual dream which hurt you. If the Neptune symbolism is more personal, it could indicate an ungrounded romantic belief in some person, one who ultimately proved less worthy than anticipated. Intense spiritual practice, especially those practices that emphasize egolessness and self-sacrifice, can move a person too far too fast, just like psychedelic drugs. Finally, there are the age-old soul-traps of narcotics, alcohol and so forth—this can mean any substance, whether it is illegal or socially acceptable, that blurs our access to the material we have been born to work on. These kinds of addictions and dependencies in a prior life may also be indicated by hard Neptune aspects.
What Was Left Unresolved: A "blurred" state in the ego-function, leaving the soul wide-open to dangerous influences in the present, and a general loss of momentum, focus, and vision.
The Possible Projection: Longing after external factors that promise to bring meaning and magic into the life—spiritual teachers, "answers" and belief-systems. A little too much faith in the idea that at any moment now

Elvis will come around in the UFO, change our DNA, and restore the earth to a state of peace, love, and understanding.

The Resolution: A need to enter into a right and healthy relationship with some kind of spiritual practice. Such practice may look "religious," but as easily it could involve harnessing creativity. Visionary experiences, independent of outside circumstances and observers, resolve the blockage.

Examples:

Squares: Albert Einstein (Taurus; eleventh). Felipe Calderon, president of Mexico (Scorpio; first). Ernest Hemingway (Gemini; tenth). Michael Moore (Libra; third). Bill Wilson, cofounder of Alcoholics Anonymous (Gemini; ninth house). Oprah Winfrey (Libra; tenth). Timothy Leary (Leo; eighth house).

Oppositions: Lauren Bacall (Leo; second house). Martha Stewart (Virgo; eleventh). Bob Dylan (Virgo; ninth). Linda McCartney (Virgo; eleventh). William Blake (Leo; second house). Anne Rice (Virgo; birth time uncertain).

Pluto in Hard Aspect to the South Node

The Affliction: "Nightmare" is a useful word when Pluto lies in hard aspect to the south node. Life is full of truly terrible possibilities: grueling, painful diseases, sadistic violence, accidents we can barely stand to contemplate, the evil acts of lost souls. Fortunately, most of us never experience them. But some of us do—and if you had such an experience in a prior life, it may very well show up as this kind of Pluto aspect in the present chart. You were touched by one of two realities: either catastrophe or flat-out evil. The word "victim" bothers some people; if ever there would be a use for the term, it would be here.

What Was Left Unresolved: Repressed memories. Faced with extremity, humans have the capacity to drive the experience into the unconscious. With prior lives, we may never remember the exact reality—but there exists in us a fear or a rage or perhaps a morbidity that afflicts our mental equilibrium in this life.

The Possible Projection: Paranoia about schemers or looming catastrophes can be projected onto innocent fabric, as if demons were afoot. This can lead to a generalized feeling of mistrust, or even one of doom.

The Resolution: There is a need to do a deep Plutonian journey into the dark. Some might take a page from the shamanic traditions and call it soul-recovery. Others might call it psychotherapy, if the work is deep enough. A critical point is that, given the difficulty of directly recalling a specific prior lifetime, it is *sufficient to contact the repressed emotions* even if we cannot understand their source—fear, rage, shame, grief. Past-life regressive techniques, such as those pioneered by Roger Woolger among others, can be very productive.

Examples:

Squares: Tina Turner (Leo; twelfth). Ram Dass (Cancer; first). Monica Lewinsky (Libra; twelfth). Diego Rivera (Gemini; tenth). Bill Wilson, cofounder of AA (Gemini; eighth). J.K. Rowling (Virgo; no birth time). Al Gore (Leo; first house). Jim Jones (Cancer; seventh house).

Oppositions: Christine Jorgensen, the first transsexual (Cancer; twelfth). Miles Davis (Cancer; second). John Coltrane (Cancer; fifth). Jim Morrison (Leo; sixth). Robert Bly (Cancer; seventh). Marilyn Monroe (Cancer; eleventh). Allen Ginsberg (Cancer; fourth house—node on cusp of fifth).

CHAPTER ELEVEN:
PLANETS IN SOFT ASPECT TO THE SOUTH NODE

Astrologers have long recognized that angles of 60 or 120 degrees between planets suggest harmony. There has been an unfortunate tendency to oversimplify that basic truth by equating harmony with "good." Two young guys with a hot new car might be in perfect harmony in their decision to "see how fast we can take Dead Man's Curve." Perhaps that's how the curve earned its name.

Harmony just means harmony. We can be harmonious in folly, in laziness, or in violence. And of course we can be harmonious in friendship and support as well. In working with trines and sextiles to the Moon's south node, it is helpful to be alert to all the possibilities. In common with all the other aspects to the lunar nodes, we also recognize that the darker interpretations are often the more productive ones. Here, as elsewhere, our karma as it emerges from the symbolism generally contains elements of issues left unresolved and of wounds still bleeding. Attending mindfully to the negative is the soul of our ultimately positive strategy of healing, even with the so-called "good" aspects.

Essentially, the soft aspects operate in one or both of two ways:

Soft aspects to the lunar nodes represent people, talents or circumstances that offered us comfort or solace in a time of trial. We carry an unresolved sense of affection, dependency, or indebtedness toward them.

Soft aspects to the lunar nodes represent people or circumstances that "helped" us get into trouble. They are the temptations we did not resist.

In my own practice, I concentrate primarily on the conjunctions, squares and oppositions. They tell the more dynamic part of the story, with the softer aspects filling in some details. Generally I will be most inclined to use the soft ones in the absence of harder aspects—when I am having to "squeeze" the chart a little harder to get a tale out of it!

One important variation on that situation occurs when there are no hard aspects to the nodes at all, but quite an array of trines and sextiles. Then the message is basically that things were *too easy* in the prior life. Just imagine a pampered rich "kid" of forty who has never had to lift a finger for anything. It is not hard to imagine the karmic results of adapting, like a perfect sybarite, to a completely unchallenging reality devoid of inspiration, edge, or consequences. In a subsequent lifetime, that kind of karma could easily be symbolized by a preponderance of soft aspects to the nodes.

The Sun in Soft Aspect to the South Node

As a person one once knew, the Sun always represents an authoritative individual who wielded great power and influence in your life. With the soft aspects, such a person was in a benign relationship to you—or at least that would have been the appearance. Certainly your basic decisions were made for you. Probably you did not object. You were shepherded.

As a set of circumstances, the Sun represents an overwhelming force to which you must adapt, abandoning all other concerns. Economic cycles, mass movements—anything whose "gravity" is irresistible. In this case, there was some benefit to you from the developments. They carried you along.

The unresolved attachment is a vulnerability to moving sheep-like into dependency upon external, charismatic, compelling influences, losing one's own center. The fascination with the "other" can eclipse one's own soul, one's own values, and one's own creativity. The treasure of freedom can be surrendered without a whimper or a twinge.

The implicit strength is that we have been schooled by powerful role models in charisma and leadership.

The higher ground lies in avoiding the comforting temptations of being a follower, and in claiming leadership—at least the "leadership" of one's own life.

Examples. Bill Moyers (Gemini; fourth house). Franklin Delano Roosevelt (Aquarius; fifth house). Jackie Robinson (Aquarius; sixth house). Stephen King (Virgo; third house). Martin Luther King (Capricorn; ninth house).

The Moon in Soft Aspect to the South Node

As a person one once knew, most simply the Moon can refer to the mother, literally. More generally, the Moon symbolizes anyone who played a nurturing role toward you in a prior life. The subjective feeling here is one of great gentleness and presumably of genuine love. And yet we must also wrestle with the weakening impact of overprotection and coddling, and with the unintentional cultivation of unnatural levels of dependency. To love someone is to give away power and autonomy—not always a bad thing, obviously. But here, the little bird stayed too long in the nest.

As a set of circumstances, the Moon most often refers to family or clan. Even today, these are monumental influences on our lives. Historically, they were even more so. With the soft aspects, we are not faced with bitter, dysfunctional prior life family dynamics—only with the blurring of individuality that is inherent in loving one's "people" unquestioningly and never doubting the rightness of the role we are expected to play. With this aspect, we must also consider the idea of the person having been weakened in a prior life as a result of the kind of "nurture" and "support" that makes us flaccid and hyper-reactive to pain.

The unresolved attachment is a vulnerability to one's own natural path through life being subsumed by the needs and expectations of others toward whom we feel devotion and affection—by "family," however we might define it. Possibly, there is an issue around self-indulgence or escapism relative to adult realities.

The implicit strength is that we have been schooled by powerful role models in "parental" behavior and sensitivity.

The higher ground lies in claiming a certain hard-headed quality relative to the need to set boundaries, to claim autonomy and freedom, and to walk away from inappropriate or excessive expectations and demands.

Examples. John Lennon (Aquarius; eleventh house). His Holiness the Dalai Lama (Virgo; third house). Jazz pianist Kenny Kirkland (Aquarius; fifth house). Edith Piaf (Gemini; seventh house). Monica Lewinsky (Taurus; seventh house). George Patton (Capricorn; eighth house). Julia Roberts (Leo; second house).

Mercury in Soft Aspect to the South Node

As a person one once knew, Mercury can represent a teacher or a student with whom you had a harmonious connection in a prior life—although immediately we must realize that you probably parroted the teacher or became enamored with the process of mesmerizing the student! The cognitive, even academic world of conceptual understanding can be seductive; we can mistake knowledge for wisdom—and that is another trap here. Mercury may also represent a good friend with whom pivotal conversations took place—again with the same caveats. Similarly, it can symbolize a beloved sibling in a prior life.

As a set of circumstances, Mercury stands for any situation or institution where knowledge is disseminated. It can represent books, quite literally—and reflect for a moment on how many human beings have comforted and distracted themselves with literature over the centuries, even perhaps when their worlds were falling apart. Although the history is shorter, we can say the same for media in general. Mercury can symbolize any situation characterized by extreme busyness, distraction and rapid change.

The unresolved attachment is a vulnerability to random fascination. Conversations, teachers, entertainment, media—these can glisten appealingly, but ultimately lead us away from our deeper priorities.

The implicit strength is that we have been schooled by powerful role models in terms of rigorous thought and communication skills.

The higher ground lies in drawing the attention inward toward the soul's still, small voice, and following its dictates.

Examples. Miles Davis (Taurus; twelfth house). Albert Einstein (Aries; tenth house). Bill Gates (Libra; fourth house). Martha Stewart (Cancer; ninth house). Tiger Woods (Capricorn; fifth house). Jean Luc Godard (Sagittarius; third house). L. Ron Hubbard (Pisces; third house). David Koresh (Leo; eleventh house).

Venus in Soft Aspect to the South Node

As a person one once knew, Venus represents the beloved. The love may be romantic or it might simply be the sweet affection of friendship. In soft aspect to the lunar south node, this other person emerges in a comforting, soothing light. If there was seduction in any sense of the word, it was one of those seductions without exploitation or malice aforethought. Inevitably, when we see someone as an embodiment of Venusian qualities, we turn a blind eye toward his or her faults. This can simply be the kindness and generosity of friendship, but it can also correlate with a gradual disillusionment—a good relationship with a decent person, which simply runs out of gas.

If the general tone of the nodal story suggests art or creativity, then Venus may represent a creative partner or an artistic influence.

As a set of circumstances, Venus suggests an environment of grace. Courtesy and propriety are themes, and probably comfort. Generally this correlates with comfortable material circumstances, and a general air of elegance. It can be vitiating and soporific. It can represent an environment that supports vanity and triviality.

The unresolved attachment is a kind of romantic and aesthetic idealism to which reality can never quite live up.

The higher ground lies in committing to the funky, difficult work of creating true intimacy—expecting difficulty there and not interpreting the difficulty as anything worse the normal, honest reality of being close to another flawed human being. There is often a hunger to achieve artistic and creative independence, to be more "raw" and direct in self-expression, and less mannered.

The implicit strength is that we have been schooled by powerful role models in relationship-building, "public relations," diplomacy, and perhaps in the arts.

Examples. Jerry Garcia (Cancer; ninth house). Adolph Hitler (Taurus; seventh house). Thomas Merton (Sagittarius; ninth house). Michael Moore (Taurus; tenth house). Franklin Delano Roosevelt (Aquarius; fifth house). Barack Obama (Cancer; fifth house). Arnold Schwarzeneggar (Cancer; first house). Georgia O'Keeffe (Libra; birth time uncertain). Sue Grafton (Gemini; third house). Ludwig von Beethoven (Capricorn; birth time uncertain).

Mars in Soft Aspect to the South Node

As a person one once knew, with the soft aspects it is not really appropriate to think of Mars straightforwardly as an enemy, although there may be elements of friendly rivalry and competition. Imagine your "worthy opponent" in chess or tennis or any other kind of contest. Or simply consider Mars as representing a comrade—someone who was *on your side* in a win/lose situation. The most obvious imagery here is that of warfare, and of the bonds of life-and-death loyalty that might be forged between people sharing that unfortunate situation.

As a set of circumstances, Mars always suggests stress and the flow of adrenalin. With the softer aspects, there is a certain thrill as well—giddy emotions of victory, the sheer energy of vented rage, the consummation and release of sexual passion.

The unresolved attachment is to an unnaturally hyped perspective on what life has to offer. Adrenalin—and drama—can be addictive.

The implicit strength is that we have been schooled by powerful role models in courage and the force of the will. We know how to pay the enormous energetic price that true excellence demands.

The higher ground lies in integrating a steady reservoir of available courage and vigor without needing constantly to test it and experience it.

Examples. Oprah Winfrey (Scorpio; eleventh house). Christine Jorgensen (Pisces; ninth house).

Janis Joplin (Sagittarius; tenth house). Adolph Hitler (Taurus; seventh house). Bill Gates (Libra; fourth house). F. Scott Fitzgerald (Gemini; fifth house). Miles Davis (Pisces; eleventh house). Sue Grafton (Gemini; third house).

Jupiter in Soft Aspect to the South Node

As a person one once knew, Jupiter can represent someone you knew in a prior lifetime who was in a position of authority, or anyone whom you perceived as being of a higher status than yourself. In the gentle aspects, there was probably affection in you toward this individual—a genuinely beloved king or bishop or boss, for example. Presumably the affection was reciprocated as well. There may in fact have been generosity directed from this person toward you. He or she may have been a patron. There is a leftover element of feeling drab and dull in comparison—the same way that modern middle-of-the-road people often feel flat in comparison to Hollywood luminaries.

As a set of circumstances, Jupiter symbolizes abundance in every sense: money, power, luxury, life governed by well-fed appetites. The soft aspects suggest that these elements of "living large" were embraced with gusto—and that "coming back down to earth" might now feel like a balloon deflating. As Freud said, "the libido never forgets a pleasure." Scaling up is easy; scaling down is hard.

The unresolved attachments are to a karmic history of things being easy, to a kind of benign ego-inflation that comes with privilege, and perhaps to excessive appetites in general.

The implicit strength is that we have been schooled by powerful role models in self-confidence and a sense of our own worth. Success feels natural and expected rather than exotic and unattainable.

The higher ground lies in a determination to sustain effort and focus in the face of insults, misunderstanding, and resistance. Success that does not come quickly is still attainable, and often sweeter than the lazy victory forged half by privilege and luck.

Examples. Jerry Garcia (Cancer; ninth house). Paul McCartney (Cancer; tenth house). Duke Ellington (Scorpio; ninth house). Douglas Fairbanks Jr. (Libra; ninth house). Timothy Leary (Virgo; ninth house). Garrison Keillor (Cancer; eleventh house).

Saturn in Soft Aspect to the South Node

As a person one once knew, Saturn often simply represents the father in a prior life. We all have one, and it is far from unusual for the relationship with him to be complicated and unresolved. The controlling and protective qualities of Saturn must be understood in the gentler form here—while you may have been stultified by your father in a prior lifetime, with the trine or the sextile you probably found the relationship comfortable. The strictures felt safe. Extending beyond taking Saturn literally as the father, we see it as any figure of august authority, typically somewhat distant emotionally, but always reliable. In spiritual contexts, it could represent a guru or master teacher.

As a set of circumstances, Saturn implies difficulty, shortage, limitation, and "making do." With the softer aspects, we must temper any overly harsh reading of these conditions. In the prior life, you found such limits acceptable or even comforting. Why might the working class kid refuse the scholarship to the Ivy League college and instead join his or her friends in going to the state school? Why is being released from prison so disorienting that many prisoners wind up back behind bars within a year or two? Limitation can feel comfortable and unthreatening.

The unresolved attachment is an adaptation to limitation. There can be a peculiar kind of unconscious or unwitting depression underlying one's attitudes—a kind of pessimism masquerading as uncomplaining realism.

The implicit strength is that we have been schooled by powerful role models in endurance, patience, and humility.

The higher ground lies in harnessing that Saturn energy to pull the chariot of greater, more ambitious and expansive dreams.

Examples. Christopher Reeve (Libra; ninth house). Deepak Chopra (Leo; sixth house). Gianni Versace (Leo; ninth house). Madonna (Sagittarius; fourth house). Frieda Kahlo (Pisces; eighth house.). Albert Einstein (Aries; tenth house). Miles Davis (Scorpio; sixth house).

Uranus in Soft Aspect to the South Node

As a person one once knew, Uranus represents what mom used to call a "bad influence." And maybe mom was right—although we must also be sensitive to the idea of this aspect indicating someone who supports us in a helpful, liberating process of questioning authority or stepping outside the box of our social conditioning. The attraction to the "outlaw" and the freedom he or she represented, even if it led down a slippery slope, was voluntary and enthusiastic.

As a set of circumstances, Uranus symbolizes "revolution" in any possible sense of the word. Things change, sometimes explosively and precipitously, and it is "an ill wind that blows no one good." In a prior life, the dam broke somehow. The social order unraveled. You saw your main chance and grabbed it.

The unresolved attachment is to "the wild side." There can be a vulnerability to get-rich-quick thinking, to cutting corners. There is a general impatience with the normal slow pace of most human events and developments.

The implicit strength is that we have been schooled by powerful role models in sheer genius—these are the "outlaws" in the best sense of the word, the ones who allow the world to change by changing our basic assumptions about it.

The higher ground lies in committing to honesty, authenticity and integrity in all you undertake. There is a focus on the *substance* of genius rather than upon its appearance.

Examples. Pedro Almodovar (Cancer; first house). Matt Dillon (Virgo; seventh house). Bob Dylan (Taurus; fifth house). Georgia O'Keeffe (Libra; birth time unknown). Dane Rudhyar (Scorpio; eleventh house). William Butler Yeats (Gemini; fifth house). Martin Luther (Sagittarius; fourth house). Maximilian Robespierre (Pisces, first house).

Neptune in Soft Aspect to the South Node

As a person one once knew, Neptune represents someone who is not living in normal relationship to the human ego. At the low end, this can be anyone given to escapism: drunkenness, addiction, and all the "transcendent" irresponsibilities they typically create. At the high end, it can symbolize an authentic mystic or spiritual teacher. In the middle ground, such a Neptune can describe a creative person, a visionary, a fellow idealist, a spiritual friend. Always, there is a theme of an attractive surreality, with the potential of ungroundedness.

As a set of circumstances, Neptune correlates with uplifting, inspiring, but not necessarily grounded belief-systems, movements, or situations. Glamour is generally present in abundance, and with it, illusion—and disillusionment. It can indicate a *Zeitgeist* of wantonness, escape, and pleasure-seeking, such as England just before Cromwell or the late 1960s in North America and Europe.

The unresolved attachment is to preferring life in another world, one full of magic and instant gratification, even at the price of illusion and self-destruction.

The implicit strength is that we have been schooled by powerful role models in creativity, psychic sensitivity, and idealism. We may have had contact with genuine spiritual luminaries.

The higher ground lies in focusing and grounding this inspiration with daily spiritual and creative discipline. The mind has become inspired but unstable in its resolve. One-pointed discipline is essential.

Examples. F. Scott Fitzgerald (Gemini; fifth house). Stephen Spielberg (Libra; fourth house). Christopher Reeves (Libra; ninth house). Bill Gates (Libra; fourth house). Kenny Kirkland (Libra; second house). George Patton (Taurus; twelfth house). Mother Theresa (Cancer; birth time unknown).

Pluto in Soft Aspect to the South Node

As a person one once knew, in harmonious aspect Pluto can represent someone who holds our secrets—a confidant or a counselor. It can be someone with whom we shared an extreme experience—a fellow survivor, a comrade, or a co-defendant. It can represent the person who sold us the gun or the drugs or the sex we wanted. Such a person is both scary and attractive; we meet at night; we think of them more by moonlight—or street-light—than by sunlight.

As a set of circumstances, Pluto generally represents anything nightmarish and frightening. With the softer aspects, we must temper that fact with one more: we humans love the feeling of aliveness that comes with taboo territory. Think of the subject matter of the movies that earn billions of dollars: violence, edgy sex, vengeance . . .

The unresolved attachment is to the thrill of extremity and of breaking taboo.

The implicit strength is that we have been schooled by powerful role models and experiences in terms of material that is typically repressed and denied. As William Blake famously put it, "The Road of Excess leads to the Palace of Wisdom."

The higher ground lies in breaking the fascination of personal involvement in these extreme passions, and concentrating on passing on the gifts of compassion and understanding they generate to others. The higher ground is simply the road of *informed compassion.*

Examples. Tom Waits (Leo; eighth house). Henry David Thoreau (Pisces; no birth time). Stephen Spielberg (Leo; second house). John Lennon (Leo; fifth house). F. Scott Fitzgerald (Gemini; fifth house). Gianni Versace (Leo;

ninth house). Frank Zappa (Leo; no birth time). Deepak Chopra (Leo; sixth house).

Ascendant/Descendant in Soft Aspect to the South Node

As a person, the Ascendant/Descendant axis is typically not relevant. It does not have a "personality" in the same way that a planet does, and so it tends to function more circumstantially and psychologically.

As a set of circumstances, the Ascendant/Descendant axis suggests unresolved karma in connection with the question of finding the right balance point between taking and giving, between necessary selfishness and generosity. Since the aspect here is harmonious, it is a strong indicator that whatever form this imbalance took, we were not challenged or confronted about it. If the rest of the nodal story suggests selfishness, then we "got away with" too much insensitivity. If the nodal story suggests giving and self-sacrifice, it was excessive—and expected of us by a demanding partner to whom we bowed down.

The unresolved attachment is a tendency to give either too much or too little, according to the logic we described above.

The implicit strength is that we have been schooled by powerful role models in giving or taking—again in accord with the logic we described under "circumstances."

The higher ground lies in learning to feel our way sensitively through the paradoxes of being loving toward ourselves while also being loving toward others.

Examples. Paramahansa Yogananda (Ascendant: Virgo). Francis Ford Coppola (Ascendant: Capricorn). Salvador Dali (Ascendant: Cancer). Hugh Hefner (Ascendant: Virgo). Stephen King (Ascendant: Cancer).

Meridian Axis in Soft Aspect to the South Node

As a person, the Midheaven/IC axis does not have a "personality" in the same way that a planet does, and so it tends to function more circumstantially and psychologically. We can personalize it somewhat as the "face" of the world and public opinion (Midheaven) and the consensus of our family or tribal group (IC).

As a set of circumstances, the Meridian axis suggests unresolved karma regarding the balancing of home life versus career, personal versus public responsibility, the joy of family-life versus the satisfactions of meaningful work in the world. Since the aspect here is harmonious, it is a strong indicator that whatever prior-life form this imbalance took, we were not challenged or confronted about it. If the rest of the nodal story suggests family or relationship themes, we probably sacrificed career. If the rest of the nodal story is more public and mission-oriented, then we turned our back on family. In either case, we were not called to account for it.

The unresolved attachment is a vulnerability to giving up career or to sacrificing family, according to the logic we just described.

The implicit strength is that we have been schooled by powerful role models in terms of building a healthy family foundation or in terms of building position in the world, again according to the logic we described above.

The higher ground lies in finding a balance between, on one hand, the ancient human need for roots and a place we can call home regardless of our worldly fortunes, and on the other hand, the need for the kind of meaningfulness that enters our lives when we feel we are serving the larger good of our community and culture.

Examples. Martin Luther King (Midheaven: Capricorn). Thomas Merton (Midheaven: Sagittarius). Peter Sellers (Midheaven: Gemini). Dan Rather (Midheaven: Aquarius). Muhammed Ali (Midheaven: Taurus). Pablo Casals (Midheaven: Taurus). Isadora Duncan (Midheaven: Capricorn).

CHAPTER TWELVE: THE RIGHT ATTITUDE

Astrology is both a science and an art. As a science, it is based on the observation of patterns in human life and their correlation with astronomical configurations. As an art, it is spontaneous and gentle, always aimed at flowering into healing.

Much of what we have explored so far can be understood as science—and, like all science, you can check it out for yourself, see if it works. Our hypothesis is clear and simple: *the prior-life stories that emerge through the analytic techniques we have been exploring leave their fingerprints on the present lifetime*. You might not be able to go back to the past and verify your previous incarnations directly in an absolutely scientific sense, but you certainly know the realities of your current experience. Observe them—and correlate the observations with your nodal story. If they mesh, you have your proof. The relevance of Evolutionary Astrology to your life does not require any particular leap of faith. You do not even necessarily need to believe in reincarnation. You only need to observe objectively the phenomena of your life and compare them with the predictions.

Those observations can be dispiriting. Potentially, they can be devastating. Imagine telling someone that it looks like he or she was once a Nazi prison guard, or a rapist, or a torturer in the Spanish Inquisition. Metaphors that are consistent with those kinds of past-life realities can easily be generated by astrological symbolism. In fact, the power of the astrological symbolism is such that it can represent literally any conceivable human condition, including the most horrific ones. Were it otherwise, astrology would have too limited a vocabulary to be useful.

A story went around the Evolutionary Astrology community a few years ago. A new student who was bright and diligent was talking about a consultation he had done for a woman. He obviously hadn't liked her very much. And he spoke of how he had "nailed" her with his X-ray of her inner condition. I suspect his analysis of the woman's issues had been accurate—these techniques are extremely powerful, and not so hard to learn. But like any tool, they are no wiser than the person using them. Other students challenged this young man on his use of the word "nailed." Good for them! Is "nailing" people our motivation? We have to be so careful of letting the ego get its grips on us in this work. It feels good to be "right," of course. We all enjoy it. But that natural desire to be correct—not intrinsically such a bad thing—needs to be allied with the compassionate desire to assist people, to make a positive difference in their lives.

I got in a little trouble with one of my students once. A name had been drawn out of a hat and I was doing an analysis in front of a class. The reading was for a woman with Pluto conjunct her south node—often an indicator that a person had become enmeshed in some kind of darkness in a prior life, typically as a result of their own choices. In the analysis I presented, I emphasized her rightness of intention in the prior life. I soft-pedaled the damage she had done, even though in this particular case it had probably entailed her ordering the death of another human being.

Later, I was taken to task for being too soft on her, but I do not regret my choice. Relatively few people intend actively to do evil, although there is obviously no shortage of evil in the world. If I steal to feed my children, I am still stealing. But I am probably thinking of their hunger rather than gloating over the futile anger of the person I am robbing. Even Nazi prison guards, rapists, or a torturers in the Spanish Inquisition mostly either believed in the ultimate good of what they are doing or at least came up with rationalizations for it.

The underlying point is that heaping guilt and shame on people rarely helps them. No one has ever been assisted by being "nailed." What we do is to enter the subjective reality of the person back in his or her prior life, and indicate as compassionately as we can the consequences of those actions. We try to leave the person's dignity as intact as possible, and encourage him or her to feel *deserving* of further evolutionary growth.

What I am saying is that, in my opinion, going from conventional psychological astrology to Evolutionary Astrology is like switching from broadswords to tactical nukes. Temper your enthusiasm for the hardware with a little diplomacy!

A Word About Language

In much of what follows, we will equate the notion of one's "karmic pattern"as revealed in these techniques with terms such as "the south node" or "the nodal pattern." Those terms are shorthand for the larger, integrated matrix of symbolism we have been exploring throughout this book. In other words, it is a lot more complicated than just the south node! The south node is only the gateway into the labyrinth. To work exclusively with it would be similar to trying to explain people's psychology on the sole basis of their gender. When we say "the south node" or "the nodal pattern" we are really referring not only to the south node, but also to its planetary ruler, its aspects, its polar relationship with the north node, and so on.

Perfection here would be nothing less than a complete and integrated understanding of *all* the present chart symbolism in the light of its origin in prior lifetimes—looking at all the planets that way, even the ones that do not connect directly with the lunar nodes, as we did in Chapter One. In short, nothing in the present chart has an independent or random origin. That whole territory is what we are exploring.

Accepting the Inevitability of the South Node

If your sister gives up smoking on Tuesday, you would not be surprised if she is really longing to light up again by Thursday. If she expresses bad feelings about herself because of that desire, we naturally comfort her. We say, "Have you smoked any cigarettes since Tuesday?" If she says, "About four hundred—in my imagination, " we congratulate her on her success. And we are sincere. Habits are hard to break; she is actually doing quite well. Even if she slips and smokes a cigarette on Saturday night, we encourage her to keep on trying to quit. There is no shame in failure, so long as she does not give up. Sunday is the first day of the rest of her life.

After a while, her desire for cigarettes will probably fall away, but that is not likely to happen quickly or easily. We all understand this, so without any effort compassion arises toward such a person. This territory is well-mapped. Humans have been navigating it for countless thousands of years. Bad habits have a long history.

Karmic patterns are far more deep-seated than a cigarette addiction. Personally, I have never seen anyone whose present life did not display the mark of their unresolved issues from prior lifetimes, as revealed in the techniques we are exploring in this volume. For the majority of us, breaking those patterns takes a lifetime—in fact, we might say that is *why we have a lifetime.* Even *becoming aware* of the patterns is a formidable spiritual accomplishment. And simply becoming aware of them, while precious, is a lot easier than escaping them.

For these reasons, our first compassionate principle is . . .

Accept that the karmic pattern as revealed through the nodal structure will inevitably manifest in your life. Take no shame in that. It is a good beginning simply to observe it.

Our second principle is *mindfulness*:

Maintain as much awareness of the karmic pattern as you can. Keep tension on it. Even in the grips of it, affirm that you are one with a power that is greater than the habit. That power will win someday.

Those two principles are the foundation. When you move beyond theory and actually walk the path of your own evolution, you will rest on these two pillars.

There is another helpful technique for unweaving the hypnotic spell of the Moon's south node. Let's explore it.

Offering the South Node as a Gift

The south node is not all darkness. If you were a torturer for the Inquisition, you know quite a lot about how the human mind operates *in extremis.* That knowledge is not inherently evil, however you came by it. If you were a Nazi prison guard, you understand the way conscience can be socialized right out of a person. If you were a rapist, you know the depths of degradation to which unresolved rage can carry a human soul. All such understandings can potentially be applied in helpful ways.

These are of course the most horrible and extreme examples. Most of the stories you will pull out of a chart are far less dramatic. South node in Gemini? You were probably good at talking and thinking on your feet. That you tied yourself in knots that way is the heart of the matter, but those Gemini skills are not inherently wrong. In Evolutionary Astrology's *counseling* context, we recognize that it is time to move beyond those old Geminian views, assumptions, and behavioral patterns—that they interfere with the present evolutionary intentions of the soul.

Theoretically, we understand that while it is generally useful to make negative assumptions about karmic patterning, we must remember that there are still likely to be many positive elements in it. In the *counseling* context, we de-emphasize those positive elements. That sounds counter-intuitive until we realize that our aim as counselors is to help a person defeat his or her attachments to the south node patterns. We do not get there by praising them! But the past was virtually never entirely negative. And even in the darkest scenarios, we may well have learned something from our mistakes.

The point of all this is simply that, while you are not going to benefit personally from repeating your karmic patterns—at best, you've already learned the lessons and have no need to learn them again—you may very well be able to use them in *support of other people*. With that Gemini south node, help someone learn English—or help someone polish that novel manuscript. A torturer in the Inquisition? Help torture victims—or help torturers themselves recover from their own awful wounds.

Accepting the inevitability of south node behavioral patterns, let them play out as gifts, support, and acts of generosity toward other people. That way, you lose your *personal attachment* to them. This paves the way for losing them entirely.

There is elegance in this strategy. We do not directly fight the ingrained power of the karmic pattern. *Instead, we fight against our tendency to identify with it.* By giving it away, we take some of the ego out of the equation. We are no longer selfishly imagining benefit to come to ourselves from the behavior. The only appetites we are likely to satisfy are mostly altruistic ones. Even if we cling to the idea of getting praise and recognition for our magnanimity . . . well, the good news is that we are tempering that natural ego-attachment with concern for others.

In his monograph, *The Planetary and Lunar Nodes*, Dane Rudhyar speaks of the south node in terms of *sacrifice.* He writes, "There are many ways of speaking of sacrifice, some quite meaningless, even actually egocentric or masochistic. But the true meaning of sacrifice is "making sacred;" and this implies a complete dedication of one's thoughts and actions to what one may call either God or mankind—or to a specific group, culture or ideal. This means a surrender of the ego-will."

Again, we cannot fight the south node directly. Instead, like serviceable dinnerware we no longer need, we give it away.

In Chapter Five, we took a quick look at a few features of the chart of Oprah Winfrey. She has a Cancer south node in the seventh house. Breaking that down, we see that in a prior life she was largely defined by a relationship *(seventh house)*. She gave away her autonomy and her power, or it was taken from her. Cancer correlates with home life, so the relationship was very likely a marriage, although it could have been some other kind of familial bond that became too enmeshed to be healthy. Uranus is conjunct the south node, suggesting that Oprah Winfrey behaved in a rebellious way, breaking out of the conventional strictures of family and marriage. She escaped. Good news—but it also set up a karmic pattern of instability in her intimate, personal life, which has continued into the present incarnation. Still, in her current lifetime she has turned this drama into a gift. She illustrates our principles well and positively. She has helped to liberate millions of stay-at-home day-time TV watchers from the two-dimensional, intellectually inert, psychologically flat, realities of the lives they might otherwise be tempted to live. Oprah has brought them books, thought, and hope. Thus, some of her "jailbreak" karmic pattern has been offered up as a gift. It continues to play out in her personal life, but her ego is less attached to it than it would be if it were all one hundred percent her own drama.

Oprah's karmic story is naturally more complex than these couple of hundred words can indicate. Still she serves splendidly as a positive example of this *strategic generosity.*

Patience

Imagine a gymnasium floor covered in grease. In the center of the floor is a stake. You are attached to it by a long rubber leash. If you struggle and run, you can stretch out that leash and get pretty far from the stake. But if you stop struggling for ten seconds, the rubber draws you back over the slippery floor. All your effort goes poof.

That is how karma works. Whenever you fall asleep at the wheel, whenever your mindfulness fails, karma pulls you back into the old patterns, beliefs and attitudes. It is automatic and relentless. If your self-awareness turns off, if your intentions momentarily weaken, karma instantly begins to consume your life. Only though diligent, sustained effort can you pull away from it.

Those are your boring vegetables. Eat 'em, they're good for you.

Ready for dessert?

Elastic fatigues over time. Think of old underpants that won't stay up anymore. The rubber leash of your karma gradually weakens as well—but only if you keep it stretched. Your mindfulness and your effort must be even more relentless than the mindless rubber leash.

These principles are intrinsic to the fabric of the outward laws of the nature and the inward laws of spirit. They may not be our favorite principles, but they will not go away. No one evolves without effort. We cannot do it without self-discipline, effort, humble self-scrutiny, ultimate faith on ourselves, and, above all, patience.

But we can do it. We are strong enough.

This attitude—this volatile, paradoxical mixture of humility and triumphant belief in our soul's power—is the engine that drives our ascent up the spiritual mountain, one step at a time. Find that balance in yourself, and bring that attitude to bear upon your clients and your friends as you explore the meshing gears of Evolutionary Astrology.

The North Node

Everything we have explored so far in this chapter has been about the right attitude toward the Moon's south node and its attendant family of symbols. Now let's turn our attention to the other side of the equation: the Moon's north node, and the evolutionary potential it represents. What are the most helpful attitudes to take there?

The north node, obviously enough, is opposite the south node. Everything we need to grasp about it derives directly from that simple observation. The south is the past; the north is the future. The south is familiar; the north is strange to us. The south is where we are smart; the north is where we are dumb—or at least inexperienced, which often looks about the same. The south is habitual; the north is waiting to be discovered. The south feels safe; the north feels insecure, groundless and, thus, dangerous. At the south node, we are suave; at the north node we are goofy and awkward. The south is boring; the north is alive.

From the perspective of the death bed, a life lived according to the inclinations of the south node and its family of symbols feels in retrospect to have been empty and pointless, no matter how overtly successful it might seem to others.

From the perspective of the death bed, a life lived pursuing the potentials of the north node and its family of symbols feels in retrospect to have been meaningful, rich, and somehow "right" from an intuitive and transcendent perspective.

To make a good death or to make a bad, sad one. Our culture is afraid of death so we break taboo even thinking this way—yet can there be a more fundamental question? Sooner or later, the issue of mortality presents itself to all of us. Avoiding the dark enchantments of the south node and cultivating the heady uncertainties and vulnerabilities of the north node is the road to a peaceful, self-assured exit from this mortal coil. That is too precious a treasure for us to allow fear or conformity to keep us away from claiming it.

Just Because It Feels Unnatural . . .

. . . doesn't mean it is bad for you! That is a critical element in framing our right attitude toward the north node. We can *count* on its feeling unnatural—that is simply because our souls are unfamiliar with it. There is no escaping that principle. When we are beginning anything, we do not have much sense of what we are doing. Culturally, we have made the word "natural" into a shibboleth. If it is natural, it has got to be good for you. If it is not natural, then beware. Personally, I think that is a profoundly helpful attitude regarding anything we put into our bodies or our ecosystems. On

the scale of individual psychology, the issue is more complex. To an active alcoholic, nothing feels more natural than having a drink. To an active co-dependent, nothing feels more natural than being agreeable and compliant with a crazy person. Breaking either of those patterns feels totally unfamiliar, strange, dangerous, awkward—and you may recognize here the family of words we used earlier to describe the north node!

They all mean "unnatural."

Karma is habit and habits are familiar. Doing north node work is unnatural business. It takes not only tremendous courage to do it, but also a willingness to improvise, to face embarrassment, to feel insecure and vulnerable.

The beat generation poet, Allen Ginsberg, had his south node in Capricorn and in the eleventh house, suggesting a karmic pattern of being defined by his identity as a member of a social group or class *(eleventh house)* which was characterized by rigid rules of propriety, "right thinking," and conformity *(Capricorn)*. His node-ruling Saturn was in Scorpio and the eighth house, adding a further detail—these prior-life social repressions left him isolated and perhaps depressed *(Saturn)*, largely because of unexpressed *(Saturn again)* taboo *(Scorpio)* sexual desires *(eighth house)*. Furthermore, Pluto opposed his south node from the fourth house and Cancer, implying a "brick wall of reality that he couldn't get around," stemming from toxic spiritual conditions *(Pluto)* within his then-family of origin *(fourth house and Cancer.)*

Ginsberg's north node was in the fifth house and Cancer. His "unnatural" task in this lifetime was to "mother" himself gently and lovingly *(Cancer)* and specifically to heal his warped relationship with Dionysian pleasure *(the fifth house)*. Establishing a right and unabashed relationship with his own sexuality was an essential part of it. Creativity and self-expression in general are critical elements in realizing the potential of a fifth house north node—and with the north node conjunct Pluto, Ginsberg's creativity needed to embrace everything that was taboo and unacceptable to "polite society."

I vividly remember hearing Allen Ginsberg read his poetry to a packed auditorium at Duke University in the early 1970s. It was fascinating to watch the body language of audience members as he launched into his exceedingly graphic—and very gay—erotic poetry. I can only imagine the "unnatural," holy journey that brought Allen Ginsberg to that stage—an "angel-headed hipster burning for the ancient heavenly connection to the starry dynamo in the machinery of night," to paraphrase his own words in his epic poem, *Howl*.

Allen Ginsberg's Moon was in Pisces and the twelfth house. As the planetary ruler of his north node, we recognize that another "unnatural" element in his evolutionary plan was to explore mysticism and altered states of consciousness, moving toward direct knowledge and experience of the Divine. All this was reflected in his fascination with psychedelic substances, and perhaps more lastingly with his explorations of Buddhism and Hinduism. In a spectacular example of the kinds of synchronistic magic we can trigger as we move upward along our nodal axis, Ginsberg met the vaunted but controversial Tibetan Vajrayana teacher Chogyam Trungpa Rinpoche "by chance" when they both tried to catch the same taxicab in New York City! The event triggered his life-long Buddhist practice.

The Medicine

If the south node is the soul's dis-ease, then the north node is the medicine that cures it. There is an underlying perfection implicit in this relationship; the complimentary fit between the south node and the north node is invariably a study in Yin-Yang harmony, once you grasp it. At the risk of being melodramatic, if the south node is the poison, then the north node is its impeccable antidote. Or as Michael Lutin put it in a lecture once, using Alcoholics Anonymous symbolism, "The south node is the bottle and the north node is the meeting."

South node in Aries? An attachment to passion, very likely to anger. The medicine? Libran peace, tolerance, aesthetics and grace. South node in the fourth house? Enmeshment in one's inner world, and very likely in family too. The medicine? Get a job! Get out into the big world and find a meaningful place there.

These are very simple "medicine" examples, based on the obvious polarities of opposite signs and houses. Understanding these polarities thoroughly is the foundation of a good education in Evolutionary

Astrology—and astrology in general, actually. We covered these complementary opposites in detail in Chapters Six and Seven. Get them into your bones if you truly want to enter this particular world of archetypal understanding.

Once we go a little deeper, the process of understanding the north node's medicine becomes more complicated, less obvious—and custom-tailored to the needs of the individual. We saw a good example in the previous section about poet Allen Ginsberg. There, his karmic predicament emerged in fairly precise detail—we certainly grasped it in a far richer and more integrated fashion than we might have through simply knowing about Capricorn or the eleventh house. Correspondingly, our understanding of Ginsberg's north node medicine was more focused and nuanced than a mere isolated understanding of Cancer or the fifth house. Once we included his Piscean twelfth house Moon—the ruler of the north node—we added a lot of clarity.

For another example, in Chapter Four, we explored in greater depth the chart-behind-the-chart of Lee Harvey Oswald. There too we were able to define the medicine that might have cured the considerable damage he had sustained in prior incarnations.

Once again, even though we refer to the "south node" karma and the "north node" medicine, it is absolutely critical to remember that those are short-hand terms for a larger theoretical perspective that ultimately and ideally would embrace *everything* in a chart.

In the final section of this book, we will demonstrate in-depth analysis of five influential people's charts—and in Chapter Fourteen, we lay out specific procedures for putting it all together.

Fear not, in other words, if you don't yet feel ready to grasp the big picture. We will get there!

The Heart of the Matter

The north node is medicine. Take it and it will work. But you have to take it. You have to stretch that rubber band we were talking about a few pages ago, and you have to keep it stretched until its tension is defeated and you are released.

Time does not do it. You do it.

Nothing But A Good Idea

The Moon's north node has no intrinsic power at all. In that, it is different from every other symbol in astrology. With everything else in astrology, one principle is certain and inescapable: the symbolism will manifest somehow in your life. It is energy, so *it can be neither created nor destroyed, only changed in form.* It cannot go away. That is true of your Mercury, your Sun, your Venus. They are all "fated" to manifest somehow in your life, depending on how you use them. The same is true of your south lunar node as well. In that sense, it works just like a planet. It has both power and inertia.

But none of that applies to the Moon's north node. It is *absolutely nothing except a completely wonderful idea,* which you are free to accept or to ignore. Furthermore, it is a wonderful idea that is shrouded in your own blindness and your own attachments—even seeing it is difficult. (Remember our key words with the north node: *unfamiliar, strange, dangerous, awkward, alien, unnatural . . .*)

There is an "automatic" element to everything else in the birthchart. But the manifestation of the north node is only triggered by *intentions.* Otherwise it remains inert—not good, not bad, not even *there* in any meaningful way.

The north node is the forgotten bottle of water in your trunk when you are thirsting to death. It is the winning lottery ticket lying unremarked in your top drawer. It is the unlocked door in your prison ten feet from where you lie sleeping.

Self Acceptance

When I see the Moon's north node in Pisces, the twelfth house, or conjunct Neptune, I will often say to my client "your intention in this lifetime is to attain Enlightenment." That raises their eyebrows! My clients are generally spiritually sophisticated people—individuals with sense enough to know that they are not likely to attain Messianic states of consciousness before running out of gas this time around. And of course in practical terms, predicting Enlightenment for anyone is dubious, given the odds against it.

The remark gets my clients' attention, though—and then I make the real point. I ask them to imagine a thousand lifetimes of meditation. I ask them to imagine that every time they sat down to meditate, they began their meditation with the humble affirmation that they will definitely *not* attain Enlightenment this time. I ask them to consider the effect of that affirmation repeated over a thousand lifetimes.

Humility is a fundamental spiritual value, prized in the mystical traditions of every religion. Losing our self-importance and our self-obsession is one of the main plazas in the City of God—no matter where we wander, we will pass through it again and again.

And yet, and yet . . . in every mystical tradition there is a countervailing principle: *you are already there.* All is one. We are all One in the Body of Christ. Buddha-nature exists in all beings. Atman and Brahman are one. The Sufi whirling dervish dissolving his illusory individuality into oneness with Allah. The Lakota Sioux in the sweat lodge saying *Mitakuye Oyasin*—All Our Relations, affirming their connections with the stars and the squirrels.

Take your pick. They are all saying the same thing—something almost too luminous to bear. This is the eternal mystical paradox. You must struggle forward indomitably, and *you are already there.*

Embrace only the latter, and you become ego-inflated and probably lazy. Embrace only the former, and you eventually become dispirited, a broken slave.

Similarly:

Evolutionary Astrology can describe with daunting precision the soul-cages in which we find ourselves. Be careful it does not "nail" you! Focusing on the south node alone is dangerous. It can break your heart.

Balance that danger with a solid, hopeful focus on the message of the Moon's north node. Above all, in working with the north node and its ruler, keep the faith! Do not lose sight of the fact that you *can* do it, that the answer is already there inside you. Wipe away the illusions and distortions of the south node, and let the light shine through the window—there is nothing between you and Enlightenment except a little grease on your window pane. Tibetan Buddhists call this *vajra pride*, and cultivate it. We might as easily call it faith. It is medicine against despair and shame. It is the soul of true self-acceptance.

And, in the long run, nothing in the outward universe nor in the demonic depths of your mind's primordial madness can stand against it.

CHAPTER THIRTEEN: WHEN THE KARMIC WAVE BREAKS

Long ago in another life in ancient Babylon, you took a stroll through the marketplace. It had been a good week in your rent-a-camel business; coins were jingling in a sack hanging from your belt. You felt right with the world and grateful to the gods and goddesses. Turning a corner, you came upon a miserable leper dressed in rags, begging. He was hideous. You had seen him before and always turned away, revolted. Today something shifted inside you. Your mood of gratitude turned to generosity and your generosity to compassion. You reached for some coins to give him. And you looked that leper in the eye and saw a human being there. And the leper saw you seeing him, soul to soul. He accepted the coins happily, but his deeper appreciation was about the real gift you had given him: seeing past his appearance into his essential humanity.

Today that leper is named Bill Gates. And he feels he owes you one.

Good karma!

As always, I am just making up a story here. I have no idea if Bill Gates was a leper in a prior life. But I have no doubt that he received acts of generosity from others from time to time. These acts of generosity are beautiful things, but they set up karmic imbalances. We feel a need to return the favor. Like most things metaphysical, you do not really have to take this idea on faith. You can just reflect on your own daily experience. If you get a flat tire on a rainy day and a stranger stops to help you out, how do you feel? Grateful, of course—but also desirous of returning the favor. That is karma too, just on a shorter time-scale.

I suspect that Bill Gates has occasionally encountered people toward whom he felt an inexplicable surge of generosity. If you were indeed the camel-dealer who looked him in the eye when he was a leper in Babylon—well, lucky you today!

But "lucky" is an imperfect word here. Luck implies a kind of randomness in the universe. That randomness is pure fiction. You and Bill Gates simply need to re-balance the karma. Superficially, it will look like his being generous toward you, out of the blue. That is how the transaction would be described in the context of consensual reality. But neither of you will *feel* exactly that way. Even if Bill Gates gives you a million dollars, his experience will be one of comfort, joy, relief—and release. You will feel happy too of course. But deep down, you will not feel awkward about receiving his gift. It will feel right to you. If you experience any goofy emotions along the lines of "I can't possibly accept this . . .", that is really only your social training kicking in. In your inner silence, you will feel something similar to what Bill is feeling: comfort, joy, relief—and release. A burden has been lifted from both of you. A debt has been repaid.

So *when* will you actually meet Bill Gates? What day should you mark on your calendar? Your act of generosity long ago set up a kind of tension, or potential energy between your soul and his. When will it burst forth? When will the karma ripen?

When will the karmic wave break?

Here is a good guess: It will break when Jupiter transits over your south node of the Moon, while something similarly expansive and "nodal" is happening in Bill Gate's chart. There are many astrological possibilities, and our deeper purpose in this chapter is to investigate them. What they all have is common is some stimulus of the nodal axis or the points most connected with it. That is when the karmic chickens come home to roost.

By the way, with transiting Jupiter moving through a sextile to his south node in 1999, Bill Gates actually was moved to express great generosity. Early that year, he made a major contribution to the International AIDS Vaccine Initiative, and in September of that year, he made the largest ever academic behest—one billion dollars—aimed at helping disadvantaged students get their educations.

Your karma is complex. Everyone's is. You may have been kind to poor Bill Gates when he was suffering as a leper. But you may also have stolen and killed, or mocked the crippled or the outcast, or poisoned the well, or oppressed the poor. The karmic well is deep and kaleidoscopic; it is a Cineplex, and not all the films showing there are from the Disney studios.

As a planet passes through an aspect to your nodes, it is like a colored filter through which you are peering into the karmic kaleidoscope. And through which the light of that kaleidoscope is being filtered before it reaches your eye—or before it reaches the world of manifestation. If Jupiter is passing through such a nodal aspect, then you are seeing karma manifesting that has a Jupiter quality—rosy! Or at least glittery. And maybe generous. The universe literally owes you one; you were kind to one of its children. That must be balanced.

But what if you were mean to one of the universe's children? Maybe Mars is passing over your south node—and another driver recklessly cuts you off in traffic, nearly causing you to collide with a truck. It is five minutes before the painful adrenalin and anger leave your system. No big deal. But it is not random either. Put out aggression—yesterday or in a prior life—and aggression will come back to you. That is not just a good idea; it is the Law. And Mars is a likely trigger for the manifestation of that kind of karma. When Fletcher Christian set William Bligh adrift after the famous mutiny on the *Bounty*, transiting Mars was on Bligh's north node. When Nelson Mandela was thrown in jail in August 1962, beginning his twenty-seven year imprisonment, transiting Mars was opposing his south node.

Similarly, each planet has a certain tone or quality that will bring forth a certain type of karmic manifestation when it contacts your nodal system. Think of your south node as emanating white light—and "whiteness" here does not symbolize purity, but rather plurality: all the colors of the rainbow of human possibility, from the lowest to the highest. The "colored filter" of a planet forms an aspect to the nodes or related points. The white light of the karma temporarily takes on that hue.

Gradually, all of your karmic potentials for this lifetime—all the ones that have ripened— are modulated into actual biographical manifestation. You experience the results of what you have created in the past, for good, for ill, for strange, for amazing.

A Few Tweaks

Everything in your chart is karmic in origin. Nothing is there by chance. But as we have been learning, karma is not orderly any more than life is orderly. Through nodal analysis, we learn to find the most quintessentially relevant past-life story. We build our central understanding around it. But we must always recognize that there are "loose ends." You might, for example, have Pluto in the Third House. As we have seen earlier, that configuration broadly indicates some issues around untruthful speech in a prior life. Perhaps you lied. Perhaps you were lied to. In any case, truthfulness, coming and going, becomes an important evolutionary theme in this present lifetime.

Now, this third house Pluto might not have any direct aspectual relationship to the nodal axis. It may not rule either node. It might, in other words, not be central to the nodal story. It constitutes a more fragmentary glimpse into the karmic well. We would not have enough information to build a real storyline around it, although we might possibly be able to connect it meaningfully to the main nodal tale somehow.

In any case, that Pluto, like everything else in your chart, represents a field of potential karmic energy. Any transit, progression, or solar arc to it will correlate with opportunities either to advance spiritually in the face of that underlying Plutonian issue—or it will correlate simply with some repetition of the ingrained karmic pattern: you will lie or someone will lie to you.

If the main nodal story were one of *deception in intimacy*—say, a fifth house Piscean south node squared by a seventh house Neptune—it would be easy to connect this third house Pluto (lies) to that storyline (intimate deception). You would not need any direct aspectual link in order to see it.

Once we understand that connection, then when the natal Pluto is stimulated by a transit or a progression, we are able to be much more precise in our advice. We will know that an opportunity to clear the air with honesty (or to repeat the pattern with lies or deception) may very well arise in the area of interpersonal intimacy. We will also know that the past life lie was more likely one we were told by another, rather than one we told ourselves—that is the nature of the specific karma in this case. The underlying karma is of being deceived rather than of being the deceiver. We can forewarn our client. We can encourage him or her to ask hard questions during this period of time. The karma is ripening.

As always, what we are seeing here is how our understanding deepens as we move away from "single factor analysis," and begin to include the whole field of astrological information with as much integration as possible. That is true not only for Evolutionary Astrology, but for every other kind of astrology as well.

Nuts and Bolts

In timing the breaking of the karmic wave, we employ the whole range of "predictive" techniques that astrology has to offer. In my own work, I rely on transits, secondary progressions, and solar arcs. (By the way, if you would like some grounding in a choice-centered approach to those methods, have a look at the second edition of my book, *The Changing Sky*. In this book, I am assuming you already understand those rudiments.) If you are drawn toward other predictive techniques, such as eclipses or tertiary progressions or converse arcs or whatever, go for it!

There are two basic categories of stimuli to consider. They are equal in effectiveness, and both are essential:

First, consider anything that stimulates the nodal axis, its rulers, or any planets in major aspect to it.

Second, consider the motions of the nodes themselves.

Stimulation of the Nodal Axis

A transit of Mercury over your south node is often a palpable astrological event, even though it will only last for a few days. As always with Mercury in general, you will notice an increase in your general busyness, more events around communication or media, more restlessness. In this case, those qualities will be relevant to your karmic predilections. Maybe you will read a book about reincarnation. Maybe that is why you are reading this book in this moment! Maybe, whether you know it or not, your guardian angels will be hearing you "talk exactly the way you did in Paris in 1875." Something connected with communication is likely to happen, and it may feel strangely familiar—or fated. When Linda Tripp betrayed her friend Monica Lewinsky by wearing a "wire" and recording Monica's trusting woman-to-woman conversations, transiting Mercury was opposing Monica's south node.

A transit of Pluto over your south node or its ruler will change your life forever. It is a much more serious astrological event than a Mercury transit, affording you a chance to really get down to the heart of the evolutionary matter. Consider: when Ram Dass was shocked by a sudden stroke on February 19, 1997, transiting Pluto was square his Venus—the ruler of his south node.

Most astrologers would not even mention that transit of Mercury in a yearly update for a client. No evolutionary astrologer would dare ignore the Pluto transit. But consider: On a day-to-day basis, each event is equally real and powerful. The difference is that Pluto has *a lot more time* in which to work! The transit thus has long enough to develop depth and complexity of meaning.

This is a critical point: transiting Pluto is not more powerful than transiting Mercury, but as *human consciousness interacts with planetary energies, the slower the event the more powerful it becomes*. It simply has time enough to become important. A good reality check on all this is to consider the *progressed* or *solar arc* Mercury crossing your south node: that is a much slower event and it will indeed leave a major mark on your biography. For Napoleon, the solar arc square of Mercury to his nodal axis meant Waterloo!

Avoiding "overwhelm" is critical in all kinds of astrology. We have to do some strategic "weeding." If we try to juggle too many configurations, our brain overheats and our hearts shut down. That is tragic because it is the heart that excels at the integrative work. For that reason, I suggest focusing exclusively on truly major stimuli of the nodes and their planetary correlates.

In my own practice, here is a list of what I use. As always, I suggest this not as Holy Writ, but only as a practical jumping-off point for your own explorations. Here we are considering moving planets contacting the natal nodes.

Transits: Jupiter, Saturn, Uranus, Neptune and Pluto. Keep an eye on up-and-coming Eris too!

Secondary Progressions: Sun, Moon, Mercury, Venus, Mars, Ascendant, Midheaven.

Solar Arcs: Everything. (Note that the solar arc Sun is identical to the secondary progressed Sun.) There are a variety of ways of progressing the Midheaven. I use both the solar arc Midheaven and the secondary progressed one as well. For a long while, I advocated paying more attention to the solar arc Midheaven. Lately I have been re-considering that practice, and finding myself preferring the secondary progressed Midheaven.

By the way, if you would like a deeper look at how all these "predictive" techniques work in the choice-centered, evolutionary context, I would recommend the second edition of my book, *The Changing Sky*.

Stimulation of the Chart by Nodal Motion

This is a much smaller category than the direct stimulation of the nodal axis via transits, progressions and arcs. Here, we are only looking at the way the nodal axis itself moves around the chart. As it does so, naturally the nodes make contact with natal planets, bringing the latent karmic potentials to bear upon them. There are three possibilities here.

The Transiting Nodal Axis. Every 6,793.39 days, which is to say every 18.5997 years, the nodal axis completes one cycle through the Zodiac. The south node returns to zero Aries, in other words. That is just a little over every eighteen years, seven months. The nodes spend about a year and half passing through a sign. Thus in the course of a normal human life span, the south node will transit through a conjunction with each of your planets four or five times. (Your mileage may vary.)

Do not count on each of these nodal transits always to correlate with something big. Often they seem to pass pretty much unnoticed. It feels forced for me to pretend to read each one as karmically important. Probably they all have some evolutionary meaning at a deep level. In my experience, the transiting nodes will be spectacularly relevant and illuminating sometimes, and other times they are duds, except perhaps in the context of adding dimensionality to other major events.

Remember our key "weeding" principle: the more slowly something moves, the more important it is. The nodal axis only takes about three months to move through five degrees—that is, through that critical 2.5 degree orb (one twelfth of a sign). That is not a huge amount of time.

The Solar Arc Nodal Axis. Of the three "moving node" techniques, this is the one I have consistently found to be most reliable. The solar arc nodes ghost along at about one degree per year. They have plenty of time to generate depth and complexity, and to pick up "assists" from other astrological events. Furthermore, solar arcs in general tend to be very event-oriented. They have the Sun's active signature deep in their nature, after all. And the Sun is about the concerns of the ego: biography more than deeper process, basically. It is less oriented to subtle inner developments. So for purposes of timing the physical manifestation of karmic potentials, solar arcs are well-suited to the task. When the solar arc nodes form an aspect to a natal planet, especially one connected to the nodal story, stand back. Karma has ripened.

The Secondary Progressed Nodal Axis. This method of moving the nodes has a tragic flaw. It does not do very much in the course of a lifetime. It is simply too slow to be of much use except at a very broad level. In the course of a long life, the nodes may progress through five degrees. It is worth paying some attention to times when one of its aspects becomes perfectly exact, or when it changes from one sign to another—although only about one in every six or eight people will ever experience that. Ditto for the nodes progressing into a new house. But there you have another problem: unless a birth has been timed to an extremely high degree of precision, you never really know *precisely* where your house cusps are. One minute error in a birth time moves the cusps about a quarter of a degree—not much, but enough to throw the date the nodes enter a new house off by over four years.

In my own practice, the progressed nodes basically fall prey to my instinct to weed things down to manageable essentials. I do not use them except when I am contemplating my own life or the lives people I love very much and know very well.

When Not to Weed

There is one big exception to this "weeding" principle. It has to do with "event charts." Let's say you have just met your true love. Naturally you want to know what was going on for both of you that day astrologically. Even the fast-moving planets are quite relevant in such charts. For example, Venus was almost exactly conjunct his natal north node when Arnold Schwarzeneggar married Maria Shriver. When the Oprah Winfrey Show debuted on September 8, 1996, the transiting north node was trine Oprah's Sun and trine her Venus too.

The key here is that we are not attempting to counsel someone in advance about their evolutionary challenges. Instead, the karmic wave has actually broken—and we know when it did. Even the quick planets are now frozen in time; we know exactly where they were. If, say, this person you have just met is *really* your true love, you will almost undoubtedly find all sorts of major (i.e., slow moving) astrological events that are very directly connected with the encounter. They will not necessarily be strictly "nodal" either—maybe, for example, your progressed Venus is making a major aspect to your Sun. But there is a good chance you'll see something going on along the lines of what we are exploring in this chapter too—some significant nodal stimulus. You may very well also see that the little "firefly" events are busy too: transiting Venus is trine your south node from the seventh house, transiting Mercury is hitting your north node. These kinds of "triggering" transits are often accurate to within a couple of days. They seem to be what actually precipitates the breaking of the karmic wave. Their only problem is that they are nearly impossible to use in advance because there are so many of them.

Say that your *progressed* Venus is making an aspect to your south node. That will be in effect for a couple of years, and is very indicative of meetings with people "who seem strangely familiar." During that two year period there will literally be hundreds of these "firefly" transits. Any one of them could "have your name on it"—or two names inside a heart.

We can tweak our techniques further, and maybe make some better guesses about which "firefly" transits are more likely candidates for triggering something big. When a major aspect is getting near exactitude, for example, you would naturally pay more attention to the quick transits. Things are heating up. Or if a great number of quick ones all seemed to be clustering around a particular date—again, mark your calendar.

While reasonably effective, these "tweaking" techniques are not completely reliable. My personal feeling is they that verge into the area of "party trick" astrology—there is too much focus on concrete prediction. I think it is far more helpful to concentrate on the deeper evolutionary meaning of a longer period of serious nodal stimulus. Then you have helped yourself—or your client—be as ready as possible to make the best use of events whenever they actually manifest.

Transiting to Progressed . . .

Look back at major events in your life, particularly ones that had that classic "karmic" signature: they felt "fated." You will almost certainly find connections with the material we have just been considering: impacts upon the natal chart.

You will also probably see configurations such as "solar arc south node conjunct transiting Pluto." These "moving to moving" events are powerful configurations, and commonly present at such times. I believe in them—but I tend not to use them very much. Here is the reason: the root structure of the birthchart, seen from an evolutionary perspective, tells a fairly specific past life story. When those specific potentials are triggered, we can be very precise—and very helpful—in our analysis of the issues. We are summing the testimony of many planets, integratively. The key here is that something moving through the chart (i.e., a transit, progression, or arc) has triggered the *wholeness* of this very precisely detailed natal potential.

We lose that deeper precision when we see, for example, a transit triggering a solar arc or a progression. Neither one is rooted directly in the detailed matrix of the natal chart.

I do repeat that such moving to moving aspects "work"—when your backpack was stolen in that train station in Dubrovnik, sure enough transiting Saturn was conjunct your solar arc south node in the ninth house. The symbolism fits. And we might possibly have even been able to take timely warning from it. Good if you can save your backpack! But it is perhaps better to understand *why* it would be stolen in the first place. And the answer to that question lies in the birthchart itself.

Coloring in the Nodes

When transiting Saturn hits a sensitive astrological point, we know that we will be faced with hard reality. We know that any healthy response will require self-discipline and effort. We should not expect "luck" or a free ride. We know that right actions here will lead to maturation—and that, deep down, we are ready to outgrow an outmoded response to the part of our lives that natal planet symbolizes. We also understand that if we do not rise to Saturn's higher calling, we will experience a dark Saturn mix of misfortune, despair, and soul-tiredness.

We know, in other words, quite clearly what Saturn brings to the table. We can refine it even further by considering the nature of our natal Saturn in terms of its strengths, vulnerabilities, and ultimate evolutionary intentions. No wonder our ancestors thought of the planets as gods. They have personalities.

Can we do the same things with the transits, progressions and arcs that trigger the nodes of the Moon? Yes, but the procedure is a little different. The issue hinges on one key question: *What exactly does the south node mean?* We know that basically it refers to your emotional or attitudinal attachment to some unresolved issues from prior lifetimes. That's it. But what are those issues? Violence? Passivity? Hubris? Despair? Given the enormous range of possibilities when it comes to karma, our basic definition of the south node is thus too vague to be of much use. That is the fundamental distinction between the lunar nodes and the planets. You know the planet's nature, but the node is more of an outline sketch. You have to color it in.

Maybe you have the south node in Libra and the twelfth house—and your karmic blind spots have to do with laziness, escapism, or letting other people define who you are. Maybe you have the south node in Aries and in the first house—and your karmic attachments are quite the opposite: authority, control, independence and force. Those two possible nodes, stimulated by transit, progression or solar arc, would be as different as Venus and Mars!

That kind of holistic thinking is good practice in astrology in general, but it is utterly critical to success in this kind of evolutionary analysis. The nodes just do not say as much *intrinsically* as do the planets. Put them in their natal contexts, though, and they say plenty!

Aspectual Orbs

Our intellects are valiant little warriors. Once they get locked onto a problem, they hang in there tenaciously, bravely suffering coffee-nerves and a wrinkled brow. Ask anyone who ever passed calculus or learned to conjugate Greek verbs. But it is the human heart that pulls everything together. Just visualize your closest friend. You know countless facts about her, but that is not what comes up inside you. When you think of her, you get a feeling. Her nature strikes something like a musical chord in you. Everything you have ever experienced about her comes together in that feeling. That is what I mean when I speak of the heart's integration. All of your myriad facts, memories and impressions of your friend dance together in that chord.

Finding that chord when you look at a chart is the essence of effective astrology. If you are too focused on individual facts, you will never get there. And if you have no facts, you won't get there either! Astrology requires a middle path between head and heart. Perhaps the greatest weakness of modern astrological tutelage is the over-centralization of academic "head" energy, at the expense of poetry and soul.

To get this balance right, we simply must keep a handle on the over-stimulation of the intellect under a barrage of facts and details. To accomplish that we must, as I have been emphasizing in this chapter, do some "weeding." And one of the most effective ways to achieve that control is through how we use aspects and orbs. Underlying everything I am about to write is one simple notion: *at some point, we simply have too much information.* We need to recognize that point—and that is easy, because the heart begins to shut down. The chart starts looking like secret code encrypted in abstruse mathematical disguises. It stops feeling like your friend.

We also need to be very systematic in terms of which facts we use and which ones we toss. Obviously, the key is to pay attention to the most important things.

With orbs—which are the "tolerances" we use for aspects—it is understood that the closer two planets are to being exactly 90 degrees apart, the more strongly that square will manifest. We also know that we may experience a square when it is as much as ten degrees away from exactitude, or even more. If, in looking for transits to the nodal axis, we allow an orb of ten degrees, the odds are fairly good we will find something. There are obviously two points that are square the node, one 90 degrees before it and another 90 degrees after it. If each one affects a span of twenty degrees (an "orb" of ten degrees on either side of the exact square), then we can plainly see that there is a 40-in-360 chance of a planet's happening to be there. That is about 1 in 9. Proceeding this way is valid astrology—a ten degree orb, while wider than normal usage, can often be seen to be effective. We feel it. But if we reduce our orb from ten to five degrees, we have eliminated about half the squares. And we have done so strategically—we have weeded out the less powerful ones and kept the stronger (more nearly precise) ones. Things are now less confusing—not so many aspects to think about. Your cerebral head is not claiming the entire energy budget anymore. Your heart can breathe a little more.

We can tweak this approach a bit by realizing that not all planets are created equal. Two factors interact here. First, we generally use larger orbs with the planets that are more important in the chart. (See my book *The Inner Sky* if you need a refresher on how planets become more or less central in a birthchart). Secondly and more importantly, a slow-moving planet generally wants smaller orbs. If we use a ten degree orb with transiting Mercury, the aspect will be in effect for a few weeks at most. If we used one with the progressed Sun, it would be effective for twenty years! And that might actually be the experienced reality—but our interpretations will enjoy better focus and punch if we limit our attention to the few years of that progression's maximum intensity. They will be especially so if we concentrate on the one year that really represents the apogee of the progressed Sun event.

Rather than give specific recommendations here, I would prefer to simply encourage you to see how far you can go without losing your emotional connection to the chart. If it goes poof, then tighten your orbs!

As a practical starting point, I would suggest not paying attention at all to any of the really quick transits. Then give the heavier, slower events an orb of 2.5 degrees—one twelfth of a sign. The peaks of dramatic timing leap out of the mixture that way. You then have a solid foundation. You could do helpful work based only on that information. If you can keep that "big picture" feeling, then go ahead and add some technical details.

Aspects

Which aspects to use? Sesquiquadrates will vex you and quincunxes will force you to adapt, while quintiles and septiles often bring visitations from the angels and muses of inspiration.

A lot of astrologers really love aspects and get good results parsing them out into ever more subtle distinctions. Mercury is in 15 Aries and Saturn is in 9 Virgo—is that a quincunx with a six degree orb, or is it an exact bi-septile? Both, really—and occasionally also the source of blood-letting at astrology conferences. I am usually not sitting at that table.

My own predilection lies in the direction of keeping it simple and thus more soulful. Ninety-five percent of the time, I personally use only five aspects: conjunctions, sextiles, squares, trines, and oppositions. They divide the circle integrally, which means that six sextiles, four squares, three trines, and two oppositions would equal one perfect Zodiac, with no remainder—all the while keeping the same degree-numbers. One could say the same about the semi-sextile aspect of 30 degrees, but no others. Again this is not Holy Writ, only my own style. I feel that these five are the most powerful and organic aspects. If I need more information, I would stretch further into aspectual esoterica. But so far these five Ptolemaic aspects have virtually always given me everything I need to speak meaningfully to my clients.

Among these aspects, there is a kind of hierarchy of strength, with the conjunction being the most energetic, followed by the opposition, the square, the trine and the sextile, in that order.

In practice, if any slow-moving planet is passing through a conjunction, square or opposition to the nodes or their rulers, I will very surely pay it a lot of attention in my analysis. These 'hard" aspects typically indicate that the karmic wave is breaking in some compelling, turning-point kind of way. Something has gone critical.

With the trines and sextiles, the drama and tension are less evident. There is typically an opportunity to make fairly easy work of an evolutionary step. The resources we need in order to succeed at it are in place and the door is open. Trouble is, we may sleep through it! With trines and sextiles, it is also particularly easy to slip backwards into the grips of an old karmic pattern. These so-called "good" aspects have a tragic liability: they love "easy" more than is good for them! Clearly, the old distinctions between "good" and "bad" aspects are not particularly helpful here in this evolutionary context.

As you get going with this branch of astrology, a good rule of thumb in working with transits, progressions, and solar arc is to focus on conjunctions, squares and oppositions with orbs of 2.5 degrees. That will get you to the heart of the matter, and you won't lose perspective on what is most central.

What if there are not any such aspects happening? You could stretch the orbs and use more subtle aspects, but a better idea I think is to stretch the scope of time you are considering: look a little further into the past and future until you find something that fits our criteria. What is happening now is all about integrating the lessons of the past and preparing for the challenges of the future.

These are the basic techniques for analyzing the breaking of the karmic wave. We will see more about their practical application as we move on into our five specific examples of analysis later in the book.

CHAPTER FOURTEEN: PUTTING IT ALL TOGETHER

"Make everything as simple as possible, but not simpler."
—Albert Einstein

Daunted by the intricacy of these techniques of nodal analysis? They *are* complicated. Let them stay that way! Listen to Professor Einstein—if we make the methodology simpler than it can honestly be, we pay a big price in terms of the depth and accuracy of the system.

With the bad news on the table, let's add that by following an orderly approach we can surf all this complexity effectively. Certainly if you have had any success with psychological astrology, these techniques are easily within your grasp.

All forms of astrology contain the same tempting pitfall: *piecemeal interpretation.* "I'm a Leo. Tell me about myself." Answering that question is dangerous! There are shy Leos, with lots of Moon-energy and their Suns in the fourth house. There are thermonuclear Leos with Sagittarius rising, the Moon in Aries, and Uranus aspecting everything in their charts.

Astrologers can speak of "Leo" as an archetypal principle, but God help them if they fall into the obvious folly of imagining that there are only twelve possible human personalities available on this earth. "Leo" has a valid abstract meaning, but its *human* meaning—its individual meaning for a specific person—depends almost entirely upon the astrological context in which it finds itself.

This is true of all the astrological symbols, including the Moon's nodes and their various modifiers.

As we learn astrology, inevitably and naturally we begin by mastering the basic language—the general meanings of the signs, planets, houses, and aspects. That is good and necessary. No one can bypass that step, anymore than we can receive an education without first becoming fluent in our native language. At this stage, there enter various catastrophic temptations—*shortcuts.* You are holding one in your hands at this very moment! Here's what I mean: In many of the earlier chapters of *Yesterday's Sky*, I have offered you stock paragraphs about the meanings of various nodal configurations. Is your south node in the third house? No need actually to read this whole, long-winded book! Just turn to Chapter Seven and cut to the chase. Neptune square your nodal axis? Make your way to Chapter Ten.

These shortcuts are the recipe for Astrology Made Easy—and often wrong. Or at least misleading. This copy/paste approach can quickly lead to the most virulent form of lie: the half truth. If you have Neptune square the nodal axis, or if your south node is in the third house, there *are* indeed various archetypal realities that are relevant to you. You can learn something about them—and yourself—from those pages. But you will be settling for Rent-a-Wreck when you could be sitting there stylishly in your brand new Porsche.

Don't do that! Be like Einstein: make Evolutionary Astrology as simple as possible, but no simpler. Bottom line, you have got to see each symbol in context. That takes some practice. A well-organized interpretive strategy helps a lot, mostly by keeping you on an even keel in the face of what could otherwise become an overwhelming load of information. We will offer such a strategy in these pages.

And you definitely do need that foundation of piecemeal understanding of the abstract meaning of each of the symbols—that is why those earlier chapters are there. They are your launching pad.

The rocket is your intelligence, your wisdom, and your imagination.

The Heart of the Matter

Twelve signs, twelve houses . . . and depending on how you count them, ten planets or so. Add the two lunar nodes. Call it thirty-six symbols. Together, they are capable of describing everything in the humanly-perceivable universe. All of the near-infinite possibilities of what is, what was, what might yet be . . . all held in thirty-six cosmic boxes.

Those are big boxes.

That simple statement is the key to the heart of the matter. Each symbol represents a huge range of meanings. Each one is an *archetypal field* containing a wide range of potential meanings.

Take the simple notion that you might have your south node in Capricorn. Even though that is only one symbol, the range of authentic potential expressions it might represent is so wide that there is no way any one human being could manifest more than a few atoms in that galaxy of potentials. But *which* atoms? Knowing that the south node is in Capricorn does not answer that question for you. So leave the question open! Make it as simple as possible, but no simpler.

Now let's say that your Capricorn south node falls in the second house. Like Capricorn, this too is one of our thirty-four basic archetypal "boxes." It too represents such a broad range of possibilities that there is no way they could all be on the stage at once.

You might think that your problem just became twice as intractable. You know the node is in Capricorn—which could mean a bazillion different things. Ditto for knowing it is in the second house. Add 'em up, and weep, right?

No, not exactly . . . what that south node is telling you is that the karmic story contains *both* Capricorn *and* second house elements. Rather than complicating things, that narrows down the field of possibilities. The true story has to pass two tests now; it has to pass through two filters.

You are looking for someone in Ohio. All you know is that she is female. That doesn't narrow the search very much. Half the people in Ohio are women. Now add one more filter: the woman you seek is blonde. That helps! The person is female—that is like knowing the sign of her south node. She is blonde—add the house.

But you are still in a mess. There are a lot of blondes in Ohio.

What if you knew she lived in Cleveland? (Which house holds the node-ruler?) South side of town? (In which sign is it?) You get the picture.

Let's say you allowed yourself to feel overwhelmed when you first saw that the node was in Capricorn. Your mind reeled as you made a mental list of the issues Capricorn could possibly signify. Reacting to that feeling, you goofed: you made an unconscious decision to simplify things—prematurely. One thing you know for sure about Capricorn is that it is about "great works." So you decide that, in a prior life, this person must have done something really huge and impressive. You ignore all the other things Capricorn might mean. You forget the rest of its archetypal field.

That error might encourage you, making you feel as if you were on track now. But not only have you turned away from a lot of what Capricorn can represent, you haven't even let the second house have a word.

The primary psychological meaning of the second house in karmic analysis is *self-doubt and insecurity*. Materially, it relates to money—or really the resources that support our survival. At this point, based on your narrow and premature "great work" assumption about Capricorn, your interpretation is almost forced into the corner of deciding that the story is one of a prior life focused on the "great work" of accumulating a great pile of cash through some enormous effort.

That might be it. That is one of the things that the combination of Capricorn and second house can fairly and honestly represent.

But say you kept your mind more open when you thought of Capricorn. You kept more of the possibilities alive and didn't jump to a conclusion. Great works—sure. That's Capricorn. But also *time-serving, limitation, pathological caution, inability to reach out for help*—those are Capricorn themes too, on the darker end of the spectrum. Mix those notions with the self-doubt of the second house, and another set of ideas emerges: perhaps here is a person who, in a prior life, failed to attain his potential out of self-doubt, and joylessly masked that failure with endless mechanical patterns of efficient responsibility rationalized as "financial necessity."

The key to this richer interpretation lies in *holding open* all the possibilities of each symbol, then *combining* them. Let it get *very* complicated, in other words, before you attempt to reach any conclusions. Put all the evidence on the table before you start tapping strange women on the back all over Ohio.

What we just illustrated only involved a sign and a house. That is a good start, but of course that south node will, at a minimum, have a planetary ruler. Ninety percent of the time that planetary ruler will add a different sign and house to the interpretive mix. The same principles apply—keep all the possibilities on the table. And note that this does not mean that you should decide what the sign and house of the south node mean, then move on to the ruler! Keep them *all* open, if you can. Let them all speak at once. Strive to hear the integrated message.

And of course this same reasoning continues as we stretch out to include any planets in aspect to the nodal axis, and so on. Let them all make their speeches. Digest them and see which way the collective wind is blowing.

Entertain simultaneously all possible meanings of all the symbols related to the nodal story. With each archetypal field wide open at the same time, look for places where the fields overlap, reinforce each other, or flow into a coherent narrative.

This process, while not easy, is far easier than it sounds. In the next section we will explore why that is so.

Your Ace In The Hole

If I suddenly name your best friend, you immediately get a feeling in your heart. Within less than a second, a certain emotional chord sounds inside your body-mind system. A visual image of the friend might form in your mind too, but I want to concentrate on the heart's instantaneous experience.

What is that feeling? *It is a kind of intuitive emotional summary of all your impressions of your friend.* Later, specific facts and memories about her might arise. If I start querying you in detail about her, you would soon be sorting through a vast library of concrete information—where you met, what her current relationship status is, her pet peeves, her favorite CDs, her Mercury and her Moon . . . the list is almost endless. But that list of facts is not what I am talking about. I am talking about that instantaneous emotional chord that sounds inside your body-mind system. In one microsecond, you feel a kind of integrated summary of all those fractal facts.

Social shorthand for this phenomenon is that we experience the world in two ways: *integratively* through the heart and *cognitively* through the head. The head is full of factual information, while *the heart is full of instantaneously accessible emotional meta-summaries of all that information.* (Astrologically, by the way, head and heart translate neatly into Sun and Moon, and these two styles of cognitive processing are represented by Gemini and Sagittarius, respectively.)

Your ace in the hole is that you can do the nodal interpretations at the heart level. You can get to know these symbols in very much the same way as you know your friends. You can feel them in your body-mind, in other words. There, keeping those vast archetypal fields wide open is not so daunting a prospect. If we contemplate attempting it with the head alone, the mind freezes—or goes into a kind of brow-wrinkling intellectual overdrive which typically accomplishes very little. But the heart can handle it.

In doing nodal analysis—or any other form of astrology—the intuitive heart must be engaged with the process. Only the heart can handle these vast archetypal fields of data without over-simplifying them.

This is, of course, a pleasing thought. But don't abuse it. There is no licence here to escape the head-work! Think of your best friend again. That emotional chord that the sound of her name strikes in you is a masterpiece you have created over time. It is the culmination of years and years of listening and loving and sharing. We have all been offended by con-artists and seducers who try to masquerade as our closest confidants twenty minutes after we have met them. No one can really know you that quickly. They have got to work at it for a while. That is how friends honor each other. That is how we know we are loved—someone thought we were worth the effort, and acted accordingly.

Our hearts come to know the archetypal fields of the astrological symbols gradually through the mental disciplines of study, memorization, observation, and experience. The spires of intuition soar upwards from the foundation of hard cognitive work

Once again, beware of the earlier chapters of this book! Try to avoid the temptation of simply parroting those interpretations. I believe that what I have provided there are fundamentally correct understandings of the archetypal meanings of the astrological symbols which are most relevant to nodal analysis. But they are all presented in vacuums. Reality does not operate that way. If your south node is conjunct Mercury, go ahead and read that section. Then look at the rest of the clues in your chart. Some of the points I made about your Mercury-node conjunction will then be underlined ten times by the rest of what you read. Others will not be supported at all. Those latter parts fall away, or at least fade from centrality.

Cosmos and Consciousness

We live in the material cosmos, but we also live in the inner world of the psyche as well. The foundational principle of astrology are that the two worlds are structured according to the same laws and that they are locked in resonance with each other. What happens inside us and what happens outside us reflect each other. One expression of this idea is synchronicity—for inward evolutionary reasons, it is time for you to go to the Dingle Peninsula in Ireland. At the same time, "by chance" a friend offers you the keys to a cottage on the Dingle Peninsula. Cosmos and consciousness dance together, and are perhaps not nearly as separate from each other as they seem.

For all that, there is one very basic difference between the inner archetypal world and the outward material one: the inner world is a lot simpler. Certainly the mind is complex! But in your mind you have the archetypal reality we call the color "yellow." How many yellow things are there in the world? In your mind you have the archetypal reality we call the "villain." How many villains are there in literature, film, history, politics?

Astrology accesses the core archetypal structure of the cosmos. As you invoke "Capricorn," it is like tapping into a deep aquifer. As the water rises into the individual psyche, it becomes more complex. As it reaches the surface of the earth and enters into material manifestation, that complexity has exploded into almost infinite diversity. So archetypal Capricorn is not simple, but it is far simpler than all the possible outward things that Capricorn can represent—which include governments, blueprints, mechanical controllers like railroad switches, business plans, mining interests, goats, regulations, macro-economics, the herb mullein, conservative business suits, the organization of your hard drive, social duties, repressive tyrannies, steep and inaccessible mountains, tundra, literary outlines, freezers . . . you get the picture.

Bottom line, it is a lot easier to keep this integrative, heart-centered approach working if you are dealing with Capricorn psychologically than if you are trying to hold all its possible material manifestations in mind!

When the archetypal field of Capricorn is stimulated in your life, we can be one hundred percent certain that some of those material manifestations will be part of the story. But tundra or social duties? Tough call.

All this explains why psychological forms of astrology typically prove more reliable than material, "predictive" forms. The psychological realm is simpler than the material one, as the archetypal realm is simpler than the psychological one. Out of unity comes diversity. Out of the mental plane emerges the material realm. This timeless metaphysical truth also provides helpful guidance for us as evolutionary astrologers. We do better to concentrate on staying simultaneously open to the psychological or archetypal significance of all the nodal symbolism. We do not need to worry about whether our client will be buying a new freezer.

A Map through the Deep, Dark Forest

There are surely many right ways to analyze a birthchart. In the battle plan that follows, no dogmatism is intended—only a set of practical suggestions which consistently work well for me. I encourage you try them and see how they work for you.

One point about which I would be dogmatic is the benefit of having *some* kind of master plan or strategy. The reason is that the load of information the nodal axis can generate is truly titanic, even if we stick to its psychological and archetypal dimensions. Even with your heart engaged, you will have your limits about how much information you can integrate. It is imperative to have priorities. Build on the most elemental bedrock first. Decorate the landscape with petunias and chipmunks later, if you haven't already reached your body-mind-spirit limits.

Below are the steps I take in the order I generally take them. Please remember two critical points. First, keep all the possibilities open with all the steps—do that by *feeling* each one rather than trying to remember dictionaries of key words. Second, look particularly for any limiting, negative, or destructive possibilities with each of these configurations.

1. Meditate on the sign of the south node.
Characterize the individual's prior-life *psychological character* and *emotional agenda.*

2. Meditate on the house of the south node.
Characterize the individual's prior-life *situation* or *circumstances*.
3. Meditate on the sign position of the south node's planetary ruler.
Add another dimension to the individual's prior-life *character and agenda*.
4. Meditate on the house position of the south node's planetary ruler.
Add another dimension to the individual's prior-life *situation*, or discover a *critical chapter in the story*.
5. Is there a planet conjunct the south node?
In the prior life, this person was the embodiment of that planet. He or she was deeply identified with it, personally and probably publicly.
6. Is there a planet conjunct the planetary ruler of the south node?
This planet is a significant "adjective," amplifying and modifying our sense of this person's prior-life nature and position.

Sit and feel for a moment. This is quite a lot of information. Let your heart have time to integrate it. Are there any repeated themes? (Mercury on the south node and the node-ruler in Gemini, for example.) Any obvious polarities, paradoxes or contradictions that could provide narrative drive to the story? (An independent Uranian type caught in a situation where he or she is defined by external relationships—for example, the node or its ruler lies in the seventh or eleventh houses, conjunct Uranus.)

The first six steps establish the identity of the person in his or her prior lifetime. Pull these clues together and feel them as a unity. We have the character. In the next steps we discover the plot.

7. Any planets opposing the south node?
What or who *opposed* this person in the prior life? What or who was *the brick wall of reality* he or she faced? What or who was *unattainable* or *impossible*? For what or who did he or she *long*? What *defeated* the person?
8. Any planets square the south node?

What or who *afflicted, blocked,* or *vexed* this person in the prior life? What was *left unresolved* or *hanging in the balance*? What *blind-sided* the person? What evolutionary *steps were skipped*?

9. Assuming there are any planets square or opposed to the south node, is one of them also its ruler?

How might this person have been his or her *own worst enemy in the prior life*? What *independent personal choices* might have led to trouble or damage to self or others? What might the *present consequences* of such prior actions be?

Again, take a moment to reflect and breathe. If there are planets making these hard aspects to the south node, you have begun to uncover a story of difficulty. How might this story have gone badly? How might the person have sustained psychological or spiritual damage as it unfolded?

Assess yourself. As far as ferreting out the prior-life story, you may have gone far enough at this juncture. There are more stones to turn, but you have looked at the primal ones. Resist the temptation of assuming that more information is always better. That is true only so long as your heart can surf the complexity. You may have enough. You may be wise to stop here. I often do myself.

Ready for more?

10. Are there are any planets sextile or trine the south node?

What or who simply *comforted* or *supported* the person in the prior-life situation? What or who *offered encouragement or support in folly*? What *temptations* were not resisted? Who *seduced* or *conned* this person? Are there *many* trines and sextiles? If so, might things have been too easy and led to lassitude and loss of evolutionary momentum?

11. Any planets square or opposed to the planetary ruler of the south node?

Not quite as telling as planets aspecting the node directly, but the interpretations of these aspects to the nodal ruler are similar to what we saw in steps 7 and 8. .

12. Any planets sextile or trine the planetary ruler of the south node?

Again, these are not as central as planets aspecting the node directly, but similar to what we saw in step 10.

These twelve steps will provide you with the bones of a helpful and evocative prior-life story. As we have discussed previously, the gold you will pan from this river is simply a helpful *parable*—symbolism is not literalism. The story that emerges *parallels* a valid, difficult karmic memory—and not a random one. Instead it is a story that is profoundly relevant to the person in his or her present lifetime, for the simple reason that it involves a haunting pattern of loose-ends, unresolved issues, unpaid—or uncollected—debts, erroneous beliefs, and general human craziness. It is a pattern which has been carried forward into the person's present circumstances and psychological profile, where its fingerprints can easily be detected as life's go-nowhere loops and dead-ends.

It may not be just one single prior-life story that we have uncovered here, either—more about that below.

If we stopped our analytic process here, we could have some fascinating results. We would have learned about a past life which lives on today. But the results of that knowledge might also be devastating. We have essentially defined the disease. We have yet to define the medicine.

Enter the North Node

The Moon's north node is the antidote, the resolution—the medicine that addresses the karmic predicament we just defined. To understand it we need to shift gears. We turn our concentration away from the immutable water-under-the-bridge of the karmic past, and enter the realm of magic: the present moment, where our future is being created. The quantum principles of uncertainty, modulated by human consciousness, take over. We abandon the boring "predictions" of the fortune-tellers—surely second only to pornographers in the strictures of their imaginations. We take enthusiastic responsibility for a future we can create intentionally.

Using the North Node to Help Understand the South Node

You can use the north node to help you grasp the south node story. When I have found myself stuck in trying to figure out the karmic pattern, I have often noticed that skipping ahead to the north node breaks up my mental log-jam.

Let's imagine a really complicated human situation. I will write it in plain English first, then translate it into the technical language of astrology in the next paragraph. You marry someone. She gets sick. She is *legitimately* dependent on you—she has no choice because of her debility. You devote yourself to a life of helping her, sacrificing most of the personal joys and comforts one might expect from a marriage. Your wife's situation is authentically tragic, but her response to it is dreadful. She falls apart spiritually. She is whiny, unappreciative, endlessly given to complaint, and completely opposed to making the slightest effort to ease your burden. You endure that hell until death do you part.

Frame that as a prior lifetime.

Astrological translation: reflecting the unresolved issues from that experience, your current south node lies in Virgo in the seventh house (the servant in the house of marriage), with its ruler, Mercury, in Virgo too, and in the sixth house (service again). The node is squared by Saturn (duty) from the fourth house (home). Jupiter is in the first house and Pisces, opposing your south node—there is your wife, opposing you. She is imperious (Jupiter), suffering (Pisces), and domineeringly self-centered (first house). She is the brick wall of reality which you cannot get around.

This sad story has many moral complications. Your wife may have been on the ropes legitimately enough—spiritually and psychologically unable to do any better. Should you have said, "Adios, honey" and walked out? Or did you do the right thing to sacrifice your own life that way? *Were you right or wrong to honor your deepest marriage vows at this fierce level of self-sacrifice?*

I would not enjoy having dinner with anyone who has too quick or certain an answer. Life is full of these kinds of slippery dilemmas, infinitely more complex than anything the Ten Commandments might address. The karma in this situation is nuanced. How do we pitch the south node story? What are the real evolutionary issues left over from this prior lifetime?

Ask the north node. Understand the medicine and maybe you are a step closer to understanding the disease. Here, the north node lies in Pisces and the first house, conjunct Jupiter. Clearly, your evolutionary future lies in *celebration* and *abundance* (Jupiter). You need to get better at the fine art of *selfishness* (first house) as a way of claiming the experiences that will trigger *mystical breakthroughs* (Pisces).

Being that way is hard for you because it is opposite all the ingrained patterns left over from that lifetime of tedious servitude and vow-keeping.

Taking all that in, we can focus our understanding of the south node story. We honor your prior-life commitment and self-sacrifice, but we realize that the experience left your soul inured to quiet, uncomplaining despair. *You assume you will be a slave,* whether or not you ever literally experience that thought consciously. You were left with a big dose of co-dependency—a tendency to go into orbit around the needs of others, however dubious those "needs" might be. There is great risk of getting into present-life marital or familial contracts that reflect the old pattern, literally or energetically.

Thus a consideration of the north node has helped us sort out what should be proudly carried forward from the prior lifetime (integrity), and what wounds need to be healed from it (too much self-sacrifice). Even better, it tells us how to heal them.

A Map into the Uncharted Future

Again I imply no dogmatism or rigidity here—what follows is intended only as a set of practical steps for analyzing the Moon's north node. Try them and see how they work for you. With experience, you may well go down a different road.

1. Meditate on the sign of the north node
Characterize the *evolutionary intentions* of this soul in terms of what *basic virtues and wisdoms* it is attempting to develop.

2. Meditate on the house of the north node
Characterize the *outward, behavioral arena of life* within which this soul can most effectively learn its lessons. What *realm of experience must it enter* in order to do its work?

3. Meditate on the sign and house positions of the north node's planetary ruler.

Add a secondary, supportive dimension to the soul's intentions. How might the soul *perfect* its evolutionary plan? What kinds of experience *trigger breakthroughs?* How might it *"make an A"* in this lifetime?

4. Is there a planet conjunct the north node?

What *core planetary archetype* is this soul attempting to integrate into its self-image? What *heroes* should it emulate? What *negative projections* onto certain types of people must it withdraw? Whom must it *stop shaming?* To what kinds of people must you guard against *giving away your power?*

5. Is there a planet conjunct the planetary ruler of the north node?

What qualities and attitudes can play *efficiently supportive roles* relative to the evolutionary intentions?

6. Any planets square the north node?

What issues must be resolved in order to *provide access* to the evolutionary intentions? How can this planetary energy, which is currently *hanging in the balance*, be made to *serve the north node* rather than falling back into repeating old dramas and reproducing old blockages? What *negative projections* onto certain types of people must it withdraw? What kinds of people can potentially *trip you up?*

At this point, assess the condition of the integrative sensing device upon which this whole procedure depends: your heart. Do you have enough information? Maybe you do. Would more overwhelm you and create mental confusion? Never be afraid to stop here.

7. Are there are any planets sextile or trine the north node?

What might be your *best resources* in support of this evolutionary work? Whom might your *best friends* or *allies* be?

8. Any planets square or opposed to the planetary ruler of the north node?

Not nearly so powerful as planets aspecting the north node directly, but the interpretations of these aspects to the nodal ruler are similar to what we saw in step 6.

9. Any planets sextile or trine the planetary ruler of the north node?

Again, similar to what we saw in step 7.

Elegant Final Touches

Everything in the chart is ultimately karmic, as we explored back in Chapter One. There is not a single planet in your chart that is not there for reasons that existed before your birth. Specifically, a planet does not need to rule or aspect the nodal axis to be there as a result of pre-existing, past-life causes. In Evolutionary Astrology—and life—nothing is random, and there are no meaningless loose ends.

For all of us, karma is complex—certainly far more intricate than any single past-life story could convey. We have all lived many lifetimes. In each one entanglements and illusions have arisen, as well as evolutionary breakthroughs. It would not be reasonable to expect the present birthchart to tell only one single past-life tale. Instead, we would expect the chart-behind-the-chart to reflect something more fragmentary, with lots of unrelated pieces.

The beauty of the nodal-based form of karmic analysis is the way it cuts through to the heart of the matter. We see the core—the *most elemental, most relevant* karmic story. We often tell one story, but we know it represents a summation of many. This reduction is a helpful simplification. But it is still a simplification.

All the planets that rule or aspect the nodal axis can be corralled into our storyline—that is basically the methodology this book is exploring. Planets that have no such technical relationship to the nodal axis are put aside, assumed to be mostly irrelevant to that storyline. Good! As we have seen, keeping a handle on complexity is a critical interpretive strategy. But you can sometimes provide an elegant final touch. *Sometimes you recognize that a planet with no relationship to the axis fits into the storyline anyway.* If you do, go ahead and use it.

For example, you may encounter a military story, full of death and darkness, such as the one we saw with Lee Harvey Oswald. Let's add that Saturn is in the seventh house, but not making any connections to the nodes in the ways we have been exploring. Toss in a little human wisdom: soldiers in combat lose friends to death, and worse. Battle-hardened, they may develop a hesitancy to get too close to anyone for fear of repeating the pain of loss. (See the Saturn seventh house connections?) Such experiences and adaptations may survive death unresolved. That seventh house Saturn has just leapt elegantly into the storyline.

> **Just because a planet makes no technical connection to the nodal axis or its rulers does not rule it out as part of the karmic story.**

How Many Stories?

An astrologer might predict how a stock will perform, or tell you where you left your wallet, or say who will win the big game or an election—those are legitimate forms of astrology, and obviously those astrologers will be concretely right or concretely wrong. The best practitioners in those fields do about as well as the long-range weather forecasts. Pretty well, all things considered.

But for the rest of us, Parables 'R' Us. We are looking for the metaphors and images that trigger recognition, reaction, and release in our clients and friends. Unless we are doing very concrete, non-psychological forms of astrology, parable-work is really all we can do.

For these reasons we never assume that there is one single "right" nodal story in any birthchart. We can recognize a brilliant analysis—a story that hits all the technical bases and still moves the heart. We can recognize a bad analysis too—the leaps are too long and unjustified, inconvenient pieces are ignored. But we know we are always, bottom line, *creating a story*. We never have "the right answer" in the envelope as we wait to see which student wins the prize.

> **What we are seeking is a past-life story which is consistent with all the clues the chart offers, leaves no clues out, and which includes nothing additional of significance which we cannot justify through technical analysis.**

Never would there be only one possible karmic scenario that fit those criteria. The symbolism is too rich for that. There are many "right answers." One of them may actually be a factual account of the literal prior lifetime. But which one? Barring psychic or intuitive information, there is no way to know.

So what if we choose the wrong story? There are dozens of possibilities, so very likely we *will* choose the wrong one. This is not nearly the disaster it might seem to be. *Our goal was never to tell the facts; it was always to tell the truth*—which is a far bigger concept. If I say that you were a solider at war, while the actual reality is that you were a street fighter in a gang in a ghetto, the essential psychological and existential point has been made.

Sequenced Stories

Sometimes a few stories appear out of the symbolism which seem to exist in an evolutionary sequence. When telling several stories in sequence makes the most sense out of all the clues, tell it that way. Typically, we are talking about familiar learning processes which often happen in the context of a single lifetime, but can also unfold over several. For example, we take a prestigious job for reasons that have nothing to do with our soul. After a few years we get sick of it, change careers, take a pay cut—and we don't hate Mondays anymore. One lifetime or many? Such a process could also unfold over several lifetimes—some of us learn faster than others!

That one feels like a single lifetime. It is easily encompassed, in other words. Other evolutions are more monumental, and seem to sit more easily in the context of a cycle of lives, all wrestling with the same core issue. In plain English, the drunk dries out and becomes the mystic. The amoral power-seeker realizes the emptiness of power and become a great leader in some larger, altruistic cause. The disciple becomes the guru. The killer repents and becomes the healer.

Decades—or centuries? Handle it as you please. The essential point is not actually affected.

In speaking of sequenced lifetimes, usually it is clear which are the lower and which the higher evolutionary states. Tell the stories in that order! Be sensitive here, though. Appearances are not always reality. A person, for example, might be so active in charitable activities that she is widely considered a saint. But her motivation might include an ego-driven need for attention and approval. Her charitable work is still helpful karma, no matter what subtle contaminations might have entered it. But karma is karma. As the seeds of her darker ego-driven karma ripen, she might move into a future lifetime in which she is self-indulgent, spoiled, and demanding. There, she will experience the unsatisfying consequences of the unbridled expression of those qualities—and that too is an evolutionary step forward—despite appearances.

In this work, in other words, be wary of the judgments this world has taught you. The thief in this lifetime may, in prior life, have been a monk who took a premature vow of poverty. The hooker might have been the nun who took a premature vow of celibacy. The woman who abandons her children may have sacrificed too much of her soul to her children in a prior life.

You now possess all the basic tools I have been using successfully with my clients for the past ten years or so. For me, they have passed the only test that truly matters: their effectiveness and relevance in the counseling room. They help people. Many of Jodie's and my students and apprentices have used these tools themselves with equally good results with their own clients. A number of them—oh happy moment!—have quit their day jobs. They now earn their livings enhancing the meaningfulness of other people's lives. If you feel drawn to such a road yourself, your next step is simply the gathering of experience. Practice, practice, practice, in other words. That, famously, is how you get to Carnegie Hall from here.

To help you get off on the right foot in that journey, we now turn to five in-depth karmic analyses of specific individuals. Three of them are famous; the other two culturally important. In choosing them, I purposely was not thinking of people whose lives would "prove" my theories—long ago, I learned that one can prove anything in astrology by that method! These techniques are sufficiently robust that there is no need to cherry-pick supportive illustrations. The criteria by which I choose these five people were as follows:

All have lived and died, and enough time has passed that we have gotten some perspective on their lives

All will, I suspect, be meaningfully recognizable to readers a decade or two from now.

All lived sufficiently colorful lives that we can readily observe the outward expression of their karmic patterns.

In each one, you will see the ghost of the past making itself felt in the shadier corners of the present biography. In at least one, the same echoing dark sun rose on another dismal version of yesterday's sky. In some, evolutionary progress shines forth triumphantly.

CHAPTER FIFTEEN: AGATHA CHRISTIE

September 15, 1890
4:00 AM-GMT
Torquay, England
Rodden Rating: A

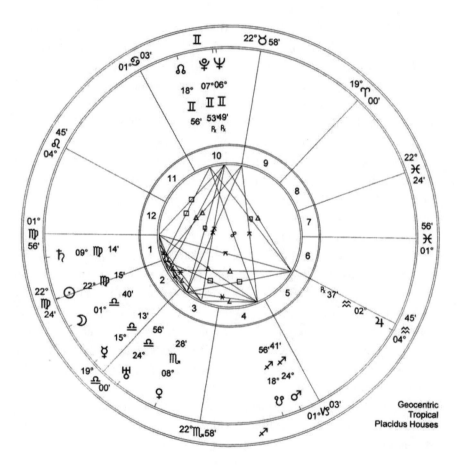

Four *billion* copies of her books are in print. She is often described as the best-selling author in history. Her play, *The Mousetrap,* is the longest continuously running one in the world, having opened in London on November 25, 1952, and still going strong as of this writing.

But it is for her murder mysteries that Agatha Christie is best known. Her work practically defined the genre that Arthur Conan Doyle launched. Her vain Belgian detective, Hercule Poirot, with his waxed mustache and his brilliant deductions, humanized the infallible "Sherlock Holmes" archetype. Poirot is the only fictional character ever to be given an obituary in *The New York Times*, after Christie killed him off in her 1975 novel, *Curtain*—such was the popularity of her work at the time. Her delightful Miss Marple, at least as brilliant as Hercule and a lot more charming, made it safe for older, middle-class ladies on both sides of the Atlantic to have a devilish streak and a gleam in their eyes.

Reading Agatha Christie's mysteries today, one might be excused for thinking that they are riddled with clichés—until we realize that she originated most of them! Arguably there is not a mystery writer today who does not owe her an enormous debt.

So who was this mystery woman?

Agatha Christie was born in Devon on the southern coast of England. Her mother was British and her father was an American stockbroker who died when Agatha was eleven. Their circumstances were comfortable—at age sixteen, for example, young Agatha went to "Mrs. Dryden's Finishing School" in Paris to study piano and voice. In 1914, she married a pilot, colonel Archibald Christie. She gave birth to a daughter, Rosalind, in August 1919. In October 1920 her first novel, *The Mysterious Affair at Styles*, was published to glowing reviews. She had written it in 1916, with transiting Uranus and the progressed Sun applying to trine to her north node. It was published with Jupiter, ruler of her south node, rising into the seventh house by solar arc.

On December 8, 1926, with transiting Sun conjunct her south node, Agatha Christie disappeared for ten days. By then she was quite famous and it was a media circus. Popular opinion held that it had been a publicity stunt, but more likely Agatha's own explanation was the truth. It was essentially a controlled and very private nervous breakdown, driven by her husband's having an affair. She checked into the hotel into which she "disappeared" *under the name of his lover*—and please keep that odd fact in mind as we get into the deeper material, below. The marriage broke up shortly thereafter, in 1928, with Saturn spending most of the year transiting back and forth over her south node.

Agatha Christie re-married in 1930. Her second husband, Sir Max Mallowan, was an archaeologist fourteen years younger than her. That marriage was apparently happy for quite a while, although it too entered darker years as her second husband also began a series of affairs. Due to Mallowan's work as an archaeologist, Christie had many opportunities to travel to the Middle East, the setting of many of her novels. Her best-known work is probably *Murder on the Orient Express*, which she wrote in Istanbul and published in 1934, with the solar arc south node trine her Moon and conjunct her node-ruling Jupiter.

In 1971, Agatha Christie was made Dame Commander of the British Empire. She died in January 1976.

Astrologically, Agatha Christie is a Virgo with Virgo rising. Thus, Mercury rules her chart and disposits the Sun. She has two planets—Uranus and Venus—in the third house (communication), and two more in Gemini up in the tenth house: a tight conjunction of Pluto and Neptune. No astrologer would be surprised to learn that this was the chart of a prolific and successful writer. "Mysteries" would naturally be the domain of Pluto and Scorpio. With her Pluto in the tenth house and her third house Venus lying in Scorpio, we can easily see astrological support for what we already know: that she was a prolific writer who wrote mysteries.

Let's see if Evolutionary Astrology can carry us more deeply into Agatha Christie's soul.

Her lunar south node lies in Sagittarius in the fourth house, in a conjunction with Mars. Sagittarius is the "gypsy." It is fiery, with little tolerance for restraint or limitation. The hunger to explore, to see the world, to learn, to expand—all those are Sagittarian qualities. Mars, similarly, is fiery by nature—and of course also occupies the fire sign, Sagittarius. It too suggests an explosive, adventurous spirit, rebelling against outward constraints in a prior life with a "live free or die" attitude. (Note the basic tension between these energetic nodal perspectives and the more cautious qualities suggested by her "double Virgo" status.)

Thus the sign of Agatha Christie's south node and the planet conjunct it describe her prior-life *nature* in vivacious and boundary-busting terms. I italicize the word "nature" here because one's "nature" is what signs and planets describe. They reflect what we *are* as human beings: our style, our affect, our energy.

But if you want to know what Agatha Christie was *doing*, then look to the relevant houses. They give the circumstances and the biographical "shape" of the life.

Agatha Christie's south node lies in the fourth house: home, family, the domestic environment. Again note the clash: a free-spirited, passionate, experience-hungry individual who found herself defined by domesticity. *She was a fiery, Mars-enhanced, gypsy-on-steroids, trapped in a home.* And she was not only frustrated about it, but also angry (Mars). The feeling this configuration invokes is of a tiger stalking in a cage or an eagle with its talons chained to the ground. The metaphor of the bomb going off inside the steel room comes to mind.

It takes a lot to contain this kind of fire. What kept Agatha Christie so trapped and house-bound in this prior lifetime?

Following our procedural outline, we would next look to the ruler of the south node. Here we immediately find at least one answer to our question. The ruler of Sagittarius is Jupiter, and it lies retrograde in Aquarius in the fifth house. As we have learned, this will give us "another dimension" of her past-life identity or "another chapter in the story" that casts light on her identity. One ancient correlation of the fifth house is *children*—and, naturally, when our first hint was "family" (south node in the fourth house), it is a very short jump to thinking about children. Those are exactly the kinds of interlocking metaphors we seek. In this case, we might speculate that we are talking about a *lot* of children as well—Jupiter tends to be expansive and Aquarius has some pertinence to groups of people.

We might add that Agatha Christie has already emerged as *passionate*—that is one message of her "hot" Mars conjunct the south node. And Sagittarius has a tendency to leap before it looks. And where did she leap? Into a home. Into the fourth house. Putting two and two together, remembering that birth control was quite dicey until recent generations, the notion that in a prior lifetime Agatha Christie found herself *bound to a home by children* leaps out.

It is doubtless relevant that she chose to have only one child in this incarnation, five years into her first marriage. And she had none in her second marriage. Nowadays such a choice would not raise an eyebrow, but in the context of her times, it was an unusual choice. People used to have more children, and the social mind-set in support of them doing so was entrenched and ubiquitous.

But in a prior lifetime children had been the lock on the door of Agatha Christie's jail-cell.

The fifth house has other meanings too. Love affairs. Creativity. Celebration. Debauchery. Let's not forget them—they are part of the archetypal field too—but let's leave them to bubble on the back burner a little bit longer.

What about hard aspects to the south node? Let's put a little more narrative into the mix if we can—planets in hard aspect to the south node always help with that. They provide the grit of plot.

The Pluto-Neptune conjunction is tantalizingly close to an opposition aspect with the south node, but it is a little too wide for us to make much of it—eleven or twelve degrees is pushing it. We will return to that aspect later as a kind of "tweak," once we have the main thrust of the story understood.

No ambiguity about the Sun though—it lies on the second house cusp in Virgo, making a solid three degree square to the south node. Here we encounter another major element of the story. The Sun always represents some force in our lives which simply must be obeyed. Sometimes it represents an overwhelming, transcendent *moral obligation*, something upon which we just cannot turn our backs—a dear friend in dire need, for example. Other times it represents a *compelling circumstance* over which we have no power—the ship is sinking and we are a hundred miles from shore. Most often the best entry-point with the Sun is to try thinking of it as a *person of compelling authority*, someone "in charge" of us, someone whose word must be obeyed.

Let's try that latter angle for starters and see where it carries us.

Agatha Christie is in a family situation and feeling bound there. Love for her children is part of the binding. The Sun here can easily indicate her partner—and we would naturally be looking for a partner in a "family" storyline such as this one. Had the south node been making her look like a hermit, we wouldn't consider that possibility. But with a domestic setting for the story, thinking of the Sun as husband or wife is natural.

What can we say about this partner? First, he or she was characterized by *dominating* (solar) *authority.* Very likely, there was a *demanding, picky* quality in the person—that is one of the darker faces of Virgo: never satisfied, always quibbling and criticizing. It is not fair to say "all Virgos are like that," but in this kind of astrology we are trying to ferret out unresolved *problems* from prior lifetimes. We do not begin our search for them at the highest levels of each symbol's expression—quite the opposite.

So, in a prior lifetime, Agatha Christie's partner was domineering and critical. That's a start.

The Sun lies at the cusp of the second house. The partner was probably *quite concerned about money.* This does not indicate either wealth or poverty specifically, only concern and worry (Virgo).

Taking the Sun more broadly as a possible indicator of compelling circumstances, we might speculate that Agatha's situation was somehow fraught with *financial issues* that could not be ignored or gotten around—not an unusual situation in families. The kids have to eat, and so forth.

Virgo can indicate *self-doubt,* a quality driven by enslavement to impossible or unreachable standards. The second house, from a psychological perspective, deals with feelings of inadequacy, of "not having what it takes." Taking the Sun as indicative of the partner, we now achieve a deeper, critical insight: *the partner, though domineering, was insecure, felt inadequate, and was inwardly self-critical.* He or she somehow held the aces of power, but was not fundamentally as strong a person as Christie herself.

So far I have been referring to Agatha Christie's prior-life partner as "he or she." Might we narrow that down a bit? Trying to scope out gender from the planets is shaky work. You can never be totally sure, although sometimes it becomes fairly clear. For obvious reasons, a story of death in a military action probably suggests a man, whereas death in childbirth would rather definitively suggest a female prior incarnation. The very rough rule-of-thumb that Venus indicates a female and Mars indicates a male must be taken with a large grain of salt—there are surely exceptions to it. Here, with Agatha Christie, seeing a fiery Mars conjunct her south node, I speculate that we are talking about a prior lifetime in which she was male—and thus a husband and a father. The Sun then would naturally become female here: Christie's demanding, self-centered, critical, ultimately insecure wife.

Going further, Sagittarius represents *philosophy, religion,* and *belief.* Generally speaking, it has a *moral quality.* With Agatha Christie's south node in that sign, we can assume that in this prior life she was quite identified with her energized sense of right and wrong. Likely, this moral framework was significantly conditioned by fourth house values: family, and "the ties that bind." *She made a religion of family.* Throw in the passionate, over-the-top qualities of the Warrior archetype, represented by Mars: she would *die* for the family, if necessary.

This kind of domestic commitment has a robust kind of moral authority to it, but it is not to be confused with love. It is not about soft feelings of connection; it is about fierce, self-sacrificing feelings of moral duty. It is surely not intrinsically indicative of happiness. We already know that she was a stalking tiger within the cage of family responsibilities: angry, not happy. But we can now add another set of bars to the cage: a moral commitment to "doing the right thing by the family," no matter what she (or he!) was feeling.

Several paragraphs back, we posed the question: What kept Agatha Christie's free spirit so trapped within a family in this prior lifetime? Now we have three answers. All are relevant. First, *children.* Second, a *demanding, insecure, needy partner* with all the manipulations that entails. Third, a compelling sense of *moral obligation.*

These were the bars on the soul-cage.

They made her furious (Mars). But the bomb went off in a steel room (the fourth house).

Cutting to the dark heart of the matter, it is the nature of Mars that it *wants to kill.* Better said, the part of humans that sometimes feels homicidal is called Mars. That is simply the name for it. We have all got one. Whenever you have felt like hitting someone, your Mars had risen up.

I postulate that, in a prior lifetime, inside this steel room of moral and practical constraints, Agatha Christie built up a pitch of *contained* (fourth house) rage (fiery Mars) at "his" wife. I feel that this rage was never expressed outwardly or directly—it remained contained within the fourth house, held in check by the bars on the three soul-cages.

I postulate that these unresolved and unreleased *fantasies of murder* found expression in her novels in this present lifetime. Beneath their mannered English facade, Agatha Christie's novels and plays are of course generally stories about "good, respectable" people killing each other, often quite horribly.

We have still got something bubbling on the back burner: the other possible meanings of the fifth house where Jupiter, the ruler of Agatha's south node, lies. *Love affairs. Creativity. Celebration. Debauchery.*

What might a passionate man do, trapped in the kind of situation we have described? How would he survive? What release might he find? He might comfort himself with life's simple pleasures: food, alcohol, toys, games, sports, friendships. There are no serious indications of a prior-life addictive problem here—no major Neptune issues, for example—but I suspect that Agatha Christie "partied hardy" back then.

Aquarius, where Jupiter lies, is inclined to break the rules. It is the *rebel*. Factoring that element into our equations, might we imagine that "he" also took some license sexually? It is always critical to remember that, with reincarnation, we are dealing with history. Sex never goes away—or we will! But it is famously malleable by custom and belief. Different periods of time have always been characterized by distinct sexual mores. Males often experienced a different set of sexual pressures, norms, and expectations than did females—the infamous "double standard," which is thankfully evaporating in many places today. "Wenching" and whoring have often been unspokenly acceptable, something "men needed to do," something verging on acceptable so long as they did not talk about it—and came home afterwards.

Jupiter loves excess; the fifth house loves pleasures; Aquarius likes to "walk on the wild side." All these hints apply to Agatha Christie's karmic story. With this Jupiter configuration ruling her south node, I think it is fair speculation that while Agatha Christie was loyal to the family in the material and practical sense, "he" was not faithful in a sexual sense.

This speculation is further bolstered by that *curious and exploratory* (third house) Scorpio Venus squaring the node-ruling Jupiter. Both Scorpio and Venus represent sexual drives, and here—through the square to the node-ruler—we see them "making trouble."

We can bolster this sexual speculation even further, but not with astrology. We turn to the actual facts of Agatha Christie's life. Her first marriage collapsed partly because her husband was having an affair. And in her second marriage, while it started brightly enough, her husband also had many affairs. He remained "with" Agatha—but married his long-time lover the year after Agatha died.

Karma is most often simply pattern-repetition, but sometimes we "reap as we have sown." I believe that Agatha Christie's promiscuous karma had ripened—the chickens came home to roost. Remember that when she "disappeared," she checked into the hotel *under the name of her husband's lover.* Why would she be *identified* with the lover? And what resonance did she feel sexually with these two unfaithful men?

We have one more element to consider about that node-ruling Jupiter in the fifth house: *creativity.* I suspect that another, healthier way that Agatha Christie survived being imprisoned in a hellish marriage with an "awfully wedded wife" was through some kind of *artistic expression.*

How many guitars are sold for every rock star? What's the ratio? How many novels are started compared to novels even finished—let alone actually published? People are creative for the joy of it. That is enough sometimes. I suspect that Agatha Christie took simple pleasure in creativity in this prior lifetime. Creativity was another diversion.

We can take that notion a little further. The Pluto-Neptune conjunction in Gemini and the tenth house *almost* opposes the south node. We might safely ignore it, but everything in a chart has meaning—even this near miss. Let's start by making a mistake—imagine the opposition to be closer, close enough to count. What would it mean then? A brick wall of reality out there in the "big world," something that could not be gotten around—and perhaps something for which Agatha Christie *longed.* What could this longing be? The two planets are in Gemini. It is an "impossible" *longing to be heard.* Heard saying what? Neptune: fantasy and imagination. Pluto: serious, perhaps shocking truth. But public opinion and cultural reality would have been adamantly opposed to such expressions. They did not happen. Public opinion and cultural reality (tenth house) were the brick wall of reality.

Remember that this "opposition" is not close enough to be truly effective. To correct our "mistake," we have to water the interpretation down. I think it is fair to say that fantasies of being heard publicly this way entered Agatha Christie's mind only occasionally in this prior lifetime, and were quickly pushed aside as impossible and unreachable. In and of itself, this "opposition" is a very minor part of the interpretation. It only puts a little spin of wistfulness on Agatha Christie's prior life creativity, which remained private. I could visualize "his" making up bedtime stories for the kids, for example—great stories that only the kids ever heard.

Pluto and Neptune take on a more serious tone when we take our analysis to the next level: to the Moon's north node in Gemini and the tenth house. *Agatha Christie came into this world with a compelling soul-intention to have her voice heard, and heard very widely.* This would be the medicine for her soul-wound. She was angry, and profoundly tired of being trapped. It was time to break out of family and into the big world. It was time to tell the unvarnished Plutonian truth about what she felt about being trapped in conventionality, marriage and parenthood.

Mercury is the ruler of the north node, from the second house and Libra. Agatha Christie needed to *prove herself to herself* (second house) as an *artistic* (Libra) *voice* (Mercury). And that proof would be inseparable from her willingness to use *imagination* and *fantasy* (Neptune) to make some distinctly Plutonian points about the darker possibilities of social and familial dynamics!

A serious "skipped step" blocked Agatha Christie's way: the Sun, squaring her nodal axis. If she was to attain her north node goal, she first needed to *create an ego*. In the prior lifetime, she had given too much power and authority to the partner. She had abdicated from her own natural autonomy in important, life-shaping matters, and only claimed it in the form of trivial, illicit pleasures which actually had the effect of keeping the situation stable—and stuck. In the end they only engendered more rage, and presumably leavened it with guilt as well.

Furthermore, Agatha Christie had projected negatively onto "the wife," whom she had perceived as demanding and egocentric. She said, from the snooty—and highly compartmentalized—reaches of the morally superior high ground, "I would *never* be self-centered and demanding like that!" What this negative affirmation actually meant was that she would create a *moral and philosophical justification for remaining in jail*—a jail that she had at least partly created herself. Presumably the umbrella of this moral self-justification extended to cover the "modest comforts" she extended to herself in terms of various escapist excesses, sexual and otherwise.

All that had to be fixed. Agatha Christie needed to claim her solar right to be *selfish*, to claim what she needed for herself. Ask any writer: you simply cannot succeed at the craft without some degree of selfishness. Otherwise you will never have time to write. Virgo represents the idea of *craftsmanship* and *skill*. Part of Agatha Christie's skipped step fell in the category of honing and polishing her skills—in this case, her gifts as a writer. Then, in full view on the stage of the world, she would honestly unload the great weight that she had brought into this lifetime—suppressed, murderous rage at the "nice" family that had clipped her wings and contributed to her corruption.

And just "talking" about it would make her feel a whole lot better! That insight is simple enough—commonplace, really. *It is the rage we bottle up that is the true soul-poison.* Get it out, put it into words, get it off your chest—we all know it helps. Even if agreements cannot be reached, it is still good to clear the air. Unprocessed anger blocks love, it locks up the heart. And we do not even need accord from a partner—often it is simply enough to know that we have been heard.

Some of us experience this healing, clearing process in a talk across the dinner table. Agatha Christie, with her Gemini north node in the tenth house, turned it into four billion books.

CHAPTER SIXTEEN: BILL WILSON

November 26, 1895
3:22 AM-EST

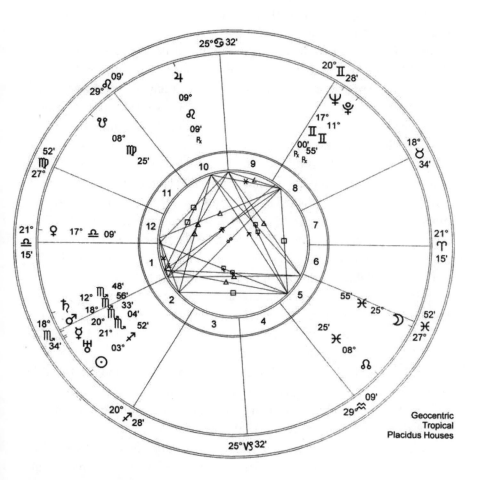

East Dorset, Vermont
Rodden Rating: B, given as "around 3:00AM" and rectified to 3:22AM

Bill Wilson may have the highest ratio of anonymity to influence of any human being in the past century. His work has saved countless lives, perhaps even countless souls. Yet unless you are directly or indirectly involved with the fellowship he founded, you have probably never even heard of him. That was, partly, his point. He was the cofounder of Alcoholics Anonymous.

In his early twenties, while serving in the military during World War One, Bill Wilson had his first drink. Both solar arc Neptune and Venus, along with the progressed Ascendant, were beguiling his south node with sextiles. Becoming an addict is famously easy. He found that a drink helped lubricate his tongue in social situations, and he quickly became addicted to alcohol. He married and became a successful securities analyst from 1919 to 1925, but booze took its predictable toll. His career collapsed. After many unsuccessful attempt to moderate his alcohol intake, including hospitalizations, he finally had his last drink on December 11, 1934. A few months later, on May 12, 1935, he met with a man known as "Dr. Bob" in Akron, Ohio at around 5:00 P.M. Many take that moment as the "birth" of Alcoholics Anonymous, although the question is murky—many in the Fellowship celebrate a date in June. Transiting Saturn was almost exactly on Bill Wilson's north node that day, and Neptune was stationing close to his south node. In addition, the transiting south node was almost exactly aligned with his Midheaven, while transiting Mercury squared his nodal axis. Karma was ripening.

By the way, Bill Wilson's birth time is given as "around 3:00 A.M." Astrologer Donna Cunningham has rectified it to 3:22 A.M. I accept her rectification as it really does seem to line up with the timing of events in Bill Wilson's life better than the 3:00 A.M. chart.

In this book, our primary concern is with karmic analysis. As we will soon discover, the root issue in Bill Wilson's prior-life dynamic is not primarily addiction. It is *pain* and *shame*. But briefly we do note his Pisces Moon—and we recognize how the Piscean "mystic" can manifest as "the drunk" unless it learns positive ways of dealing with its own sensitivity. The Moon is late in the fifth house, which can correlate with "debauchery." Potentially escapist Neptune squares it. Furthermore, Venus rules the chart, and Venus always seeks *release of tension*—and plays a far larger role in the charts of people with addictive tendencies than many astrologers recognize. Venus also lies in the twelfth house, underscoring the mystic/drunk themes. Finally, Bill Wilson is a solar Sagittarian with Jupiter trine his Sun—more indicators of a possible vulnerability to excess.

Handed this chart, no astrologer would be shocked to hear that the person it represented had experienced issues with substance abuse. But what would an evolutionary astrologer see that the conventional one might miss?

The Karma

The Moon's south node lies in Virgo in the eleventh house. Here, in the context of a prior lifetime, we discern in Wilson a person eager to be competent and effective, and perhaps in some kind of "service" role. He is given to fretting and worry, and fraught with self-doubt. All that is the Virgo message.

Placed in the eleventh house, we see Bill Wilson's prior self operating in the context of a group, swept along by the currents of the group, and defined by his role in the group—that is the meaning of the eleventh house. Integrating Virgo's "servant" archetype with the eleventh house symbolism, we recognize that his role within the group was a subordinate one. He was following guidance or orders from above. In some sense, he was "in uniform," although so far we have no reason to think of it as a military uniform. So far it might just as well have been a baseball team! All we know is that he is part of a group, striving to be competent, and under someone else's command.

Mercury rules the south node from Scorpio in the second house. We hit a vein of gold here—Mercury is in a stellium, tightly conjunct Uranus, very close to Mars and less than eight degrees from Saturn. That is a lot of information to take in. Get the big picture first. The theme of *self-doubt,* first suggested by the Virgo south node, is now underscored by the second house placement of its ruler. When a chart repeats a theme this way, it is like adding exclamation marks. We must use emphatic language to convey the meaning of the symbolism. Thus, in this prior life, Bill Wilson emerges as a man *overwhelmed* and *in over his head.*

Scorpio, in the context of nodal analysis, often represents the extreme aspects of life—death, betrayal, taboos broken, sexual storminess. In other words, whatever overwhelmed Bill Wilson might have overwhelmed you or me too! Note that we are not seeing anything that compels us to think of him, in the prior life, as wimpy or cowardly. He was up against something big. It could have overwhelmed anyone.

Now throw in the specific significance of the three planets that are conjunct the south node ruler. All of them add three-dimensionality to his prior life identity. Uranus, lord of earthquakes and lightning bolts. Mars, the god of war. Saturn, classically the indicator of failure, despair, and impossibility. Clearly, Bill Wilson's south node ruler is directing our attention toward a tale of considerable drama. And remember what we already know from the south node itself—he is being swept along by *collective currents*, playing a *subordinate* or *functionary* kind of role in this explosive situation.

Saturn is the weakest of these three modifying influences simply because it is furthest away from the node-ruling Mercury. It echoes the idea of "orders" and "duty," strengthening those themes. Orders and duty were grafted onto his identity.

Mars is quite powerful, being less than three degrees from Mercury. It also lies in Scorpio, the sign of its traditional rulership. Remember, the ruler of the south node always gives us information about the *identity* of the person in the prior life context. Was Bill Wilson actually a solider? Mars can certainly indicate that, as we saw earlier in the chart of Lee Harvey Oswald. Surely Wilson was in a *competitive situation* in which *passionate anger, resentment* and perhaps *violence* were present.

Uranus is less than one degree from the Mercury—and thus provides us with our most powerful modifying signature: Bill Wilson was identified with the *archetype of the rebel*. He broke the rules. He stood up to authority. He got into trouble. That is what Uranus does.

That Uranian theme is extremely powerful. We cannot overlook it. But note how it jars us—everything else we have seen so far is suggestive of Wilson playing a *subordinate role within a hierarchy*, expected (and expecting) to do his duty. Now suddenly we are seeing rebellion. These themes contradict each other, yet they are both there. Both must be true. How can that be? Perhaps he first obeyed, then rebelled. It is tempting to run with that theme, but let's be patient a little longer. There are clues we have not yet explored.

There are no planets in opposition to Bill Wilson's south node, but when we look for squares we hit the jackpot. The Sagittarian Sun in the second house squares the nodal axis, while Pluto in Gemini in the eighth house squares it from the other side. In addition, Neptune is conjunct Pluto, and falls a bit over eight degrees away from the nodal square as well—close enough to be a factor, for sure.

Let's start with the Sun. Always a *force majeure*, the Sun represents that which must inevitably be obeyed. Planets orbit the Sun whether they like it or not. Similarly there are people or situations that simply command our attention and submission. They hold all the aces. Try, for example, telling the government that you are not in the mood to pay your taxes this year, that you don't believe in taxes anyway. Now, *you can do that*—but of course the consequences are such that the action is practically unthinkable. That is the way the Sun works. Something—probably someone—of such an undeniable, powerful nature *afflicted* Bill Wilson. Whoever or whatever it was, was Sagittarian too—which here means cocksure, impulsive, good at philosophical rationalization, and self-righteousness.

Recall how we have repeatedly seen the theme of *orders* and *hierarchies?* The Sun we have just been exploring is very probably their source: something undeniable, inescapable, and all-powerful, *which controlled and vexed Wilson.* And remember that earlier Uranian suggestion of rebellion? Rebellion against what? And remember all the weakening influences in terms of Wilson's confidence? Now the story begins to look like the futile rebellion of the mouse against the tyranny of the cat. Futile frustration and pique build against an immovable dam.

Pluto awaits. It too is square the nodal axis. Pluto is always evocative of extremity and nightmare, especially when it lies in the eighth house where it is so strongly accentuated. The eighth is the traditional house of death. With Pluto there, it can point toward horrific forms of death—or the psychologically-sapping, pervasive threats of them.

Remember the symbolic trinity of Pluto, the eighth house, and Scorpio—and remember that Wilson's four planets in Scorpio are all part of our nodal story as well. *The symbolism of nightmare and horror is mounting.* Every word in the astrological lexicon that can indicate nightmare is present here in this nodal drama, in spades.

Gemini, Pluto's sign, correlates with speech, as does Bill Wilson's node-ruling Mercury. Therefore, a theme of *speaking up rebelliously to authority* is gathering momentum.

Incidentally, Gemini is also linked to *respiration*, and in the context of the house of death, our attention is directed to ways that life can be ended through the direct interruption of breath.

Finally, Neptune squares the south node, although less precisely than Pluto. Might Bill Wilson, in a prior life, have been afflicted by *ungrounded idealism*? That is always one of the darker potentials of Neptune. Might he have had a *martyr complex* (remember the eighth house)? What about a tendency toward *problems with alcohol* or some other substance? That is certainly a potential Neptunian issue. Given the facts of Wilson's present life, the interpretation is not only tempting, but eminently plausible—still, emphatically, it is not central to the story. Of all the "afflictions" in this nodal configuration, Neptune plays the weakest role. The chart tells us not to overdo it, whatever the realities of his present life might suggest. Always trust the symbols!

Before we pull the threads together into a coherent narrative, what about supportive aspects to the south node? There is a striking absence of them—only Saturn sextile the node from Scorpio and the first house. I suspect there were superiors who liked Bill Wilson in that prior lifetime—or who at least liked his competence and dutifulness. Perhaps he was more at peace with solitude than many of us.

But the real message is that when we look for support, there basically is not any. This man was alone, isolated and exiled within a group.

War has never been in short supply, and perhaps the easiest way to ground this story in reality is to imagine that, in a past life, Bill Wilson was a low-ranking soldier pressed to perform dark acts of violence *(Mars; Scorpio)* which he began to find reprehensible. There is the feeling of an escalating collision between what was, on one hand, initially a true sense of duty, and on the other, an increasing feeling of abhorrence and shock in the face of death and killing. Likely, there was some manner of "true believer" in a position of absolute authority over him *(Sagittarian Sun)*. Probably some element of shock-based Uranian emotional dissociation entered the mix. Perhaps alcohol soothed the wounded conscience and sensibilities for a while, but one day something snapped in Bill Wilson. The resentments boiled over. He spoke up. He rebelled, futilely.

I suspect he was hung for it.

I have no compelling reason to insist on framing Bill Wilson's tale as a war story. All I know is that he was part of a hierarchical organization linked to some extreme activity redolent of death and skirting the edge of taboo. Even though a Scorpio Mars conjunct the ruler of his south node gives some further support to the idea that we can identify him as a solider in a prior life, we do not need to limit our imaginations to that one single possibility—although it may well be significant that he had his first drink in 1917 as a solider in World War One.

To keep our work honest and open to the nuances of metaphor, I could almost as easily imagine Bill Wilson as a minor figure in a large corporation who became appalled at some corrupt practice, indicated that he might "blow the whistle," and was silenced—forever. Or perhaps he was a member of a "crime family" who similarly reached a point where moral shock and anger boiled over despite his loyalty to his clan—and do remember that Uranus can indicate a criminal.

Whatever the story, the interpretive key is to note the sense of *absolute, irreconcilable conflict*—a moral situation that left no life-affirming choices. On one hand, betraying his tribe was morally unacceptable—not to mention completely terrifying in its personal implications. On the other hand, there is a mounting sense of alienation and shock. Finally, there is the Uranian element, suggesting that "one day, something snapped." That explosive feeling is augmented by the precipitous tendencies of Mars and Mercury in Scorpio. It was as if he were "caught between a rock and hard place" or "damned if he did and damned he didn't."

In the end, Bill Wilson had no option that did not involve some manner of self-destruction. Alcohol abuse probably began to creep into his behavior as a "solution," but indications are that the behavior did not have time to build into what would be perceived socially as full-blown alcoholism. Alcohol is not the center of the past-life story. Pain, shame, rage, resentment, and impossibility are.

It is interesting to note that what drew Bill Wilson to alcohol first in this lifetime was that he found it very difficult to speak up in front of people without it. His voice had gotten him into a world of trouble n the prior life.

Uranian things happen quickly. In the prior life, I can imagine words popping out of his mouth, words that were unforgivable in that social context—and fatal. Reincarnating, how would he then feel about speaking up spontaneously?

What about the north node? It lies in Pisces and the fifth house. God kicked Bill Wilson out of heaven this time around, saying, "I want you to go down there and have a good time!" That is the fifth house. But Wilson did not really know how to do that. Like all of us, he had a tendency to behave ignorantly in the areas symbolized by his north node. A shot of whisky may make us feel happy, but how does a bottle of whisky make us feel?

The deep meaning of the fifth house is *joy*. High Piscean energy is about *surrender* and *ecstasy*. The man needed to become re-enchanted with life. He needed to recover a child-like quality of innocence. Bill Wilson had suffered terribly in a prior lifetime, as we have outlined. His suffering had been moral and spiritual. He had felt the sting of mighty evil triumphing over powerless, futile good. He had felt utmost alienation, a complete lack of support or understanding. Indifferent, murderous injustice had been his last perception. He entered this world in an unresolved state of soul-agony.

Contemplating all this, the familiar phrase "I really need a drink" leaps to mind. And many people throughout human history have taken innocent comfort in a glass of wine. But wine is no medicine for this kind of pain—and if we ask more of wine than it can deliver, it of course begins to become a further source of pain, one which we can perhaps not handle because we were already so burdened at the moment of the first breath.

The higher ground in Pisces is mystical and spiritual. Those among you who know anything about Alcoholics Anonymous know that the program revolves around surrendering to a "Higher Power," however that principle might resonate in the individual conscience. In this life, after experiencing the bitter echoes of his unresolved karma, Bill Wilson seems plausibly to have leaped forward into the message of his north node's sign. He found his "medicine." It was spirituality.

The fifth house is often about creative self-expression. While we do not think of A.A. in terms of art, the "telling of one's story" to a receptive, supportive audience is a significant part of Bill W.'s "cure." The fifth house is also very much about the present tense, which brings to mind the A.A. adage "One day at a time."

It is telling to see that Bill Wilson's progressed Midheaven made a conjunction with his south node in 1939 when he wrote the seminal volume, *Alcoholics Anonymous*, commonly known as "The Big Book." At the same time, his solar arc Pluto had also come to his Midheaven. Had Bill Wilson chosen a lesser path, these symbols could easily have indicated a descent into utter depravity—or the kind of death that "serves as a lesson to others." Instead, reflecting the highest meaning of the Midheaven, he claimed his mission in the world and left behind a gift that has benefitted countless lives.

We can take faith and courage from Bill Wilson's story, even if we have never felt oblivion's call ourselves. It is a story of a soul falling into the gravitational well of its own karma and managing to climb out again. Bill Wilson eventually seized the spiritual joy of his north node—and he made a gift to the world out of the lessons he learned from his south node. We can take wisdom from his story too in that it teaches us to look beyond obvious surfaces. Alcoholism was only a symptom of his karmic story, not the source of it. With that reality understood deeply, we experience compassion arising for the wound Bill Wilson brought into this world. We experience respect for the futile courage that ripped this pain into his soul so long ago. And we celebrate that same courage as it blossomed into healing in this lifetime—a healing whose ripples extended way beyond the shores of Bill Wilson's own life.

CHAPTER SEVENTEEN: ADOLPH HITLER

April 20, 1889
6:30 PM-LMT
Branau, Austria
Rodden Rating: AA

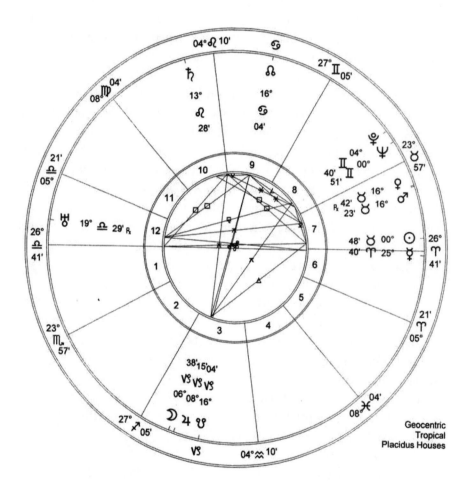

Geocentric
Tropical
Placidus Houses

Human history is not short of villains. It takes a special kind of guy to sweep all the votes for the top of the list. One man accomplished that. The way "Einstein" has come to signify genius or "Bill Gates" wealth, Adolph Hitler has become the standard metaphor for evil incarnate. What kind of karma can lie behind someone holding such a place in history?

Hitler's birthchart is famously deceptive. It has been used for an example so many times that most beginning astrology students learn to recognize it and thus avoid making apparent fools of themselves. But let's look at it honestly from a conventional astrological perspective. It's not as mean as one would expect. Hitler was a seventh house Taurus—not a belligerent placement for the Sun. One might imagine a reasonably cooperative, peace-oriented, solution-oriented, practical approach to human relationships.

Libra is rising, again echoing the notion of a "let's all get along" attitude. Venus, goddess of peace, is thus the ruler of the chart—and is placed in the seventh house and in Taurus. The planet of love could hardly be stronger.

The Moon lies in Capricorn, once more suggesting a practical, grounded theme, along with basic reasonableness. The Moon is aligned with Jupiter—and while the combination of those two bodies in Capricorn can be ambitious, there is also a certain bigness of heart and generosity of spirit typically associated with a Moon-Jupiter conjunction.

What's going on? Given the actual realities of his life, Hitler's chart just does not "work" very well.

Some astrologers, in an effort to line the chart up with the horrific realities it represents, glom onto the fact that chart-ruling Venus is retrograde and tightly conjunct Mars, the god of war. They point knowingly to controlling Saturn in the ambitious tenth house and in kingly Leo, squaring the Mars-Venus conjunction.

But, like Hitler, Charlie Chaplin had a Venus-Mars conjunction in Taurus squared by a Leo Saturn! So did game show host, Merv Griffin—although in his case the planets are in different signs.

Give us a break, in other words.

The basic vocabulary of astrology, taken in sum, would clearly not suggest that Hitler's was the chart of the man whose very name would come to epitomize the depths of evil and human depravity. Astrologically, Adolph Hitler looks like a nice, if somewhat pedestrian, fellow.

Hitler's chart is one of those, like that of Lee Harvey Oswald which we explored earlier in the book, in which evolutionary astrology really shines. As we will see, when the karmic pattern is very different from the "obvious" thrust of normal birthchart analysis, the karmic pattern always makes itself felt in an undeniable way. If we ignore the karmic pattern, our interpretation will be significantly off the mark. If we include it, we penetrate to the heart.

Often the karmic analysis is not so dramatically distinct from the conventional one. To keep this book honest, I have generally chosen charts more randomly so that they reflect the range of realities you will actually see. But when I want to make an argument for evolutionary astrology, it is a chart like Hitler's or Oswald's that I use. Where an astrologer ignores the underlying nodal pattern *when it is very distinct from the conventional view of the chart*, the astrologer consistently winds up with egg on his or her face.

Hitler's south node of the Moon lies in Capricorn, suggesting a *drive toward accomplishment, a hunger for control*—and a willingness to do whatever it takes to attain those goals. That south node also implies an underlying mood of *solitude, self-sufficiency* and perhaps *loneliness*, along with a "wintry" feeling in the heart.

Always remember that one of our basic procedural principles in karmic analysis is to accentuate the negative! As we have maintained throughout this book, that attitude is helpful simply because unresolved karma is *by definition* problematic.

The third house placement of the Moon's south node implies a *mental* quality in Hitler's prior life, one of *improvisation* and quickness of response. It has a reliable correlation with *language skills*, which presumably were very pronounced in the prior life. There is also a certain *amorality* in the third house—it is helpful to recall that it lies opposite the principled, philosophical ninth house. This does not make the third house "immoral," but rather it emphasizes an *immediate* and *practical* response to whatever comes up. Linked to Capricorn, the pragmatic, even calculating qualities of the third house are further illuminated. The word "cunning" comes to mind.

To be fair, Capricorn often stands for situations that are inherently difficult, even survival-oriented. In a prior life, Hitler might have found himself *improvising his own survival*. As anyone who has ever lived on the streets knows, moral and philosophical niceties do not buy you many doughnuts.

Jupiter conjuncts the south node, as does the Moon from just under ten degrees away. The presence of the "king of the gods" on Hitler's south node carries us a giant step forward in our understanding. Up until now, we could have been looking at an orphaned street urchin putting food in his belly through animal cunning—and in fact, deep in the wells of soul-memory, there may be such themes in Hitler's karmic story. But the more immediate karma is Jovial. The prior-life ambitions were vast; he wanted to be on top. *There is a hunger for material wealth, glory and worldly power—the things of Jupiter.* And Jupiter brings extraordinary gifts to the table—in this case, outstanding abilities in the area of *rhetoric and persuasion* (third house) and gifts of *calculation and strategy* (Capricorn).

The Moon falls just within our arbitrary ten degree orb for aspects to the south node. We must include it in our thinking, but also be careful to de-emphasize it due to the wide orbs of the aspect. Like Jupiter, although less so, the Moon too represents something with which Adolph Hitler was identified in a prior life. Above all, it would signify *his own needs* and *emotions*, from which he could not easily distance himself. Those are standard lunar concepts, and here we already know something about the nature of those needs and emotions—we have been exploring them for a few paragraphs now: *ambition, control, authority.* Further, the Moon often relates strongly to our *roots*, in some sense of the word: our family, our home, our ethnicity, our land. This echoes Hitler's obsession with his mythical Aryan "master race."

The Moon is, of course, nurturing and typically gentle. Those expressions are somewhat constrained here, both by Capricorn and the third house, neither of which much support those kinds of energies. Also, we remember that the conjunction is right at the outer limits of relevance. Jupiter can be generous, but in this Capricornian context, jovial *ambition* is more central.

There is another reason to downplay the nurturing elements of the Moon symbolism, one that trumps everything else. Let's meet it—we have one more card to turn over. In this case, it is an ace. Saturn rules the south node, and thus represents another critical dimension of Hitler's story. It lies in Leo and in the tenth house. *The symbolism of "father" and the symbolism of total control* (Saturn) *converge with the tenth house* (worldly power and public authority) *in the sign of the King* (Leo).

Note that there are two symbols of kingship in astrology: Jupiter, the king of the gods, and Leo the Lion, the king of the beasts. Here we have Jupiter conjunct the south node, while the south node's ruler lies in Leo. Hitler's karma says "king" twice over. In addition, kings are often addressed as "Sire," which of course means father—and Saturn and Capricorn are the classic astrological symbols for fatherhood, so both "king" and "sire" are supported here. Finally the tenth house, while not directly related to "royal" symbolism is surely related to an elevated position within a community—or at least the hunger for one.

In evolutionary analysis, we are seeking *reinforced, repeating themes.* And almost everything we have so far seen in Adolph's Hitler's karmic analysis is about the drive be on top. Any nurturing themes we might detect must be placed in that larger context. Hitler, in a prior life, nurtured ambition and those who could support him in attaining it. As Bruce Springsteen put it, "Poor man wanna be rich. Rich man wanna be king. And the king ain't satisfied 'til he rules everything."

While we are speaking of "father," we might as well add that the Moon is usually taken to correlate with the Mother archetype, adding another "parental" element to Hitler's karma—and nothing here is suggesting blissful domestic parenthood, free of more mundane ambitions. This "parenthood" is about dominion over many lives, wearing the hat of some elevated and controlling personage within a broader community.

In a prior life, Adolph Hitler might have risen, in somewhat calculating fashion, to be the mayor of a small town in Bratislavia. He might have unscrupulously cornered the market for shoes or hats in southwestern Macedonia. Or he could have been one of the other famous tyrants of human history—Vlad the Impaler, Genghis Khan, Pol Pot, Hernán Cortés.

Outwardly, those are very different conjectures. But karma is not directly about outward matters. It is a matter of consciousness, attitude, values, and motivations. Inwardly, all those stories are basically the same, from the most tawdry and forgettable to the ones that leave a historical body-count.

Our next procedural step is to scan the chart for aspects to the lunar south node. We do not always find them, but in this case we immediately see that we will get some help from that direction. We have a number of aspects to consider. They add more of an element of plot to the lines of character we have already unearthed.

Uranus is tightly square the south node from Libra and the twelfth house.

Mercury falls just within our arbitrary ten degree orb for the square to the nodal axis. It lies in Aries. And we can have more confidence in this Mercury than we might have for another aspect so wide. That is because the planet is inherently so strong, being almost exactly angular, conjunct that seventh house cusp. As such it would throw wider orbs than it might otherwise. There is also a natural resonance between Mercury and the third house placement of the south node itself.

Conjunctions, squares, and oppositions typically tell most of the story, but we have a very precise and dramatic trine from the Venus-Mars conjunction in Taurus and the seventh house to the south node. The importance of that conjunction to our story is further amplified when we note that it also lies square to Saturn, the south node ruler. Obviously, there is a lot of Hitler's story yet ahead of us.

All of the planetary aspects to the node listed above have one common theme: *relationship.* Mercury is at the cusp of the seventh house *("marriage").* The Venus-Mars conjunction lies in the seventh house, and Venus is the goddess of love. Even Uranus lies in Libra, the sign which Venus rules.

Who can rise to power alone? King-making is a group effort, and it inevitably involves making enemies as well as friends. It is helpful to recall that historically the seventh house was not just the house of marriage—it was also the house of *open enemies.* In that light, of these four planets, two (Venus and Mars) are in harmonious relationship to the south node and two (Mercury and Uranus) are in harsh relationship to it. Very simply, these indicate friends and enemies, respectively—although let's be a little more circumspect about these "friends." Mars and Venus may trine the south node, but they also square its ruler. And of course having Mars, the god of war, sitting on Venus does not always support harmony. Thus, in Hitler's prior life story, we have clear enemies—and ambivalent friends.

Hitler's Capricornian solitude and blind ambition existed in tension with his practical need to elicit the cooperation of allies. Venus is retrograde, further suggesting his tendency toward relationships with people who held something back, or who had something to hide. We are looking at fair-weather friends at best, and at relationships based on perceived personal advantage and mutual manipulation. We are also looking, through Mercury, at *open enemies* with considerable leverage (Mercury is almost exactly Angular) and a warrior-attitude of anger or competitiveness (Aries) toward Hitler.

This brings us to Uranus in Libra and the twelfth house, closely squaring the south node. Uranus represents *shock*. It correlates with the unexpected, the bolt from the blue. The twelfth house, in this inimical context, correlates with *loss*. Often it indicates the total, catastrophic loss of everything: the bottom falling out. Linking house and planet, we see an "affliction" in Hitler's karmic story that reflects *the sudden, unanticipated, total loss of everything.* In one moment, his world fell apart.

What could he have lost? We already have a good hint about the answer from the previous analysis. *What had meaning for him?* In a prior life, he rose to a position of tremendous power, probably through Machiavellian means—and one day it all ended in an existential train wreck.

We might add that a classic meaning of Saturn in the tenth house is a rise to power, followed by downfall. That depressing prophecy emphatically does not always work out in practice! But here, with Saturn ruling the south node and our attention directed toward darker and more dire interpretations, it makes sense. Always, when we see two configurations independently confirming the same idea, as we do here, it pays to take the message to heart: Hitler, in a prior life, rose to the top then lost everything.

We have one more hint: Uranus lies in Libra, and thus it participates in the general theme of difficult relationships we have already contemplated. Likely, Hitler's prior-life downfall came from an enemy he did not know he had—remember that in traditional astrology the twelfth house is often described as representing "secret enemies," contrasting with the "open enemies" of the seventh house. In a prior life, Hitler was brought down from inside. His world exploded. Prior-life suicide is a possibility. So is assassination.

The Moment the Karma Ripened

A full analysis of Adoph Hitler's chart, including his lifelong transits, progressions and solar arcs would require another book. Our ambitions in this volume are narrower. Rather than watch his whole story unfold, let's instead take one early astrological snapshot: the moment in which I think it is fair to say that Hitler's karma ripened. On July 29, 1921, he was first introduced as the *Fuhrer* of the National Socialist Party. Jail still lay ahead for him; *Mein Kampf* was not yet written. But this was clearly the surfacing of his karmic pattern. On that day Adoph Hitler was declared *king of the Nazis.*

Transiting Mercury was crossing his north node—and of course opposing his south node—at that moment. Transiting Jupiter was within close orbs of a trine to his south node and also to his Venus-Mars conjunction. Opportunity (Jupiter) knocked, in other words, and invited him to speak up (Mercury).

As we have seen, two planets square Hitler's nodal axis. Both of them were also triggered around this time. Two days before he became *Fuhrer*, on July 27, transiting Mars squared his natal Mercury. On August 1, two days later, transiting Mercury squared his Uranus. July 29 falls right in the middle, and thus both transits, admittedly minor, were in effect on that fateful day.

As usual, the unfolding of the larger karmic pattern is indicated by heavier, slower planets. The quick-moving ones operate only as triggers for the deeper themes. Transiting Pluto was triggering Hitler's ambitious—and very karmic—Jupiter by opposition aspect at that time. Meanwhile, solar arc Pluto was opposing his Moon. Thus, on the day he was declared *Fuhrer, both of the planets that Hitler had in natal conjunction to his south node were simultaneously receiving oppositions from Pluto!* One was by transit, the other by solar arc. Given Pluto's predilection for dredging dark material up from the psychic depths, this was a momentous and unusual pair of events. The karmic wave was breaking.

Completing the picture, transiting Neptune *(illusion; glamour)* was crossing through the conjunction with his tenth house Saturn—the ruler of his south node.

It was a perfect astrological storm, in other words. The nodes were stimulated; the planets conjunct them were stimulated; the planets squaring them were stimulated. And the ruler of the south node was stimulated.

Again, the karmic was ripening.

Hitler's Possible Evolutionary Future

Karma is habit, the compulsion to repeat patterns. We all re-enact the south node story to some extent. That is understandable and we need to have compassion for ourselves there. The evolutionary journey is long and difficult—although punctuated with roses, good friends, and music! As we can see, Adolph Hitler's life hewed very closely to the outline of his karmic pattern. But unlike Agatha Christie and Bill Wilson, there was no overt indication of any progress. Given the enormity of his acts, it is easy to speculate that he had dug this karmic hole quite deeply—that he had been down this dark road before, worn in the grooves. Speculating as we did earlier that Hitler might have been among us previously as someone such as Vlad the Impaler, Genghis Khan, Pol Pot, or Hernán Cortés is not unreasonable.

Certainly, in any case, it is fair to say that the techniques of evolutionary astrology correct our tendency to see Hitler's chart as mild-mannered and reasonable! Underlying that "kind-hearted" seventh house Taurus with Libra rising was another beast entirely, one with a very different agenda. The "personality" of the chart that emerges through conventional astrological means was simply a tool in the hands of a soul that had long been walking a darker road.

And that is practical evolutionary astrology in a nutshell: *letting the karmic perspective underlie the conventional psychological approach, molding it and informing it.* Let the symbolism of the present psyche and that of the ancient soul dance together—there you not only get the deeper insights, but you also see the practical realities a lot more accurately.

In fairness, the conventional astrological view would not be completely wrong. History records Hitler's famous charm and seductiveness, his love of the arts, his brilliant oratorical flair—much of what such an astrologer might see is actually true and verifiable, although we can only keep a balanced perspective in this case through the lens of evolutionary astrology.

Could Hitler have possibly taken a higher road? That is a mystery beyond my fathoming. I can only know what I would have told him had he come to me as a young art student looking for some guidance in his life.

Probably I would have been careful about laying out the karmic story as straightforwardly as I have done here. That could potentially be damaging. I would emphasize the Cancer north node, and the need for *rest* and *healing* in this lifetime, after prior life trauma. I would underscore the ninth house and the importance of a life lived according to one's *highest values*—and I would suggest that in his case, Cancerian values would provide a good foundation. Those would imply the benefits of prioritizing *home life* and *family*, and certainly keeping them higher on the motivational list than ambitions of a career nature. I would emphasize how imperative it was to his ultimate happiness that he face the unresolved issue of *good, clear communication in the intimate context* (Mercury in Aries and the seventh house, squaring the south node). That would include the healthy communication of *anger*. With an eye on that node-squaring Uranus, I would encourage a highly independent (Uranian) exploration of *authentic spiritual values and experience* (twelfth house), perhaps through the arts and certainly through some degree of intimate dialog with a trusted partner (Libra). I would frame these "skipped steps" as necessary prices of admission to his real goal, which would be to create a gentle, loving life based on values in which he could truly believe until his last breath—the basic meaning of a Cancer north node in the ninth house.

All those words would represent deep truth, tempered with kindness. In practice, I would wait for signals—words, body language, encouragement—from young Adolph before I broached the darker themes. If he gave me indications that I could go forward without doing more harm than good, I would bring in the meaning of his north node-ruling Moon being conjunct the south node: *to go forward, he must go back into the past.* There are debts to be paid, truths to be faced, karmic chickens that will hatch in this lifetime.

And all that remains true. Somewhere in this universe, the mindstream that was Adolph Hitler is facing two eternal realities: unquenchable evolutionary possibility and the consequences of his previous choices.

CHAPTER EIGHTEEN: CHRISTINE JORGENSEN

May 30, 1926
9:00 AM-EDT
New York, New York
Rodden Rating: A

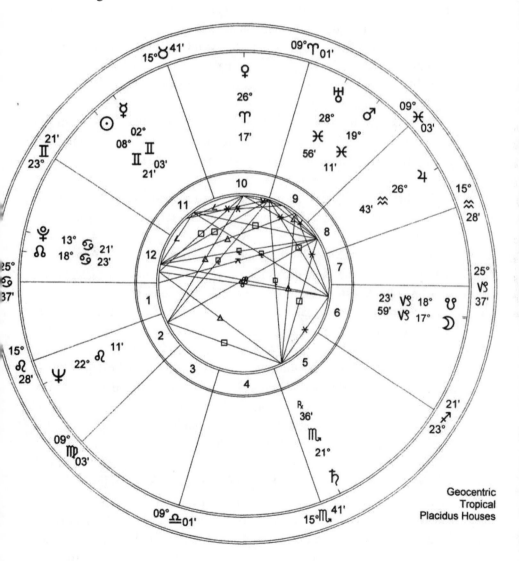

Geocentric
Tropical
Placidus Houses

Christine Jorgensen was born as George Jorgensen, but always felt "that nature had made a mistake." Inwardly, he felt like a woman. More than attitude and psychology were in play here—George's male physiology had not developed in typical fashion either. George went to Denmark in 1950 and came back two years later as Christine. In the subsequent media storm, the surgery was dubbed the first sex change operation in history. The statement is not quite true—physical conversions had been done in Germany as early as the late 1920s. But with Christine, a critical missing ingredient was added to the process: female hormones. For that reason, and arguably for cultural reasons, it seems fair to call Christine Jorgensen history's first transsexual.

Born physically a man, but psychologically a woman—what kind of karma could lie behind such an existential predicament? And of course this is not simply a question of Jorgensen's being gay. The majority of gay men think of themselves as men, not as women.

In Christine Jorgensen's birthchart, the south node of the Moon lies in Capricorn and the in the sixth house. Tellingly, it is very tightly conjunct the Moon itself.

The history of the last few thousand years is basically sexist. Astrologers have breathed that air and drunk that water—or, to put it more charitably, they have adapted to the cultures into which they were born. In that context, many astrologers in the past—and, sadly to me, in the present too—were convinced that the Moon and Venus were female and everything else except some asteroids were male. To me, that is not only blatantly sexist, but also simply bad observation. Has there ever been any shortage of male artists—those epitomes of Venus—in the history of the world? Any shortage of courageous Mars-women? Male chefs? Female accountants? All of the planets can express themselves through either gender. That is the root reality, as I have written before in these pages.

But, given the way sociology and culture enforce gender roles, I think it is fair to entertain the notion that when we see a major signature of Venus or the Moon on the south node that we are looking at a female prior incarnation. This is especially plausible for prior lifetimes, which naturally tended to occur in more uniformly gender-rigid societies. That Christine Jorgensen was actually a woman in a prior life is well-grounded speculation, given this nodal situation.

Going further, we must recognize that Venus and the Moon are not interchangeable. In the traditional social and mythic context, Venus represents the *attractive, beguiling* face of the feminine. The Moon reflects its *fertile, pregnant, nurturing, mothering* dimensions.

Later we will reckon with the fact the Christine Jorgensen's south node is squared by Venus. Suffice to say here that Venus is part of the karmic picture too. Bottom line, something of the "sexy, desirable" feminine *afflicted* him, while he was *identified* with the "nurturing, helping" aspect of the feminine.

Here the plot begins to thicken, as we know it must. Most of us have reincarnated in a different gender without the slightest thought of heading for Denmark to correct "Nature's mistake." Long ago, in a prior lifetime, something went wrong here,.

The south node of the Moon lies in the sixth house, the classic house of *servants.* And it is in Capricorn, emphasizing *duty* and *responsibility.* Normally it is good practice to begin with an analysis of the south node's sign and house, then proceed to the planetary modifiers. In Christine Jorgensen's case, the Moon signature leaps out so dramatically that I cannot not resist bringing it up right away. Immediately, in the context of the dutiful implications of the sixth house and Capricorn, we see the lunar theme of "nurturing" taking on a far more *slavish* connotation—hardworking Capricorn interacts powerfully with the house of servants, producing obedience, obligation, and efficiency. This "mother" was defined by a situation of duty and service. The love she felt may have been sincere, but it was given under constraint, in circumstances of *humility* and *restriction.*

Delving more deeply, our standard strategy now requires us to consider the condition of the ruler of the south node, which in this case is Saturn. We know that an analysis of this planet will give us another chapter or another dimension of the story, with a focus on a deeper grasp of Christine Jorgensen's prior-life identity. ("Plot" comes later, with the aspecting planets.)

Saturn lies retrograde in Scorpio and in the fifth house. The fifth is often connected to joy and creativity, but neither of those themes are very consistent with anything we have seen so far, nor with Saturn in Scorpio. Classically the fifth house was also the house of children—and here we hit the jackpot. Mothering—not to mention duty, service, and responsibility—are themes that naturally light up when we think of kids. They are a lot of work! We have found a way that the south node themes sit comfortably and reasonably with the Saturn themes: *the duty of nurturing and serving the needs of children.*

The interpretation is beginning to click.

While we are here, let's make note of another reinforced theme: both Scorpio and the fifth house have natural correlations with *sexuality*. There is an obvious connection between sexuality and procreation, and thus one more potential link to the issue of children appears right away. Yet the fifth house often refers to sex *outside of marriage* or *before it.* So let's just make note of that sexual question and keep it in the back of our minds. Sometimes a loose end such as this just falls away as we crystalize a nodal story. Other times, it becomes critical. It pays to notice the elements that do not initially seem to be fitting the puzzle. That is especially true when, as in this case, the chart has brought up the theme twice—again, both Scorpio and the fifth house can reference sexuality, and that is where we find the ruler of Christine Jorgensen's south node.

Still ahead, we have Venus squaring the node and Pluto opposing it. We will get to them. But what we have so far is a sense of who Christine Jorgensen *was* in this prior lifetime. Clarifying that information is the job of the node, its ruler, and any planetary conjunctions with it. Let's assess what we have learned about her "character" so far, and then see what Pluto and Venus might add in terms of "plot."

About her character, we have good reason to believe that in a previous lifetime, Christine Jorgensen was a female in a position of service. Thus, she had a master or masters. She was taking orders, dutifully and meekly. And her tasks were hard and relentless (Capricorn), as well as oriented to the work of the Moon: nurturing, feeding, cleaning, caring—the scut work of survival, or what, under the patriarchy, was often called "women's work." She might have been literally a slave—not in the cotton fields, but in the context of a home. Her duties very probably were oriented to children, as her fifth house Saturn attests. Likely, these were not her own children.

Very probably, Christine Jorgensen was what we would today call a *maid* or a *nanny.* In terms of her personal character, the combination of Capricorn (south node) and Scorpio (its ruler) energies suggest that she was at least *serious* by nature, and very probably *sad* or even *depressed.* That makes sense since there was no exit from this "slavery," no escape. Outwardly, she was bound by the demanding circumstances of endless responsibility Inwardly, she had internalized a "humble" self-image.

A servant serves a master. Whom did Christine Jorgensen serve? Opposite the south node we find Pluto in Cancer and in the twelfth house. This planet is good candidate for representing one who had authority over her. The opposition aspect tells us that her master was "unattainable" and also that he represented "the brick wall of reality," something she literally could not get around.

Here we are *personalizing* Pluto as her master. As we have seen in previous chapters, often turning planets which aspect the node into actual people works very well. And seeing a sixth house south node almost demands that we seek some evidence of a master and some information about his nature and agenda.

Still, it is helpful not to lose sight of the fact that Pluto in this oppositional position can also suggest something less personal—nightmarish, inescapable realities in general, which she could not get around. We can, for example, speculate easily enough about the "brick wall" of economics and social structure which might lead a young woman into a position of service which allowed her to survive. How many scullery maids in seventeenth century England would have preferred life on the streets? How many had better options than remaining in servitude?

For now let's focus on Pluto as representing the master himself. What does that tell us? He is "Plutonian" and thus probably moody, demanding, and dark. The influences of Cancer and the twelfth house hint strongly at something *hidden or private* about him, something behind the scenes, something that could not "stand the light of day."

And he held all the aces. He was the brick wall of reality. You obey the master, period.

Remember that earlier we had a possible loose end? Saturn, ruler of the south node, is in Scorpio and the fifth house, with their sexual connotations—but not the connotations of married sexuality, rather something suggesting "sex outside of marriage or before it." And of course Saturn carries the implication of duty, of *that which must be done whether we like it or not.* It is time to weave those loose ends into our storyline.

I believe that Christine Jorgensen's master took sexual advantage of her in a prior lifetime and that she felt powerless to resist him, not because of desire but rather because of the practical "politics" of the situation. Furthermore, she was compelled to keep the secret. The consequences of revealing it were far more nightmarish than the consequences of keeping it. As a simple reality check, we reflect that naturally, in situations of radical social, gender and economic inequality, women have borne this particular risk throughout history.

We have yet another clue to the plot of Christine Jorgensen's unresolved karma. Venus lies in Aries and the tenth house squaring the south node. Thus, it represents something that *afflicted* her in the prior lifetime and something that was *left unresolved* from it.

Let's start with the affliction. As we saw earlier, in historical contexts, Venus can often be taken to connote a female, particularly one displaying the Aphrodite function of sexual attractiveness and desirability. Through the square, we see that such a woman was in an inimical relationship with Christine Jorgensen. That antithetical feeling is further underscored by Venus lying in Aries—the woman was forceful and probably given to outbursts of temper. With Venus in the tenth house, she was a person of power and position. Likely, she was hard, ambitious and competitive—tenth house Arian qualities.

Given that Jorgensen was a servant, one natural notion is that this Venus represents her female master—her *mistress*. Very concretely, Venus lying in the tenth house declares that from Christine Jorgensen's perspective, this woman was above her in the social hierarchy. That clue supports the "mistress" interpretation without any strain; it is probably the simplest reading of the configuration, all things considered. Furthermore, this Venus represents a powerful, passionate woman, elegant but probably too hard to be considered beautiful—and one who noticed her servant only when the servant created an annoyance or failed in some trifle.

We have of course already met the master in the form of Pluto—and Pluto's maleness here is further supported by the process of elimination, since we have convincingly got the mistress in the form of Venus.

Interestingly, Pluto and Venus themselves are square by sign, although the orb is too wide to call it a technical square. To me, this suggests a discordant relationship between Jorgensen's two prior-life masters, but one in which they managed to avoid conflict by avoiding each other. And Christine Jorgensen was "squared" by one and "opposed" by the other, as if she somehow functioned as a bridge between them. But a battered bridge—the wife afflicted her with temper and anger, while the husband created an even more inescapable, fundamental and degrading problem.

Any harmonies or supports? Saturn sextiles the south node. Christine Jorgensen probably actually *liked the children.* She was intrinsically a nurturing type. Love for the kids could have "supported her in folly," to use one of our standard phrases for easy aspects to the south node. In this case, her love of the children would suggest yet another reason not to rock the boat and to remain in the protective role.

Mars also sextiles the south node from Pisces and ninth house. She may have derived some comfort from *religion*, which can be symbolized by both the sign and the house here—perhaps a religion which emphasized the virtues of *courageous martyrdom* (Mars; Pisces). Christianity and Islam both provide good illustrations.

A planet square the south node always represents something *left unresolved* from the prior lifetime, something which must be experienced or gotten right if we are going to get to the north node resolution. Often, the great difficulty with squares to the south node lies in the fact that we are *angry* at the person or thing that afflicted us. That makes it hard to 'withdraw the projection" and claim the energy in ourselves.

Picture yourself in Christine Jorgensen's position, and consider how the mistress looked to you. She dressed in finery—you probably dressed her yourself, so you knew every detail about her clothing, make-up, and jewelry. Perhaps you even furtively tried something on once or twice, terrified that she might return and find you in her things. She treated you harshly. Generally it was as if you barely existed. And yet she was like a haughty goddess of sophistication and elegance—something so far above you that you knew you could never attain it. You longed for that glamour, and were afraid to long for it.

And in this present lifetime, there was a need for Christine Jorgensen to resolve that unresolved issue—to claim that personal relationship with Aphrodite. *Men can do this without surgery!* Maybe we would have to translate a bit, and call Aphrodite "Dionysus" or "Apollo." It is an open secret that men can be vain and desirous of sexual admiration too. It is not a female province. There are mysteries in Christine Jorgensen's life which I do not claim to understand. But one that I do understand is that integrating Venus was a skipped step for her. She had to do it. For some reason, she needed to do this in the literal form of integrating the feminine realities of

Aphrodite. Perhaps the reason lies in her fundamental sense of *duty toward the Moon archetype.*

How interesting that after her operation, Christine Jorgensen was not content simply to live the quiet life of an average woman. She wanted to be glamourous. She wanted to be noticed. When she got home from Scandinavia, she made the headlines. With transiting Uranus on her north node, *The New York Daily News* blared, "Ex-G.I. Becomes Blonde Beauty." She became a cabaret singer, dressed in glittering gowns. She would sing songs such as *I Enjoy Being a Girl,* and switch into a *Wonder Woman* costume (think Aries Venus!) during the finale of her act.

Her "unresolved issue" was not simply with the broad notion of the feminine, but with the very specific notion of an Aries, tenth house expression of pure, confident, in-your-face Aphrodite energy.

Surely, Christine Jorgensen was the brunt of many jokes at the time. ("She went abroad and came back a broad," was a popular one). Yet we can admire her courage and vehemence in claiming back her relationship with the archetype of the *femme fatale* from her harridan of a mistress.

Pluto presents a fiercer challenge, both intrinsically and through the opposition aspect. As always Pluto symbolizes the darkest potentials life has to offer. When it lies in opposition to the south node, a person faced horror in a prior lifetime—and came into this lifetime with that nightmare still intact and powerful. In the context of Jorgensen's nodal structure, we have let Pluto represent the sexually oppressive and exploitive master.

In dealing honestly with Pluto, we must be prepared to be uncomfortable—that is simply the nature of the planet and what it represents. What is the darkest conceivable expression of male energy when it is in a position of total, unquestioned dominance over fertile, lunar female energy—a female energy which depends upon the male for its survival? If we are older than twelve, the question answers itself.

But yet again, by the immutable laws of spirit, healing the unresolved issue that Pluto represents involves the withdrawing of the projection. How could Christine Jorgensen make peace with male energy when the face of it she knew was practically Satanic? Given these realities, how could she even think of her feelings as "psychological projection?"

(How could a Jew in Dachau forgive the Nazis? How could a Lakota at Wounded Knee forgive the white man?)

There are answers to those kinds of questions, but let's first engage compassionately with the enormities they pose. The wounding experiences reflected in Christine Jorgensen's karmic signature did obvious direct damage to her soul, but they also shattered her dignity and her sense of self-worth. She was dismissed by the epitome of "Venusian" female energy (her mistress) and then exploited sexually by male energy (her master).

Given this kind of prior life experience, imagine the shock of being reborn in a male body! This is what "George" Jorgensen faced from the instant of his birth. Think of the rage and psychic horror directed at his own penis. The stunted development of his male physiology was a physical effect of the ingrained karmic pattern. That is how profound these imprints can be.

Christine Jorgensen's story is a radical one. As we might expect, the nodal tale is correspondingly extreme. The critical astrological point in understanding her reality lies in the interaction of three forces. First, her deep identification with the wounded feminine. Second, her deep loathing and fear relative to the masculine. And third, her skipped step in connection with the public celebration of Venusian desirability.

The north node of the Moon lies in Cancer and the twelfth house. Those symbols direct our attention to Christine Jorgensen's underlying themes of regeneration and evolutionary possibility. Cancer implies the need for *self-care* and *healing*. After a wounding experience, we naturally feel the need for quiet, for some distance between ourselves and the world. We might prefer to stay home rather than to go out. We may simply need to cry for a while. These are all Cancer signatures—and part of her healing strategy.

Similarly the twelfth house invites us to take solace in our spirituality, and again like Cancer to withdraw from the world. Ultimately, the healing for Christine Jorgensen lay in those directions.

But there is more. A critical point is that the Moon, ruler of the north node, lies conjunct the south node. Thus her evolutionary future is directly tied to a need to re-visit her karmic history. With the ruler of the north node on the south node, *the road to the future routes through the past.* To evolve beyond the soul-cage we have described, Christine Jorgensen had to go back and face the lunar wounds directly. These wounds were not something that could simply be "gotten over." Elements of the drama had to be re-lived from different perspectives.

This theme is echoed further when we come to terms with Pluto lying conjunct her north node. Here we see a different face of Pluto than the daunting one we have met in opposition to the south node. Instead of the monstrous manifestations of the dark Pluto, we encounter the higher ground: Pluto, the master psychologist, the shaman leading us into the underworld—and back out again—to recover the stolen parts of our own souls. As with the Moon ruling the north node but lying on the south node, Pluto tells us that Christine Jorgensen had to re-live the past. That is Pluto work: digging down into the strata of honest psychological history, be it present-life or past-life material.

Furthermore, we have already understood Venus as a "skipped step." In order to go forward and gain access to the healing, Christine Jorgensen needed first to have an experience of pure Venusian power. She needed to be *Wonder Woman.* Her shame needed to be dissipated in the healing rays of glory, applause and attention. Only then would she be strong enough to do the inner Plutonian work—the transcendence, the forgiveness, the empowerment.

Did Christine Jorgensen succeed? Was a physical sex change actually necessary to this process? I cannot be the judge of any of that—and, in all honesty, I don't think that you can be the judge either! As an evolutionary astrologer, all I can say is that she had some deep unfinished business with both genders. I would add that, given the humiliations of the karmic past, her way forward lay in feeling the energized and powerful aspects of her own possibilities. *It lay in the category of making a radical, Plutonian free choice in the direction of her own healing as she understood it.* That would represent the ultimate medicine flowing from the highest dimensions of a Cancer north node to a soul carrying such a wound: "I love you. You are worth it."

The interaction of flesh with spirit, of body with mind, is a complex phenomenon. It is folly to ignore any element of the system. Ultimately, the manifest physical world proceeds from the reincarnating, ever-learning mind. It is there, in deep mindfulness, that our most profound work must occur.

But if the physical act of putting on a *Wonder Woman* suit impacts the mind in a helpful direction, then pass the cape and the sparkly shoes.

CHAPTER NINETEEN: CARL GUSTAV JUNG

July 26, 1875
7:32 PM - GMT
Kesswil, Switzerland

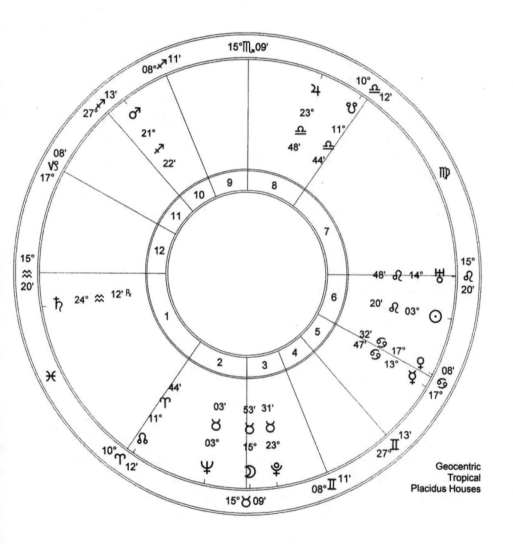

Rodden rating: A

The craft of psychology is about a century old. Anyone who looks at its early history constantly encounters two names: Sigmund Freud and Carl Gustav Jung. Each was a genius in his own way. And Freud came first. Yet today most modern psychological astrologers feel a deeper kinship with Jung. Like ourselves, he loved symbolism. The world, the mind, and all the stories that have ever existed—all were like dreams awaiting his interpretation. He was an astrologer himself. Perhaps more importantly, he made the ancient *wizard* archetype plausible in the twentieth century. He kept that flame burning when it was in danger of being extinguished.

Without Carl Jung, psychological astrology might not exist at all. He laid the foundation on which the rest of us stand. He carried us out of the darkness of fortune-telling and gave us direction. For myself, I know that I owe Jung a far greater intellectual and spiritual debt than I owe to any of my purely astrological ancestors.

Jung's sheer genius is amply reflected in his birth chart. He has Aquarius rising, with chart-ruling Uranus sitting angular on the western horizon. His "elder" persona is signaled by Saturn in the first house—that was his "mask" in the world, his *persona*. And how often do you see pictures of a *young* Carl Jung? He of course was young once, but history wants to remember him in the full flower of his Saturnian elderhood. That Saturn is in Aquarius too—another indication of genius, mixed with that beautiful wizard archetype.

The Sun is in Leo, the sign of the king. Yet it is in the sixth house, suggesting his sense of *lineage* with the other myth-makers of history, as well as his prodigious capacity for sheer hard work—a quality echoed by that powerful Saturn. I would not want to try to carry the collected works of Carl Gustav Jung on my back! But I would carry them a thousand miles to save them if I had to. They are holy books, precious to my soul. His third house *(writing; teaching)* contains a conjunction of the Moon and Pluto, both in Taurus. Earthy, grounded instincts, a respect for the "primitive," and a trenchant capacity to penetrate the surface of things—all are indicated here.

So who had this great soul been before he took birth as Carl Gustav Jung? How did he arrive here with this gift to give? And, more aligned with our purposes here, what unresolved karmic issues was he born to face? Hagiography is dangerous and not our intention. We aim here to see Jung more nakedly than that—as a man, as an evolving soul, not as a paragon. What baggage did he bring into this life?

As always, we enter our karmic analysis through the Moon's south node, which lies in Libra on the cusp of the eighth house. We know that where these two vast archetypal fields—sign and house—intersect and reinforce each other, we will find the core of the story.

Libra: Balance, grace, courtesy, civilized values, relationship, aesthetics, creative skill, tolerance for paradox and ambiguity, the capacity to get along with others.

Eighth house: Depth, psychological insight, a conscious relationship with death, sexual bonding, complex interpersonal process, inheritance, intrinsic charisma or worldly power, contact with the magical or shamanic realms.

All that is helpful—we can see most of these good qualities operating in Jung the practicing psychoanalyst. But with the south lunar node, we know that we must always be alert to the *Shadow,* to use his own term. Fundamentally, the south node represents wounded places to which we are attached and by which we are conditioned. In simple terms, it is always some combination of things we got wrong in a prior life—or damage we sustained in getting them right. And the most reliable practical principle of evolutionary astrology is that we will see at least the fingerprint of these unresolved issues in the present biography. Typically we see large segments of them simply reproduced whole cloth.

So let's re-frame these Libran and eighth house qualities in a more cautious and critical way:

Libra: Indecision and dithering, inability to choose and commit to a course, hypersensitivity and nervousness, vanity, relationship dramas, dependency, indolence and laziness, fawning insincerity, obsession with comfort, hypocrisy.

Eighth house: Moodiness, self-absorption, morbidity, obsessive fear of death, power-tripping, exploitive seductiveness, sexual compulsivity and drama, deceit, treachery.

While we can be confident that many of the positive and neutral elements we listed above will be present in Carl Jung's life, we can also count on some of the darker pieces making themselves felt as well.

What *patterns* are we seeing? Relationship themes, absolutely. They are central to both Libra and the eighth house. There is also elegance and civility in Libra and often the eighth house represents *power,* not to mention inheritance and "other people's money." There is thus a suggestion that in a prior lifetime, Jung had known *comfort* and *position* in a social sense, and that they had either come to him through *upwardly-mobile marriage* or that he had been born into that class and married "appropriately." Ideas such as those emerge where Libra and the eighth house intersect and reinforce each other.

In reality, Carl Jung's mother had come from a wealthy family, but his father was a poor minister in the Swiss Reformed Church. Jung grew up humbly—and yet he affirmed from his earliest days that he was possessed of two personalities. The first was exactly what he appeared to be—a schoolkid in Switzerland. And tellingly, the second was "a dignified, authoritative and influential eighteenth century man." (Jung tells this story in his autobiography, *Memories, Dreams, Reflections.)*

I suspect that this was a literal karmic memory.

On Valentine's Day 1903, Carl Jung married Emma Rauschenbach. She was from one of Switzerland's wealthiest families. From that moment on, Jung was a wealthy man. He had courted her for seven years. On his wedding day, he was twenty-seven years old—and his solar arc Moon was half a degree past an exact trine to his south node. The karmic chicken of "inherited" wealth and position had come home to roost.

Libra sees the other person's point of view. In the realities of eighth house intimacy, that perspective is often challenging, simply because our own wounds, needs, and fears are crying out so loudly. With his south node in this position, there is every indication that prior to this incarnation, Carl Jung had experienced not only socially comfortable intimacy, but also "deep" intimacy. And that means *complex* intimacy, fraught with raw emotions and ghosts from the pasts of both partners. The passionate road is not an easy one, at least not beyond the first mile or two.

Given the sticky nature of the south node, we cannot assume that Jung in his prior incarnations was always successful in rising to these interpersonal challenges—and in fact this notion of *intimate failures* will emerge as the major theme in this analysis. But, to his credit, Jung did experience these storms very directly in prior lifetimes. He undoubtedly learned from them as well as sustaining damage from them. He walked the road of passion and had scars and wisdom to prove it.

I believe that prior-life experiences in the psychological cauldrons of complex sexual intimacy are central to the foundation of Jung's gifts in this lifetime. This is how he came to know about *anima* and *animus, complexes, archetypal dramas*, the *persona*, the *Shadow*, and the rest. Before this lifetime, he saw them up close, both in himself and in the other.

We cannot rule out the idea that Carl Jung had some *occult training*. Obviously that is a minority theme across the general population, but it is very much part of core eighth house symbolism. For *mysticism,* look to the twelfth house, but for white and black magic, divination, shamanism, witch-work, and "powers," it is the eighth. The outward evidence of Jung's biography supports that interpretation in his case, although it is often too exotic for widespread relevance. He was fascinated with alchemy, astrology, shamanism—these "fringe" or "occult" traditions.

More about that further on. We are only beginning.

Let's turn our attention now to the planetary ruler of the south node. With the node in Libra, that points our attention to Venus, which lies in Cancer on the cusp of the sixth house and in a conjunction with Mercury in the fifth house. That is a lot of information. We can count on it adding a lot of detail and focus to our emerging interpretation.

Cancer is the Crab, a creature that survives because of a shell. Psychologically, it indicates sensitivity's eternal need to defend itself. Vulnerability requires walls between itself and the hard realities of the world. Thus, it orients naturally to *family,* to *home* and *hearth.* More often than not, Cancer manifests *shyness*, or at least a somewhat cautious social quality. As a Water sign, it is emotional—and, through Venus, these are the emotions of love, especially love of a romantic nature. Linked to the nurturing archetype of the Great Mother, Cancer also correlates with *kindness* and the urge to help, nourish and support others. That latter theme—helpfulness—is immediately underlined by the presence of Venus in the sixth house, which indicates *service,* and *supportive roles* in general.

Do we have a contradiction here? A little while ago, we were looking at symbols of elegance, socially advantageous marriage, and a graceful position within society. Now we see a servant?

The key to resolving this apparent paradox lies in a richer understanding of the sixth house. Not all "servants" are in lowly social positions. We can be very high on the social totem pole and still be taking orders. In fact, in some ways, the orders grow stricter the higher we go. Who has more actual daily freedom, the child of a single working class mother or the child of a

President? A hobo or the copilot of a 747?

Furthermore, the sixth house carries an implication of *lineage*. We are initiated into some tradition by those older than ourselves, then we are expected to carry that tradition forward. With the Cancer symbolism and all the marriage symbolism in the mix, in Jung's case this could indicate a *family tradition* connected with maintaining a place in society. It could also be the tradition of some art or craft.

A few paragraphs ago, based on the eighth house position of Carl Jung's south node, we speculated that he may have had prior-life contact with occult traditions. Now we can take the notion a step further. With Venus ruling the south node from the sixth house, we see Jung in a position of "receiving orders." He was, in some sense, a "servant." What might that mean in the context of, say, shamanism? Immediately the phrase *the sorcerer's apprentice* leaps to mind. What about in the context of a mystery school? Jung might have been an *initiate*.

The eighth house tends toward the sexual, although it can have other meanings. With Venus involved in the mix, it would be prudish to ignore the erotic undercurrents here. And there are many occult traditions that consciously embrace and employ sexual energy—certain branches of Tantra being the most obvious illustration. I strongly suspect that Carl Jung, in a prior lifetime, received initiation and training in such a tradition.

Time to assess where we are in the clue-gathering process. We have got "a good marriage." We are looking at a subordinate role coupled with some degree of social status. We've got sexy witchcraft.

We are all over the map, in other words. Don't worry! That is exactly where we want to be at this stage. Remember, the key to our interpretive strategy is to keep all indicated possibilities on the table for as long as we can. We need to see the whole picture before we can reliably decide where the main threads run, and what can be safely ignored. Let's keep going. We have more balls to juggle.

Shaky ground, but classically Venus was seen as *feminine*. As we have often emphasized in these pages, it is imperative that modern astrologers adapt realistically to changing gender roles and expectations—and basically that means realizing that at present any planet can be actualized by a person of either gender. But historically it was not like that. When we see a strong Venus signature connected with the south node, we must remember we are dealing with a past life—something back in history, when "boys were men and women were girls." Thus, it is often productive to speculate that we are dealing with a female prior incarnation—keeping in mind that it could also easily be a reference to a male *artist* or *diplomat*. Or perhaps to a gay man.

We may, in other words, be looking at a prior lifetime of Carl Jung's in which he took female birth and had a female experience.

There are more clues. Venus is modified by Mercury via the conjunction, also in Cancer, but in the fifth house, not the sixth. A planet conjunct the south node's ruler operates the way an adjective flavors a noun. We know Jung was "Venusian." Now we learn that he was a Venusian with a fifth house, Mercurial flavor. Let's see what that adds to our understanding.

Mercury here implies that Jung was *curious, eager to learn*, and perhaps a *student*. He was oriented to experience and stimulation. Mercury, in horary astrology, is also often taken to indicate a *young person*. Young people are restless and speedy compared to older ones, and often more eager for fresh experience—those are the basic reasons behind the association of Mercury with youth. It is critical to remember that Mercury can indicate other possibilities too, just as Venus would not always reliably indicate a female. Mercury can deliver newspapers. It can be a linguist; it can be a thief. But certain experiences are uniquely available to young people. Courtship, especially historically, leaps out as the most obvious possibility—and we also note that courtship and love affairs are quite central to the fifth house. So that theme is reinforced. Whenever we see such thematic reinforcement, we take it seriously.

With Mercury in this mix this way, it can be helpful to hold in our minds the possibility that we are dealing with Jung as a young person—that is, with pivotal experiences that were laid down *early* in one of his prior lifetimes. Given the strong relationship orientation of everything we have seen so far—and framing that fact in the context of sixth house subordination—thinking of Jung as a young person is consistent with the larger picture. Younger people are generally somewhat under the thumbs of their elders. The idea sits easily in the matrix of all of the emerging metaphors. And that flowing consistency is what we are seeking.

Libra and Venus relate archetypally to *symmetry* and to attractive *balance*. We find their expressions pleasing to the eye and the ear. Carl Gustav Jung, in a prior life, was quite likely physically attractive. Taking it further, most of us figured out early that there is a difference between "pretty" and "sexy." We all know people who fit one category, but not the other. But Carl Jung, in a prior life, fit both. The eighth house is sexy. Venus and Libra are "pretty." Thus, we have a lot of reasons to believe that Jung was attractive—and with the chart making such an effort for us to see this element, we know this information must be pivotal.

If we assume Jung to have been female, we can add a third point. From a coldly clinical point of view, most of the attributes that heterosexual males read as compelling sexual attractiveness in a female are in fact biological indicators of fertility—curves, breasts, apparent youth, the appearance of *not* being pregnant already, and so forth. And fertility is in the domain of Cancer, where both Jung's karmic Venus and Mercury lie. Even were he male, these Cancerian qualities often suggest "good husband" to a heterosexual female.

The world greatly values these qualities of physical attractiveness. But, with your wisdom hat on, ask yourself: are there dangers connected with being young, female, privileged and sexually desirable? A prize—or a trophy? Or a young male, but otherwise the same? Might either of those conditions lead to someone landing in a "privileged" position, but one in which he or she was constrained by orders and servitude?

Before we draw any of the obvious inferences, let's see if there are any more clues for us to add to our growing pile. Remember—as always, our overall strategy lies in laying all the clues on the table before we draw any hard-and-fast conclusions.

Are there any planets conjunct the south node? Jupiter is twelve degrees away—too far to be central to our emerging interpretation, but quite consistent with our themes of privilege. It adds some confidence to that interpretation, but not much more.

What about hard aspects to the south node? That familiar Venus-Mercury conjunction squares it—and that compels us to consider these two planets from a second perspective. Mercury is quite close to the exact square, only a couple of degrees away from perfection. Venus is wider, but well within the orbs at a little under six degrees. We are looking at something here that created trouble for Jung in the prior lifetime, something that vexed him.

Let's focus on Venus first. It is clearly playing a dual role here—ruler of the south node, plus square the nodal axis. We can stand by all that we have seen so far, but there is more to discover through the square. For starters, we immediately know that we can add another exclamation point to the notion that Carl Jung's karma is profoundly Venusian. The planet appears twice in the nodal analysis.

Formally, the planet ruling the south node (or a planet conjunct it) says something about our *prior-life identity*. It is connected with our *values, motivations*, and *self-image*. It has a lot to do with how we looked to other people and what they came to expect of us.

Formally, a planet square the south node is something that created a problem for us. It *afflicted* us, attacked us, bothered us. Often it represents another person who was in an inimical or challenging relationship to us. Whatever issue this planet represents, we know that it was *left unresolved* as that prior life ended. Therefore it still *haunts* us now in the present life as something *left hanging in the balance.* Facing that issue, *withdrawing our negative projections* from it, and integrating the energy in a helpful way, constitutes a *skipped step* from the past—something which must be gotten right if we are to go forward.

In Carl Gustav Jung's chart, Venus plays *both* of these roles. It simultaneously represents him in the prior lifetime and also something that afflicted him. *Thus he afflicted himself.* He created his own troubles. He "shot himself in the foot." He was, in other words, *his own worst enemy.*

Furthermore the troubles Jung created for himself were Venusian in nature. We must keep perspective here—most of us have gotten ourselves into difficulties as a result of romantic missteps! In fact, with a little wisdom and maturity, we easily recognize that such missteps are just part of life's learning curve. Nobody can grow up right without a few of them. If you passionately kiss two different people during the same week when you are sweet sixteen, it is probably not going to show up as your south node in your next incarnation! We must, in other words, be looking at something more complex and more charged than simple youthful sexual experimentation. There are a lot of ways we can get into situations of jeopardy with our sexuality. What is the root issue here?

Start by reviewing what we know about that Venus. It lies in Cancer and in the sixth house. It may be devastatingly attractive, but it is also *obedient* (sixth house) and probably *shy* (Cancer). It is *oriented to family.* And families, of course, often give orders.

What kind of orders might a "good family" give their lovely young daughter? There are a variety of possible answers, but the most obvious ones lie along the lines of chastity, the avoidance of scandal—and above all, the making of a good marriage and the production of children. Not forgetting that Jung might have been male in this prior life, how might those orders have changed? Probably not very much—although there might have been less emphasis on chastity. And what was "marriageable age," historically? Appallingly young, of course—at least so it seems by the standards of our present world. And Jung obeyed. He probably found himself "well married" at a tender age. There are two indications of *fertility* as well—Venus lies in Cancer and Mercury, also in Cancer, is in the fifth house *(children)*. With Venus in the house of servants, Jung served three masters: *children, spouse, and family.*

Many people have found fulfillment in marriage and parenthood. In this prior lifetime, Jung did not. Remember that he was "afflicted" by Venus. The drive to experience *passionate, naked, and transformative intimacy*—the root meaning of the Libran eighth house south node—clashed with his being framed as an idealized object of beauty and service, whether he was female or male. Likely, he was considered "cute." He was probably patted on the head.

There is another basic tension here, one of some complexity. Let's count it on both hands, as follows.

On the right hand, we have strong symbolism of *loyalty to family*, of *dutifulness* and *fidelity*. The eighth house bonds very deeply. There is no casual sex there. Libra seeks to please and it refers to ongoing partnerships. Cancer is oriented to home, and opens up only slowly. The sixth house obeys the rules.

On the left hand, we see a highly *curious* quality in the planet Mercury, modifying his Venus. It wants experience and knowledge. In the fifth house, it is drawn to courtship—to the delirious processes of mutual discovery and mutual fascination. It reflects the natural developmental needs and behaviors of the young as they begin to integrate their sexuality: experimentation, wide experience, testing the waters.

We might total up the balance and conclude that the right hand outweighed the left hand. But we would be missing the core point: the root of our analysis is always the south node's placement in terms of sign and house. *It was Jung's soul-intention to experience that passionate psycho-sexual intimacy* we described a few lines ago. That drive was not going to disappear—nor was it likely to be satisfied within the context of a "proper marriage," especially one basically chosen by Jung's prior-life parents rather than being based on his own natural desires.

Furthermore, Carl Jung, in this prior life, was Libran and Venusian—he (or she!) *aimed to please.* Especially with the sixth house in the mix, we are looking at a *biddable* quality. And, given the realities of the world, what kinds of "bids" might an attractive young person receive? Remember that Venus squares the node: Beauty (Venus) and kindness (Cancer) were *afflictions* here. *How could Jung refuse the fervent supplications of others, particularly when what they were offering was the very thing for which he longed?* The right hand battled the left—and the left won, at least from time to time.

Finally, we have one more clue on the table which definitively tips the scales toward the "left hand." Venus, the ruler of the south node, also squared the south node. Carl Jung was his own worst enemy. And the battlefield was defined by Venus, Libra and the eighth house. The battlefield where he shot himself in the foot was sexual.

Right at the beginning of our analysis, thinking about the Libran south node, we put "relationship dramas" on the list. Under the eighth house, we listed self-absorption, seductiveness, and sexual compulsivity. We listed many other ideas too, but in the light of the larger analytic context, these are the ones that are underscored.

One more point: For reasons we described earlier, we cannot be completely sure we are looking at a female prior incarnation. The strong Venusian and Cancerian signatures do suggest that interpretation of the clues, and it may well be correct. But in one way I find myself tempted by the alternative interpretation—that Jung was male in that lifetime. My reasoning is simple, if sad. The historical reality is that, in most cultures, for a male to behave promiscuously outside a marriage has often been more socially acceptable than the same behavior would be for a female. In that light, I note the absence of strong Uranian signatures in *direct connection with the karmic indicators.* With a female, based on that behavior, we would expect social condemnation (Uranus). With a male, typically less so. Note that Jung's chart in general is of course highly Uranian! The point here is that Uranus figures in the karmic analysis only through a sextile to the south node, as if he were living in a society that actually *supported* marital infidelity. There have been societies in which both genders were expected to behave that way, but they are outnumbered by the ones governed by the infamous "double standard."

Confused about Jung's prior life gender? Reframe your confusion as understanding. His chart makes solid arguments in both directions. Our goal is to come up with a story that fits all the facts, adds nothing significant that we cannot substantiate, and leaves out nothing of importance. My conclusion is that both gender possibilities are true. Jung had been both male and female. Likely, at least two lifetimes are reflected in this symbolism. We are probably looking at a long-term karmic pattern of these kinds of sexual complexities, one which Jung experienced from both gender perspectives.

Time for a reality check. Carl Jung's marriage to Emma Rauschenbach raised his social status and lasted until she died in 1955. They had five children. Throughout the marriage, Jung was openly unfaithful. He carried on long affairs with at least two former patients, Sabina Spielrein and, more famously, Toni Wolff.

Jung and Wolff began their relationship in 1914. Solar arc Venus had opposed his Saturn in September of the previous year, presumably amplifying the underlying karmic tendency towards romantic and sexual hunger. Their bond lasted into the 1940s—three decades, in other words. There we see Jung's oddly ambivalent karmic signature—the Libran, Cancerian, and eighth house *fidelity* mixed with the wilder, more promiscuous elements. With Toni Wolff, Jung had an affair that lasted longer than many marriages. But even within the affair, Jung was not faithful. There were others as well.

Emma Jung was at first devastated by Jung's relationship with Wolff, then she made outward peace with the situation. Wolff was even a frequent Sunday dinner guest in the Jung home—again, note the oddly domestic (Cancerian) quality of the affair. Yet when Toni Wolff died in 1953, Jung did not attend her funeral. They had parted over a disagreement about his study of alchemy, much as he had parted with Freud many years earlier. More about that later.

The mention of alchemy brings us back to our "occult" themes—the hypothesis that, in a prior life, Carl Jung received some sort of *occult empowerment* (eighth house south node) as an *apprentice* (sixth house node ruler) and *student* (Mercury), and that the initiation included elements of a *sacred sexual* nature (eighth house; Venusian themes).

One might dismiss this line of interpretation as "too weird." The more conventional marital and sexual analysis is obviously represents a statistically more likely scenario—philanderers outnumbering shamanic initiates at the typical garden party! And we also have definitive evidence for the conventional analysis: the karmic marital and sexual themes are echoed in detail, as we have seen, in the realities of Carl Jung's personal life. We therefore know that they are correct. They pass the reality test.

But so does the more exotic story of mystical initiation. In reality, Carl Jung was a wizard—a protean man in the "Age of Science" who felt a fascination and a kinship with occult matters. Freud pressed him to abandon "the black tide of occultism." Jung's refusal to do so was one of the main causes of their split. His lover of three decades, Toni Wolff, was afraid that Jung was damaging his reputation because of his obsessive interest in alchemy—and he abandoned her over it, and did not even attend her funeral.

Toni Wolff may have been right! Today, Jung is mostly ignored in mainstream academic rats-in-a-maze psychology. In some ways, he actually did sacrifice his place in history through his fidelity to the realms of the occult and of human spirituality. Even among academic Jungians today, there is a tendency to downplay Jung's profound and lifelong fascination with astrology, for example—in my experience, they "pat him on the head" a bit about it.

In any case, the main point is that we have substantial biographical justification for accepting the notion that Carl Jung had a prior lifetime in which he was an occult initiate. It is suggested by the karmic analysis and echoed in the realities of his life. It too passes the test.

What can we learn from it? First, my sense as I mentioned earlier is that we are looking minimally at two or three different prior lifetimes here. I suspect the lifetime of the occult initiate occurred earlier. Always, we look to the nodal analysis to reveal problems and unresolved issues from prior lifetimes. I postulate that *premature sacred sexual initiation* basically fried Carl Jung's capacity to function in a normal, conventional marriage. Through the impact of a teacher, he experienced a spiritualized sexuality *which he could not have experienced without that teacher.* This opened up doorways to occult wisdom, but it also left him with a hyped hunger for a kind of sexual experience which he could not find in this world with a partner who was on his own plane of consciousness. Not that he didn't search for at least two or three lifetimes: the one as Jung himself, and the one or two that emerge in our more conventional karmic analysis.

Here is an archetype we all know, and which Jung would have easily recognized—the sorcerer's apprentice gets into deeper waters than he can handle. It happened to Mickey Mouse. It happened to Carlos Castaneda. And I believe it happened to Carl Jung.

How could Jung go forward?

The purest, highest expression of Venus in Cancer in the sixth house is one of *humble, committed devotion in the context of a home.* Immediately, let me emphasize that astrology is not puritanical. It is equally adept at positively describing sexual styles that would make a shy person blush—try Venus conjunct Uranus and Jupiter in Gemini and fifth house, for example! But in Jung's case, we are looking at a Venusian placement that, ideally, would suggest relationships that were stable and steadfast. That is simply the nature of Venus in that sign and house.

But remember: Venus is square Carl Jung's nodes. It represents a skipped step, something he left unresolved and undone, something not gotten right in the prior life—and something which haunts him in this life. To accomplish his larger soul-intentions, Jung needed to deal with that skipped step. *He needed to experience himself effectively and righteously supporting a partner and a family.* He needed that dignity. He needed that quintessentially manly experience—and here the word "manly" stands in contrast to "boyish."

A conventional psychological astrologer would point, correctly, to rule-breaking Uranus ruling his chart and lying on the cusp of his house of marriage. That is commonly taken as an indicator of intimate instability. No argument! That configuration can indeed correlate with unconventional choices within marriage, and often suggests rebelliousness against the strictures of commitment. Clearly, even in a healthy marriage, Jung would need more "space" than most people. Continuing a conventional analysis, even though that dramatic Uranian placement really stands out, there are mitigating factors. That powerful Uranus would exist in tension with the innate conservatism and self-control of Jung's strong Saturn, the stability preferred by a Taurus Moon, and the generally Fixed quality of Jung's natal chart. Looking at everything integratively, it would be a tough call for a skilled conventional astrologer to determine whether Jung would experience instability in marriage—or a solid marriage characterized by unusual elements of independence and chafing.

But from the evolutionary perspective, we know that Jung's Uranus had a powerful ally in the "skipped step Venus" and the rest of the underlying karmic pattern. When there is ambiguity in a conventional analysis and the chart-behind-the-chart takes a side, it usually casts the tie-breaking vote. With Carl Gustav Jung, that wilder expression is certainly the case in terms of the bottom-line biographical facts.

Carl Jung is an inspiration to many of us, myself included. Uncomfortably, we must note that there was an element of basic coldness, even cruelty, in his intimate behavior. He put his wife Emma through emotional torture. He made his lover a regular guest at Sunday dinner. After three decades of intimacy, he left her over a professional disagreement. He would not attend her funeral. And she was not his only lover—there are other intimate figures in his life. Carl Jung left a trail of blood and broken hearts behind him.

A relevant piece of the biographical puzzle lies in Carl Jung's relationship with his mother, Emilie, who was moody and depressed, and who spent many hours alone in her room "communing with spirits" when Jung was a child. In *Memories, Dreams, Reflections*, he writes that as a result, his attitude towards women was that they had an "innate unreliability." He refers to this as the "handicap I started off with."

One can make obvious sense of that information from a conventional psychological perspective. But what about the karmic perspective? If Jung was female in the prior life we are discussing, then she *experienced herself* as "innately unreliable." If he was male, he experienced females as both entrapping and disposable.

However we look at the nodal story, Carl Jung had been immersed for lifetimes in the alchemical cauldrons of the Shadow. Spiritually, we might say that he "grew up fast," but most people who are forced to grow up fast also grow up damaged. He dived, or was hurled, into the dark. He came up wiser—and wounded. At his prior death, these issues were not resolved. They still had momentum, a momentum which he demonstrably carried forward into this present life.

The ultimate medicine for that karmic momentum, as always, lies in the Moon's north node. In this case, it falls in Aries at the cusp of the second house. With the second house, we are always looking at the need to "prove one's self to one's self." There is a basic *insecurity* which must be addressed—an insecurity connected with the Aries archetype: the Warrior, in all its independent, self-sufficient glory. Opposite Libra, the sign of partnership, Aries is profoundly self-directed. Carl Jung needed, above all, to integrate *the realization that he could exist outside of intimate relationship.* This was a foreign, alien idea. All his assumptions about himself and about life—his south node, in other words—suggested to him that sexual intimacy was essentially the purpose of life. Paradoxically, that hyped belief in the power of sex was preventing him from experiencing intimacy. *He was looking for so much from another human being that no one could ever fulfill it.*

With the tables turned, he himself could not fulfill it.

When marriage failed to meet the impossible demand, he sought to fulfill it in multiplicity and breadth of experience. And he failed there too.

The answer lay in greater Arian self-sufficiency and a less romanticized view of sexual love. And the road to that answer, as we have seen, lay through his skipped step—that Venus-Mercury conjunction in Cancer. It was about *unconditional commitment* (Cancer) to a single partner, and probably to their *children* (Cancer again, plus Mercury in the fifth). As we put it a few paragraphs ago, it was about that quintessential *manly* mystery—making a stand.

An appropriate partner would have to be Jung's *intellectual equal*, and fully capable of holding her own in conversation with him—there is the Mercury element, shaping the natural expression of skipped-step Venus. In Emma, he had the loyal wife and the mother of his five children. Probably in Toni Wolff he had his intellectual peer, or something close to that. Others filled in the cracks and gave temporary relief to the compelling karmic hunger. He pieced it together, in other words.

But it was not supposed to be "pieces." That is not the Cancer way.

It would not be fair, in my opinion, to call Jung's life a failure in terms of his own evolutionary intentions. Even intimately, his "piecing together" elements of his ultimate goal was at least a tentative step in the right direction. He remained with Emma until her death. He remained with Toni Wolff for a very long time. Also, more importantly, recall that the heart of the matter lay in his attaining Arian independence—proving to himself that he did not need to be defined by the "life-giving" dramas of sexuality, or by the approval of any "master." There is evidence of ample progress on those fronts—for the latter, witness his split from Freud.

The gravitational field of the karmic story compels us to contemplate

Carl Jung's life from the perspective of his intimate, marital, and sexual successes and failures. Those are the karmic themes. Of course there was more to his life than that, and much of it was directly related to his north node process. Certainly he bravely pioneered a new field *(Aries)*, and proved himself to himself by the creation of a substantial body of work *(second house)*. Going further, Mars is the ruler of his north node, and it lies in Sagittarius and in the tenth house. Thus, a critical arena for this evolutionary expression and development of his Arian independence was the realm of career—or better said, his mission in the world. There he was invited to *defend against all attackers* (Mars) a set of *fervently-held beliefs and principles* (Sagittarius) and to do so on the stage of the world. I think it is fair to say he took that step. In a very dark hour, he kept the world safe for "the black tide of occultism," for which I thank him!

Ultimately, no astrologer can make a final judgment on another person's life. That is not what this work is about. Its real purpose simply lies in holding the clear mirror before another soul, and letting that soul make its own judgments. Carl Jung's teachings were pure and powerful. But he was as human as the rest of us—and, just maybe, that is why his teachings have the impact and authenticity they do.

CONCLUSION: BEYOND DESCRIPTION

When I was a kid, the astrology I encountered was purely descriptive. You could recognize the signs by their signature behaviors. Capricorns wore suits and Virgos put things in alphabetical order, while Leos were haughty and Aquarians dressed in purple. To this day, the only way I can grasp how something that dumb could have hooked me is to get a little mystical about it. Even at thirteen, I could see how trivial that kind of astrology was—and not only trivial, but also wrong a lot!

I was a "science track" child, mostly interested in astronomy anyway. And in science-world, it was difficult to find a printed sentence that contained the word "astrology," but did not contain the word "superstition." Nothing in my environment encouraged me to give astrology more than a moment of dismissive thought.

But it sunk into my bones anyway. Astrology became my hobby. If I wanted to win popularity in the astrological world, I would now write the following sentence: "Then I discovered that beyond the silly astrology of sun signs lay the rich, persuasive world of serious technical astrology in all its cerebral glory." But that would be a lie. What I actually found was that, while the mental crossword puzzles of technical astrology became a lot more demanding, the serious astrology of the 1960s I encountered was not that much different at heart than the silly sun sign stuff: it too was merely descriptive, given to dogmatic prediction, often trivial in its conclusions—and still wrong a lot. (To be fair, there was better work going on, but I had no idea how to find it, so deeply was it buried.)

Still, I stuck with it. I began to gather experience with astrology, closing the books and opening my mind and heart instead to my friends and their birth charts. As I recounted in my first book, *The Inner Sky*, I realized that people were changing and growing even though the books described them in static terms. That simple observation was like a catalyst. Something went "click." It took all the conventional astrology I had absorbed, reorganized it, and made it come alive.

The process took a few years, but in retrospect it was utterly simple. I can recount it now in a single paragraph. In the astrological literature that I read, I had learned that Leos were self-important *(a bad thing)*, but I had also learned that Leos could be colorful and creative *(a good thing)*. Most of the then-current descriptive material about the signs fit that pattern—a mix of bleak or embarrassing characterizations, speckled with encouraging, hopeful possibilities and virtues. What I came to me years ago was the realization that *I could take the bad stuff and the good stuff and arrange it on an evolutionary continuum.* We would start out our lives with a great vulnerability to the bad stuff, but gradually, through (optional!) work on ourselves, we might move more toward the good stuff. A little bit of compassionate psychological thought carried it the rest of the way. For example, Leos behaving in ways that appeared self-important were actually driven there by an insecurity which they could address through authentic creative self-expression. Voilà.

Suddenly, for me, astrology went *beyond description—into prescription.* Based on the configurations in a person's chart, I could caution them about their dark side and also aim them toward the higher ground. It worked beautifully. People loved it. It helped them. By my twenty-eighth birthday, I was able to quit my day job.

Hallelujah.

An added happiness was the realization that everything I had sweated to learn about conventional astrology was actually all still quite useful. It had all been worth the effort. All it needed was that one catalytic insight—a precise system of conscious evolution—to light the fuse. Even as my work has grown more sophisticated over the years, that happy realization remains intact: burning the midnight oil learning conventional astrology is far from a waste of time. It is essential.

Currently the astrological world is in ferment. There are many distinct kinds of astrology vying for primacy. Modern psychological astrology. The Vedic, or Jyotish, tradition. Hellenistic and Renaissance astrology. Cosmobiology. Sidereal systems. Uranian astrology. Often there is acrimony among the diverse camps. So long as the various traditions are practiced with loving kindness, I have no ax to grind against any of them. All of them seem to produce good results in the right hands. I grew up in the heyday of modern psychological astrology. That is the basic language I learned to speak. I have built my own brand of Evolutionary Astrology on that chassis. I suspect that, had I learned Jyotish as a young man, I would have married the evolutionary techniques to that system. That might even have been easier, given Vedic astrology's roots in the great metaphysical Hindu tradition.

Evolutionary Astrology as I practice it has many nuts and bolts—they are what this book has been about. But more than a set of techniques, it is *a philosophy or an approach to understanding life.* At a practical level, Evolutionary Astrology is grounded in the simple, objective observation that most of us learn, grow, and change in the course of our lives. That is hardly arguable since we experience it quite directly. Alone, that observation refutes the purely static, descriptive kinds of astrology. Virgos *can* get over being critical. Capricorns *can* stop being controlling. And people with fourth house Moons in Scorpio square their Plutos *can* get over their mother issues. Some of them don't even have mother issues, for that matter!

So personal evolution itself is really not in the realm of philosophy, although many philosophies are based on it. No one with their eyes open can deny its reality. Where Evolutionary Astrology does enter the realm of personal belief is when we start asking the larger questions: *why* do you have this particular chart, these blind spots or vices, these exact evolutionary possibilities? There, for our purposes in these pages, we have been assuming reincarnation. As we saw in Chapter Two, there is good reason to accept its reality—anyone who wanted to dismiss reincarnation as superstition would have quite a lot of objective evidence to counter.

But, to be fair, reincarnation is a belief. There are other ways of making sense of life. People who do not accept the idea of our living many lifetimes are welcome in the world of Evolutionary Astrology. In terms of its practical applications and relevance, it can stand alone without reference to past lives. Obviously enough, in practice those who are drawn to the system are generally also open to reincarnation. Socially, it is a world of yogis and meditators, metaphysicians, people drawn to eastern religions, born again (and again) pagans, with a smattering of mystical Christians, Sufi dancers, psychical researchers, and Kaballists. That is the natural community for this kind of work. It is large, vibrant, growing, and a lot of fun. For an increasing part of the astrological world, Evolutionary Astrology provides a good philosophical and cultural fit.

And for many people, it does not. Certainly, as an astrologer, I am bound to respect human diversity. We are not aiming for converts; we only ask for a fair hearing. The five essential points for us are very simple.

The unresolved prior ife issues indicated through evolutionary analysis are demonstrable in the present life.

Often these unresolved issues and tendencies are not detectable through any other form of conventional astrological analysis.

These points are not subtle; often they completely change the tone of an interpretation.

We can evolve beyond them; the chart tells us how to do so.

One way of understanding these unresolved issues is to think of them as leftovers from a prior lifetime.

The reality that will not go away is that these techniques correspond directly and undeniably to the stories that people live. We can observe that. It is real. All the branches of astrology do that, but Evolutionary Astrology sees elements they often miss.

Generally. in my experience, the astrological community has been open and receptive to Evolutionary Astrology. Attendance at our lectures is encouraging. Our books get sold. Our students develop thriving astrological practices. But inevitably, the field has attracted opponents too. We welcome the ones who ask hard questions—they make us stronger. The ones who sadden me are the ones who dismiss the system without understanding it. Some of it is the inevitable whisper campaign. A shake of the head, then, *"They're flakes . . . they all think they were Cleopatra,"* wink, wink. That is no more than trial by gossip. No one can really defend themselves against that kind of mischief.

More frustrating are people who try to dismiss Evolutionary Astrology by framing it as unverifiable. "You can say *anything* about a past life and who can possibly prove you wrong?" That point is completely valid, of course. And completely beside the real point, as our five statements above demonstrate. Evolutionary Astrology is the *most* verifiable form of astrology that I have ever encountered.

I have spoken of Evolutionary Astrology as if it were one unified system. Emphatically—and happily—it is not. In the introduction to this volume, I spoke of my partnership with Jeffrey Wolf Green. His technical approach is a work of genius in the deepest sense of the word: it is original. It is also significantly different from my own, although our underlying aims are the same. Several paragraphs ago, I wrote that Evolutionary Astrology was "more than a set of techniques, it is a philosophy or an approach to understanding life." Jeff and I shared that perspective and so we worked very easily together for two or three years before illness sidelined him. We each have had large teaching programs, and I am delighted that we have shared a great number of students. I find the cross-fertilization between our two systems very exciting, and I have heard Jeff say that he does too. We had some good moments imagining ourselves as old codgers out to pasture, and our students taking the best from us—and adding their own best to it.

At the beginning of the book, I mentioned Raymond Merriman, currently the president of the International Society for Astrological Research and as far as I know the originator of the term Evolutionary Astrology. His techniques are totally different from either Jeff's or mine. I have not explored them rigorously enough yet to evaluate them and incorporate them into my own work, but I do know that Ray has been gracious about the widespread use of what he might have defended as "his brand name." He too sensed that this was simply bigger than any single personality. I thank him for that. Recently at a conference I had the pleasure of meeting Jan Spiller, author of the bestselling *Astrology for the Soul*, a very popular mainstream book about the lunar nodes. Her techniques again are distinct, but she shares the same core "philosophy or approach to understanding life." Out of curiosity I asked her if she calls herself an evolutionary astrologer. She said that she did not actively use the term, but she was quite open to it. She knew the shoe fit, once I described the shoe.

These shoes fit an increasing number of us. I feel a pull toward listing names here, especially of those up-and-coming younger astrologers who are already publishing and teaching in this realm. But such a list is not really the point; those who have written books are listed in the Recommended Reading section, and those who have studied with Jodie or me for any length of time are listed in a Directory on my website. Go to www.sevenpawspress.com, then hit "Training," then "Forrest Trained." I recommend them all.

A generation ago, Martin Shulman, whom I have never met, did some critical work on the lunar nodes from a reincarnational perspective. The same basic philosophical views are often quite apparent in the seminal work of Stephen Arroyo. They occasionally peeked through in the writings of Dane Rudhyar a generation or two earlier. More or less contemporaneously with Rudhyar, one might reference Alice Bailey and the Theosophists or Isabel Hickey. None of them used the term "Evolutionary Astrology," but I think of all of them as part of the tribe.

The point is that the field of Evolutionary Astrology is vibrant, diverse, and thriving. Modern western astrology has been hungry for a coherent philosophical foundation. For a good while, it simply lacked one entirely—it had descended into mere description. Whatever the surface erudition might have looked like, underneath it was agnostic nihilism: we were silly personalities going through the predictable motions of life in a random situation-comedy universe. With Evolutionary Astrology, *meaning* enters the system. The added psychological and existential accuracy is only the cherry on top of the sundae.

Will Evolutionary Astrology ever become a single, coherent, unified system? Mostly I hope not—that sounds too much like the beginning of the end to me! It needs to walk its own talk about evolution. It is more a movement to integrate astrology and metaphysics than it is a rigidly defined craft. As such, I suspect it will prove open-ended. But I suspect that over the next century there will be some convergence in the techniques. And of course many new techniques will emerge.

I would like to reflect a bit on where we might go next. As I write these words, I am in the midst of my second Saturn Return, and thus entering the cycle of the Grandfather. I think of *Yesterday's Sky* as a companion to my first book, *The Inner Sky*, which I wrote coming out of my first Saturn Return, at the beginning of my middle years. In a sense, this book contains what I now realize was only hinted at in the first one. It completes the picture. In my mind, *The Inner Sky* and *Yesterday's Sky* together form the foundation of my understanding of the astrological birthchart—the alchemical fusion of personal psychological work and the larger evolutionary intentions of the soul. The passions of youth and midlife, and all the psychology they stir up, are natural grit in the evolutionary system. In them, we experience our karma very directly. It is the dream we do not realize we are dreaming, the one from which it is so difficult to awaken. Much of *The Inner Sky* sits in that realm—and hopefully points a way forward through it.

Entering now into the last third of my life, the mind naturally cools and clears a bit. The waters are less turbulent, the mud settles a bit. The personal dramas gone by are remembered more structurally and elementally; patterns emerge. *Yesterday's Sky* comes out of that emerging, older place in me, taking in the broader scope of life's meaning in the stark light of life's brevity. From this "grandfather" perspective, I would like to speculate about where Evolutionary Astrology might next go—not only about where my own interests are trending, but also about what might develop after I am gone, while I am having my "little rest upon the wind," as Kahlil Gibran put it many years ago.

Physical Evolutionary Astrology

If I had to critique my own system as presented in these pages, my biggest problem with it would be the lack of focus on the physical body. Karma is behind a lot of health issues—people who were hung on the gallows in prior lifetimes are often prone to sore throats today, for one typical example. We may have a birthmark in the present life where we were stabbed to death in a prior one. I imagine that there would be many applications of Evolutionary Astrology to health and to the affairs of the physical body: early warning about potential problem areas, diagnosis, maybe even healing and prevention. The *timing* of the application of remedies and preventive measures is one example that leaps to mind. Instinctively, I believe that as we progress toward our north node "medicines" and resolutions, many underlying causes of illness can be eliminated. I am not advocating any one-dimensional views of disease here, but it is surely true that many such physical conditions have their origin not in biochemistry but in the ancient mind, which is then reflected in the physical realm.

There are people doing good work in medical astrology—Dr. Ingrid Naiman comes to mind. Jeffrey Wolf Green has contributed significantly here too. Noel Tyl's book, *The Astrological Timing of Critical Illness*, is helpful and relevant. I am quite excited watching the nascent work of my student, Dr. Robert Finnegan, who is beginning to marry his Western medical training with his deep understanding of evolutionary astrological principles. I would also mention the work of Kim Marie, a long-time student of Jeffrey Wolf Green's. I am sure there are many others—as I mentioned, this is not an area of astrology with which I am particularly conversant.

My own north node lies in Taurus *(body consciousness)* and in the sixth house *(health and illness)*, so I am probably the *last* astrologer in the world to qualify for leading this endeavor—although it would do me good to participate, so you never know. As to that possibility, the synchronistic elements are already in place: circumstances have drawn me into an active ongoing involvement with the integrative medicine movement. Maybe someday I might become brave enough to contribute something to the field as my soul inches forward . . .

In the meantime, I simply name *physical* Evolutionary Astrology as the next gold field in this ongoing work.

Hypnotic Regression and Trance Work

In Chapter Two, "Why Believe in Reincarnation?", I described the work of Roger Woolger and Patricia Walsh. Essentially, Roger is one of the pioneers of using visualization techniques as a way of helping people gain access to their prior life memories. As recounted earlier, his partner, Patricia Walsh, trained under Jeffrey Wolf Green. She is beginning to correlate the results of astrological karmic analysis with the actual content of people's regressive work. She is working on a book. For now, all she has published to my knowledge is an article titled "Astrological Observations from Past Life Therapy." It appeared in *The International Astrologer*, the Journal of the International Society for Astrological Research (ISAR) in the Leo issue, 2006, Volume XXXVI, #3. The article details very precise correlations between the results of trance-based recovery of past-life memories and the results of evolutionary astrological analysis.

From a purely logical perspective, it is always compelling when two completely independent systems come to the same conclusion. Proving reincarnation or Evolutionary Astrology will probably always be an elusive goal—but if an astrologer sitting in one room reads the karmic pattern in a chart and people sitting in another room consistently come up with similar stories via regression techniques, it will give the skeptics a serious headache. As Patricia Walsh has proven, that is exactly what is happening.

Far more importantly, regressionists and evolutionary astrologers can learn from each other. Evolutionary hypotheses can be tested against personal reality. For one specific illustration of what I mean, consider the vexed question of determining prior life gender. In this volume, I have conjectured that Venus might often correlate with a feminine past life birth and Mars a masculine one. I have described my hesitations about this idea, but I do often use it in practice. If, in hypnotic regression, people recall stories that clearly fit the karmic outline, but gender seems randomly distributed . . . well, we will have learned to drop that Venus/Mars notion! Or to trust it, if the opposite happens. A second opinion is always a help!

Hypnotic regression and trance work have probably been the most productive disciplines in the west in terms of supporting reincarnation. It underlies the work of Helen Wambach, Brian Weiss, Peter Ramster, and others, all described in Chapter Two. I have not been through Woolger's Deep Memory Process training myself, and I am too busy with clients, and my writing and teaching, to practice it anyway. But I am very excited about what might happen when a hundred people trained in both disciplines start comparing notes.

Psychic Work

The "second sight" is a reality. It is almost impossible to have any contact with the field of psychic phenomena without becoming a believer. Like astrology, it is slippery and hard to prove in a scientific way, but totally compelling case by case. Many psychics work with prior lifetimes, recovering stories from the *Akashic Record*—the universal memory where everything is stored and nothing is forgotten. In Chapter Two, I detailed the work of Edgar Cayce, for one spectacular example. There are psychics in most communities of any size in the western world.

With psychic work, the essential point is the same as what I described a few lines ago regarding hypnotic regression. The idea is that we would gauge and document agreement and disagreement between psychics and evolutionary astrologers, and thus presumably let each field independently confirm or question the other's results. Confirmation would be a compelling result, which might lend more credence to both modalities and thus draw more people into the work. More precious is the knowledge that would come to us—knowledge of error too. Reincarnational "data" is slippery. Psychics can help evolutionary astrologers strengthen and clarify their techniques.

It is often said that everyone is a little bit psychic. As we contemplate our own charts from the evolutionary viewpoint, inevitably intuition is stimulated. The symbols may trigger a chain of more detailed and specific past life memory. Obviously, for most of us, such intuitions are subject to a variety of distorting influence, starting with movies we saw before we were five years old! Still, with hundreds of evolutionary astrologers comparing notes on their personal intuitive experiences, useful patterns of information are likely to emerge.

Linked to this notion is another one. As I am writing these words, news has just come to me of a set of astrological Tarot cards aimed specifically at triggering prior life memories. Designed by Ingrid Zinnel, Peter Orban, and Thea Weller, these "Symbolon" cards link astrological symbolism to European mythic motifs. Obviously, many of us have lived in non-European cultures as well, but these cards seem well suited to marriage with Evolutionary Astrology in terms of catalyzing the recovery of prior life memories.

Astromapping

Where exactly did you live your previous lives? I personally know of no reliable astrological techniques for answering that question, but I believe they might exist. The reason is that astrologers have developed methodologies for determining how we might react in practical present life terms to any particular location on earth. I suspect karmic themes underlie these methodologies, awaiting discovery.

The two main techniques are *Astrocartography* and *Local Space* astrology. Both generate a set of "planetary lines" crisscrossing the earth—lines that with fair consistency coincide with places in which we have lived or in which we have had experiences in the present life. These lines cast light on our experiences in those places. Astromapping is complex and obviously beyond the scope of this book. But I wonder about its relevance to the *locations* of prior lifetimes. Personally, I have done no more than fiddle a bit with "evolutionary astromapping." I have compared my own karmic intuitions with my own astromaps. I have stretched a little further, into the lives of people with whom I am close—and who wanted to fiddle along with me. The results have been intriguing—astromapping really seems to generate some "hits" that resonate intuitively with our notions of significant prior life locations. But it misses a lot too—just as it seems to miss important geographical connections in more conventional applications.

I feel that astromapping is another goldfield waiting for someone to come along and discover it. Working *as a community* with our present mapping techniques and applying them to evolutionary questions could be highly productive—and I emphasize "community" because otherwise it truly is only fiddling. Something may "work" for me purely by chance. It is dangerous to assume it will work for everyone else. We need many astrologers comparing notes. That is how the field has always advanced.

Buddhist and Hindu Practice

These two spiritual traditions have kept the flame of reincarnational understanding burning for thousands of years. As I mentioned in my introduction, I could not have written this book without standing on the shoulders of the Buddhist lineage. And Buddhism bears approximately the same relationship to Hinduism as does Christianity to Judaism. In both cases, the latter sprang from the former and carries the marks of its origin. So I am grateful to the ancient lineage of Hindu sages as well, although I have had less direct contact with it.

Astrologers have no business dictating belief systems to their clients and students. That is not my intention here, any more than it has been to turn all astrologers into hypnotic regressionists, physicians or psychics. But we have gems to mine here: these Eastern spiritual traditions have long explored the subtle principles of cause and effect that underlie karma and rebirth. They have given me the principles and philosophy to test against the realities of my clients lives. And they have passed that test.

Someone here in the western world might earn a Ph.D. in psychology and thus be recognized socially as an expert in questions of mental health. And yet such a person, quite demonstrably, might be visibly insane—dangerous, incapable of maintaining relationships, cold, unloving, whatever. Exactly the same catastrophe might happen today in the realm of Evolutionary Astrology. Anyone with good intelligence can learn these techniques. Thus empowered, such a person could do terrible damage, as do bad psychologists. With a knowledge of karmic analysis, we can devastate people. It is possible to shame them, disempower them, and discourage them spiritually. This is sacred knowledge, and thus it comes with risks. It is the kind of knowledge that, in the past, might have been kept secret, available only to the initiated.

Buddhism and Hinduism are scholarly traditions. But the scholarship unfolds in the larger context of *mind-training*: meditation, service, and the generation of feelings of loving harmlessness toward other beings. My prayer for the future of Evolutionary Astrology is that it might follow a more integrated spiritual pattern rather than the perilously one-dimensional western academic approach. Evolutionary Astrology is a medicine too strong for the soul to handle without that larger spiritual context to ground it and give it stability.

So far, I am encouraged. Most of the evolutionary astrologers I know have some kind of spiritual practice. They are not by any means all Buddhists or Hindus. Some are Christian. Many follow Native American paths. Yogis abound, as do people who meditate. A few have come from Muslim backgrounds—and they are particularly welcome, given the present polarization of the world. The nature of anyone's path is his or her own business. But I am encouraged to see the direction the culture of the Evolutionary Astrology community is going.

In Closing . . .

I cannot prove what I am about to say, but my intuitive feeling in developing the principles that underlie this book was more one of *remembering* something than of creating it. I believe that the knowledge of most of these principles has existed in the past.

To be sure, there is no recorded precedent in astrological history for these particular techniques. From any academic astrological perspective, they are new. For whatever their worth, they were clearly created by a group of astrologers, mostly in North America, over the past two or three generations.

But my guts tell me to question that.

We do know that a personal astrology, vaguely reminiscent of modern forms, emerged rather suddenly twenty-three centuries ago in the Hellenistic world. That is generally accepted as the beginning of astrology as we know it. Vedic astrologers claim a much more ancient origin for their system, going back at least 25,000 years—a claim that is roundly dismissed by western academic historians.

Pyramids in Egypt and Mexico, Stonehenge, Angor Wat, New Grange, Tiahuanaco—all are proof set in stone that our ancestors felt a strong connection with celestial phenomena. Unless we imagine them to be doing purely scientific research, we must acknowledge that this was astrology in the most general sense: the feeling that there are meaningful messages for us in the heavens. Our ancestors felt this idea strongly enough to create massive monuments of earth and stone reflecting celestial configurations.

There are maverick scholars who believe that there was a civilization on earth prior to the present accepted storyline of history, a civilization that was destroyed by natural cataclysms at the end of the last Ice Age about eleven thousand years ago—basically, precipitous flooding and a sudden, coast-drowning rise in the sea level. Their arguments are not as flaky as they sound at first blush—just google Graham Hancock and read for half an hour, if you are interested. I am not going to summarize his work here, but it is impressive. For whatever worth my own untrained opinion might have in these matters, Graham Hancock's exhaustive research has convinced me. I am not a scholar, but neither am I a fool. The Vedic claims of a more ancient origin for personal astrology are plausible to me in this context. I honor them and I accept them.

We can take this path further.

East and west, there have been *mystery schools* characterized by secret teachings only passed on to students when they were deemed ready. Nothing, or very little, was ever fully committed to writing for fear of its falling into uninitiated hands where it could be damaging. This is still very much the present-day case in Vajrayana Buddhism, for one example. Jesus also spoke of deeper secrets that would be revealed only later to the disciples. To this day, there is no clarity about what was taught in the Eleusinian mystery schools of Greece, or what Druids taught their acolytes.

I believe that, speckled throughout history, wherever astrology, a belief in reincarnation, and mystery schools converged, the core principles of Evolutionary Astrology—and other deep astrological principles as yet unknown—have been kept alive.

I also believe that this precious chain of lineage has been broken many times, but that it always reknits itself. How? First, these principles, like those of science, are simply there to be rediscovered over and over again once someone simply asks the right questions. They are hidden in plain view. They are not like a secret handshake. One can rediscover them through thoughtful observation and correlation. Second, through reincarnation, those beings who once held this knowledge may return again—old wine in new skins, to turn the parable on its head.

Evolutionary Astrology is in renaissance now, and its future looks bright. I can imagine a future historian of astrology crediting me—or Jeff Green, or Jan Spiller, or Martin Schulman, or Ray Merriman—with "inventing" this or "originating" that technique.

I cannot speak for the others, but I just smile at the thought of such a historian. Subjectively, I honestly feel that I have created nothing . . . only remembered.

Years ago, when people used to ask me how long I had been doing astrology, I would often answer with a wink, "Four thousand years." Nowadays I actually think that number might be fairly accurate. That would make me a youngster in the field, by the way.

My own lunar south node lies in Scorpio *(secrets)* on the cusp of the twelfth house *(spirituality)*. Along with the formidable psycho-muck that goes along with any nodal structure, this symbolism is consistent with prior-life initiations into secret mystical traditions. I feel that I have sat at the feet of masters—and in fact that extravagant blessing has echoed a few times in this present lifetime as well. Karma, as ever, repeats. I feel that these spiritual masters have sometimes taken a personal interest in "my case," despite everything. I can honestly say that this thought fills me with feelings not of arrogance, but of humility. The masters were a lot wiser than me. They still are. Nothing takes the starch out of the ego faster than sitting before someone who is undeniably, perceptibly, millennia ahead of you.

I have a Mars-Mercury conjunction on the cusp of the third house *(teaching; speaking),* tightly squaring my nodes—that configuration represents my unresolved prior life affliction and thus my present life "skipped step." Fear not, I will not subject you here to a long, self-indulgent exegesis of my own karma. Instead I will cut to the bottom line: in a prior life, I misused my voice *(third house),* my reason *(Mercury)* and my skill at verbally conveying contagious passion *(Mars conjunct Mercury).* Furthermore, I was "my own worst enemy," as per our theories—that jumps out because Mars, traditional ruler of Scorpio, both rules my south node and quite precisely squares it. In a prior life, I afflicted myself. I was my own worst enemy.

Specifically, I have come to understand that I let my voice and my reason serve a very dark purpose: the Christian justification of torture visited upon the native people in what we now know as Mexico during *La Conquista.* I did not realize my complicity in evil at first. That took a little while.

When I was twenty-two, Marian Starnes, a wise and loving psychic who was my first true spiritual teacher, told me that I might face deafness later in this lifetime. The reason she gave was that "in a prior life I could not stand the sound of the people screaming." Those were her exact words. She said no more. Now I understand what Marian was too kind to say. What I could not stand was the sound of human beings enduring torture—torture which I myself had justified theologically based on my Christian shock at the Aztec practice of human sacrifice. I did not perform the torture myself. But I gave encouragement, support, and the blessing of the Church to those who were doing it.

In the name of Jesus.

And now at nearly sixty, I have been wearing hearing aids for several years. Marian was right. Encroaching deafness is the major nightmare of my present personal life. The karma has ripened.

From a conventional astrological perspective, Mars *(trouble)* afflicts my Mercury *(hearing)* in my third house *(hearing and communication again)*. Accurate enough—I even had a speech impediment as a child—but that conventional interpretation misses so much. It misses the *meaningful origin* of my deafness.

Let me add one strange twist. As of this writing, even though my work takes me all over the world, the only foreign country I visit on a regular basis for my teaching is Mexico. I have taught there, mostly right in Mexico City, many times. Circumstances have dictated that I stay in the very neighborhood that historically housed the Spanish rulers of the conquered Aztecs.

Here is one more twist: my astrological work has been translated into at least a dozen languages, some of them relatively obscure from the English perspective—Turkish, Romanian, Dutch, Czech, Italian. *But never into Spanish.* It is as if I am still karmically forbidden from having my voice heard in that language.

And Spanish is the only language in which I can really communicate at all except for English.

Just like everyone else with a planet square the nodes, the resolution of my karmic dilemma depends on my resolving the skipped step. Mercury (in Capricorn) and Mars (in Aquarius) must now serve my evolutionary intentions, or I will fall back into old patterns. My passionate "preacher's voice" is *hanging in the balance.* In spiritual matters, I must speak the truth of Natural Law as I see it, no matter what the practical consequences—that is the righteous expression of my Mars-Mercury configuration.

I must make my passionate voice serve my north node, which lies in Taurus (*instinctive awareness of the laws of nature*) in the context of the *lineage-honoring* sixth house. Thus I bow to those teachers who have gone before me and who have taught me what I know and how to see it directly.

I promise to carry this flame diligently so long as the brief light of my own eyes endures.

And I bow gratefully to those of you who may carry this flame forward into the human future. Thank you!

It is in that spirit that I offer this book.

Every word in it is the highest truth I know.

—Steven Forrest
Borrego Springs, California
April 27, 2008

RECOMMENDED READING

Please note that I've compiled this list of recommended books with an eye to directing your attention to works that I have either quoted or mentioned in Yesterday's Sky *or which have immediate relevance to it. Thus, your favorite (or my favorite) basic astrology book may be missing. The focus here is on reincarnation, its historical context, and the kinds of astrology that speak to it.*

Arroyo, Stephen, *Astrology, Karma & Transformation: The Inner Dimensions of the Birth Chart*, CRCS Publications, Reno, Nevada, 1978.

Bache, Christopher M., *Lifecycles: Reincarnation and the Web of Life*, Paragon house, 1994.

Bogart, Gregory C., *Astrology and Spiritual Awakening*, Dawn Mountain Press, Berkeley California, 1994

Borstein, Agneta K., *The Moon's Nodes: A Churning Process of the Soul*, Crescentia Publications, West Hartford CT, 2004.

Brown, Mick, *The Dance of 17 Lives: The Incredible Story of Tibet's 17th Karmapa*, Bloomsbury, 2004.

Dalai Lama, *Illuminating the Path to Enlightenment*, Thubten Dhargye Ling Publications, 2002.

Dzoghen Ponlop Rinpoche, *Turning Towards Liberation: The Four Reminders,* Siddhi Publications, Vancouver, Canada, 2000.

Dzoghen Ponlop Rinpoche, *Mind Beyond Death*, Snow Lion, 2007.

Dzongsar Jamyang Khyentse, *What Makes You Not A Buddhist*, Shambhala Pubications, Boston, 2007.

Fernandez, Maurice. *Neptune, The Twelfth House and Pisces*, Trafford, Victoria, Canada, 2004.

Forrest, Jodie. *The Ascendant,* Seven Paws Press, Chapel Hill, NC, 2007.

Govinda, Lama Anagarika, *The Way of the White Clouds: A Buddhist Pilgrim in Tibet,* Shambhala Publications, 1966.

Green, Jeffrey Wolf. *Pluto: The Evolutionary Journey of the Soul, Volume 1.* Llewellyn Publications, St. Paul, MN, 1998.

Green, Jeffrey Wolf. *Pluto: The Soul's Evolution through Relationships, Volume 2,* Llewellyn Publications, St. Paul, MN, 2000.

Guirdham, Arthur, *The Cathars and Reincarnation,* Wellingborough, England, Turnstone Press, 1982.

Hancock, Graham. *Fingerprints of the Gods*, Three Rivers Press, New York, 1995.

Hancock, Graham and Santha Faiia, *Heaven's Mirror: Quest for the Lost Civilization,* Crown Publishers, New York, 1998.

Hanh, Thich Nhat, *The Heart of Understanding: Commentaries on the Prajñaparamita Heart Sutra,* Parallax Press, Berkeley, California, 1988.

Head, Joseph and S.L. Cranston, *Reincarnation: An East-West Anthology,* Theosophical Publishing House, 1961.

Landwehr, Joe, *Tracking the Soul,* Ancient Tower Press, Mountain View, MO, 2007.

Langley, Noel, *Edgar Cayce On Reincarnation,* Warner, 1967.

LoFreddo, Alice, *Perfect Together: Astrology, Karma and You,* Sterling House, 2007.

Lutin, Michael, *SunShines: The Astrology of Being Happy,* Fireside, New York, 2007.

Mann, A.T. *The Round Art of Astrology*, Vega, 2003.

Merriman, Raymond A, *Evolutionary Astrology: The Journey of the Soul Through States of Consciousness,* Seek-It Publications, W. Bloomfield, MI, 1991. (Note that in 1977 a handwritten version of this work came out in an edition of 1440 copies. To the best of my knowledge, Ray Merriman is thus on record as being the first person to go to print with the term "evolutionary astrology.")

Meyers, Eric, *The Arrow's Ascent: Astrology and the Quest for Meaning*, Astrology Sight Publishing, Longmont, CO, 2004.

Meyers, Eric, *Between Past and Presence: A Spiritual View of the Moon and the Sun*, Astrology Sight Publishing, Longmont, CO, 2006.

Meyers, Eric, *Uranus: The Constant of Change*, Astrology Sight Publishing, Longmont, CO, 2008.

Oken, Alan. *Soul Centered Astrology: A Key to Your Expanding Self,* Crossing Press, 1996.

Rahula, Walpola. *What The Buddha Taught,* Second Edition, Grove Press, New York, 1979.

Railey, David R., *The Soul Purpose*, iUniverse, 2003.

Ramster, Peter. *In Search of Lives Past,* Somerset Films & Publ., 1992.

Rudhyar, Dane. *The Planetary and Lunar Nodes,* Humanistic Astrology Series #5, CSA Press, Lakemont, Georgia, 1971.

Sagan, Carl. *The Demon Haunted World,* Random House, 1995.

Schulman, Martin, *Karmic Astrology: the Moon's Nodes and Reincarnation*, Samuel Weiser, York Beach, ME, 1975.

Shaneman, Jhampa & Jan V. Angel, *Buddhist Astrology*, with a Foreword by His Holiness the Dalai Lama and an Introduction by Steven Forrest, Llewellyn Publications, St. Paul, MN, 2003.

Spiller, Jan. *Astrology For the Soul*, Bantam, 1997.

Spiller, Jan (with Karen McCoy), *Spiritual Astrology*, Simon and Shuster, 1998.

Stevenson, Ian:
    Twenty Cases Suggestive of Reincarnation. 1966. (Second revised and enlarged edition 1974), University of Virginia Press,
    Cases of the Reincarnation Type Vol. I: Ten Cases in India, 1975. University of Virginia Press.
    Cases of the Reincarnation Type Vol. II: Ten Cases in Sri Lanka. 1978. University of Virginia Press.
    Cases of the Reincarnation Type Vol. III: Twelve Cases in Lebanon and Turkey. 1980. University of Virginia Press.
    Cases of the Reincarnation Type Vol. IV: Twelve Cases in Thailand and Burma. 1983. University of Virginia Press.
    Unlearned Language: New Studies in Xenoglossy. 1984. University of Virginia Press. *Reincarnation and Biology: A Contribution to the Etiology of Birthmarks and Birth Defects.* 1997. (2 volumes), Praeger Publishers.
    Where Reincarnation and Biology Intersect. 1997, Praeger Publishers. (A short and non-technical version of the scientific two-volumes work, for the general reader)
    Children Who Remember Previous Lives: A Quest of Reincarnation. 2001. McFarland & Company. (A general non-technical introduction into reincarnation-research)
    European Cases of the Reincarnation Type. 2003. McFarland & Company.

Sugrue, Thomas, *There Is A River: The Story of Edgar Cayce*, 1942.

Tarnas, Richard. *Cosmos and Psyche*, Plume, 2006.

Khenchen Thrangu Rinpoche, *Buddhist Conduct: The Ten Virtuous Actions,* Name Buddhist Publications, 2001. page 24.

Van Toen, Donna, *The Astrologer's Node Book,* Samuel Weiser, York Beach, Maine, 1981.

Walsh, Patricia, "Astrological Observations from Past Life Therapy," article in the *Journal of the International Society for Astrological Research,* Leo 2006, Volume XXXVI, #3.

Wambach, Helen *Reliving Past Lives* and *Life Before Life,* both published in 1978 by Bantam. The updated *Reliving Past Lives: The Evidence Under Hypnosis* was published in 1984.

Weiss, Brian L., *Many Lives, Many Masters,* Simon and Schuster, 1988.

Woolger, Roger J., *Other Lives, Other Selves,* Bantam, 1988.

STEVEN FORREST'S
ASTROLOGICAL APPRENTICESHIP PROGRAM

The aim of Steven Forrest's Astrological Apprenticeship program is to provide a practical education in client-centered evolutionary astrological counseling. This process is inseparable from a commitment to one's own personal and spiritual growth. Both aims are incorporated into the teaching. Students who do not intend to establish a professional practice of astrology are welcome. Currently, there are two programs, both located in California. Each program meets twice a year for four full days of training. Topics vary, and new students may join the program at any time. The only requirement is a familiarity with the astrological basics—internalizing Steven's and Jodie's books is a good start.

Once a student has attended a single four day session, he or she has access to recordings and, in many cases, transcripts of all previous meetings. That way, it is possible for the motivated student to fill in any blanks and catch up. For reasons of confidentiality, these recordings and transcripts will never be made public in their present form. The heart of the apprenticeship program lies in the direct experience of astrological energies in the personal lives of the students, and so all the personal information revealed is held to be strictly private.

A certificate is awarded after a student has attended three full four-day sessions (96 hours). This also qualifies the student to be listed on Steven and Jodie's web site, which provides good support for growing an astrological practice. A Level Two certificate is awarded after six sessions (192 hours), and currently plans are taking shape for a Master Class. Over the past ten years, over four hundred people have passed through Steven's program. Many have gone on to become successful astrologers, astrological writers, and teachers.

For more information, current topics, costs, and so forth, please visit www.sevenpawspress.com and click on TRAINING at the top of the opening page.

JODIE FORREST'S
ASTROLOGICAL MENTORING INTENSIVE PROGRAM
From Theory to Practice

My Astrological Mentoring Program is separate from Steven Forrest's Astrological Apprenticeship Program, and is meant to be a stand-alone program in and of itself, as well as working in mutual support with his. You may of course attend classes in either or both programs, according to your schedule and your interest in the topics presented.

An effective evolutionary astrologer is something like a spiritually-oriented life coach, a perceptive counselor, and an engaging, memorable teacher all rolled up into one flexible and adaptable package. While this mentoring program certainly covers evolutionary astrology theory, its intent is very much geared toward the nuts and bolts of astrological practice and presentation: how to do evolutionary astrology readings, how to work one-on-one with your clients as you interpret their charts for them. That sort of practical, hands-on material is perhaps best learned from coaching and mentoring by someone who's been working with clients for a long time, rather than learning only from books. For an evolutionary astrologer, practicing effectively means learning how to establish rapport, how to listen to clients and dialog with them—how to relate to your clients, not just to their charts. It means acquiring a wide variety of interpretive tools, so that you can choose lots of different ways to present frequently complex astrological material to different sorts of clients. That's what this program is for. I want to help give you more tools.

If you feel comfortable that a birthchart refers to a set of questions that life is asking of that person—is or her soul's lesson plan——not his or her predetermined responses to those questions, then you'll fit right in. Some knowledge of Steven Forrest's and my work, and/or that of Jeffrey Wolf Green and the astrologers who've worked with him (www.evolutionaryastrology.org), would be helpful but not required.

Astrological Mentoring Program Intensives are now meeting 4-5 times annually in California: in Lakeside near San Diego in southern CA, and in Oakland in the Bay Area in northern CA.

For dates, topics and fees, please visit our website's Events section (www.sevenpawspress.com). Programs are often two days long, Saturday and Sunday, rather than four days. Format is a combination of lecture and application, theory and practice. Once we go over theory, we practice with students' charts. There may be some experiential techniques and some group work, but the primary focus is on theory and application. Recordings of the programs will also be available to my students only, and confidentiality applies. Certification and Forrest Trained directory postings both operate as with Steven's program, with the difference that hours toward certification with me may also be earned outside of the program classes by one on one tutoring, either by appointment on the phone, or by a pre-arranged, in-person intensive, usually in Borrego Springs, CA. For details, please see the website and also email me, shazam92004@yahoo.com. Mentoring intensive programs and tutoring can work particularly well together, since you can tailor the tutoring for where you think you need the most practice.

I hope to see you in class!

—Jodie Forrest

Please visit the website of
Jodie Forrest and Steven Forrest

www.sevenpawspress.com

for complete information
about our products and services:

* various types of astrological consultations
* written, computerized astrological reports
  based on your birth data
* our schedule of astrological workshops,
  intensives, lectures and other classes
* recorded lectures and DVDs
* books by the Forrests
* astrological software
* how to order a copy of your birth certificate
* and lots more material!